JOHN ANDERSON
VISCOUNT WAVERLEY

JOHN ANDERSON, VISCOUNT WAVERLEY

JOHN ANDERSON

Viscount Waverley

BY

JOHN W. WHEELER-BENNETT

LONDON

MACMILLAN & CO LTD

NEW YORK · ST MARTIN'S PRESS

1962

MACMILLAN AND COMPANY LIMITED
St Martin's Street London WC2
also Bombay Calcutta Madras Melbourne

THE MACMILLAN COMPANY OF CANADA LIMITED
Toronto

ST MARTIN'S PRESS INC
New York

PRINTED IN GREAT BRITAIN

FOR
RUTH
WITH LOVE

AUTHOR'S NOTE

IN the great convolutions of history it is true to say that events are either loosed or controlled by outstanding individuals or that they produce eminent persons who in their turn exercise notable influence on their times. Such men as Winston Churchill, Franklin Roosevelt and Woodrow Wilson, in the interests of freedom ; such men as Hitler, Stalin and Lenin in the name of authoritarianism—all held the fate of the world in their hands. They moulded or rent it, built or destroyed, wrought constructively or destructively upon the wide panoramic stage of history. They were 'the lords of their events', the titanic artists who 'splashed at a ten-league canvas with brushes of comets' hair', the great forces of good or evil who, born of the concatenation of the stars, clashed in the firmament of world affairs.

But there are other men who evolved more slowly and gradually along established lines to spheres of achievement which, though perhaps not comparable to those of the category of mighty leaders, nevertheless enabled them to perform the highest services to the nation — less spectacular but no less profound ; they established for themselves positions of honour and respect which are imperishable, and have left their mark no less deeply and indelibly upon the national life of their country.

In this second category is John Anderson, first Viscount Waverley. The greatest public servant of his day, he stands out as the apotheosis of the Civil Service, combining a mighty intellect, an astounding — almost an encyclopaedic — knowledge, and a genius for government which carried him successfully to Ireland and to India and to the highest offices of the realm. A Scottish background and upbringing, a natural dignity of manner and a gravity of mien, which some found forbidding, masked a nature of great kindness, great understanding and great justness. But above all he was A Man, unshakable in judgment and integrity.

In writing Lord Waverley's life I have not been over-blessed with a richness of written material. He was not one who committed himself easily or unnecessarily to paper and his official minutes, though clear and to the point, were not numerous. As a correspondent, however, he was admirable and I have been fortunate in having been given access to the many letters which he wrote to his father, David Anderson; to his first wife, Christina Mackenzie; and to his second wife, Ava Wigram. These give excellent examples of his vivid perception, his purity of style and his passing flashes of humour. For permission to use these letters and for help in complementing them I have been greatly indebted to Lord Waverley's family, to whom I am profoundly grateful for having entrusted me with the task of writing the life of this great man. His widow, Lady Waverley, has been a never-failing source of information and she has given me the benefit of her indefatigable and invaluable interest throughout the writing of the biography. To his son, Lord Waverley ; his daughter, Lieut.-Colonel the Hon. Mary Anderson ; his sister, Miss Katherine Anderson ; and his sister-in-law, Miss Helen Mackenzie, I am greatly beholden for much help and information of his intimate life.

Apart from these sources I have consulted the works listed in the Bibliography at the end of this book. I have also been in correspondence, or in personal contact, with over 250 men and women who knew John Anderson in varying stages of intimacy during one or more phases of his remarkable Protean career, and I have travelled to Ireland, Denmark, the United States and Canada to supplement what they have told me. To all of them I offer my warmest thanks. Dictates of space prevent my acknowledging all personally, but certain of those who have given me particularly valuable assistance I must thank by name :

Lord Attlee, Sir William Gorell-Barnes, Sir Isaiah Berlin, Professor Niels Bohr, Mr. L. A. Boosey, Lord Bridges, Sir Henry Bunbury, Dr. Vannevar Bush, Viscount Chandos, Mr. Alan Chapman, Mr. J. R. Colville, Lord Cottesloe, Dr. W. M. Crofton, Sir Charles Cunningham, Sir Henry Dale, The Earl of Drogheda, Sir Leslie Ford, Dr. A. F. Giles, Sir Ernest Gowers, Sir Alexander Gray, Sir James Grigg, Professor Denis Gwynn, Sir Alan Herbert, Mr. E. A. Hogan, General Lord Ismay, Mrs. R. S. Jamieson, Sir Alexander

Johnston, Mr. O. C. Kerrison, Viscount Knollys, Sir William Mabane, Sir Roger Makins, Vincent Massey, Sir Alexander Maxwell, Sir Frank Newsam, Mrs. A. N. Odling, Sir Thomas Padmore, Lady Paterson, Sir Kenneth Pickthorn, Mr. L. G. Pinnell, Lord Robbins, the late Sir Bejoy Prasad Singh Roy, Lord Salter, Viscount Simon, Lady Rachel Sturgis, Sir George Thomson, Sir John Tyson, Sir Percival Waterfield, Sir David Webster, Sir John Woodhead, Mr. Justice Wylie and Mr. Roger Young.

From first to last I have been deeply conscious of the great debt which I owe to Sir Norman Brook. As censor, critic, counsellor and friend he has given me most generously of his time, his wisdom and his encouragement. The book could not, and would not, have been written without his aid, and my most sincere thanks are now offered to him in the fullest measure.

I would also especially thank my secretary, Miss Frances Coulson, for the efficiency of her work, the accuracy of her research and the tireless patience with which she has battled with my handwriting and with the typing and retyping of drafts.

I must also tender my sincere thanks to Mr. Rex Allen and Mr. T. M. Farmiloe for their meticulous and painstaking work in proof-reading, and to Mrs. H. W. Bawden for her compilation of the index ; and, finally, my keen appreciation of the great care and trouble which my publishers, Messrs. Macmillan, and the printers, Messrs. R. & R. Clark, have taken in the final production of the book.

JOHN W. WHEELER-BENNETT

GARSINGTON MANOR,
OXON.
February 1959–February 1962

ACKNOWLEDGMENTS

The author wishes most gratefully to acknowledge the gracious permission of Her Majesty the Queen for access to the Royal Archives at Windsor and to reprint the telegram from King George V on page 143 and the letter from Queen Mary on page 307.

He also wishes to acknowledge his indebtedness to the following, who have kindly given permission for the use of copyright material : Sir Henry Bunbury, Sir Henry Dale, the late Lord Dalton, Captain N. W. Fisher, R.N.(rtd.), Sir Alexander Gray, Viscountess Greenwood, Rt. Hon. Sir James Grigg, Lord Hankey, Brigadier J. A. Hopwood, Lady Graham Kerr, Mr. O. C. Kerrison, the late Rev. Robert E. Lee, Rt. Hon. Harold Macmillan, Sir Alexander Maxwell, Sir James Peck, Lord Robbins, Lord Salter, Viscountess Templewood, Sir George Thomson, The Marquess of Willingdon, Hon. Mr. Justice Wylie, and the authors and publishers named in the text.

CONTENTS

CONTENTS

ILLUSTRATIONS

I

A Man in the Making

1882–1905

ON the 27th of September 1881 a young couple were married in the parlour at the home of the bride's parents at 12 Saint Giles Street, Edinburgh.

The bridegroom, David Alexander Pearson Anderson, was three months past his twenty-sixth birthday. The eighth of eleven children of a poor dominie in Dunfermline, he had come to Edinburgh as a youth to be apprenticed to the printing trade. He had worked diligently and on the completion of his indenture had found good employment. Now at the time of his marriage he was 'on his own', the proprietor of a small fancy stationer's shop at No. 8 in the Princes Street Arcade, for which he was paying an annual rental of £270.

Short and stooping in stature, David Anderson had a good intellect and had longed to go to the University. This advantage having been denied him, he set himself to improve his mind by all means which came to his hand. He possessed a retentive memory and had become an omnivorous reader, with a great fondness for poetry and music and a keen interest in flowers, birds and animals. His personality was gay and vivacious. But, above all, he was a shrewd and ambitious business-man, determined to make his way in the world.

David's bride came of a more varied background. Some time in the early nineteenth century, Franz Bregelmann, a young German sailor from Oldenburg, variously described as a seaman and a ship-master, made his appearance in Leith. It is not known why he came there, whether as a result of shipwreck or as a deserter from his ship in a successful attempt to escape from the Napoleon-dominated continent of Europe. However, having found asylum in Scotland he speedily became a naturalized British subject, and in November

B
1

1815, being then twenty-five years old, he married a Dundee girl, Janet Mustard, and settled down to earn a living by letting out seamen's lodgings in Leith, first at 28 The Shore, where they also kept the Old Bridge Hotel, and later, in addition, at 73 Constitution Street.

To Franz (now Francis) and Janet Bregelman there was born a son on September 4, 1816, to whom they gave the somewhat unexpected names of Charles Wildgoose. Of his early life little or nothing is known, but he must have been something of a wanderer, for at the age of thirty-one he was established in Dublin as a mechanical engineer and there he married in July 1847 a Leith girl, Catherine Beveridge. At this time Charles Wildgoose spelled his surname Briggleman, but, on his return to Scotland some years later, he shortened it still further to Briglmen. It was their daughter Janet, born in 1850, who married David Anderson in 1881 — her father, Charles Briglmen, being then established in Edinburgh in the engineering business ; a man of some substance, with an interest in house property.

Janet Kilgour Briglmen was a handsome young woman ; tall and upstanding, with a graceful carriage and something of the physique of her German ancestry. She was thus in some distinction from her more diminutive fiancé, a distinction which was the more marked by her shy and retiring nature. In other respects, however, they had much in common. Her parents had sent her south to school in London where her naturally acute mind had been well formed and stimulated. She was very well read and, like David, was fond of music and singing. They were a well-matched couple — and from their union evolved the remarkable mind of John Anderson, first Viscount Waverley.

David Anderson and his wife set up housekeeping in two rooms on an upper floor of 1 Livingstone Place, off Melville Drive to the south of The Meadows. The house was owned in part by Charles Briglmen and he charged his son-in-law £19 : 9s. a year, an average rental for the district. There at three o'clock in the morning of July 8, 1882, their first child was born, whom they called John. Subsequently they had three other children : a second son, Charles, born in February 1884, who died seventeen months later of cerebro-spinal meningitis, and two daughters, Catherine ('Katie') born in October 1886 and Janet ('Nettie') in January 1889.

In the first eight years of his married life, therefore, David Anderson had added considerably to his responsibilities. But he was already what the Victorians called 'a warm man' and had used his outstanding business ability to the fullest capacity. By the time his youngest child was born he had acquired the lease of two further shops in the Princes Street Arcade and had added photography and the sale of leather goods to his original activity of fancy stationery. So strong was his personality that the Arcade soon became locally known as 'Anderson's Arcade'. He had also acquired an interest in house property and his feet were firmly set upon the road to the further betterment of his position. In May 1890 he moved south from Livingstone Place to the Braid Hills district. There he bought, in his wife's name, No. 17 Braid Crescent and borrowed £500 to pay for it. The house was an unlovely, solid, terraced eight-room villa built of red sandstone. The Andersons lived in Braid Crescent for the next ten years, during which time David Anderson steadily improved both his financial position and his social standing. In 1899 he disposed of a part of his business interests to the well-known firm of fine art printers and publishers, Valentine & Sons of Dundee. They agreed to give him £2900 for the deal and he accepted 290 Ordinary Shares of £10 each. In February of the following year David was elected a director of the firm and so continued for nearly half a century. Valentine's became his chief business interest, though he continued to operate his shops in the Arcade until 1907. Throughout his long association with the firm he retained the high regard and affection of his colleagues, who learned to respect his opinions and the meticulous fairness of his judgment — though it is recorded that he was a great stickler for claiming expenses.

It was David Anderson's ambition, even in the more striving period of his fortunes, to give his son those educational advantages which had been denied to him by reason of the poverty of his parents. In accordance with this aspiration, in the autumn of 1888 he entered the seven-year-old John in the Lower Division of George Watson's College for Boys.

David Anderson's choice of this great school was influenced by three factors. First, the standard of education was of the highest in Scotland — and therefore very high ; secondly, it was near by, for at this time George Watson's was not housed in its present splendour in the Colinton Road but occupied the buildings of the former Merchant Maiden Hospital in Archibald Place ; [1] and was therefore separated from the Anderson home in Livingstone Place only by the breadth of The Meadows, a distance of some few hundred yards (later John Anderson walked the two miles and more to school from Braid Crescent). The third reason was that it was cheap. When John entered the Lower Division the fees were £1 : 15s. a quarter (*i.e.* £7 per annum) and when in due course he reached the Higher Division they were only a guinea a year more !

The 'Wee School', as John Anderson knew it, was a gaunt, unlovely building of four storeys, separated from the Royal Infirmary by a high wall but with its classrooms enjoying an uninterrupted view of the 'Infectious Diseases' department of that institution. 'To-day such contiguity would be regarded with consternation', wrote one of Anderson's contemporaries, 'but we enjoyed it. We could, and did, lighten the labours of the day by watching the nurses moving about the wards. We found it a great relief from the burden of abacus and blackboard.'[2] Later, when John passed into the Higher Division, he may have noticed — if he gave any thought to it at all — the beauty of its eighteenth-century architecture.

John at this time was a solemn little boy. Tall for his age — both he and his sister Katie inherited the fine physique of their mother — he does not appear to have outgrown his strength, and, from the moment he first entered the school till the moment he left it eleven years later loaded with honours, he was immersed in the serious business of education. On this business he concentrated with an almost ferocious intensity, to the exclusion of games, student activities or any other form of recreational distraction.

John was undoubtedly, both now and at all later periods of

[1] At the death of George Watson, first Accountant of the Bank of Scotland, in 1723, it was found that his will made provision for the founding of a new hospital 'for entertaining and education of the male children and grandchildren of decayed merchants in Edinburgh', and this institution was opened in 1741 in a part of Heriot's Croft on the south side of Lauriston, bordering on The Meadows. In 1870 the Royal Infirmary took over the original site of the Hospital, which moved into the buildings of the former Merchant Maiden Hospital in Archibald Place. At the same time the Governors of the Hospital decided that George Watson's original benefaction could more usefully be fulfilled by the establishment of a Day School. In 1929 the development of the Royal Infirmary again threatened to displace George Watson's, which moved out of the metropolitan area of Edinburgh to new buildings on the Colinton Road, which were formally opened by H.R.H. The Duke of Kent in 1932. [2] *The Watsonian*, vol. xxiv, No. 1, December 1927.

his school and university career, 'a swot' and when he entered
Watson's there is good reason to believe that, like most small boys
of his age, his habits of personal cleanliness were no better than they
should have been. But, withal, he was a sturdy, craggy little boy,
angular, perhaps, in mind as well as body, but of good stamina. He
had need of it, for the curriculum at the 'Wee School' was stern
and demanding. Classes began at nine o'clock and it is to be hoped
that young John began the day with a good oatmeal breakfast inside
him before starting across The Meadows from Livingstone Place —
or later before his two-mile walk from Braid Crescent — for there
was only a half-hour's break at noon, just time to go up to
'Chirnsides' for a bun and a glass of milk, and he would only get
his main meal of the day on his return home from school after
3 p.m. The sheer frugality of those days is not easy to realize to-day,
for those boys whose 'people' were better off than the Andersons
'did themselves' little or no better than the rest. Such is the fundamental democratic spirit of the Scot ! Most of the youngsters,
however, survived and indeed throve on this Spartan régime —
amongst them John Anderson.

As the years passed, his personal interests — those over and above
his formal studies — began to manifest themselves. He developed
a devotion to birds and animals, keeping many pets and giving
first-aid to broken wings and other ailments. At the same time his
interest in flowers and trees began to show itself and also a certain
aptitude in geology. As he grew older he would take his hammer
and go for long walks in the Pentlands, returning home with his
pockets filled with specimens. Never a great reader outside his
school subjects he seemed to take in facts 'through the pores' and
would startle his family and his contemporaries by the variety and
unfailing accuracy of his information. These characteristics were
not always fully appreciated by his schoolmates.

John was not primarily a classical scholar. His aptitude was
always towards science and mathematics and he was fortunate in the
latter part of his time at Watson's in coming under the influence of
that eminent philomath, Dr. John Alison, who later became Headmaster of the school. Alison's magnetic authority stimulated the
already budding genius into its full flower of achievement and John
was ever conscious of the debt which he owed. When Dr. Alison

retired in 1926 his former pupil contributed to the school magazine
an article which reveals his capacity to analyse and delineate character with sure clarity, and also the sincerity of his gratitude.

> Of his work as Headmaster I have no direct personal know-
> ledge [wrote the Rt. Hon. Sir John Anderson, G.C.B., then
> Permanent Under-Secretary of the Home Office], but as Mathe-
> matical Master I knew him well, for I sat at his feet for four years.
> The admiration I had for him as a schoolboy was enhanced as
> wider experience gave me a better appreciation of the difficulties
> of his task.
>
> Alison never taught us as if his subject was the only one that
> mattered. He was careful to let his pupils know that he took an
> interest in their progress in other studies. In marked contrast
> with some of his colleagues, he seemed pained to learn that one
> of his bright boys was thought backward in other branches of
> study. From his conversation out of school anything in the nature
> of 'shop' was rigidly excluded. He wisely discouraged any
> tendency to specialize prematurely. A boy who showed special
> aptitude was given no excuse for thinking that he could make his
> way in life on the binomial theorem. But he was by no means
> a negligent teacher. He taught sympathetically and thoroughly
> from first principles. His choice of text books was marked by
> care and discrimination. He was quick to take advantage of any
> improvement in this respect, and in his own presentation of the
> subject always used to the full the gift of lucid exposition. Look-
> ing back I realize that among the secrets of his success was the
> fact that he taught as one realizing keenly the difficulties of the
> average boy.
>
> ... My debt is greatest to Alison, for he first guided my
> faltering footsteps along the path that it has been my lot to tread.
> I am only one of a multitude.[1]

And indeed the pupil was worthy of his master. In his last year
at Watson's John Anderson gained the Dux Medal — being the
first mathematician and non-classicist to do so. He was, in Ciceron-
ian phrase, *omni laude cumulatus*, for he was also awarded the Jenkins
Prize in Anglo-Saxon and Old English and the Lizars Modern
Language Prize. Thus, laden with honours, he turned his eyes
towards Edinburgh University.

[1] *The Watsonian*, vol. xxii, No. 2, April 2, 1926.

Anderson never forgot in after life the debt of gratitude which he owed to his school. He was among the most loyal of Watsonians, welcoming an opportunity to visit the new building at Colinton when he was in Edinburgh and attending with pleasure and interest the dinners of the Watsonian Societies in London and in Calcutta.

Students entering on an Arts or Science course in the University of Edinburgh sit for an examination to decide an order of merit for the various bursaries and scholarships which are available. In the examination held in October 1899 candidates from George Watson's School seem to have swept the board. In the list of results their names appear in the first, second, fourth, sixth, seventh and eighth places, and none was lower than twenty-second. John Anderson was eleventh on the list and was awarded a bursary of £100. He was seventeen years old.

In his first year at the University John's promise was fully justified. At its close he was first in his class in both senior mathematics and natural philosophy, receiving a medal and a Certificate of Honour in both subjects. He was weaker in Latin, only achieving ninth place and a second-class certificate.

The year 1900 had a further significance for the Anderson family, for in that November David decided to take his wife and children out of Edinburgh to the neighbouring village of Eskbank, about seven miles from the University. There he purchased for the sum of £1700 (with a mortgage of £1000) a pleasant rambling property called Westland House, of which the centre portion was of some age and the two wings, of which one was an octagonal tower, were of later addition. The whole was faced on the south by a conservatory. The property abutted on to the railway, within a stone's throw of the station, this being an attraction in those days when transportation to the city was either by rail or by carriage, and the Andersons, though they had come a long way socially, had not yet set up their carriage.

Their new home offered more room for the younger members of the family and of this facility John took full advantage. The previous owner had been something of an amateur photographer and astronomer and the curious octagonal wing on two floors had housed a massive telescope. John annexed this wing for his own quarters, fitting up the upper storey as bedroom and sitting-room and equipping the ground floor as a working laboratory. Here he pursued his chemistry studies at night after he returned from the University, developing his natural bent for scientific research.

The year 1902 was destined to be one of some significance in Anderson's life, for in the summer, accompanied by a young man of his own age, Charles Lyall Philip, one of the few friends he had made at Watson's, he undertook a bicycle tour of France and Switzerland. One's first glimpse of the great world outside is always momentous, and John's horizon had been bounded hitherto by the city of Edinburgh and its environs, with occasional summer holidays in the Highlands. Now he and Philip crossed the Channel, saw strange faces and stranger sights, essayed their respective gifts in French and German, and accomplished the whole adventure at the total cost of £10 per head. John returned home with memories of the snow-capped majesty of the Alps and of the broad swift-running reaches of the Rhône. He had also acquired a juvenile respect for good food and good cooking which matured with time into a keenly appreciative gastronomic sense.

The excitements of foreign travel, however, had not dimmed the pleasures of the return home, and on reaching England John wrote to a friend, Miss Chrissie Mackenzie :

> I felt sorry our holiday was over, but it was a relief, I can tell you, to be in a place where you could make your wants known with something like fluency. The first policeman I asked the way of I nearly addressed in French but I could hardly resist shaking hands with him when he answered in decent English, though it was a bit cockney.

At the University John became a leading light in the Chemical Society and in his final year was elected its Vice-President. It was in this capacity that he read before the society a paper on 'Explosives'. Both in style and content the composition was of more than usual merit and though, read now in the light of modern knowledge, some of the speculations contained in it are known to be incorrect, it is remarkable that such speculations were made by a young man of twenty-one more than half a century ago. Indeed, in the opinion of an eminent modern scientist to whom it was recently submitted, 'as a constructive undergraduate paper, written before chain reactions or, really, shock waves were known about, it is obviously more than usually powerful'.

John's membership of the Chemical Society was almost the full extent of his participation in student activities. Certainly the lighter aspects of student life did not appeal to him. He was a very serious-minded young man, with a contempt for anything bordering on the frivolous. He was, however, capable of relaxing to the extent of indulging in occasional three-handed 'Skat' — a German card game — with his friends William Gentle and Alexander Gray.

John's friendship with Gray was perhaps one of the most important personal factors in his university life, and it continued — at least in some degree — until his death. Their association was certainly not based on an affinity of temperament or disposition. They were rather the antithetic complement of one another. Gray was a boy of brilliant intellectual powers but in addition he had a wit, a vibrant sense of humour and of frivolity, to which Anderson could never aspire. He was a gay laughter-maker and, among the very few of John's associates, he could, and did, make him unbend by 'pulling his leg'. John responded well to this treatment and their friendship became warm and lasting.

Anderson's career as an undergraduate at Edinburgh closed in 1903 in a blaze of academic glory comparable to that which had marked his departure from George Watson's. During his four years as an undergraduate he gained eleven medals and, in addition to many other prizes and certificates, the Hope Prize in Mathematics and the Vans Dunlop Scholarship in Chemistry. In the latter subject his final examination results were so brilliant that Professor Crum Brown twitted, instead of censuring, him about certain minor errors in his written paper. He graduated with the degree of Bachelor of Science, with special distinction in Mathematics, Physics and Chemistry, and as a Master of Arts, with first-class honours in Mathematics and Natural Philosophy. He had swept the field and his intention was the pursuit of scientific research.

By the age of twenty-one John had developed amazingly, both physically as well as intellectually. The craggy little boy who had stepped into life across The Meadows had passed through the period of gangling, coltish adolescence and had emerged into manhood. Tall, even lanky in stature, yet well favoured in looks, he stood on the threshold of virile maturity. The life of a man opened before him.

Life in the Anderson home was somewhat austere. John's mother was shy and retiring, and his father, though vivacious himself and devoted to his children, was much occupied in his spare time with politics—in which he was a strong Gladstonian Liberal—and with the affairs of his local church — of which he was an elder. He was also a strict teetotaller and non-smoker, and regarded card-playing, in however mild a form, as influenced by the Evil One. John and his sisters, Katie and Nettie, were thrown much upon the society of their young Briglmen cousins for company and gaiety, and through them they made the acquaintance of the Mackenzie family, their near neighbours.

Andrew Mackenzie, a commercial traveller, and his wife Mary had five daughters, and of one of them, five years his junior, John became early enamoured. She was named Christina and it was to her that John had written on his return to England from France. Their love began as an idyllic affair of childhood. John would wait for Chrissie outside her school to walk home with her, carrying her books, and, on the excursions which the three families frequently took together, he always wanted her to be with him. On one occasion during a party on Loch Awe when he found that she was in a different rowing-boat from himself he insisted on her changing into his in the middle of the loch, a proceeding as risky as it was uncharacteristic of his usually careful way of life!

Their friendship ripened with the years, and by the time John left Edinburgh University in 1903 it was more or less an open secret that they purposed marriage. Chrissie was an attractive girl of middle height with fair hair and a fresh complexion. She was gay and charming, and perhaps a little frivolous by nature, and in her company, and in that of her sisters and the Briglmens, John found an outlet for that lighter side of his life and for that sense of humour and fun which, though it undoubtedly existed, he kept somewhat rigorously suppressed in other surroundings.

In his own family, while John held his father in great reverence and fondness and was devoted to his two sisters, his filial affection centred upon his mother, whom he loved deeply and sincerely. 'I just worshipped her', he would say simply.

The summer of 1903 was a tragic and momentous time in the history of the Anderson family. As was their not infrequent custom, they had made plans with the Briglmens and the Mackenzies for a holiday in company at the village of Newburgh, near Foveran, on the Aberdeenshire coast, each family taking a separate house but making their plans for excursions and pastimes in common. The Andersons rented Stewart Villa for the month of August but almost from the beginning their visit was overshadowed by tragedy. Scarcely had they arrived when Mrs. Anderson's brother, Francis Briglmen, fell ill. He had been a phthisic case for some time and had been in ill health before they left Edinburgh. A cold contracted on the journey to Newburgh turned to pleurisy and on August 3 he died of heart-failure.

Mrs. Anderson was saddened by the loss of a brother to whom she was fondly devoted, but they continued with their holiday and the younger members of all three families enjoyed themselves with the usual diversions of the beach and countryside. John found recreation in tennis and swimming, for the bathing off the estuary of the river Ythan was good, though at times dangerous. There was, however, a pool, between the shore and a low ridge of sand, which was believed to be safe at all times.

The three families had arranged to return to Edinburgh by an afternoon train on Saturday, August 29, and in the morning, Nettie Anderson, with Chrissie Mackenzie's sister Nellie and some Briglmen cousins, went to the shore for a final bathe. The sea was rough and, though it still lacked two hours to high tide, the waves were washing over the sandy ridge and filling the pool to a considerable depth. The youngsters, none of whom was a strong swimmer, were amusing themselves in shallow water at the top of the ridge when a heavy sea dashed over the barrier and carried Nettie and Nellie and another girl into deep water. With the aid of two boys of the party, Nellie Mackenzie and her friend managed to scramble to the shore, but Nettie Anderson failed to regain her footing, nor could they see her body, for the receding wave had sucked her back over the ridge. The desperate cries of the boys and girls to some adjacent salmon fishermen went at first unheeded, for the party were daily bathers and frequently shouted to them in fun. Eventually, however, the fishermen realized the urgency of the situation, but too late, for the strong current had carried Nettie far down the estuary and her body, choked with sand, was only recovered later that evening, four hundred yards below the spot where the accident had occurred.

As the horror-stricken little group made their way back towards the village they encountered John Anderson and Chrissie Mackenzie, who had set out to join the bathing party on the beach. Shocked as he was and deeply moved by the death of his much loved sister, John at once took command of the situation, assuming the responsibility of breaking the news to his parents and postponing the plans for their departure. It was, moreover, he and not his father who made the official notification of Nettie's death before the local Registrar on the following day.

The bathing fatality of that summer had an important effect upon John Anderson. He had suddenly been brought face to face with the stark realities of the abrupt transition from life to death and, though he had always been older than his years, this incident placed the seal upon his manhood. He had met an emergency with calm courage and efficiency. The loss of his much loved sister had not paralysed his capacity to take the necessary measures. In all he had conducted himself with complete self-possession.

Moreover it gave him a deeper insight into the sufferings of others. The sorrow of the death of their beloved daughter Nettie had settled down like a pall over the minds of her parents. Their grief was deep and continued ; John shared it, displaying a depth of understanding unusual in one of his years.

Time hasn't been able to efface the memory of last August yet [he wrote to Chrissie almost a year later]. I know myself how the recollection comes back every now & then & knowing how it makes me feel, I think I can partly realize what it means to Father & Mother. Little things continually occur to freshen the pain — just last Sunday I heard a hymn sung to the melody of 'The fisherman and his child are drowned' ; do you remember Nettie's singing that the spring before last ?

Chrissie, I know what it is to weary but anything I have ever felt must be nothing compared to the wearying & longing of parents for a dead child ; my love, we may have to go through it ourselves & till then we will never realize what it means.

In another sense the affair had further determined Anderson's course of action with regard to his own life. At this moment he was set upon being a scientist and to this end he had enrolled for a year's study in the University of Leipzig, but he was also resolved to marry Chrissie Mackenzie as soon as was possible after his return from the Continent, and it was with this resolution that he went to Germany.

At the beginning of this century many young men from Britain, Canada and the United States went to study Chemistry in Leipzig, and Anderson found among his fellow Scotsmen, Forsyth James Wilson, afterwards Professor of Organic Chemistry at the Royal Technical College at Glasgow ; Joseph Maclagan Wedderburn, later an eminent Professor of Mathematics at Princeton University ; and William Wilson, now Professor Emeritus of Physics at the University of London and a Fellow of the Royal Society. These four young men became fast friends. Together they visited Prague and Dresden and made excursions into the lovely land of Weimar, perhaps then almost the happiest state in the world, where Goethe's spirit still animated the Gästenhaus and the Grand Ducal Palace, and the city had not given its name to a transient democratic régime in Germany. The river Saale was the 'holy river' of the German students of that time, who used to assemble at the Rudelsburg, a ruined castle on a hillside above it. Anderson and his friends were fortunate enough to be asked to join one of these gatherings, an experience which greatly impressed them. They also visited the University of Halle, where Hamlet and Horatio once studied philosophy, and spent an idyllic day or two rambling in the mediaeval forest and sleeping at a tiny woodland tavern.

John was young and happy in these new and interesting surroundings. He wrote regularly and often to Chrissie Mackenzie, telling her of his life and work and adventures. How he had been to worship in the Scottish-American Church of Leipzig, what the Minister had preached about and how long. How his work was going and what he and his friends were doing in their vacations.

We had some difficulty in finding the proper place [he wrote of their visit as tourists to the royal palace at Dresden]. At first we got up the wrong stairway & found ourselves in the private apartments of the Princess Mathilda, whereupon we made matters worse by ringing a bell marked 'court ladies', when a superb dame came out & told us in a reproachful voice that we must go away.

Nor did the romantic side of life escape him. He was very much in love and very lonely for his Chrissie. In May he and his friends were in Prague and there, standing on the historic bridge in the moonlight above the swift-flowing Voltava, he thought of her :

> Darling, have you been looking at the moon lately ? [he wrote.] Last night it was just lovely & I was wondering if it looked the same at home & if you were admiring it & thinking of me as I was of you. You can't imagine, Chrissie, how I miss your letter this week but it means that I shall get two within a short time & that is some compensation. . . . I am, my darling, ever your own loving John.

Anderson had intended to study at Leipzig under the great Professor Wilhelm Ostwald, but scarcely had he arrived at the Ostwald Institut when the Master abandoned the teaching of chemistry for philosophy, thereby demonstrating the true academic freedom of his university! In effect, therefore, Anderson did most of his work under the guidance of a certain Dr. Luther, who was among the first to investigate radioactive materials in Germany. His fellow students were, as he wrote to Chrissie, 'a truly motley crowd':

> My right hand neighbour is a Bohemian, my left a nondescript with a beard a foot long & a Jewish countenance — immediately behind me is a Russian & immediately in front a Frenchman. There are 6 Americans, 2 Scotsmen, about 5 Russians, a Finn, & a few Poles & Czechs in the room besides ; and as for names! How do you like Balorowski, Muscat Muskowski, Wesziletski ? But these are only some of the least formidable — there are others that I would not even venture to spell.

John chose for his special study the subject of uranium, the radioactivity of which had been discovered by the French scientist Becquerel in 1896. He devoted his researches, however, to the chemical rather than the radioactive properties of uranium, and on his return to Edinburgh he wrote a paper on this subject which he submitted to the University and which was adjudged remarkable for its perspicacity.[1]

That any young science student in the early years of this century should have selected uranium for his researches is not in itself without interest, but that John Anderson should have done so, in view of his later intimate association with this precious mineral, is very remarkable indeed.

Why, it may be asked, with all his interest in science and all his promise of success, did John Anderson forsake this field for that of the Civil Service ? In either the practical or theoretical branches of chemical science there is every reason to believe that he would have achieved high distinction and, indeed, had he followed this line, he might well have been awarded the Order of Merit as a distinguished scientist instead of as a distinguished public servant. Why did he thus abandon a career for which he seemed clearly to be destined and eminently well suited ?

The answer to this question is, perhaps, twofold. In those days Edinburgh University regarded it as virtually a *sine qua non* that its best scholars should take the Civil Service Examination. Any boy considered of appropriate calibre for such a calling underwent very considerable pressure of persuasion to do so from the University authorities, from his parents and from his fellow students. It was deemed to be a duty to himself, to his family and to his Alma Mater to pass, and pass high, into the Civil Service, and the corollary of this attitude lies in the many Edinburgh men who have risen to the highest places in the service of the State, the Empire and the Commonwealth.

John Anderson was certainly subjected to some degree of this compulsion and it undoubtedly influenced his decision, but there was another and more material factor involved. He was deeply in love with Chrissie Mackenzie and his one desire was to marry her

[1] Unfortunately the text of this paper is no longer in the possession of Edinburgh University, having been lost in the processes of time. It has been widely believed that it was written by Anderson as a dissertation for a Doctorate of Philosophy at Leipzig University (see an addendum by Sir Henry Dale, O.M., F.R.S., to the memoir on Lord Waverley by Lord Bridges in *Biographical Memoirs of Fellows of the Royal Society*, vol. 4, November 1958). This is not so. Anderson did not take any degree at all from the University of Leipzig, which he only attended for a year. He never, in fact, received a Ph.D. from any university.

at the earliest possible opportunity. It was here that his father played a part.

David Anderson was a shrewd man who had made his own hard way up the ladder from virtual poverty to a very comfortable competence. Though he was justly proud of the fine record which his son had achieved and had given him every assistance in his power to further his success, he could not but feel that science as a source of bread-and-butter represented something ephemeral and uncertain.[1] His discerning advice to his son was, in effect, that if he wanted to get married he should eschew the attraction of a scientific calling for the more certain and substantial security of a Civil Service career. 'And Jonathan harkened unto his father.' He chose the Civil Service and he and Chrissie became engaged.

Thus perhaps Britain lost a great scientist, but thus also did she gain a great public servant, whose record in the service of the State has been equalled by few and surpassed by none ; one whom his contemporaries did not hesitate to acclaim ungrudgingly as 'among the greatest men of our generation'.

In order to prepare himself for the Civil Service Examination in the summer of 1905, John spent the previous year at Edinburgh University, taking an honours course in Economics and also in Political Science, his final performance in both subjects being well up to his usual brilliant standard.

In the last days of July 1905, accompanied by his friend and fellow candidate for the Civil Service, Alexander Gray, John Anderson travelled from Edinburgh to London. They stayed at a rather grimy, but certainly cheap, little boarding-house in Gratton Road, off the Addison Road, kept by a Mrs. Cliff, and on August 1 they presented themselves at the offices of the Civil Service Commission in Burlington House for their examination.

John was now twenty-three years old, five feet ten and a quarter inches tall, with a 38-inch chest, and weighing 11 stone. His lanky body was all bone and sinew, without an ounce of superfluous flesh on it. His long face was lantern-jawed and his eyes deep set. The mouth was stern, yet a smile, even a grin, lurked about it and

[1] 'The War Office assessment of the value of trained chemists was expressed in 1905 in the offer of a commencing salary of £150 a year', Sir John Anderson informed the Manchester Joint Research Council on December 12, 1945.

when it succeeded in emerging his whole face lit up very pleasantly.
'I have perfect confidence in him. He is a young man of high
character, conscientious and upright', wrote the Rev. Maclachlan,
one of his referees. His other character reference was Chrissie's
father, Andrew Mackenzie, who described him as 'a lifelong
abstainer' — which was not entirely true as John had certainly
imbibed mild alcoholic refreshment in Mr. Mackenzie's own
house! — and added with enthusiasm : 'I would trust Mr. Anderson
in or for *any position* ; he is undoubtedly the finest young gentleman with whom I am acquainted. In fact I cannot speak too highly
of Mr. Anderson.' Very proper and promising sentiments in a
prospective father-in-law!

In those days — the custom was discontinued after 1905 — a
candidate for the Civil Service Examination could offer any number
of subjects, his total marks thus depending upon the number of
subjects offered. John offered fourteen,[1] and out of a possible 7500
marks he obtained 4566, the highest (save one) ever to have been
achieved. He was top of the list. Alexander Gray, who had
offered sixteen subjects, came second with 4107 marks out of a
possible 7900.[2]

As might have been expected, John's strongest subjects were
Mathematics, Chemistry, Physics and Geology. His weakest were
Roman History, Political Economy and Economics, and Political
Science. In this last paper he received only 126 marks out of
500 and his examiner's remarks included such trenchant comments
as : 'Limited in scope and not clear in plan' ; 'Dull. Does not
know how to group and give points to his facts' ; 'Pedantic' —
which might not have been considered to augur well for a future
Cabinet Minister! In view of this it is of interest that years later,
when asked which subjects learned at Edinburgh University had

[1] These were English Composition ; English Language and Literature ; French
Language and Literature ; German Language and Literature ; Mathematics (Pure
and Applied) ; Advanced Mathematical Subjects ; Chemistry ; Physics ; Geology ;
Roman History ; Political Economy and Economic History ; Political Science ;
English Law.

[2] This was indeed a vintage year for Edinburgh University for the first three
places fell to its candidates, the third being John Charles Hirschfeld Macnair. It
was the first of only three occasions during the present century when a candidate
from Oxford or Cambridge was not top of the List.

John Anderson was not the first Watsonian to be first in the Civil Service
Examination ; this had been John James Nairne in 1890. A brilliant Indian Civil
Servant of great promise, he died of cholera in 1897 at the age of twenty-five.

been of direct use to him in his subsequent career, Anderson at once replied 'Chemistry' — then after a pause : 'Well, perhaps I should add Economics — at least it enabled me to know when the economists were talking nonsense!'

It was also characteristic of him that having himself excelled, he should sit down and analyse, for the benefit of others, the best means by which, in the light of his experience, he believed they could do likewise. In an article contributed to *The Watsonian* entitled 'Sidelights on the Civil Service' — into which, incidentally, he had barely himself been initiated! — he commented on the Civil Service Examination :

> As this joint examination for the three dignified Services of the Home Country, the Great Dependency, and the Crown Colonies is beyond doubt the most severe competitive test in the country, both on account of the scope and variety of the subjects, and from the fact that success in it is a cherished ambition of many of the most earnest students in every one of our universities ; a few suggestions from one who has had occasion to give the matter some thought may be of service to young aspirants.
>
> There are two rules which, if followed, will be found to supplement and to fortify each other. The first is : having once decided to compete, never for a moment falter ; here, as in other things, he who hesitates is lost. The second is this : never 'cram'. To keep the ultimate end in view is sufficient, avoid cramming and a sound educational course may be followed.[1]

Having laid down these two fundamental — and eminently sound — precepts, the writer proceeded to elaborate them at some length and detail. It is possible to detect in this passage, and indeed in the whole article, a touch of self-conscious pride, even perhaps of smugness. Some may even descry therein the beginnings of that portentousness which, later in life and quite unjustly, earned Anderson the sobriquet of 'Pompous John'. But in all fairness it must be remembered that he *had* just accomplished a prodigious intellectual feat and might be justly proud of it and, moreover, at this stage of his life at least, he was prone to a certain form of mildly facetious humour, to which may be attributed the otherwise intolerably patronizing passage on advice to 'young aspirants'.

[1] *The Watsonian*, vol. ii, No. 1, December 1905.

For John's triumph had been very real indeed. The choice now lay open to him of appointment to either the Indian Civil or the Home Civil Service. It was customary in those days for most leading candidates to give preference to India, where the salaries paid by the Government of India were higher than those at home and there were, in addition, allowances for housing, servants, etc. It was an alluring prospect to young bachelors. But with an eye to imminent matrimony, John eschewed the fleshpots of the East. This was in all probability due in some degree to his desire not to inflict the climate of India upon Chrissie and partly to a certain opposition on the part of his parents to his leaving Britain. In addition, although the salaries in India might be higher, the opportunities for 'home leave' were not frequent and, all in all, John chose to remain in London. He was accordingly appointed a Second Class Clerk (Higher Division) in the Colonial Office at a salary of £200 *per annum*.[1]

[1] His salary scale was that of £200–£500, rising by annual increments of £20.

II

A Civil Servant in Peace and War

1905-1920

(i)

THERE were precious few fleshpots in the life of the two young Civil Servants — Alexander Gray had been appointed a clerk in the office of the Local Government Board — when they took up their quarters in London in the late October of 1905. Having no local knowledge, they elected to return to the crowded, though welcoming, hospitality of Mrs. Cliff in Gratton Road, but they soon tired of these not very salubrious surroundings and began to look about for better quarters. It was John Anderson who found them. By good fortune he discovered that the son of an old family friend at Eskbank, William Paterson, whom he knew and liked well, was living in rooms at 14 Killarney Road, Wandsworth Common, and it was amicably arranged between him and his landlady, a redoubtable lady named Mrs. Annie Nelson, that Anderson and Gray should move in with him. The transition took place in the early months of 1906 and the three settled down very contentedly together under the motherly care of Mrs. Nelson, whom they addressed, to her intense delight, as 'Madame Annie'.

They were all hard-working young men, Anderson and Gray in the vocation of their choice — though Gray was later to forsake the Civil Service to find renown in academic fields [1] — and Paterson in the early stages of the water-engineering business which he had founded some four years earlier and which was to bring him wealth

[1] Alexander Gray transferred from the Local Government Board to the Colonial Office in 1909. He worked with Anderson both there and in the National Insurance Commission until the establishment of the Ministry of Health in 1919, when he left the Civil Service to become Professor of Political Economy at the University of Aberdeen in 1921, transferring to the University of Edinburgh in 1935. He retired as Professor Emeritus in 1956, having been knighted in 1947. He has achieved great literary distinction for his translation of poems and ballads from the German and Scandinavian languages.

and fame.[1] Their recreations were few, consisting mostly of long walks during the week-ends and a regular attendance on Sundays at the Presbyterian kirk at the top of Wandsworth Hill. John's were even fewer, for, whereas the other two went out occasionally in the evenings to visit friends or to the theatre, he never joined in these excursions. He was saving up for his marriage and would embark on no junketings which would involve him in what he regarded as unnecessary expense.

On the other hand, he appeared to do very little at home. He was never seen to read a book,[2] or indeed anything but the *Daily Chronicle* and the *Evening News*, which he perused meticulously from beginning to end, advertisements and all, doubtless absorbing as much information from the latter as from the news columns. He would play chess on Sundays but otherwise their evenings together were mainly spent in endless conversation.

(ii)

John Anderson began his career in the Colonial Office on October 23, 1905, in the West African Department, then under Mr. Reginald Antrobus.[3] He was at once christened 'young John Anderson' to distinguish him from a senior member of the Office of the same name,[4] and at first his speech was in such broad Scots that his colleagues had great difficulty in understanding a word he said. But his outstanding ability was never for a moment in doubt, manifesting itself from the outset, and he was marked down as an unusual recruit. He already displayed that gravity of appearance and that maturity of judgment which he showed throughout his life and, in addition, there was his astounding fund of accurate information.

[1] William Paterson founded the Paterson Engineering Company in 1902, which became one of the leading water-engineering firms in the country with wide ramifications abroad. He was knighted in 1944 and remained closely associated with John Anderson through many years of his life. He died in 1956.

[2] In later life John Anderson developed a greater, though still limited, capacity for reading. He came to know his Walter Scott and Robert Louis Stevenson very thoroughly and could read in Anglo-Saxon, also learning passages of Chaucer by heart and finding relaxation in works on logarithms.

[3] Later Sir Reginald Antrobus, K.C.M.G. (1853-1942), Assistant Under-Secretary of State in the Colonial Office, 1898-1909.

[4] This was Sir John Anderson, G.C.M.G., K.C.B., who later became Governor of the Straits Settlements and Permanent Under-Secretary of State for the Colonies. He died in 1918.

'The mathematics maketh men subtile ; natural philosophy, deep', wrote Francis Bacon, and John had assuredly graduated with honours in both these subjects. Nevertheless, there lies herein something of an enigma in his character, which is difficult of explanation. Though he was rarely seen to open a book, it would be quite wrong to say that he read nothing. What he did was to confine his reading to his 'In-Tray' and allied official papers. But yet he seemed to soak in extraneous knowledge mysteriously and without effort, from an assiduous reading of the newspapers and from conversation — or simply just 'through the pores'! His ability to make himself complete master of a subject in an extraordinarily brief space of time soon gave rise in the Office to the half jocular, but very nearly true, remark that if John Anderson had minuted a paper there was nothing that one could add in passing it on to higher authority. It was soon apparent that the higher authorities held much the same opinion. Mr. Antrobus did not hesitate to describe him as the most brilliantly able junior he had ever had and that this view was shared is shown by John's appointment as Secretary to two important Committees on West African questions within a few years of his entering the Office.

The first of these was Sir Kenelm Digby's Committee on the Northern Nigerian Lands which sat during the summer of 1908. This did not give him an opportunity to visit Nigeria, for in those days it was rarely that committees investigated situations *in situ*. They summoned colonial administrators to give evidence and remained themselves in London. Throughout their deliberations the Digby Committee were constantly and gratefully aware of the ability of their young Secretary and paid him a handsome tribute in their Report.[1] John emerged from this venture with an enhanced reputation, Mr. Antrobus remarking that 'young John Anderson', although a junior, should really be the head of the Department!

John was already showing that good conceit of himself and that complete fearlessness in dealing with those with whom he had to deal which characterized his whole career. He was never backward in offering his views, nor was it in him to suffer gladly the opinion

[1] The Northern Nigerian Lands Committee signed its Report (Cmd. 5102) on July 29, 1908. The report was not, however, presented to Parliament until April 1910.

of others, no matter how august they might be, if it differed fundamentally from his own. There was soon current in the Office a story that the then Assistant Under-Secretary of State, Sir George Vandeleur Fiddes, himself an awesome personage, had remarked after an official conversation with Anderson that he had felt like a peccant schoolboy being admonished by a headmaster.

In June 1909 John spent five days in Hamburg on a visit to the recently established Kolonial Institut, with the dual object of obtaining full information about the arrangements for training German colonial officials and also of finding out what he could about the method of selection of candidates and about staff arrangements generally.

The Kolonial Institut was largely the personal idea of the then State-Secretary, Dr. von Dernburg, who, being an intensely practical person, was strongly impressed by the unpractical features of the prevailing system for the training of colonial officers. German colonial officials were nearly all recruited from the home civil service and many of them were totally ignorant of the conditions in the lands and territories which they were sent out to administer. By means of the Institut at Hamburg, Dr. von Dernburg sought to improve the system whereby a new official spent the best part of his first tour of duty in an unhealthy climate in gaining knowledge which he could acquire under better conditions at home before appointment.

Anderson's knowledge of German was good and fluent. His conversations and reading of reports soon placed him in possession of facts on which he made certain comments of interest. Students at the Institut spent one academic year studying courses covering some twenty-five subjects, with certain optional courses in addition. It was Anderson's opinion that altogether too much was being attempted in this curriculum, and he also commented that, despite the multiplicity of subjects, accountancy was not included.

All in all, however, he was not deeply impressed with what he had seen, and he returned to England convinced of the superiority of British Colonial Service methods over German — a conviction which time proved to be entirely correct. It was his considered opinion that the scheme employed by the Institut had many faults characteristic of German educational methods. The British legal course was perhaps capable of further development, and he recommended that a course in Mohammedan law should be established.

The question of anthropology would also, he felt, become more pressing before long. Apart, however, from these superficial points there was little doubt in his mind that the Colonial Office would be well advised to adhere to the general lines on which they had begun.

Some two years later Anderson was appointed Secretary of the Departmental Committee set up under the chairmanship of Lord Emmott 'to enquire into matters affecting the currency of the British West African Colonies and Protectorates'. Having sat for six months, the Committee completed its report on June 5, 1912, recommending, *inter alia*, the introduction of a distinctive local currency for British West Africa and also the establishment of a Currency Board. Throughout their deliberations the chairman and members of the Committee had been fully — and indeed gratefully — aware of the fact that, in the facilitation of their work and the formulation of their ultimate conclusions, they had owed much to the personality and efficiency of their thirty-year-old Secretary. In the final paragraph of their report they paid him more than the conventional compliments : 'Both in the conduct of our enquiry and in the preparation of our report, his knowledge, zeal and ability have been of the greatest possible value to us.'[1]   Some years later, in congratulating John on his appointment as Chairman of the Board of Inland Revenue, one of the members of the Committee, Mr. Leslie Couper, wrote : 'So the "knowledge, zeal and ability" displayed by the Secretary of the Committee on West African Currency in 1911 have carried you to high places.'

Had Anderson remained in the Colonial Office there is little doubt that his outstanding ability would have been rewarded in due course perhaps by Colonial Governorships abroad and certainly by the office of Permanent Under-Secretary, in which post his grave dignity would have been well graced by the scarlet mantle of the Order of St. Michael and St. George, of which he would have been, *ex officio*, Secretary.   But, though his conspicuous talents would inevitably have brought him recognition and eminence in public life, it is, perhaps, doubtful whether this would have occurred so rapidly had it not been for the first of several fortunate incidents.

It so happened that in 1912 Mr. Lloyd George, then Chancellor

[1] The Report of the Committee was presented to Parliament as a Command Paper (Cmd. 6426) in October 1912.

of the Exchequer, had introduced amongst his programme of social reforms that of National Health Insurance. Having secured its adoption by Parliament, with no little difficulty, he had to establish a Government Department to administer it, and at the head of this he placed that brilliant, if erratic, genius of the Civil Service, Sir Robert Morant. A staff was recruited by levying upon the other branches of the Civil Service in Whitehall and, to his satisfaction, John Anderson received an invitation from Sir John Bradley, of the Treasury, to transfer to the National Insurance Commission. He at once accepted, and with him went Alexander Gray.

There was something of a gamble attached to this decision, for though the Civil Service is a faithful mistress, wife or mother — in whichever capacity one cares to consider it — to throw up the certainty of a successful career in the Colonial Office for the comparative uncertainty of a new department, which in those early days was considered doubtful of survival, demanded some degree of courage and confidence. These qualities, however, John had never lacked. Words written years later of a great English churchman are singularly applicable to him also : 'I believe he must have learnt very young what some people never learn — that if you are sure of yourself, it does not matter whether or not you are sure of what you are going to meet round the corner.' [1]

The valedictory to John's service in the Colonial Office was written in the polished prose of the Secretary of State himself. Mr. Harcourt [2] minuted : 'Mr. Lloyd George and Sir R. Morant have done well for themselves, an ill-service to the Colonial Office, and, I hope, good to Mr. Anderson, whose admirable services I gratefully acknowledge'.

(iii)

Before following John Anderson's career as a Civil Servant, it is necessary to go back a year or so in consideration of his personal affairs. Since coming to London in 1905 his fixed ambition had

---

[1] These words written by Lionel Smith, for many years Rector of Edinburgh Academy, of his lifelong friend, Archbishop Temple, are included in his biography by the Rev. F. A. Iremonger (*William Temple, his Life and Letters* (1948), p. 501).

[2] The Rt. Hon. Lewis, 1st Viscount Harcourt, was Secretary of State for the Colonies from 1910 to 1915, being raised to the peerage a year later. He died in 1922.

been to place himself in a sufficiently good financial position to enable him to marry Chrissie Mackenzie. For two years he had pinched and saved to this end on his somewhat exiguous salary, eschewing both alcohol and tobacco, and many other small luxuries and recreations. He now considered that his salary, which, with his annual increments, amounted in 1907 to £140 *per annum*, plus his savings, placed him in what he regarded as circumstances commensurate with the responsibilities of matrimony. His income was by no means princely, but he calculated that they could just manage on it.

There had been other difficulties also to be overcome. Though the older generation of Andersons, Mackenzies and Briglmens had been friendly, and John and the Mackenzie girls had always been on the best of terms, there had been some feeling in his family that he was 'throwing himself away' on Chrissie ; and, though this had never for a moment affected his love for her, it remained, nevertheless, a factor with which he had to contend. But his mother and father, who had agreed to his engagement at the time of his departure for Leipzig, were now equally ready to acquiesce in his marriage, if this was his unwavering intention and his happiness depended upon it.

So in the spring of 1907 John applied for leave from the Colonial Office ; the bachelor triumvirate at 14 Killarney Road was broken up and, with his two friends, he journeyed to Edinburgh where, on April 2, he and Chrissie were married in St. Andrew's Church, Drumsheugh Gardens. Alexander Gray was his best man and the witnesses were Chrissie's sister Kate and William Paterson. John was twenty-four and Chrissie twenty.

From first to last John and Chrissie's married life was one of great devotion. They were young and very happy and, though in the days of their courtship she had displayed certain neurotic tendencies, these diminished as their lives blended together. Chrissie was sweet, charming and pretty, and John adored her. Her intellectual attainments were not outstanding but she was shrewd and clever, and she understood the secrets of married felicity. John might appear to be portentous to his fellow Civil Servants, but this was not the case at home. Chrissie teased him and twiddled him round her little finger, and he delighted in it. Occasionally she lost her temper with him — once at least going so far as to slap his

JOHN AND CHRISSIE ON THEIR WEDDING DAY,
APRIL 2, 1907

face — but he laughed at her in his turn and chose to treat it as an endearment — which perhaps it was! With her he was gay and carefree ; love and laughter had come into his life ; and though, as a matter of principle, he would not allow himself to be dominated by her, in ordinary matters of life he deferred almost invariably to her wishes.

On their marriage they rented a small furnished house in Throwley Road, in the Surrey suburb of Sutton, and there they led a frugal but contented life. Chrissie was a good cook and John himself liked to go into the kitchen during the week-ends, though his culinary accomplishments did not extend beyond pancakes and the Scottish sweetmeat known as 'tablet'. If there was a fly in the ointment of Chrissie's early married happiness it was that, like many another young bride, she was lonely when her John was away at the office and, in consequence, she was homesick. While he was wrestling with the problems of West Africa, she had little to occupy her time, for the housekeeping in their tiny home was not a demanding task. Outside her immediate intimate circle Chrissie was shy, and this reserve kept her from making friends in the neighbourhood.

John solved this dilemma with the same masterful aplomb with which he was to resolve other and greater problems. He discovered in the local doctor, Robert ('Jimmie') Jamieson, a former contemporary and friend at Edinburgh University, who was just about to be married. With him and his young wife, Chrissie soon found that companionship which she had lacked. In addition, both Alexander Gray and William Paterson soon followed John's lead into matrimony and there resulted an extension of the old friendship of Killarney Road.

But it was with the Jamiesons that the young Andersons spent many of their week-ends in company. The four of them would play golf on the Banstead or Woodcote course and then return to supper and bridge in each other's houses. John was an excellent bridge player but, at this period of his life at any rate, an indifferent golfer. He was intolerant of his faults at this game and, on one occasion at least, is known to have broken a putter across his knee!

During his annual leave of absence they visited their parents in Scotland, with sometimes a Highland holiday by themselves. In other respects Chrissie did not impinge upon John's official life.

She never wanted to go with him to official parties in London or to meet his colleagues, and there is no evidence that she accompanied him on his five-day visit to Hamburg in the summer of 1909. What she really enjoyed was a shopping expedition, and perhaps a matinée at the theatre, with Mrs. Jamieson or another woman friend, returning to Sutton in time to welcome John home from the office.

In due course there came other occupations and distractions. A son was born to them on February 18, 1911, and they were justly proud of their first-born. They named him Alastair, with the second name of David, in honour of John's father.

In the following year, John's fortunes having prospered, he bought a house, 'Locksley', in Sherwood Park Road, Sutton. This was a milestone in their lives. They had at last acquired a home of their own, furnished with their own belongings, and Chrissie's cup of happiness seemed to have been filled to overflowing when, on February 3, 1916, she gave birth to a second child, a daughter, Mary Mackenzie.

Anderson's home life in these years was the normal complement to his career as a dedicated Civil Servant. His work in the Colonial Office, and later in the National Insurance Commission, was bringing him the recognition by his superiors which it deserved. His pattern of life became regular and almost rigid, and though the outbreak of the European War increased the volume of his work it did not materially change the rhythm of his daily routine. He would lunch each day at the Reform Club, to which he had been elected in 1914, sitting at the same table with the same people, and the conversation was very apt to run daily on the same lines. In the evening he would return to Chrissie's loving welcome and would listen to her news of the day and the doings of his son and daughter. Within their circumscribed and somewhat monotonous suburban limitations, and secure in the affection of his family, he was extremely happy.

(iv)

In his new work with the National Insurance Commission John was concerned with the beginnings of a social revolution. In these days of the mid-twentieth century the undoubted benefits of the Welfare State have come to be taken for granted as an accepted part of our national life. As such there is a strong tendency to consider them, if any thought is given to their origins at all, as purely an emanation of the great social revolution effected by the Labour Government between 1945 and 1951, and not as the latest steps in a long progress of social reform, initiated by the Liberal Government of Mr. Asquith in 1911 and continued by the Conservative Government of Mr. Baldwin in 1925. It was indeed the radical fervour of Mr. Lloyd George which blazed the trail and ultimately laid the foundations of our present benefactions.

Believing that not less than one-third of the poverty in Britain was caused by sickness rather than by unemployment, and that there was in the country a vast mass of unacknowledged destitution, the Chancellor of the Exchequer proposed to raise for the purposes of insurance a fund of £27,000,000 in a full year, partly by grants from the State and partly by contributions from employers and employees. Everyone in receipt of wages of not less than £3 a week would be covered by this new system of insurance, based on a compulsory weekly levy against ill-health and unemployment. It had been his original intention to expand his scheme at a later date to include provision for widows', orphans' and contributory old age pensions. This he was not able to achieve, but the foundations which he had laid were found adequate to bear this later superstructure when it was eventually brought into being by Mr. Baldwin's Government in 1925, in which legislation John Anderson was to play a leading part.

The National Insurance Bill, introduced into the House of Commons on May 4, 1911, became a part of what came to be known as 'The People's Battle', which so gravely embittered the political and social relations of the country — and, in respect of the Parliament Act, even threatened a constitutional crisis. But, on its introduction, the Bill received as warm a welcome from the Tory Opposition benches as from the Government supporters.[1] Mr. Lloyd George looked for an easy passage for his Bill and it was only in the Committee stages that it received a rough handling.

In the country at large, however, it was far from popular. 'Never

---

[1] 'The House of Commons was a wonderful sight', that indefatigable commentator, George Riddell, recorded. 'The Tories were almost as enthusiastic as the Radicals, and treated L. G. as if he were the saviour of mankind. Arthur Balfour all smiles and cordiality' (Lord Riddell, *More Pages from My Diary* (1934), p. 33).

was legislation more needed; never was it less wanted', said its author in later years. Indeed it is difficult at this distance of time to recapture the climate of bitter hostility which this piece of inspired legislation engendered. The medical profession was acutely divided, many doctors believing that their practices would be ruined by the introduction of the panel system provided by the Bill, and deputations of angry medicos made their representations to the Chancellor, threatening to boycott the system if it were enacted. Nor were the workers carried away by Mr. Lloyd George's catch-phrase of 'Ninepence for Fourpence' — the proposed contributions being, the State 6d., the employer 3d., and the employee 4d. — and there were many who would have preferred a non-contributory scheme and a slogan of 'Ninepence for Nothing'.

A strong element, moreover, among the Friendly Societies regarded the new system as an encroachment upon their preserves of working-class insurance. But by far the most spectacular of the hostile movements was that directed against the inclusion of domestic servants in the new scheme, when it dawned upon mistresses that they would have to stamp their servants' insurance cards. Drawing-room meetings, at which mistresses and servants alike pledged their opposition to the Bill, were held all over the country, and the nadir of vulgarity was reached when revolting little plaster figures of the Chancellor made their appearance in many homes, of which the tongue was made of rubber sponge, and which bore the legend: 'Let 'im lick 'is stamps 'isself'.

The Tories were in a difficult position. Much of what Mr. Lloyd George was proposing to do was in accordance with the progressive Conservative tradition of Disraeli, Lord Randolph Churchill and Joseph Chamberlain. Yet they were furious with the Liberal Government over the passage of the Parliament Act and would have dearly liked to defeat it by capitalizing on the hostility in the country at large. This, to their great credit, they did not do. Recognizing the Bill as a really valuable essay in constitutional social legislation, they gave it a grudging, and somewhat ungracious, approval. It received the Royal Assent on December 16, 1911.[1]

---

[1] Malcolm Thomson, *David Lloyd George, the Official Biography* (1948), pp. 199-202 ; Frank Owen, *Tempestuous Journey : Lloyd George, His Life and Times* (1954), pp. 203, 206-209.

(v)

Such was the political background of the new venture on which John Anderson embarked in February 1912, with the rank of Principal Clerk. Preliminary arrangements for the working of the National Insurance Commission had been in the hands of William Braithwaite who, with a very small staff— 'most of us scrambling round one large table in the Privy Council room'[1]— had built up a skeleton administration with infinite difficulty and stupendous effort. However, with the passage of the Insurance Act and the formal inauguration of the Commission, the central office came under the dynamic personality of Sir Robert Morant.

This remarkable man, whom Sir Harold Nicolson has described as 'the supreme Civil Servant', has remained, even after his death, a figure of acrid controversy.[2] A man of the highest intellect, 'he had a passion for making the instruments of public service more effective, and was consumed and destroyed by it', wrote one who worked closely with him. 'There was no intermittence in his volcanic energy. He knew no rest and enjoyed no leisure.' Another colleague, perhaps less well-disposed, described him as suffering from 'chronic diarrhoea of the pen'. Unfortunately there was an immediate clash of temperaments between him and William Braithwaite and with the latter's resignation the Commission was deprived of one of the brightest assets of its earliest days.

Nor was Braithwaite the only one with whom Morant fell out. There existed a vendetta between him and Sir Robert Chalmers who had recently become Permanent Secretary of the Treasury, and their disagreement very nearly wrecked the gigantic enterprise of the National Insurance Act. For only with Chalmers' approval could Morant procure the quantity and quality of staff which he needed and at the salaries he thought right, and it did not seem that this approval would be forthcoming. However, after weeks of mutual recrimination Morant eventually won the day and the word

[1] R. W. Harris, *Not so Humdrum, the Autobiography of a Civil Servant* (1939), p. 123.
[2] For encomiums of Morant see the article in *The Dictionary of National Biography, 1912–1921*, by Sir Lucien Amherst Selby-Bigge, and an essay by Violet Markham in *Friendship's Harvest* (1956). The other side of the picture is given by Lynda Grier in *Achievement in Education* (1932) and by Michael Sadleir in his memoir of his father, *Michael Ernest Sadler*, published in 1949.

went forth for Warren Fisher of the Treasury to take 'a loan collection' to Morant's assistance. This group were not placed under Morant's orders and all had 'return tickets' to their departments whenever they cared to use them ; they were to establish contact with the heads of Morant's departmental divisions, of whom Anderson was one, seeing that they got what they wanted in staff, money and accommodation and keeping a general eye on their activities and progress. And, when the 'loan collection's' work was done, as Sir Ernest Gowers has written, 'the storm-tossed Morant at last found the ballast that he so sorely needed in the level-headed sagacity of the two young men who are now Lord Waverley and Lord Salter'.[1]

But what a galaxy of stars gathered around Morant to assist in the gigantic task of getting this machinery working in the space of a few short months. The staff of the Commission was a veritable forcing-ground of future great reputations. In the autumn of 1912 there were no fewer than four Fellows of All Souls working in the department (William Graham-Harrison, Maurice Gwyer, Dougal Malcolm and G. M. Young) and two others (Frederick Liddell and Wilfred Greene) who had between them drafted the National Insurance Act. Three of Anderson's colleagues (John Bradbury, Arthur Salter and Claude Schuster) later received peerages in addition to himself, and a fourth (Warren Fisher) might have had one if he had wanted it ; whilst among those whose subsequent careers were of at least sufficient distinction to win them knighthoods were Laurence Brock, John Brook, Henry Bunbury, Noel Curtis-Bennett, William Graham-Harrison, Alexander Gray, Ernest Gowers, Maurice Gwyer, Adair Hore, Robert Johnson, Dougal Malcolm, John Maude, Alexander Maxwell, James Roe, Ernest Strohmenger, William Sutherland, Aubrey Symonds, Sylvanus Vivian, Alfred Watson and Arthur Woodgate.

Morant was the man to make full use of such a *corps d'élite*. Once he was sure that his colleagues and subordinates were loyally working for the ends which he had set before himself and them, no-one was more generous in welcoming their criticism, in leaving them a free hand if they came up to his standards of ability and industry,

---

[1] *The Economist*, September 7, 1957, p. 753. Review of Wm. Braithwaite's memoirs, *Lloyd George's Ambulance Wagon.*

and in giving them full credit for their achievement ; and of no-one was this more true than of one of the more junior of his colleagues, John Anderson.

In the early days of the Commission, Anderson was once asked what he was doing and replied with a grin, yet laconically : 'Exceptions and Exemptions'. This terse phrase summed up the dealings of the small branch of which he was the head with certain committees which investigated all sorts of strange problems about the position under the Act of such part-time employments as those of puppy-walker and knocker-up, and whether professional footballers and 'leggers' — men who propelled barges through canal tunnels by using their legs on the roof of the tunnel — could claim to fall under the category of 'manual labour'.[1] Perhaps it seemed small beer after the larger problems which he had handled in the Colonial Office but he was undaunted. He had boldly chanced his luck in coming to the Commission and he more than justified himself. From the outset he dominated — or at least made his presence felt — at every discussion in which he took part. The distinctive qualities which he developed throughout his later career could already be discerned ; the obviously outstanding intellectual ability, which, without vanity, became confident of itself ; the *gravitas*, poise and air of authority ; ambition directed towards securing a position which would make real achievement possible rather than the incidental rewards and honours.

That these qualities were recognized and appreciated by Anderson's superiors is manifest from the fact that they called him, a comparatively junior head of section, more and more into their inner councils.

> I soon discovered that my chief was concerned with a far wider range of subjects than those assigned to his branch [writes Sir Alexander Maxwell, then one of Anderson's subordinates and later to succeed him as Permanent Under-Secretary at the Home Office]. He was often in conference with the heads of the office on major questions of policy, and it was a frequent practice for members of other branches to come to him for advice on their problems, although he had no official duty or authority to give them guidance.[2]

[1] Harris, p. 174.
[2] Letter from Sir Alexander Maxwell to the author, July 23, 1959.

D

This was also the first occasion on which John had had the opportunity of demonstrating his abilities as a chief. It was not a large staff that he administered in the branch of 'Exceptions and Exemptions' but they at once felt the impact of his character. Though unaffected and friendly, he had it not in him to evoke affection, or even friendship, among his fellow-workers, but they readily gave him their respect and their admiration, and that unstintingly — and there was even a little fear. Both now and later he would not hesitate to delegate work and, if satisfied that a subordinate knew his job, he was quite content to leave him a free hand. Moreover, as time went on, he developed that uncanny genius of the efficient administrator for knowing exactly what anyone in his branch or department was doing without interfering with them. On the other hand, if one of his juniors got into trouble, John would be the first to help him out of the mess and would fight for him 'to the steps of Caesar's throne'.

It is a matter of record that when at this time two of his elder colleagues were speculating on Anderson's future, one of them said that, if he had gone into the Church, he would have ended as Archbishop of Canterbury, while the other averred that his natural sphere was the law and, had he followed this vocation, he would inevitably have been appointed Lord Chief Justice. The subject of their discussion at this moment had just had his thirtieth birthday.

It was not surprising, therefore, that, when in May of 1913 the position of Secretary to the National Insurance Commission fell vacant through the appointment of its previous incumbent, Sir Claude Schuster, to the post of Permanent Secretary to the Lord Chancellor, John Anderson's name should be considered to succeed him. The natural successor was the Assistant-Secretary, Mr. Lawrence Brock, and the non-official members of the Commission were keenly in his favour. But Robert Morant, whose judgment of men was rather better than his handling of them, was convinced that John Anderson, though still a junior both in years and in service, was the right man for the post, which at that time demanded quite exceptional qualities. He failed to carry the Commission with him, however ; they knew and liked Brock and had barely heard of Anderson.

I recall Morant one day came to my room [writes Sir Henry Bunbury] and asked me first if I thought that Anderson should be the new Secretary. On my replying 'Yes', he asked me, as I was supposed to have some influence with the dissenting Commissioners, if I would see them and try to bring them round to his view. I tried and failed.[1]

What eventually settled the matter was the action of Lawrence Brock himself, who had got wind of what was going on, and without hesitation advised the Commissioners that Anderson was in his opinion the right man for the job. Impressed with this frankness in a potential rival rather than by their Chairman's advocacy, the dissentient Commissioners withdrew their opposition and John was appointed.[2]

It is no little to his credit that, while his appointment occasioned no surprise among his colleagues, it also caused no resentment, though his promotion meant the passing over of several men considerably older and senior to himself. He was liked and respected and it was clearly recognized that he was no careerist and that anything in the nature of intrigue was entirely foreign to his character. But, apart from the general recognition that the ablest man among them had got the job, there was also a consensus of opinion, perhaps in part unconscious, that John could team up with and control the volatile genius of Morant, in a way that Schuster had not done, and

[1] Letter from Sir Henry Bunbury to the author, August 8, 1959.
[2] It should be explained that the machinery set up under the Health Insurance Act consisted of four Commissions for England, Scotland, Ireland and Wales respectively, with a co-ordinating Joint Committee under the Chairmanship of the responsible Minister, the Rt. Hon. C. F. G. Masterman. Since the Scottish, Irish and Welsh Commissions had really only been created to satisfy the national sentiments in those countries, the major bulk of the work fell upon the English Commission, which was composed of members with very different origins, temperaments, interests and outlooks. They were Sir Robert Morant, Chairman, Sir John Bradbury, David Shackleton (Trade Union), Lister Stead (Friendly Societies), Dr. Whitaker (British Medical Association) and Mrs. Mona Wilson (Women's Trade Union League). The appointment of Secretary to the English Commission was therefore an *English*, not a United Kingdom appointment, and, on the day that Anderson was appointed, a Scottish Commissioner came to Arthur Salter (then Private Secretary to the Minister) with the remark : 'This is a feather in the cap of Scotland. The English Commission has been obliged to go to Scotland for its Secretary.' 'No,' replied Salter, 'the English Commission was not obliged to. It appointed Anderson because he was the best man available without regard to the fact that he is not "English". Now, I will put a direct question to you. If the Scottish Commission find that the best man available for its Secretary is an Englishman, just as much superior to the next candidates as Anderson was, will you appoint him ?' 'No, of course we shall choose a Scot', was the reply. 'Then', said Salter, 'don't you think that what has happened to-day is at least as much to the credit of England as of Scotland ?' (Letter from Lord Salter to the author, June 23, 1959 ; see also Lord Salter's *Memoirs of a Public Servant* (1961), p. 54.)

Brock might not have been able to do, and perhaps this view had even been in the mind of Brock himself.

'Once Anderson was there I felt that the Act was in good keeping', writes William Braithwaite in his memoirs,[1] and there is no doubt that John gave to Morant that calm and sagacious support which he needed. Their relationship, from which the work of the Commission derived such inestimable benefit, was based partly upon mutual respect, partly upon a strange affinity of complementary qualities and attributes, and partly upon John's unflinching fearlessness in dealing with a chief some twenty years his senior in age. For Anderson asserted his opinion to Morant with that same courage and confidence which he had shown in facing Sir George Fiddes in the Colonial Office and, as before, he was successful.

Once when he was trying to explain a point to Morant who, as was his custom, was offering frequent interruptions with what seemed to be irrelevant questions, John's patience was tried very hard. At each intromission he would forbearingly begin his exposition again but with an ominous calm which betokened increasing irritation. Finally, he broke out and, glaring at his chief, exclaimed : 'Look here, Morant, how *can* I explain this thing to you if you constantly interrupt me in what I am saying ?' Sir Robert collapsed into silence like a schoolboy in the presence of a justifiably scolding master — and, be it remembered, Morant was Morant. Yet he never held John's independent attitude against him, either on this or on any other occasion, and the only criticism he was ever heard to make was the remark that : 'The trouble with young John Anderson is that he is always so damned right'.

(vi)

The outbreak of the First World War in August 1914 found the provisions of the National Health Insurance Act working smoothly in an England which, under the soothing influence of its benefits, had quite forgotten the *brouhaha* which had attended its birth two years earlier, and for this great credit must be given to the efficiency

[1] *Lloyd George's Ambulance Wagon, being the Memoirs of William J. Braithwaite 1911–1912*, edited, with an Introduction by Sir Henry N. Bunbury, K.C.B. (1957), p. 302.

of the administration which emanated from the gifted partnership of Morant and Anderson.

The sudden transmogrification of England at peace to England at war had its inevitable effects upon all Government departments and not the least upon the work of the National Insurance Commission. Thanks in great measure to Anderson's organization, the machinery of the Commission was in better condition than that of many other departments in Whitehall to meet the new demands now made upon it, and not the least of its assets was the personality and scientific training of its Secretary.

Two immediate problems faced the Government in the medical field. The first was the mobilization of doctors and surgeons for war work in such a way as to equate fairly the respective needs of the armed services and the civilian population. Thanks to the good relations which had eventually been established between the Insurance Commission and the medical profession it was found possible to arrive at a speedy and efficient solution of this problem.

The second was more difficult of elucidation. Among the more serious predicaments with which the Home and Service Departments were confronted was that due to the sudden failure of the supply of a large number of important medical and surgical requirements, for which Britain had hitherto been dependent upon Germany. The crisis caused by this abrupt stoppage was the more acute at a time when so large a part of the nation's manhood was being hurriedly recruited for the fighting services. Anderson was deputed to deal with this emergency and he did so with competence and dispatch, using as a means the resources of the Medical Research Committee which had recently been created in connection with the National Health Insurance Scheme.

Amongst the more vital shortages was that of '606', an arsenical compound made by the German firm of Bayer and extremely effective in the treatment of syphilis. Its exact composition was unknown except to the makers. Meanwhile supplies were running short and the British Expeditionary Force — despite the injunction of Lord Kitchener that 'while treating all women with perfect courtesy, you should avoid any intimacy' — was in dire need of it.

Anderson moved quickly. He commandeered a portion of the supply of '606' available in Britain and called together the heads of the chief British drug manufacturing firms. After consultation it was revealed that several of them were doing research work on arsenical compounds but no one had got very far. Anderson asked them to pool their research resources and, after certain initial difficulties had been overcome, an effective partnership was achieved. As a result of their united efforts they were enabled to produce '606' by December 1914 and the demands of the Army were met in full.

After this success the pooled research team, at Anderson's instigation, began the investigation of the composition of salicylates, another German patent, with the result that, in due course, they discovered the formula for the aspirin tablet.[1]

John was also appointed a Government representative on the advisory committee set up by the Royal Society to organize chemical research for the purpose of meeting other particular wartime needs. Here he was in his element and his sound grounding at Edinburgh and at Leipzig stood him in good stead. The respect on both sides was mutual. On the one hand was Anderson's instinctive reverence for anything connected with the Royal Society ; on the other, the respect with which any suggestion coming from him was received by the other members of the Committee — all of them chemists of high standing and most of them his senior by many years. They were deeply impressed by the fact that a senior Civil Servant could talk some chemistry with them in its own language and could take an effective part in discussions dealing, in some scientific detail, with plans and enterprises for chemical research. There were to be other occasions on which he was to surprise professional scientists by the extent and variety of his knowledge in their field.

It was not only, however, John's knowledge which impressed his learned colleagues, but also his presence and his personality. Though he never asserted himself or his authority, they were conscious that in this young man of thirty-two, in the words of one of them,[2] there was

> a maturity of manner and judgment, a habit of caution and restraint in making a decision or expressing an opinion, such as are attained before the later years of middle-life by very few,

[1] Many years later Lord Waverley gave some account of these events in an address at Alderley Park to the Pharmaceutical Division of I.C.I. (*Alderley Park Review*, October 1957.)   [2] Sir Henry Dale, O.M., G.B.E., F.R.C.P., F.R.S.

even among men of the highest ability and the widest ranges of knowledge and experience. I found it difficult, in fact, to feel at ease and to do justice to my own opinions in face of what seemed in him then to be so premature, though in fact so well justified, an instinct for, and an assumption of, authority.

Yet it was these very qualities which evoked respect from John's seniors that certain, at any rate, of his contemporaries and juniors found insupportable. 'If that's the kind of man they have in the Civil Service I am afraid I have come into the wrong profession', was the reaction of one who served under him in the Insurance Commission, and there did not lack those who spoke of him as 'pompous John'.

In this they were less than fair. The truth is that John was consciously aware that he was, in a sense, the victim of his own rapid promotion and the causes which had prompted it. He was not ignorant, and certainly not ashamed, of his own great gifts and he would not hesitate to assert his opinion, if necessary, against those of the highest authority. But he was never either arrogant or discourteous — though, in later life, there was a tendency to be superior. He was fundamentally a humble man, but he realized that he had been called, by force of circumstance and his own outstanding merits, to a position in which he had to deal on terms of equality with men who were in most cases nearly twice his age. He therefore cultivated a certain austerity of manner, which indeed was not alien to him, and a severity of mien, which again was in character. He never pretended to be what he was not, but he allowed his natural authority to manifest itself in a way which gave him an appearance of being older than his years. Beneath this dour exterior he was very tender to ordinary humanity and, moreover, sensitive and vulnerable for himself.

An instance of this vulnerability occurred now in his life. In these first years of the war the streets of London were infested by young women who, in expression of a misplaced patriotic zeal, presented white feathers to any young man not in uniform. Officers on leave from France who, braving the wrath of the Provost Marshal, grasped at the opportunity of getting into civilian clothes, were not immune from these attentions — nor were Civil Servants. John Anderson was once the recipient of one of these badges of cowardice as he crossed Whitehall, and he was deeply hurt by it. Though technically of military age, he was a senior Civil Servant in prosecution of the most important needs of the State and, as such, had been urged not to volunteer. He did, in fact, register under the Derby Scheme and was placed on the Army Reserve pending a call to service. Honour had been more than satisfied and there is certainly nothing in his career, either then or later, which could give the remotest indication of lack of moral or physical courage, yet the thoughtless action of an irresponsible young woman wounded him to the quick. It rankled within him for many years. He said nothing of it at the time and, so far as is known, mentioned it very rarely, but the wound remained and it had an important influence on his subsequent career.

(vii)

On December 7, 1916, the first Coalition Government under Mr. Asquith fell and the reins of power passed to Mr. Lloyd George. The fortunes of the Allied Powers were at this moment in sad disarray. The great offensive on the Somme had bogged down in a morass of mud and blood. The Gallipoli adventure, after heavy casualties, was about to be liquidated, and the very life-lines of food and munition supplies to Britain were acutely imperilled by the intensification of the U-boat campaign. In addition to disastrous losses, the problem of shipping was further complicated by the ever-growing military demands upon sea transport. Allied anxiety was great and the chief burden fell upon the British Government.

Mr. Lloyd George acted with characteristic courage and disregard for convention. He took the control and requisition of merchant shipping out of the hands of the Admiralty and set up a separate Ministry of Shipping under a Controller, Sir Joseph Maclay, a Glasgow shipowner, who became a member of the Cabinet but not of the War Cabinet. The Transport Division of the Admiralty was transferred to the new Ministry *en bloc*, as were small sections of the Board of Trade, but the staff was pitifully small for the volume of work they were called upon to do and, above all, they lacked the wisdom of senior Civil Servants. Little by little loans were effected from other departments and a first-class team was eventually assembled, including Henry Bunbury, Arthur Salter and Cyril Hurcomb, but these yet lacked someone who could share with the Director-General, Sir Graeme Thomson, the combined responsibilities of chief executive and of adviser to the Controller on policy and administration.

The natural inclination of his former colleagues was to secure John Anderson for this rôle in double harness. Bunbury was deputed to obtain Morant's approval for the transfer and he, with the passionate patriotism that was characteristic of him, agreed that the needs of Sir Joseph Maclay were more pressing than his own. Anderson was formally seconded and took up his post as Secretary to the new Ministry on January 8, 1917.

Again John made his mark at once. The world of shipping and its problems was entirely new to him and, though Sir Joseph Maclay and those of his fellow shipowners who served as his advisory committee were his fellow Scots, they were nearly all from Glasgow, between which city and Edinburgh there is a great gulf fixed, and few of them were accustomed to the ways of doing business in a Government department. It was not an easy team to handle, but in a surprisingly short space of time John had succeeded in welding it into a harmonious and efficient organization. It soon became a pillar of strength to the Controller, who had somewhat unorthodox ideas of doing business. Maclay's forceful decisions, though often vitally necessary in an emergency, were nevertheless sometimes calculated to bring him into conflict with officialdom, and it was frequently due to Anderson's tactful handling of delicate situations that no ill feelings resulted on either side.

Though he would often sit watchfully silent at meetings in the Controller's room, his mind was never dormant and he was quick to seize upon the opportunities presented by situations with which he had previously been quite unfamiliar. Towards the end of the war, for example, Arthur Salter and his French opposite number, M. Jean Monnet,[1] having seen the imperative need for a supreme Authority to arrange allocations of shipping between the Allied Maritime Governments, had worked out a plan — then a novelty —

---

[1] The paths of John Anderson and Jean Monnet were to cross again some twenty years later when, in the early days of the Second World War, both were members of the Anglo-French Co-ordinating Committee.

for Programme Committees headed by an Allied Maritime Transport Council and Executive. They explained the scheme to Anderson who at once recognized its importance and became convinced
of its necessity. He threw the whole weight of his influence and
advice behind it. Its ultimate adoption and success owed much to
his prudence and wisdom, and his understanding of the official
machine.

The problems of shipping did not end with the termination of
hostilities and John found himself summoned to the Peace Conference at Paris to advise on various aspects of the Peace Settlement, among them the surrender to the Allies of the German
Mercantile Marine. This matter, difficult enough in itself, was
additionally complicated by the fact that it became involved in the
three separate, yet related, issues of reparation, famine relief and
blockade. Briefly the story is as follows : Germany had not been
required under the terms of the Armistice of November 11, 1918,
to hand over her merchant shipping to the Allies but, fifteen days
after the signing of this agreement, the Board of Trade, in accordance with a previous instruction from the War Cabinet, presented on
November 26 a Memorandum on the Economic Considerations
affecting the Terms of Peace, in which they recommended that 'as
an essential part of Reparation, the whole of the shipping belonging
to the Central Powers above 1600 tons gross . . . should be handed
over to the Allied Maritime Transport Council, to be employed by
them to the best advantage during the reconstruction period, and
thereafter allotted to the various Allied States in proportion to their
losses through illegitimate action by the enemy'.[1] These losses at
sea had been very great indeed and the major share of them had
been borne by Britain.[2] It was not surprising, therefore, that the
War Cabinet accepted the recommendation of the Board of Trade
as one of the substantial elements in the claims for Reparation which
they proposed should be included among the terms of peace ultimately to be imposed upon Germany.

The issue became more urgent, however, by reason of the half-

[1] David Lloyd George, *The Truth about the Peace Treaties* (1938), i, pp. 451-452.
[2] The total shipping losses by enemy action sustained by Allied and neutral
countries during the 51 months of the war, amounted to 6604 ships sunk with an
aggregate of 12,850,814 tons. Of this Britain lost 2479 ships representing an aggregate of 7,759,090 tons.

promise contained in the Armistice Agreement to the effect that, though the existing blockade of Germany was to be maintained, the Allied and Associated Powers 'contemplate the provisioning of Germany during the Armistice as shall be found necessary' (Art. XXVI). That this necessity existed there was no doubt. Germany was very short of food and there was considerable apprehension amongst certain of the Allied statesmen that, if she were reduced to actual starvation, she would fall a prey to Bolshevism. But the extra shipping necessary to supply food to Germany could not be found from Allied sources and it was therefore decided to require the German Government to hand over their merchant marine at once for use in their own revictualling and as a contribution to the relief of the famine conditions then prevailing in Central Europe generally. At the negotiations at Trier for the prolongation of the Armistice in January 1919, therefore, a committee of Allied experts, on which Arthur Salter and John Anderson represented the United Kingdom, concluded an agreement with the Germans for the surrender of their merchant shipping for these purposes, 'without prejudice to the ultimate disposition of the vessels'. (January 17, 1919.)

For various reasons the fulfilment of the Trier Agreement hung fire. The Germans were unwilling to part with their ships unless the Allies agreed to lift the blockade completely. The Allies, for their part, had no intention of thus depriving themselves of a weapon with which, in the ultimate issue, they counted upon compelling a possibly recalcitrant Germany to accept the terms of peace. Further negotiations between the Allies and the Germans at Spa early in March, at which Anderson was not present, proved abortive. Meanwhile conditions in Germany had become so desperate that General Sir Herbert Plumer, commanding the British Army of Occupation, reported to the Prime Minister that the morale of his troops was affected, that they were giving away their own rations to the German civilians, and that he could not hold himself responsible for their discipline 'if children were allowed to wander about the streets, half starving'. These facts were placed by Mr. Lloyd George before a memorable session of the Supreme War Council on March 8, as a result of which it was agreed, largely at the insistence of the British Prime Minister, that, if the Germans would formally acknowledge their obligations under the Trier Agreement and would undertake to hand over their ships accordingly, the Allied and Associated Powers would proceed forthwith with the revictualling of Germany.

The representatives of the German Government were accordingly summoned to another meeting with the Allies at Brussels on March 13, to receive what amounted to an ultimatum on shipping, food and finance. Some stiff bargaining followed, the shipping negotiations on behalf of Britain being handled by Sir Joseph Maclay and John Anderson. In the end the Germans capitulated. They surrendered their ships and in due course Allied supplies reached Germany. The vessels were ultimately divided among the Allies as a part of reparation in kind.[1]

Though Anderson had played second string to Maclay and Salter in their meetings with the Germans, both of them paid high tribute to the contributions which he had made to the negotiations.

(viii)

At the termination of his work in Paris for the Ministry of Shipping — on which he was later to write the article in *The Encyclopaedia Britannica* — Anderson was appointed to four important Government posts in quick succession. In April 1919 he was made an additional Secretary to the old Local Government Board, but when in July of the same year this body and the Health Insurance Commission were merged in the new Ministry of Health, he became Second Secretary of that Ministry under Sir Robert Morant, who had made his own acceptance of the post of Permanent Under-Secretary conditional upon his having his former colleague as his right-hand man.

It was now that recognition of John's public services began. He had been made a Companion of the Bath in the New Year's Honours List of 1918, and in the Birthday Honours of June 1919 his promotion to Knight Commander in the same Order was announced.

---

[1] Under Annex III to Part VIII of the Treaty of Versailles, Germany ceded to the Allied and Associated Powers all her merchant ships of 1600 tons gross and upwards. This amounted to 1,824,828 gross tonnage, of which Britain received 1,330,000 gross tons and 450,000 gross tons of prize and detained ships. (*The Times*, April 20, 1920.)

He did not remain long at the Ministry of Health. In the autumn of 1919 the post of Chairman of the Board of Inland Revenue fell vacant. John was appointed to it on October 1st. It was one of the 'plum' jobs of the Civil Service, carrying with it a salary of £2000 *per annum* with a War Bonus of £300.[1] He was thirty-seven years of age.

Though he was not destined to serve long in this position, John Anderson left his unmistakable and indelible impression on the Inland Revenue. On assuming office he pursued the same technique that he had found indispensable during his many and varied mutations in the Civil Service. For the first three or four months he lay completely quiet, but was far from inactive. During this period he read extensively in the background and present problems of his new department and, in addition, summoned his chief advisers whose brains he picked exhaustively. As a result, when in February 1920 he was called to testify before a Select Committee of the House of Commons appointed to consider the question of levying a duty on wartime increases in wealth, he gave a very impressive performance as a witness extending over more than one day, to the admiration and amazement of the Committee. The Board had put in a long memorandum, on the detail of which Anderson was supported by Mr. Richard Hopkins,[2] but he had himself answered about 500 questions before Hopkins was called in separately to give evidence, and had displayed, in addition to the specific subject in hand, a complete mastery of the history and practice of the Inland Revenue.[3]

Nor was he backward in asserting his authority in his own house. Dissatisfaction had arisen among the ranks of the tax inspectors in the Revenue Office by reason of objections to the promotion of younger men to senior posts. A deputation of the disgruntled waited upon John Anderson who, after listening to their case and giving it his consideration, turned it down. The discontented inspectors had the temerity to take their case over the head of their

[1] On March 1, 1920, the salary, in common with those of all Permanent Secretaries, was increased to £3000 p.a. with a £500 War Bonus.

[2] Rt. Hon. Sir Richard Hopkins, G.C.B., succeeded Anderson as Chairman of the Board of Inland Revenue and subsequently served under him, when Chancellor of the Exchequer, as Permanent Secretary to the Treasury.

[3] *Report from the Select Committee on Increase of Wealth (War)*, presented to the House of Commons, May 13, 1920.

chief to certain Members of Parliament, whom they lobbied in their interests. Justifiably annoyed at this breach of Civil Service etiquette, which he considered to be an attempt to take advantage of a young Chairman, John took severe disciplinary action. From that moment he had established his authority for as long as he remained at Somerset House.

Thus at the beginning of the year 1920, John Anderson might truly say with the Psalmist that his 'lines were fallen unto him in very pleasant places'. He had achieved a high position in the hierarchy of the Civil Service at a very young age and there was every reason to believe that he would go higher. The rhythm of his life had fallen into a well-worn, satisfying and protective routine : the morning train from Sutton, the business of the Office, and luncheon at the Reform with such friends and colleagues as Cyril Hurcomb, Alfred Watson, Horace Hamilton, and sometimes William Paterson. These luncheon discussions gave him relaxation and he would unbend with his equals. If he started pontificating, as was his wont, the others at the table would laugh at him and he took their banter well. Sometimes he would interrupt their laughter to warn them, with a grin, that this was a subject he really knew about and they had better listen to what he had to say! Back at Somerset House there would be appointments and committee meetings in the afternoon ; and then the evening train back to Sutton and Chrissie's warm and loving welcome ; the exchange of news, the doings of the children, and perhaps a rubber or two of bridge with the Jamiesons after dinner ; the week-ends spent on the golf course and round the card table. It was a life that was a little limited, perhaps, on the social side ; but it was all very assured and satisfactory.

III

Dublin Castle

1920–1922

(i)

JOHN ANDERSON'S happy little world, seemingly so safe and so secure, was destined to crash about his head with appalling suddenness. On May 9, 1920, his beloved Chrissie died under an operation for cancer.

She had not been ailing for long and her illness and subsequent death came as a heartbreaking shock to her husband. John and Chrissie had been very close in their affection. She was only thirty-three at her death and the thirteen years of their married life had covered the early period of John's apprenticeship in the Civil Service, had seen his rise to prominence in the Insurance Commission and his further advancement during the war. They had lived very happily, if domestically, in Sutton, passing from one house to a better as his status and financial position improved. Together they had shared — but so briefly — the honour of his knighthood and she was to have been presented at Court in June. The devotion which had marked their Edinburgh courtship had continued through the years. She had borne him two children. They had loved greatly. She had been so gay and pretty ; the love of his heart.

There is no doubt but that John Anderson sorrowed deeply in his bereavement, yet he made no show of his feelings. His two closest friends, Alexander Gray and William Paterson, went immediately to him to express their sympathy and to keep him company. In so far as they could see he was in complete command of his emotions, talking on every subject save that which was nearest to his heart. But at the funeral not even his iron control could mask his deep affliction, yet with native punctilio he insisted upon his

47

small son Alastair shaking hands with all present, a duty which the boy performed with the utmost reluctance.

Thus, at the age of thirty-eight, John found himself a widower with two motherless children of nine and four. His duties as a Civil Servant would keep him fully occupied ; he could give little time to their upbringing. His sister-in-law, Nellie Mackenzie, now came again into his life. She was in the course of training to be a nurse at St. Thomas's Hospital, but on Chrissie's death she threw up her career without hesitation and offered to take charge of John's household. He accepted gratefully, and for the next twenty years she gave herself unstintingly to the welfare of John and his children.

Yet, though Nellie Mackenzie's generous gesture had solved his immediate domestic problem, it was apparent to his senior colleagues in the Civil Service that John Anderson had suffered a grievous blow. Not that the standard of his work was affected ; his deep sense of duty and of the proper order of things was too great for that ; but his granite visage and his increased dourness of manner spoke eloquently of the loneliness of spirit which he would not otherwise divulge. His work as Chairman of the Board of Inland Revenue, though of importance and ranking high in the hierarchy of Whitehall, was not perhaps sufficient to occupy and drug his mind against the sense of loss. Something more vital, more all-absorbing, was necessary for this purpose of psychotherapy.

It was now that fate, in the person of Sir Warren Fisher, intervened in his interests. The Head of the Civil Service had been instructed by the Prime Minister and Sir Hamar Greenwood, the new Chief Secretary for Ireland, to make a thorough survey of the organization of the latter's office in Dublin Castle. Fisher, together with three other Civil Servants, accompanied Greenwood to Dublin when he took office there on May 6, 1920, and from their own observations it became clear that a stern hand wielding a new broom was a vital necessity. On his return to London, partly perhaps out of sympathy for his friend but certainly because he believed him to be the best man for the job, Fisher offered John Anderson the post of Under-Secretary. John accepted without hesitation, grateful for an opportunity which would fill every moment of his day. Within a week of Christina's death and only seven months after his appointment to the Inland Revenue he found himself upon the strange and largely hostile shores of Ireland.

(ii)

To appreciate the full significance of the task which John Anderson had assumed it is necessary to survey briefly the history of Anglo-Irish relations for the preceding years.

Partly as a measure of their traditional Gladstonian political inheritance and partly in payment of the debt which they had incurred to the Irish Party in the House of Commons for the support given in the passage of the Parliament Act of 1911, Mr. Asquith's Government introduced on April 11, 1912, a Home Rule Bill for Ireland ; a measure which, while making no provision for the exclusion of Ulster, conferred upon the proposed Irish Parliament only very limited powers. At once the Protestant North sprang to the defence of what it regarded as its inalienable right to remain a part of the United Kingdom, free, above all things, from the juris-diction of a government in Dublin ; at once the Conservative Party, smarting from its recent failure to prevent the restriction of the power of the House of Lords, rallied to the support of the Ulster Unionists, who were predominantly Conservative voters. The backing offered by the Conservative Party stopped little short of inciting armed resistance to the King's Government on the part of Ulster in the event of any attempt at coercion. 'If such an attempt is made', declared Mr. Bonar Law at a Conservative rally in the park of Blenheim Palace on July 29, and speaking with the consider-able weight of his position as Party Leader, 'I can imagine no length of resistance to which Ulster can go in which I should not be prepared to support them.' With such encouragement it was not surprising to see the Solemn Covenant signed in Belfast on September 28, to be followed a year later by the formation of the Ulster Volunteers.

On January 16, 1913, the House of Commons passed the Home Rule Bill, which satisfied only the Irish Nationalists. The Govern-ment took no heed of the fact that on the 23rd the Sinn Fein National Council adopted a resolution refusing anything short of an inde-pendent Republic of Ireland. The House of Lords finally rejected

E

the Bill by a majority of ten to one on July 15, and on September 25, in defiance of the accepted legislation of His Majesty's Government, Sir Edward Carson announced the formation of an Ulster Provisional Government in Belfast with a Military Committee attached.

There followed the growing threat of civil war. In March 1914 occurred 'the Mutiny at the Curragh', when Brigadier-General Hubert Gough and fifty-seven other officers of the 3rd Cavalry Brigade declared that they would prefer to accept dismissal from the Army if they were ordered north to Ulster to enforce Home Rule; the following month saw the gun-running episode at Larne for the purpose of arming the Ulster Volunteers. In June the Liberal Government, bowing before the storm, passed through the House of Commons an Amending Bill abandoning the enforcement of Home Rule upon the predominantly Orange counties, and to this measure the House of Lords agreed with drastic amendments (July 8).

A round table conference, called at Buckingham Palace on July 21 on the initiative of King George V, dispersed three days later having completely failed to find any feasible solution to the Irish question. The spectre of civil war was brought measurably nearer on July 26 when another gun-running incident at Howth, this time in aid of the Irish Volunteers, found its tragic sequel in the 'Battle of Bachelor's Walk', when men of the King's Own Scottish Borderers, marching back from Howth to Dublin with the arms they had intercepted and seized, encountered on the quays a crowd which greeted them with jeers and then with stones. A number of the troops were injured and (whether with or without a definite order has never been established) they fired into the crowd, killing two men and a woman and wounding thirty-two others.

The shots fired by Gavril Princip at Sarajevo a month previously had sounded a warning note which, in Mr. Churchill's words, 'cut through the clamour of the haggard, squalid, tragic Irish quarrel which threatened to divide the British nation into two hostile camps'. In the great surge of patriotism which followed the British declaration of war on Germany on August 4, 1914, the question of Ireland seemed to have receded into the background. The Conservative Party, however, was greatly irked by Mr. Asquith's action in placing the Home Rule Bill on the Statute Book on September 15, even though this was accompanied by legislation postponing its operation until a year after the termination of hostilities and an undertaking given to Sir Edward Carson that there should be no coercion of Ulster.

On the following day (September 16) John Redmond, on behalf of the Irish Nationalists, made a stirring appeal to the people of Ireland to take their part in the war effort. He also asked that Irish recruits should be kept together in an Irish corps under its own officers. This request was refused by Lord Kitchener, recently appointed Secretary of State for War, with what Mr. Lloyd George later described as 'a folly amounting to malignity'.

Throughout the year 1915 and the first months of 1916 there ensued the widening split between the Irish Nationalists and Sinn Fein and the growing agitation of the latter for complete independence. The increasing power of Sinn Fein was belittled by the Nationalist leaders in the House of Commons, partly on the score of prestige and partly because they genuinely underestimated the strength of the new force in Irish affairs. Frequent warnings from Dublin, emanating from the Chief Secretary's Office and the intelligence department of the Royal Irish Constabulary, were ignored, with the result that the Easter Rising on April 24, 1916, though not unexpected by Dublin Castle, came as a grim surprise to His Majesty's Government in London.

The Easter Rising, ill organized in itself and for which the people of Ireland were unprepared, lacked any great degree of popular support in the country as a whole. The people of Dublin were irritated by the upheaval, as quiet respectable citizens might well be. They did not rise in support of the Republic of Ireland proclaimed by the 'Provisional Government' from the General Post Office, and when the surrender was made at last on April 29, a young British officer, placed in charge of a body of rebels being marched to an internment camp, found that he and his escort were not so much concerned with the possible escape of their prisoners as with protecting them against the hostile demonstrations of the Dublin mob. 'If only the people had come out with knives and forks!' was Commandant De Valera's bitter comment after his surrender of the Sinn Fein garrison at Boland's Mills.

It must be remembered that in the spring of 1916 the tide of war against Germany was not running in favour of Britain and her allies. Ireland had been stripped of troops for service in France and Flanders and in the Dardanelles and, in addition, there was reliable evidence that Germany was prepared to support the forces of Sinn Fein, at least in the supply of arms. Popular clamour in England cried aloud for stern measures against the Dublin rebels and it did not seem that the execution of fifteen men was too stern a measure of retribution for a rebellion in arms which had cost the lives of over a hundred British officers and men.[1] But among the fifteen men executed were included the seven signatories of the Irish Declaration of Independence and four of the five captured commandants of the rebel forces in Dublin.[2] Moreover, they were tried and condemned by special military courts sitting in secret and without any provision for means of defence. The death sentences were executed within a few hours of being passed.

It is always easy to rewrite history by the light of hind-sight. It is not even difficult to understand that a weak and divided Coalition Government in Westminster, over-burdened with the problems of a war for survival and of which the two component parties had played fast and loose with the fortunes of Ireland for years, should swing from a policy of vacillation to one of ruthless severity born of panic. Be that as it may, there is little doubt to-day that had the leaders of the Easter Rising been accorded a public trial, if necessarily in England, with provision for defence counsel, and sentenced to long periods of imprisonment in English jails, the forces of Sinn Fein might not have established their vital grip upon the sympathies of the Irish people and Ireland might have achieved self-government within the British Commonwealth of Nations by peaceful means instead of by the tragic and bloody process which

[1] 103 British officers and other ranks were killed in the Easter Rising, 357 were wounded and 9 were reported missing ; of the Royal Irish Constabulary, 14 officers and constables were killed and 23 wounded ; 3 members of the Dublin Metropolitan Police were killed and 3 wounded. The complete Irish casualty list was computed at 450 killed, including civilians, and 2614 wounded.

[2] The fifth was Eamon De Valera, who, condemned to death on May 10, received a commutation of his sentence to penal servitude for life on the following day. This decision has been variously ascribed to intervention by the United States authorities on the grounds that, having been born in New York, he was technically an American citizen, to the intercession of John Redmond and Bernard Shaw, and to the general protests of the British and American press and public against the continued executions. (Dorothy Macardle, *The Irish Republic* (Dublin, 1951), pp. 186-187 ; Denis Gwynn, *De Valera* (New York, 1933), p. 41 ; Mary C. Bromage, *De Valera and the March of a Nation* (1956), p. 59 ; Seán O'Faoláin, *De Valera* (1939), p. 40 ; M. J. MacManus, *Eamon De Valera* (Dublin, 1947), p. 47.)

lay ahead of her. As it was, the death sentences meted out in secret to Padraic Pearse, James Connolly and their fellow insurgents converted the rising, from the Sinn Fein point of view, from an inglorious failure into a glorious success. Not for the first time in history was a cause saved by the gratuitous provision of martyrs.

In London the sequel to the Easter Rising was the Prime minister's statement, on May 25, that he had commissioned Mr. Lloyd George to negotiate with Mr. Redmond and Sir Edward Carson for a compromise which would enable the Government of Ireland Act to be brought into immediate operation. The negotiations finally broke down in July because, according to Mr. Lloyd George, of the intervention and intransigence of Lord Lansdowne, the irreconcilable Conservative leader. 'But in Ireland it will always be thought that he [Mr. Lloyd George] had given contradictory promises to North and South.'[1] In the meantime a Royal Commission appointed, under the chairmanship of Lord Hardinge of Penshurst, to investigate the circumstances surrounding the Easter Rising, had presented a report which contained, *inter alia*, a scathing indictment of the system of government in Ireland.

A new fillip was given to the urge to arrive at a solution of the Irish problem by the entry into the war, on April 6, 1917, of the United States of America, with the consequent implication of President Wilson's doctrine of self-determination of small nations superimposed upon the not inconsiderable political influence exercised by Irish-Americans. With a view to such a solution, Mr. Lloyd George, now Prime Minister, invited representatives of the Nationalist Party, the Southern Unionists, the Ulster counties and Sinn Fein to meet in an Irish Convention for the purpose of devising some schemes for self-government for Ireland. As an earnest of good faith, a Royal Amnesty released all Sinn Fein prisoners arrested after the Easter Rising and held in British jails so that they might attend the Convention. The liberated Sinn Fein leaders at once rejected any idea of participation in the Convention and addressed an appeal to President Wilson for support in establishing an independent Republic of Ireland.

The Irish Convention met in Dublin on July 25 and its discussions dragged on without much result until the following spring.

[1] Hon. Frank Pakenham, *Peace by Ordeal* (1935), p. 25.

On March 15, 1918, it rejected a resolution to exclude Ulster from the jurisdiction of the Irish Parliament, whereupon the Orangemen withdrew. In the absence of the representatives of both Ulster and Sinn Fein the Convention finally adopted on April 5 a scheme for the establishment of a parliament for the whole of Ireland.

At this moment another faulty appraisal in London of the situation in Ireland resulted in a further and unexpected advantage for Sinn Fein. Prompted by the serious shortage of man-power in the British Army at a critical period of the war, Mr. Lloyd George introduced into the House of Commons on April 9, 1918, a Conscription Bill which included a provision for the extension of its powers to Ireland. He believed that Sinn Fein was a spent force and that the Irish Parliamentary Party would be amenable. He was woefully wrong on both scores. When, on April 17, their amendment to exclude Ireland from the provisions of the Bill was rejected, the Nationalist Members left the House of Commons and, on the following day, formed an alliance with the leaders of Sinn Fein at the Dublin Mansion House to protest against the enactment of conscription. The result of this temporary alignment was disastrous to the Nationalists and a source of infinite increase of prestige to Sinn Fein. All Ireland now seemed united behind them.

The *riposte* of the Government was to order widespread arrests of the Sinn Fein leaders and their imprisonment in England. Among those apprehended was Eamon De Valera, in whose papers evidence was discovered of the elaborate detail in which plans for the establishment of an Irish Republic had been prepared.[1]

But the tide of Sinn Fein success could not be turned by the mere arrest of leaders. In the course of the General Election of December 1918, which followed the surrender of Germany, the historic Irish Party, the Party of Parnell and Tim Healy and John Redmond, went down to final defeat at the hands of Sinn Fein. Only six Nationalists followed Mr. Devlin back into the House of Commons. The seventy-three Sinn Fein members refused to go to Westminster and constituted themselves the first Dáil Eireann, sitting in the Mansion House in Dublin in January 1919. There they declared themselves to be governing in the name of the independent Republic of Ireland, set up a Cabinet and declared war upon the King's Government in

[1] *Documents Relative to the Sinn Fein Movement*, Cmd. 1108 of 1921.

Ireland. Cathal Brugha, acting President of Dáil Eireann at this time, laid proposals before its executive Committee, which were embodied in an editorial pronouncement in *An toglách* on January 31, 1919. These proclaimed that a state of war existed between the Irish State and England and that, consequently, the National Volunteers had now become the Army of a lawfully constituted Government elected by the people and were entitled morally and legally, when in the execution of their duty, to slay officials and agents of the foreign invader who was waging war upon their native Government. They were entitled to put to death all spies, informers and all Irishmen who acted as agents of the foreigners in the warfare against them.[1]

A secret attempt by Lord Haldane, at the invitation of the Viceroy, Field-Marshal Viscount French of Ypres, to effect a settlement on the basis of the abandonment of violence in exchange for the release of Sinn Fein prisoners held in British jails, as a preliminary to the grant of self-government with the status of a Dominion under the Crown, proved abortive. Haldane, however, left Ireland with the impression that 'The Sinn Fein leaders are not murderers. They are idealists with a fanatical belief in what they believe to be principles, tempered by a shrewd recognition of realities and of what is practically possible.'[2]

(iii)

Thus began that hideous penultimate chapter in Anglo-Irish relations, a period of 'undeclared war' which has become known as 'The Troubles', the Anglo-Irish War and, more recently in Eire, 'The War of Liberation'. Its first signs were organized attacks upon barracks of the Royal Irish Constabulary and the ambush and cold-blooded murder of individual members of this splendid and long-suffering police force. These attacks led inevitably to reprisals, terror was followed by counter-terror, and, five days before Christmas 1919, an attempt was made in Dublin to assassinate the Viceroy, Lord French, as he drove from Ashton Station to Viceregal

[1] Piaras Béaslái, *Michael Collins and the Making of a New Ireland* (Dublin, 1926), i, pp. 273–276.
[2] Dudley Sommer, *Haldane of Cloan, His Life and Times, 1856–1928* (1960), pp. 362–363 ; Major-General Sir Frederick Maurice, *Haldane, 1915–1928* (1939), pp. 64–67 ; Béaslái (*op. cit.*), pp. 260–261.

Lodge in Phoenix Park. In the following spring Mr. Lloyd George decided upon more drastic measures. He was determined to solve the Irish Question either by the way of force or by the way of negotiation, but to achieve either solution he felt that a complete change was necessary in the governmental hierarchy in Dublin Castle and in the military command.

In April 1920 General Sir Nevil Macready, who had recently served as Commissioner of Metropolitan Police in London, in which capacity he had dealt forcefully with the police strike of 1919, was appointed General Officer Commanding in Ireland. His first task, not made easier by the weakness of his units and the alternation of government policy between repression and conciliation, was to try to suppress the Sinn Fein rebellion.

In the same month Mr. Lloyd George persuaded Sir Hamar Greenwood, a tough Canadian who, like his compatriots, Sir Max Aitken and Mr. Bonar Law, had successfully entered British politics, though in the Liberal Party, to become Chief Secretary for Ireland; the fourth and last individual to fill that unhappy office since the resignation of Augustine Birrell after the Easter Rising of 1916.[1] With Sir Hamar there came to Dublin Castle a completely new team of Civil Servants of whom the seniors were Sir John Anderson as Under-Secretary, Mr. Alfred Cope as Assistant Under-Secretary and Mr. Mark Sturgis as a sort of Assistant Under-Secretary *in petto*.[2]

The executive government of Ireland was entrusted by constitution to three officers — the Lord-Lieutenant, sometimes called the Viceroy, who was also Governor-General; the Chief Secretary; and the Under-Secretary.[3] The Lord-Lieutenant was resident in

---

[1] Sir Hamar Greenwood's three predecessors in the office of Chief Secretary were the Rt. Hon. Henry Duke, 1916–1918; the Rt. Hon. Edward Shortt, 1918–1919, later Home Secretary, 1919–1922; and the Rt. Hon. Ian Macpherson, 1919–1920.

[2] The remainder of the party who accompanied John Anderson from London to Ireland were Mr. Geoffrey Whiskard and Mr. L. N. Blake Odgers of the Home Office; Mr. M. T. Loughnane of the Ministry of Pensions; Mr. T. P. Fairgrieve of the Privy Council Office; and Mr. A. P. Waterfield, Mr. W. T. Gilbert and Mr. B. W. Matthews of the Treasury. There was also Mr. Basil Clarke, a journalist and war correspondent who became Director of Information.

[3] 'Theoretically the executive government of Ireland is conducted by the Lord Lieutenant in Council, subject to instructions which he may receive from the Home Office of the United Kingdom. Practically it is conducted for all important purposes by the Chief Secretary to the Lord Lieutenant.' Sir William Anson, *Laws and Customs of the Constitution*, ed. 1892, p. 189.

DUBLIN CASTLE, 1920

(*Standing*) Basil Clarke, G. N. Crutchley, L. N. Blake Odgers, M. T. Loughnane, J. P. Fairgrieve

(*Seated*) Geoffrey Whiskard, Alfred Cope, John Anderson, Mark Sturgis

Ireland at Viceregal Lodge in Phoenix Park.[1] By the terms of his patent of appointment he was responsible for the civil government of the country and the naval and military forces of the Crown in Ireland were under his orders. For many years, however, the office had been much the same as that of a constitutional sovereign, having the exercise of the prerogative of mercy as its sole executive function. Proclamations issued in the name of the Lord-Lieutenant were signed by him but without previous consultation. Information on the state of the country was only sent to him if he asked for it and then only as a matter of courtesy. The naval and military forces, nominally under his command, took their orders from the Service Ministers in Whitehall.

There had been occasions in Irish history since the Union of 1800 when both the Lord-Lieutenant and the Chief Secretary had been in the British Cabinet, but more usually it was only the latter who was a professional politician, who changed with the Government. The executive administration of the country, therefore, was entirely in the hands of the Chief Secretary, subject to the control of the Cabinet. His policy was that of the British Government as a whole and it was held to be impossible that there should be any other independent authority in Ireland.

As a member of the British Cabinet sitting in London, however, he was necessarily to a great extent an absentee from Ireland, for, although his position was equivalent to that of a Secretary of State, he had no Parliamentary Under-Secretary and upon himself therefore fell the full burden of answering questions and defending the Government's Irish policy in the House of Commons.

His seat of Government was in Dublin Castle with a subsidiary establishment, known as the Irish Office, in London.[2] In many respects the position was regarded as the Cinderella of any Cabinet and, as an Irishman has written, not unfairly : 'the congratulations which a Chief Secretary for Ireland receives on his appointment from his friends in England are mingled with expressions of

---

[1] Now the official residence of the President of the Republic of Ireland.

[2] The position of affairs was the reverse of that in Scotland where the Scottish Office, the executive department, is in London with a branch office in Edinburgh. The Irish Office in London was a branch of the Chief Secretary's Office in Dublin, having no separate establishment of its own except an Office Keeper. The officials of the Irish Office were sent over from Dublin and remained only while Parliament was in session.

sympathy, and perhaps sometimes even of regret. He is congratulated as a man who is promoted to an office on the Gold Coast is congratulated ; for Ireland is the grave of many English political reputations.'[1]

The unhappy incumbent of this office was of necessity greatly dependent for information and advice on the reports of his Under-Secretary in the Castle. In theory this official could only take action under the authority delegated to him by the Chief Secretary. In practice, however, he was often compelled to take action on his own instinct and initiative. His duty was to keep his chief fully and fairly informed, to give his advice freely and frankly as to what should be done and then loyally to carry out the instructions of the Chief Secretary without regard to any personal opinion of his own.

The Hardinge Commission, which had reported in June 1916 on the circumstances attendant upon the Easter Rising, had expressed the opinion that 'if the Irish system of government be regarded as a whole, it is anomalous in quiet times and almost unworkable in times of crisis'.[2] Since nothing had been done to improve the machinery of government in the intervening four years, it may very well have so appeared to John Anderson when he first set foot on Irish soil at Kingstown (now Dun Laoghaire) on the morning of May 16, 1920.[3] Indeed his position was even more difficult and complicated than that of previous Under-Secretaries by reason of local conditions and current events.

In the first place, he was not sole ruler in his own kingdom. He had not been sent to supersede his predecessor — the Rt. Hon. James MacMahon, an Irish Civil Servant of the old school who had occupied the position for some years — but to share the office of Under-Secretary jointly with him.[4]

---

[1] R. Barry O'Brien, *Dublin Castle and the Irish People* (1912), p. 15.
[2] *Report of the Royal Commission on the Rebellion in Ireland*, Cmd. 8279, 1916.
[3] He was sworn of the Irish Privy Council on June 3.
[4] The Office of Under-Secretary had been established in 1777. He was the permanent head of the Chief Secretary's Office and of the Civil Service in Ireland, receiving an annual salary of £2500, with an official residence in Phoenix Park. Because, however, MacMahon was occupying this house, John Anderson's salary had to be adjusted accordingly. He received £3800, made up as follows : £3000 salary ; £300 as equivalent of house allowance ; and £500 War Bonus. This was, in effect, his salary as Chairman of the Board of Inland Revenue, plus a house allowance ; he received no salary as Under-Secretary.

This dichotomy of rule might well have been the source of difficulty and discord had it not been for the good sense of the two men concerned. Anderson knew nothing of Ireland and its problems ; he was alien to the climate of ideas surrounding him, and the severity of his Scottish disposition was not one which quickly responded to the Irish temperament. MacMahon, on the other hand, had all the charm and urbanity of his race. Long years of experience in Irish politics had given him a deep insight into the world of men and affairs and provided an invaluable reservoir of background knowledge which Anderson fully appreciated and on which he did not hesitate to draw. MacMahon was also close in the councils of the Roman Catholic Church and this too was a major asset. Under the new divided authority MacMahon was not averse to sitting back and letting Anderson do the work and Anderson was ready to accept this arrangement and to profit by the greater local experience of his elder colleague.

In addition to his position of Joint Under-Secretary, Anderson was also senior representative of H.M. Treasury in Ireland, thus uniting in his own person the supreme authority in administration and finance. This dual responsibility sometimes produced slightly anomalous results. Proposals involving expenditure might, with the Under-Secretary's express or assumed authority, be put up by the Chief Secretary's Office, of which John was the head, to the Irish Treasury, only to be turned down by that department! The subordinate participants in this procedure were not always sure how far Anderson was a party both to the original proposal and to its subsequent rejection but it was symptomatic of his ascendancy that incidents of this kind in no way derogated from his authority.

But it was on the political side of Anderson's work that the chief complication arose in respect both of personalities and of powers. Of his two Assistant-Secretaries, one, Alfred William Cope, known to all affectionately as 'Andy', was destined to become a controversial figure in the last fourteen months of the tortuous history of Anglo-Irish relations. Of humble origins Cope, now aged forty-three, had begun his career as a detective in the Department of Customs and Excise, a calling which had taught him the intricacies of under-cover work and the technique of dealing on terms of intimacy with gunmen and lawbreakers. Later he had served in the Ministry of

Pensions, where he had attracted the attention of Mr. Lloyd George, many of whose more devious and *rastaquouère* attributes he shared and with whom he established a close affinity.

Cope had been one of the Civil Servants who had accompanied Warren Fisher on his preliminary survey of the Castle organization in May 1920, as a result of which John Anderson had been appointed, and he now returned, ostensibly as Assistant Under-Secretary and Clerk of the Irish Privy Council but actually as the Prime Minister's personal and secret envoy for the purpose of establishing contact with the Sinn Fein leaders with a view to negotiating peace. Thus, though the avowed policy of the new régime in the Castle was to re-establish law and order in Ireland by the suppression of the rebellion, there was from the beginning a left-handed approach to peace by way of compromise.

All this was highly unusual and irregular by the strict canons of Civil Service procedure on which Anderson had been nurtured, but he was big enough and intelligent enough to appreciate the necessity for a double policy, and the only restriction which he imposed upon Cope was the strict injunction that he should do nothing as a go-between in respect of Sinn Fein and the Prime Minister without his (Anderson's) knowledge.

Of very different gifts was the other Assistant Under-Secretary, Mark Sturgis, who came from the great world of society and politics. Married to the daughter of the Earl of Wharncliffe, he had already, at the age of thirty-six, served as Assistant Private Secretary to Mr. Asquith both as Chancellor of the Exchequer and as Prime Minister. However, at the time of the parting of the ways in the Liberal Party, he had followed the Lloyd George faction and had served in the Treasury, whence he had now been summoned to Dublin. Though in all respects an Assistant Under-Secretary, Sturgis was not officially gazetted thus for nearly two years, ostensibly for fear of wounding Cope's susceptibilities. Thus he held office, as it were, *in petto*, though cognizant of all, or nearly all, that went on in the fantastic world of intrigue, murder and reprisals in which he found himself. Anderson used Sturgis as a very effective liaison between the Castle and Viceregal Lodge, where the Master of the Horse, Richard Wyndham-Quin (now Lord Dunraven), an intimate friend, provided a valuable source of intelligence. Sturgis was also an effective deputy for Anderson during his periodic visits to London.

One other of Anderson's colleagues at this time must be noted, his legal adviser, Mr. William Wylie, than whom he had no greater admirer.[1]   An Ulsterman and the son of a Presbyterian minister, Wylie loved Ireland passionately, but as a Liberal found himself torn between a deep desire for the upholding of the sanctity of the law and a hatred of the policy of repression.   Nevertheless his shrewd judgment was never lacking when necessary and his high courage never deserted him.   Though known to be a man of moderate views, he had prosecuted for the Crown at the courts-martial following the Easter Rising and was therefore a marked man.   He had later appeared fearlessly in courts where a score of gunmen had revolvers ready in their pockets and where women spat in his face. His reputation as a horseman and sportsman was perhaps his protection, for whenever he could steal a day from his legal work he was out with the hounds in Meath, and the Irish respect such a one.

Such was the little group, the Junta, as they came to be called, in whose hands lay the effective policy of government, for the Chief Secretary was but a transitory figure.   He visited Dublin seldom and was chiefly concerned with the House of Commons.   And a strangely assorted team they were : Anderson, the personification of a senior Civil Servant with his deep-set inscrutable eyes, barely visible while in thought, masking his whole countenance, yet, when open, conveying something of reserve, something of humour, giving a touch of lightness to his long dark face ; Andy Cope, the fiery democrat, consumed with a deathless hatred of militarism and a passionate desire for peace, unorthodox to a degree, temperamental to the point of neurosis, a victim alike to ebullient optimism and devastating despair ; and then Mark Sturgis, ever the observer, 'the looker-on who sees most of the game', the secret chronicler of those Castle days, more detached than his colleagues, more cognizant of the great world outside, a man of infinite charm and humour, who found relief in deceptive superficialities.

'What a strange lot you are', Wylie once said to Anderson after

[1] Hon. William Evelyn Wylie, Q.C. (Ire.).   Legal Adviser to the Government of Ireland, 1919–1920 ;   Judge of the Supreme Court of Jurisdiction of Ireland, 1920–1924 ;   Judge of the High Court of the Irish Free State, 1924–1936 ;   Chairman of the Committee of the Dublin Horse Show, 1924–1960.

dinner in the Castle mess. 'How did you all get together ?' 'I will explain the matter to you', John replied in measured tones. 'I came in by the front door ; Andy came in by the back door ; and Mark, there, came in through the drawing-room window.'

But if there were diversities of character among the team, there was also that basic essential, a fundamental loyalty. All three appreciated the excellent qualities of the others and both his Assistants were united in recognizing John's great qualities of leadership. There was no doubt as to who was the captain of that team.

Once in a blue moon the open competitive examination for the Civil Service brings to light a man of his [Anderson's] exceptional type whom no power on earth can prevent from sprinting like a flash to the top of the ladder [a shrewd and well-informed observer wrote at this time]. I doubt very much, however, whether in the whole history of the British Civil Service any of these supermen had a heavier responsibility thrown upon them than Anderson had in taking on the part of Chief of Staff to the English in Ireland at this critical period. It was only a few like myself who obtained passing glimpses of what was going on behind the scenes who could realize the forces he was up against, what with his own parliamentary chiefs and the Press and the public, while always before his eyes was the daily bulletin of disheartening crime and the hopeless outlook for the future. But he stood it with courage and infinite patience ; he saw passing events, appalling as they were, in their true proportion to the whole problem, and he never appeared to be unduly cast down or uplifted over the day's work. . . . He was the captain of the ship in more than name, and his final word on any subject went, and when the vessel was having a bad time among the shoals and breakers he was always to be found on the bridge with his hand on the engine-room telegraph.[1]

Anderson threw himself into his task with tremendous energy and a clear mind. He worked very long hours with no apparent fatigue, and showed the greatest courage and fortitude in the face of physical danger. Nor was he greatly disturbed by the see-saw policy of the British Government which it was his duty to carry out. Occasionally he would break out in forceful condemnation

[1] Rt. Hon. Sir Henry Robinson, Bt., K.C.B. (last Vice-President of the Local Government Board of Ireland), *Memories : Wise and Otherwise* (1923), pp. 292-293.

of his masters' futile attempts to combine coercion with conciliation and at their inevitable vacillation between the two. But usually he preserved a grim equanimity, devoting his attention precisely to the matter in hand yet never losing sight of the future, never mistaking the trees for the wood. His supreme authority, both among his civilian and his military colleagues, was recognized, accepted and respected.

It was indeed a moment in which both leadership and authority were badly needed. When the 'Anderson machine' took over in Dublin Castle the situation in the country was appalling. As a result of a year's open warfare, more than eighty of the Royal Irish Constabulary had been killed without any of their killers being brought to justice.[1] Immobilized behind steel shutters in small barracks, their numbers depleted by casualties, resignations and lack of replacements, and the constant target of a campaign of calumniation in Ireland and in Westminster, the morale of the Constabulary was at a very low ebb ; nor was that of the Dublin Metropolitan Police much better. A part of the 'new policy' in the Castle inaugurated by Hamar Greenwood and John Anderson was the reorganization of the police forces. These were grouped under the command of a 'Police Adviser', Major-General Hugh Tudor, a friend of the Secretary of State for War, Mr. Winston Churchill, having, as his deputy and chief of combined police and military intelligence, an officer whose record and temperament were as exciting as his name — Brigadier-General Ormonde de l'Épée Winter. An intensive replacement campaign for the R.I.C. carried out in England, Scotland and Wales resulted in a considerable accretion of recruits, most of whom were recently demobilized members of the armed services, lured from the drabness and austerity of 'civvy street' by promises of high pay and adventure.

Because this sudden influx of replacements had caught the R.I.C. establishment somewhat unprepared it was found impossible to equip them with the regulation police uniforms. They were issued, therefore, as a temporary measure, with khaki service dress and a dark green Constabulary cap, and this bi-coloured outfit earned

---

[1] A Treasury Instruction of this period authorized the purchase of coffins for the police at wholesale rather than retail rates in order to get the benefit of reduction for orders placed in quantity.

them the immediate nickname of 'Black and Tans' after a famous pack of hounds of that name in the West of Ireland.

In addition to this force there was also formed an Auxiliary Division composed entirely of ex-officers, who wore a dark blue uniform with a dark green balmoral bonnet. This force was commanded by Brigadier-General E. P. Crozier.

It is no part of the task of John Anderson's biographer to reopen the controversy as to the apportionment of blame between the Black and Tans and the Auxiliaries for certain lawless actions on the part of the forces of the Crown in these disastrous days. Let it only be said that the term 'Black and Tans' has been used loosely by historians and writers of the period to cover all the police forces in Ireland at this time and to attribute responsibility for acts committed with equal lack of discrimination.[1]

The fact cannot be avoided, however, that since they formed an ancillary part of the Royal Irish Constabulary, both the Black and Tans and the Auxiliaries came under the administration of the Castle and were therefore the responsibility of the Chief Secretary and, under him, of John Anderson. Their acts of lawlessness were placed at his door and there occurred a rising tide of criticism in London. Hamar Greenwood became the target of frequent attacks in the House of Commons, and King George V expressed the view that the Black and Tans should be disbanded and the Constabulary subjected to military discipline under the command of Sir Nevil Macready.[2]

For acts of lawlessness there certainly were, among which the burning of Cork on the night of December 11, 1920, was one of the most shocking. No one deprecated them more fervently than Anderson, for not only was his respect for law and order as a Civil Servant outraged but his essential humanity, a deep-seated characteristic of his, was deeply shocked. He did his best to induce better discipline in the police forces and ultimately succeeded in bringing them under control. Equally he opposed the imposition of martial law until this became an absolute necessity, and, when it had been imposed in the southern counties, he resisted for some time the

---

[1] For a careful history of this body see Richard Bennett's *The Black and Tans* (1959).

[2] Sir Harold Nicolson, *King George V, His Life and Times* (1952), p. 348.

pressure by the military for its extension to Dublin. He was not going to be stampeded by the soldiers into any precipitate action. His, and his alone, was the responsibility and he would allow no impinging upon his prerogatives. 'If circumstances justify the extension of Martial Law the Irish Government, on whom the responsibility has been placed by the Cabinet, will act. . . . I hope you have got rid of your rheumatism', he once wrote to Sir Nevil Macready, the General Officer Commanding.

But if there were outrages by members of the Crown forces they had ample provocation. Members of the Constabulary had been assassinated in cold blood without compunction and there came that evening in the high summer of 1920 when hundreds of police barracks went up in flames. Soon thereafter Angier Street in Dublin became known to British troops as 'the Dardanelles', so often were they fired at and bombed in it. Next came the sinister warning that the comings and goings of the high officials in the Castle were being shadowed. On their arrival in Ireland, Anderson and his colleagues had taken up residence in the spaciousness of the Marine Hotel at Kingstown — a half-hour's drive from the Castle — and they could also enjoy a round of golf on the Foxrock course. Now word came that they would be well advised to abandon their pleasures and retreat into the well-guarded though cramped and narrow precinct of the Castle itself.

So the migration to No. 4 Upper Castle Yard was made and the mess established. For exercise Anderson took up riding. This was possible in the guarded seclusion of the grounds of Viceregal Lodge in Phoenix Park whither he would proceed to and from the Castle either by armoured car or under heavy police escort. Anderson was taught the rudiments of equitation by Mark Sturgis and Dickie Wyndham-Quin, whilst astride one of the quieter of the latter's polo ponies. He learned the hard way, frequently falling off but always remounting undaunted.

For relaxation in the evening, when the Castle took on the aspect of a besieged fortress, there would be bridge or poker after dinner and endless talk of 'shop'. There was some badinage and some bickering, as was inevitable under such conditions and in so tense a period. Sometimes there was a musical evening when each member of the mess contributed a song, more often than not from

F

Gilbert and Sullivan or *The Beggar's Opera*; while now and then Andy Cope would oblige with a solo rendering of Henley's 'Invictus' — a truly memorable performance to those who were privileged to hear it.

Sometimes, in lieu of other forms of diversion, they resorted to the pencil-and-paper games which then tended to be fashionable. When Anderson was there it was the rueful experience of the participants that he almost invariably — indeed inevitably — came out top! Whatever the subject was, his knowledge of it tended to be so encyclopaedic as to flatten all other contestants. Once, when the exercise involved the enumeration of fish with names beginning with random letters of the alphabet, Anderson's list was more than twice as long as its nearest rival!

In these informal gatherings John was apt to be the least responsive. Bridge and poker he loved and was proficient at both of them, but he was not one to relax round a piano. Moreover his recent sorrow which, with characteristic reserve, he left his colleagues to discover for themselves, still dominated his mind when it was not drugged with work. 'He would laugh with us quietly, rather tolerantly and benignantly, with no signs of superciliousness, but not as one of the same age and status as ourselves', one of his subordinates later wrote of him. Nevertheless, there was about him that something of condescension which is not infrequently found in shy and reserved persons and this became exaggerated by some of his colleagues into a suspicion of self-importance, so that he became known as 'pompous John' in certain circles. One of his fellow Civil Servants once wrote to Warren Fisher during one of Anderson's visits to London, urging him to indicate to John that a slightly less ponderous attitude towards his colleagues would be welcomed. On his return to Dublin a distinct improvement in this respect was noted, but it was not until some time later that the writer of the letter learned — but not from Anderson — that John had been standing behind Fisher when he opened it and had read it over his shoulder. No mention was ever made of the incident. 'Jonathan *is* a good fellow', wrote Mark Sturgis somewhat shamefacedly in his diary. 'He never told me of this and took it well.'

But in the execution of his official duties Anderson's formidable personality and his complete intellectual ascendancy soon made themselves felt. His position as Under-Secretary and representative of the Treasury gave him powers which no other Civil Servant had ever exercised in Ireland and he used them to full effect. Inevitably it rendered him somewhat autocratic, not so much towards his inferiors as towards his superiors or his equals in rank.

Deliberate yet swift in judgment [one of those who worked with him in those days has written], without superfluity, grasping the pith of the matter in a moment, he disclosed that remarkable versatility which enabled him to hold his own with men who had made a life study of what he had first heard of but yesterday. What he lacked in knowledge of detail, he made up partly by intuition, partly by bluff, for he was sensitive to being in the wrong, or appearing uninformed. For this reason he was an adept in covering up his tracks if he made a false start or set out on a wrong trail, but he scorned the littleness that would make a scapegoat of a subordinate to save his own face.[1]

One source of his strength lay in his readiness to trust his colleagues and to delegate work to them. He consulted his senior subordinates readily and gave them his full support. Under his dynamic leadership the creaking and cumbrous machinery of the Government of Ireland began to function as never before.

General Tudor, for example, was given a free hand, unfettered by Treasury restrictions, in reorganizing and re-equipping the police forces and, as a result of this encouragement, the Royal Irish Constabulary regained its morale and its efficiency in dealing with Sinn Fein flying columns. The inevitable difficulties of co-operation between the police and the military were largely overcome by Anderson's tact and authority and this redounded further to the enhanced prestige of the forces of the Crown. Yet always it was his policy to stop short of action which in the eyes of the world might label Ireland as a hostile country and England as engaged in a war of reconquest.

Soon Anderson had become the most powerful force in the

[1] 'The Last Days of Dublin Castle', *Blackwood's Magazine*, August 1922. This article originally appeared under the pseudonym of 'Periscope', but the identity of the author can now be disclosed as that of Mr. George Chester Duggan, C.B., O.B.E., a member of the Finance Division of the Chief Secretary's Office under Sir John Anderson and transferred to the service of the Government of Ireland in 1922. He retired from the position of Comptroller and Auditor-General of Northern Ireland in 1949.

Government of Ireland. The Chief Secretary was very frequently in London and his deputy had necessarily to act upon his own initiative and judgment. His hand was upon the pulse of every governmental activity. His word was law.

In order to keep contact with his Ministerial masters in Whitehall and to be assured that they themselves were kept fully informed of a situation which often shifted from day to day, it was necessary for Anderson to make brief visits to London, not depending too greatly upon the security of the long-distance telephone. These comings and goings had initially to conform to the strict but necessary security measures in force at the time, and though John recognized the necessity for these precautions in Ireland, he was anxious to dispense with their inconvenience in London. This desire for freedom from surveillance nearly had fatal consequences.

On one occasion, as he walked across the Horse Guards Parade from the Irish Office to the Reform Club, Anderson encountered the Home Secretary, Mr. Edward Shortt, who apparently did not know he was in town and greeted him : 'Why, Anderson, what are you doing in London ?' 'I am going to lunch.' 'But what protection have you ?' asked the Secretary of State, somewhat daunted by this strictly factual reply. Anderson answered that he regarded the danger of assassination in Whitehall as being comparatively negligible and passed upon his way. But the Home Secretary would not rest until he had telephoned to Scotland Yard and given instructions for the proper protection for the visitor from Ireland. Late that evening, as John was returning to his home in Sutton, he approached his house and in the dark saw a figure move suspiciously in the shrubbery. Without hesitation he whipped out a revolver and the Special Branch was in grave danger of losing one of its best officers. 'Cabinet scolded me to-day for not taking police precautions', he wrote later to Mark Sturgis. 'They did not mind my being assassinated but objected to prospect of kidnapping.'

Anderson's letters to Sturgis at this time are indicative of his desire to keep up the spirits of his deputy in Dublin and also of the impatience which he himself felt on occasion with what he deemed the dilatoriness and irresponsibility of the House of Commons. 'You gloomy old thing', he wrote on one occasion from the Irish Office in Old Queen Street. 'Here am I pulling strings as hard as

I can and what anyone engaged in such a despicable game wants is cheering up. Go to!' And again in reply to a despondent letter from Sturgis : 'My dear old Mark, what do you mean by "I'm through"? That's exactly what we are not, worse luck! If you had written like that to-day I should have put it down to natural depression resulting from absence of a chatty letter from me!! I meant to write but spent every minute in that rotten House from 3-11, and what a gloomy performance. Talk, talk, talk and no headway. . . . I seem to be on a chain here. When the other votes will come on I don't know. But I'm for Dublin at the earliest moment.'

(iv)

The mandate with which Sir Hamar Greenwood and his team had been sent to Dublin was primarily to restore law and order in Ireland, in which country the validity of the King's Writ had become seriously imperilled. In furtherance of this objective Mr. Lloyd George's Government had introduced into the House of Commons a bill for the Restoration of Order in Ireland which received the Royal Assent early in August 1920, before the House rose for its summer recess. The Act conferred upon the authorities of the Crown in Dublin sweeping emergency powers. They could arrest and imprison without trial, or even charge, and for an indefinite time, anyone suspected of dealing with Sinn Fein. Prisoners could be tried by court-martial, potential witnesses could be held in custody and heavily fined, or jailed for six months, for failure to produce evidence, and military courts of enquiry could be substituted for coroners' inquests.

These powers were intended to aid the Crown Authorities in their struggle against the forces of Sinn Fein. It was the duty of Sir John Anderson to implement the new measures in conjunction with the police and the military. They were put into immediate effect. On August 12 the Lord Mayor of Cork, Terence MacSwiney, a fanatical Sinn Feiner whose predecessor in office, Thomas Mac-Curtin, was alleged to have been murdered by the police, was arrested in the City Hall of Cork, court-martialled on a charge of being in possession of treasonable documents, and transferred to Brixton jail. He at once went on hunger-strike and on October

23, 1920, he died, on the seventy-fourth day of his self-imposed abstinence. His death caused a sudden upsurgence of public opinion in support of Sinn Fein in Britain and in America, and gave Mac-Swiney himself a position of international repute as a martyr.

But the purpose of the new régime in Dublin Castle was not only to repress the Sinn Fein rebellion but to bring, if possible, a peaceful settlement to Ireland, a country so lovely and persuasive in its charm, yet so ravaged by dissension, murder and hatred. Sir Hamar Greenwood had announced on his arrival in Dublin : 'I will do my best to bring peace', and as early as December 22, 1919 (only two days after the attempt to assassinate the Viceroy, Lord French), Mr. Lloyd George had stated that in the forthcoming session of Parliament his Government would introduce 'a Bill for the better Government of Ireland'.

It was among John Anderson's duties to advise Ministers in this respect. The counsel which he, after consultation and agreement with his colleagues, put forward was for the granting of Dominion Home Rule to a united Ireland provided that, as a *quid pro quo*, all overt acts of hostility against the Crown should cease. The only alternative policy was one of all-out combined action by the military and police to crush Sinn Fein, and this he had always sought to avoid. His disregard of the claims of Ulster to exclusion from the jurisdiction of an Irish Parliament is in sharp contrast with the strong support which he later gave to Ulster's claims after Partition, but it is believed that at this time the policy which he advocated was based on a desire to retain some potential bargaining factor in dealing with Sinn Fein.

This advice ran counter to the views held by the Cabinet, who still retained the hope that the problem could be resolved by the ordinary methods of *rapprochement* and that it was merely a matter of jockeying for position. Moreover they were divided over the question of Ulster, Mr. Lloyd George confiding to his Irish advisers that, while he personally was not opposed to a united Ireland, Mr. Bonar Law and the 'Die-hard' Conservative elements in his Government were against it, and that he was not prepared to see the Coalition Ship of State founder upon the rock of Ireland.

There ensued, therefore, during the latter half of the year 1920, a period of frustrating stalemate during which neither side could make up its mind to make the first overture. It was now, however, that the clandestine activities of Andy Cope began to show results. From his undercover contacts with Sinn Fein he had discovered that there, as in London, there were divided counsels. The renewed energy with which the Government forces were retaliating against the attacks made upon them and the steadily tightening grip which they were applying, not only to the rebels themselves but to their sources of supply, were having their effects. A situation had been induced in which, while the more fanatical, irreconcilable republicans still thought in terms of fighting Britain to a standstill, a growing minority, among whom were numbered some of the longer-headed of the Sinn Fein leaders, were beginning to doubt the successful issue of the arbitrament of arms. These latter, it seemed, were prepared to consider negotiations, at any rate for a truce and possibly a settlement, in the hope that, with the support of certain elements of public opinion in Britain and America, they could achieve better terms by peaceful means.

It came about, therefore, that as the summer of 1920 waned to autumn, those in the Castle found themselves in receipt of a series of 'peace feelers'. Both John Anderson and his two Assistant Secretaries were involved in varying degrees in these activities, but Anderson preferred, on the whole, to leave such matters in the hands of his subordinates, perhaps wisely. In him the Sinn Fein leaders recognized — and respected — a man of authority and integrity, but without that flexibility of mind which they counted upon for negotiation. Equally Mark Sturgis failed as a diplomatic force because he could not come to grips with the real power behind Sinn Fein. The would-be negotiators regarded him — though unjustly — as a dilettante, lacking authority, and one not to be taken seriously.

But Andy Cope was in his element ; bursting with energy and living on his nerves, now riding the crest of the wave, now wallowing in the Slough of Despond ; deeply sincere in his desire to bring about peace ; fiercely denunciatory of the influences in Dublin and in Westminster which opposed him, yet revelling withal in the whole crepuscular nature of his work. He laboured untiringly and fearlessly for a settlement and, to his eternal credit, succeeded not only in winning the confidence of the Sinn Fein moderates but also in retaining that of his own colleagues and his superiors. No move was made by him without Anderson's knowledge and, though he had personal and direct access to No. 10 Downing Street, in using it he never abused the trust which Anderson reposed in him.

The first move came from Sinn Fein and on a high level. Through Judge Wylie's contacts it became known that Arthur Griffith, joint Vice-President of the Sinn Fein organization, 'Vice-President of the Irish Republic' and, in the absence of Eamon De Valera in America, the highest ranking among the insurgents, was prepared to meet a British official 'of equal status' to see whether a truce could not be arranged pending discussions for peace. Wylie thought Anderson should meet him and John was prepared to do so, subject to the consent of the Chief Secretary, which was forthcoming.

The rendezvous was arranged for Sunday, September 26, 1920, in the offices of a solicitor in St. Andrew's Street, but the authorities are at odds in their record of what occurred. According to Mark Sturgis, who made his record on the same day, the two principals never actually met. They went to the office and were put into separate rooms. Griffith saw Wylie but would not consent to talk with Anderson without a written statement that the British Government would treat with Dáil Eireann as an equal. Since Anderson was in no position to give such an undertaking, there was no more to be said and the two left the building without having encountered one another. In Judge Wylie's recollection, however,[1] the affair went somewhat differently. He recalls that Anderson and Griffith did indeed meet, that their conversation lasted for about an hour but that, though friendly, it was inconclusive. The biographer is, therefore, left in somewhat of a dilemma, there being no good reason to doubt either source! The important fact, however, is that whatever the circumstances, nothing came of the incident — though it is of interest to speculate on the type of conversation between these two highly diverse personalities which could have extended over an hour.

By early November, however, it was alleged that Michael Collins had secretly joined Griffith in his anxiety for a truce. Two

[1] Conveyed both to the biographer and in a letter to Lord Bridges dated July 14, 1958.

intermediaries came forward : Dr. W. M. Crofton, an eminent Dublin medical figure who had served with the R.A.M.C. in France ; [1] and General Wanless-O'Gowan.[2] It was their opinion, based on conversations with certain of the Sinn Fein Party, that peace would be accepted on the basis of Dominion Home Rule, on the lines of the Bill then before Parliament in Westminster with certain amendments providing for financial independence for Southern Ireland and a general amnesty. Anderson thought well of their proposal and considered their *bona fides* as authentic. He wrote as much in guarded terms to Mr. Bonar Law, while Andy Cope wrote more enthusiastically to the Prime Minister.

The emissaries duly went to London where Mr. Lloyd George was favourably impressed by them. Indeed the Prime Minister, elated by the results of his Coercion Act and what he deemed to be the consequent peace-feelers, was moved to state publicly : 'We have murder by the throat' (November 8) and the peace envoys returned to Dublin to report optimistically to Anderson. How far Jonathan considered this ebullience of spirit to be justified may be judged from the fact that on the night of November 15/16 a raid upon the home of the I.R.A. Chief of Staff, General Richard Mulcahy, though it failed to effect his arrest, nevertheless produced an amazing haul of documents indicating the most thorough and complete plots for the murder of individuals in Ireland and in Britain, for the poisoning of troops and, *inter alia*, for the blowing up of the Manchester Ship Canal.

Just how far divorced from reality was the optimism of both the Prime Minister and the peace envoys was finally disclosed in the early morning of Sunday, November 21 — 'Bloody Sunday' — when no fewer than fourteen officers were murdered by Sinn Fein gunmen in cold blood, many of them in their pyjamas and some in the presence of their pleading, horror-stricken wives. 'It has been a day of black murder', wrote Mark Sturgis in his diary. 'What they hope to gain by it, God alone knows.'

Not unnaturally the inmates of the Castle were concerned for their own safety ; for who knew when and where the bloody hand

[1] Dr. Crofton (b. 1879) had taken a leading part in forming the Irish Centre Party, which later became the Dominion Home Rule Party.
[2] Major-General Robert Wanless-O'Gowan, C.B., C.M.G. (1864–1947), had commanded the 13th Brigade and later the XXXI Division on the Western Front.

of murder might strike next; and had it not been reported that Michael Collins had remarked that 'the deaths of Smith [the Inspector-General of the R.I.C.] and Anderson would put us on the road to victory'? But whatever qualms the others may have had, all bear witness to the calm and courage of John Anderson. Completely unperturbed, he inspired confidence and fortitude in his colleagues and merited to the full the encomium which Mr. Winston Churchill wrote of him at this time : 'a man of singular capacity and firmness of character, sagacious and imperturbable amid gathering peril and confusion'.[1] Nor was this admiration for John's imperturbability in the face of constant danger restricted to his own side. Even the under-cover men whom Michael Collins had planted within the Castle in the lower echelons of the detective personnel and who did not hesitate to shoot when off duty outside the confines of the Castle, paid tribute to his coolness and intrepidity.

The reply of the British authorities to 'Bloody Sunday' was the rounding up and arrest of a number of Sinn Fein leaders, Arthur Griffith among them, and the proclamation of martial law in the counties of Cork, Kerry, Tipperary and Limerick (December 10). Yet London still blew hot and cold, vacillating between conciliation and repression. A new mediator presented himself in Dublin in the person of the Most Reverend Dr. Patrick Joseph Clune, Archbishop of Perth, Western Australia, who during the war had been Roman Catholic Chaplain-General to the Australian Forces. Dr. Clune arrived in Dublin early in December empowered by Mr. Lloyd George to place before the leaders of Sinn Fein proposals for an armistice and a peace conference. He saw Arthur Griffith in jail and Michael Collins in hiding and also made contact with Andy Cope, who kept Anderson informed of the *pourparlers*.

Dr. Clune returned to London on December 9 bringing with him a tentative offer to call off violence provided that the Dáil should be free to meet and debate. The Prime Minister summoned John Anderson to a conference in London and there were prolonged discussions, the main point of debate being whether a surrender of arms by the I.R.A. should be *conditio sine qua non* of a truce. The view of Anderson and his colleagues in Dublin was that insistence on such a condition would inevitably wreck all chances of an agree-

---

[1] Winston S. Churchill, *The Aftermath* (1929), p. 322 f.n.

ment, but the Cabinet finally decided that this was a demand which they could not forgo. Once again a 'peace feeler' had proved abortive.

Anderson, Cope and Sturgis were all deeply depressed at the failure of the Clune negotiations. To them it seemed that the British Government in Whitehall had no real conception of the magnitude of the risks at stake, nor of the dangers involved in complete failure. The insistence upon the surrender of arms seemed almost an irresponsible decision in face of the possibilities of a truce, and the three senior Civil Servants found themselves at variance with the views of their political chief, Sir Hamar Greenwood, who shared the opinions of his Cabinet colleagues. 'I *can't* help being uneasy that we are not taking a *big* enough view of the position', Mark Sturgis wrote in his diary. 'Not only the future of the Irish is at stake but the future relations of the two countries which must ever live side by side and there is so much talk as if we had nothing to do but to beat our enemy.' In the event the counsel offered by Anderson and his colleagues was accepted. When the Truce came eventually to be signed six months later, there was no mention of the surrender of arms.

But by the end of the year two important events had taken place. With the connivance of the British Authorities, Eamon De Valera, President of the Dáil Eireann and of the Sinn Fein Movement and titular 'President of the Irish Republic', had returned to Dublin from his prolonged sojourn in America ; and the Royal Assent had been given to the new Government of Ireland Act, by which provision was made for separate parliaments in Dublin and in Belfast and for a joint Council of Ireland.

The enactment of this measure rather aggravated the situation than otherwise, in so far as Southern Ireland was concerned, and the first three months of 1921 saw an intensification of hostilities. Martial law was extended to the counties of Wexford, Waterford, Kilkenny and Clare, and from January 21 to March 31 the casualties were estimated at : Crown forces, 174 killed, 228 wounded ; I.R.A. and civilians, 317 killed and 285 wounded.[1] But, both in the councils of Sinn Fein and of the British Government, there were increasing influences in favour of peace, and in England particularly

[1] Macardle (*op. cit.*), p. 429.

there arose a steadily growing weight of public opinion against the continuance of hostilities.

Again through the agency of Andy Cope, tentative peace-feelers were initiated in January 1921 on behalf of Sinn Fein by Father O'Flanagan, joint Vice-President of Sinn Fein with Arthur Griffith, who, with the approval of John Anderson, was accompanied to London by Cope, Mark Sturgis and Lord Justice (Sir James) O'Connor. The basis of the new offer was the new Home Rule Act, plus fiscal autonomy for Southern Ireland — virtually the same as that put forward by Dr. Crofton and General Wanless-O'Gowan in November — but though the talks dragged on throughout the month, with many comings and goings between Dublin and Whitehall, they too proved of no avail. One of the disgruntled Irishmen remarked to Andy Cope that he was sure that had free powers to negotiate been in the hands of Sir John Anderson, without reference to London, they would now be in a fair way towards peace.

Gradually, however, as spring drew on to summer, the factors in favour of peace became increasingly imperative on both sides of St. George's Channel. Public opinion in Britain was turning generally against the Coalition Government of Mr. Lloyd George, and its failure to bring about a solution of the bloody situation in Ireland was among the more formidable weapons of criticism. In Ireland the Roman Catholic hierarchy became more and more vehement in their denunciation of bloodshed and violence and, moreover, the material fortunes of war were running against Sinn Fein. As General Richard Mulcahy, Chief of Staff of the I.R.A., was later to admit publicly, his army had almost exhausted its reserves of ammunition, while its casualties had been so heavy that it could not hope to carry on much longer.[1] Indeed by midsummer nearly 5000, or one-third, of the Irish Republican Army had been captured. Peace was to come to Ireland by sheer necessity.

Now was the moment when Andy Cope's long-term and indefatigable efforts were to bear fruit. He was active in both Dublin and in Belfast, with the result that Sir Edward Carson met Father O'Flanagan in London in February, Lord Derby crossed to Ireland in April for secret talks with leading figures in the Government, Church and Sinn Fein circles, and Sir James Craig and Mr.

[1] Gwynn (*op. cit.*), p. 165.

De Valera had a conversation of some length in a country house outside Dublin in May. Though these meetings produced no positive results, the fact of their taking place at all was welcomed as a step in the right direction and prompted Cope — with Anderson's blessing — to renew, with fresh hope and energy, his efforts in London.

Meantime it was Anderson's duty to effect the implementation of the new Government of Ireland Act, a task condemned in advance to failure in the Twenty-six Counties. The Act had provided for a Senate and a House of Commons in Dublin and in Belfast. The Southern House was to consist of 128 members, with 33 representatives in the Imperial Parliament; the Northern House to consist of 52 members, with 13 representatives at Westminster.

On May 3 a new Viceroy took office in the person of Lord Edmund Talbot, uncle of the Duke of Norfolk and recently created Viscount Fitz Alan of Derwent, the first Roman Catholic to hold the position of the King's Chief Representative in Ireland. He at once issued a proclamation authorizing elections for the Southern Parliament on May 19 and for the Northern Parliament on May 24, both to be held under the system of Proportional Representation.

The Sinn Fein movement decided to regard the elections as being not for parliamentary representation under the Act but for Dáil Eireann, and both in the North and the South the remnant of the Nationalist Party agreed not to contest seats against Sinn Fein.[1]

In both elections the results were a foregone conclusion. In the South Republican candidates were returned in all the 124 seats filled by popular vote and in the 4 seats allotted to the National University. The opposition consisted of 4 men elected unopposed by Trinity College, Dublin. In the North the Ulster Unionists won 40 of the 52 seats and the Republicans 12; Eamon De Valera, Arthur Griffith and Michael Collins were elected for both Northern and Southern constituencies.

The Northern Parliament was opened by King George V on June 22 amid scenes of wild enthusiasm, and the Speech from the Throne on that occasion contained what was regarded — and

---

[1] Sinn Fein also decided not to contest the Senate seats in either parliament since, as these were partly elected and partly nominated, the system was regarded as undemocratic.

intended — as a gesture of peace from London to Dublin. Andy Cope had been busy in Whitehall and was more than hopeful that this gesture would be translated into definite terms of a Truce offer, but, to his horror, there came news on the night of the 22nd that a search party of the Worcestershire Regiment, while making a raid in Dublin, had arrested a man who proved to be none other than De Valera himself. Hamar Greenwood and John Anderson had gone to the North for the opening of Parliament and were still in Belfast. The telephone wires buzzed between the two Irish capitals with the result that, armed with an imperative order from Anderson, Cope personally effected De Valera's release over the protests of the military.

Meantime the Prime Minister had summoned Anderson, Cope and General Macready to London, whence they returned on June 24 with the historic letter from Mr. Lloyd George to Mr. De Valera inviting him to London for consultations for a truce.

These vital activities on a high level rendered even more anti-climactic the already inevitably farcical meeting of the Southern Parliament in Dublin. But Anderson had to go through with it and he did so with grim and humourless determination. The session took place in the Council Room of the Department of Agriculture in Upper Merrion Street on the afternoon of June 28 and was attended by fifteen Senators and a House of Commons composed of the four Trinity College representatives. The Speech from the Throne was read by the Lord Chief Justice, in the absence through illness of the Lord Chancellor of Ireland, and having taken the Oath, the Parliament adjourned until July 13. By this date there had occurred the two meetings at the Mansion House between Mr. De Valera and the Unionist leaders (July 4 and 8) and the Truce, so long hoped for, had been signed. Mr. De Valera was already in London for his first conference with Mr. Lloyd George when the Southern Parliament met for its second, and final, session on July 13. It adjourned *sine die* 'pending His Majesty's pleasure', thus ending what must surely be the shortest and most inglorious record of any parliamentary institution in the history of the British Common-wealth.

The crowded and eventful months which passed between the delivery of Mr. Lloyd George's letter to Mr. De Valera on June 24,

1921, and the signing of the Anglo-Irish Treaty on December 6 have been recorded in detail by many historians. John Anderson was retained in London as one of the Prime Minister's principal advisers throughout the Treaty negotiations and, during the many crises and vicissitudes which occurred he never seems to have lost heart, believing that, since matters had reached this point, it was inconceivable that an agreement of some sort should not be reached.

Outside the conference itself his chief problems were to prevent Andy Cope from making some hysterical outburst which might jettison the achievement for which he had worked so long and fearlessly, and to keep up the spirits of Mark Sturgis, who had been left behind in Dublin with the difficult and tricky task of acting as chief liaison officer with the Sinn Fein authorities for the proper execution of the provisions of the Truce Agreement, violations of which were frequently being alleged by both sides. Anderson was successful in both these tasks and with the signature of the Treaty he returned to Dublin for the final arrangements for the transfer of power.

But these were unexpectedly postponed. Though the Treaty was ratified on December 16 by big majorities in both Houses of Parliament at Westminster, its passage through Dáil Eireann, sitting in the National University in Dublin, was marked by the most acrimonious debates, which found their ultimate fulfilment in fierce and bitter civil war after the Free State had been established.

To those in Dublin Castle who watched the tide of battle swing this way and that in the Dáil debate, the suspense and the prospect of possible frustration were almost unendurable. Had they come this long way in the cause of Anglo-Irish peace to see the cup of the fulfilment of their hopes thus dashed from their lips ? What indeed could follow a rejection of the Treaty by the Dáil ? Mr. Lloyd George had spoken of Draconian measures to be taken in the event of a breakdown of the negotiations, but would it be possible to put them into force now that the Treaty had been signed and Britain had ratified it ? And, furthermore, would British public opinion tolerate a resumption of hostilities in Ireland ? These were the nightmares which haunted the dreams of John Anderson and Andy Cope and Mark Sturgis, and there is reason to believe that it was in this month of uncertainty that Anderson's morale, for the first time since his arrival in Ireland, reached a low ebb. He felt that now he was beset by forces quite outside his control or influence.

At length the suspense was broken. The 'Big Talk' in the Dáil ended on January 14, 1922, with a vote for the ratification of the Treaty, and thereafter those in the Castle were fully occupied in their tasks of handing over the administration of Ireland to the Provisional Government of the Free State, headed by Michael Collins.[1] Anderson found him a diverting character, with infinite charm and a quick sense of humour, and was interested to discover that one of his favourite books was Chesterton's *The Napoleon of Notting Hill*.

Coming into Anderson's room one day, Judge Wylie found him closeted with Collins. He was struck by the irony of the situation. The Crown forces, of which Anderson had been in ultimate control, had put a price of £10,000 on Collins' head but had failed to effect his capture, while it was known that Anderson's name had figured on the list of targets for Sinn Fein gunmen. Wylie himself, as Crown Counsel, had sent numerous Sinn Feiners to execution and imprisonment, yet himself had always escaped assassination. Now the three of them were engaged in the business of the transfer of power. Anderson, with characteristic punctilio, greeted Wylie and then turned to Collins : 'You've met the Judge before, of course ?' he asked. The Big Fella roared with laughter. 'That's the damn silliest question I ever heard', he cried. 'Would I be here now if I'd met the Judge before ?'

At another of these meetings Collins was accompanied by his brilliant and equally quick-witted colleague, Kevin O'Higgins. The topic under discussion was the vexed question of how payment should be made for the enormous amount of damage done to Irish property during the previous years. John Anderson explained the British point of view with technical exactness and that detailed grasp of his subject which characterized him. His Majesty's Government, he said, would only pay compensation for what had been commandeered by the forces of the Crown, and not what had been confiscated, which would become a liability of the Free State

---

[1] Until the Free State Government was formally established, Arthur Griffith remained in office as President of Dáil Eireann, with Michael Collins as head of the Provisional Government.

Government. Somewhat to his surprise, his sober and strictly factual statement provoked laughter in O'Higgins and Sir John was not used to this effect upon his audiences. O'Higgins at once offered both apology and explanation.

'I was thinking', he said, 'of old Pat Murphy who had been riding on his bicycle from Maryborough to Dunmore. He gets tired and sits down by the side of the road and rests himself, and, maybe, he takes a few pulls at his pipe. While he is sitting there some Black and Tans come driving past, stop their lorry, put his bicycle in it and drive away. I can see poor Pat puzzling out for himself: Now was that bicycle confiscated or was it commandeered?'

For once John was beaten. He was forced to admit that, after all, there were certain difficulties involved of which his precise definitive decision had not taken cognizance, and the agreement was adjusted on more liberal lines.[1]

Anderson did not attend the ceremonies of the formal transfer of Dublin Castle by the Viceroy to the Provisional Government, which took place on Monday, January 16, 1922. He was in Dublin but there is no mention of his name among those present. The only Privy Counsellor to attend Lord Fitz Alan was James MacMahon.[2] Why he absented himself is not known. It has been suggested that he did so out of consideration for MacMahon, who had held the office of Under-Secretary for a longer period than he. It is possible that he just did not want to witness what the Irish press did not hesitate to term 'The Surrender', yet it was unlike him to be either sentimental or romantic.

He crossed to London on the night of the 16th, leaving Southern Ireland for the last time at the close of two eventful years, though he was still to play an important part in the setting up of the Government of Northern Ireland.

His contribution to the Irish Settlement, and to all that had gone before, was widely and deservedly lauded and his appearance at a number of public functions was greeted with applause. None

[1] Terence de Vere White, *Kevin O'Higgins* (1948), pp. 92-93.
[2] It is a matter of record that while this ceremony was in process in the Privy Council Chamber of the Castle, the house of the Deputy Inspector-General of Constabulary in Lower Castle Yard was burgled and his watch and some jewellery stolen!

G

gave him greater pleasure, however, than the annual dinner of the London Watsonian Club on February 17, 1922. Before a distinguished audience, including his old mathematics master, Dr. Alison, now Headmaster of George Watson's, he listened to a glowing eulogy by none other than Sir Hamar Greenwood, who paid full tribute to the high value and indispensability of his services.[1] Official recognition came in the New Year Honours List of 1923 by the award of Knight Grand Cross of the Order of the Bath.[2]

His years in Ireland, however, had brought to John something more important perhaps than kudos and honours. He had gone to Dublin almost as the apotheosis of the dedicated Civil Servant, with the well-disciplined brain which would as easily have made him a leading academic, a first-class scientist or an eminent jurist. Humanly speaking, however, he was circumscribed; but under the heavy strain of the Castle days his great powers had developed amazingly. No longer did he look at men and affairs with the purely detached assessment of Whitehall. He had become a man of mature insight and experience, with first-rate judgment of acute political difficulties. In the exercise of these qualities he could remain unruffled in the face of emergency, and he never allowed his heart to be governed by his head.

[1] 'I wish to take the opportunity of thanking you for the assistance which you were always willing to give me during the time that you were Under-Secretary in Ireland', Sir Hamar Greenwood wrote to Anderson on October 23, 1922. 'It was always a matter of great satisfaction to me to know that the Government had in you an Under-Secretary on whom they could implicitly rely to carry on their Policy in Ireland. I am most grateful to you for the assistance which you were always ready to give me, personally, both in Ireland and in this country.'

[2] General Sir Nevil Macready received a baronetcy; Mark Sturgis and General Tudor were appointed K.C.B.s; Percival Waterfield, Geoffrey Whiskard and Captain Wyndham-Quin became C.B.s and Brigadier Winter received the K.B.E. Andy Cope had already been knighted and received the K.C.B. in 1922 after the conclusion of the Treaty negotiations.

IV

Home Office

1922–1932

(i)

AFTER he returned to London from Dublin John Anderson continued his peripatetic progress through Whitehall. Since leaving the Ministry of Shipping in the spring of 1919 he had served in four separate Government departments, his longest period being in Dublin Castle. Yet throughout his appointment as Under-Secretary and Treasury Representative in Ireland he had continued to hold nominally the Chairmanship of the Board of Inland Revenue and it was to this post that he returned in January 1922.

He was not to remain at Somerset House for long. In March 1922 the Permanent Under-Secretary of the Home Office, Sir Edward Troup, retired and John was appointed to succeed him. Thus, at the age of forty, he had attained the highest stratum in the hierarchy of the Civil Service and he was destined to hold this position for ten years. He was modestly aware that there were other elements in his success than his own very great abilities. 'As a civil servant I have been very lucky & in nothing so much as in my colleagues', he wrote to Sir Henry Bunbury in acknowledgment of his congratulations at this time. 'Your very kind letter only brings home to me once again the fact that without their constant support & goodwill I should have done nothing & got nowhere.'

Anderson's service at the Home Office covered a period of great political activity in our national history. He came to the Office under the Coalition Government of Mr. Lloyd George and left it under the National Government of Mr. Ramsay MacDonald, serving in turn no fewer than seven Home Secretaries.[1] During this

---

[1] These were Mr. Edward Shortt, Mr. William Bridgeman, Mr. Arthur Henderson, Sir William Joynson-Hicks, Mr. J. R. Clynes, Sir Herbert Samuel and Sir John Gilmour.

period Britain faced proximate revolution in the General Strike of 1926 and near disaster in the Economic Crisis of 1931, and in both of these emergencies Anderson played his part. Indeed it was during these ten years that John brought to maturity those great gifts of administration and judgment which had developed while he was in Dublin Castle. When he came to the Home Office his reputation was of the highest, but when he left ten years later it had been even more greatly enhanced.

When Anderson took charge of the Home Office in 1922 it comprised only seven administrative divisions. These dealt with a wide range of differing subjects, which might indeed have been handled by seven different Departments — Factories and Shops, Aliens Control, Crime, Children and Probation, Police, Northern Ireland, and the Channel Islands — and a great miscellany of subjects that fall to the Home Office as residual legatee for all matters not specifically assigned to other Departments. Each of these divisions was in the charge of an Assistant Secretary. Between these heads of divisions and the Permanent Secretary there were only two superior administrative officers ; neither of these was a genuine Deputy — each had a rather specialized rôle. One of them, Ernley Blackwell, was a lawyer who concentrated on murder cases and other outstandingly important criminal cases. The other, Malcolm Delevigne, was in charge of the industrial welfare work of the Department but specialized increasingly on its international aspects. Thus, for the most part, Anderson dealt directly with the heads of the various divisions — devolving on them a much larger measure of responsibility than is enjoyed by Assistant Secretaries nowadays. They were men of mature experience, with detailed knowledge of their own subjects ; and he allowed each of them to run his own division, though he encouraged them to go to him for guidance and advice.

All who worked in the Home Office while Anderson was its Head were conscious that there was a strong hand at the helm. He was always very much the Head of the Office — and he gave to all below him a feeling of confidence in his strength, administrative experience, sagacity and judgment. But it is probably true that, when he departed after ten years, he left little imprint of his personality on the Department.

There are several reasons for this. John had no special interest in Home Office subjects — apart from its fundamental responsibility for law and order.[1] He was interested more in the art of administering than in the subjects administered. He had, for example, no personal enthusiasm for penal reform. His inclination was to administer efficiently and smoothly within the limits of existing policy. Although he had unerring judgment, he showed at this stage of his career little of the type of imagination that goes with the initiation of great reforms or major changes of policies. There is no doubt, however, that his judgment was one of his great qualities. When faced with a choice between alternative courses of action, he had a great capacity for making up his mind — when others would go on 'swithering' — and the event would usually show that he had chosen rightly. In other words, he was not only decisive but shrewd in judgment. But an even more remarkable quality was that, in those circumstances, he had the gift of making others feel that the course which he preferred was in some way the inevitable choice. He did not leave the impression that out of, say, three possible courses one was probably the best on balance. He could present the choice in such a way that the preferred course stood out as the one which must be followed. This must have been comforting to him : it was certainly most reassuring to those whom he led or advised.

He wrote sparingly and left, therefore, little of his own composition on the departmental files. If he dissented from proposals submitted to him, he rarely put a minute on the file explaining why he preferred a different course. On these occasions his decisions were usually given in discussion with the subordinate concerned — and he left it to others to draw instructions, or to draft letters or memoranda, in accordance with his decision. This was not because he lacked competence as a draftsman. On the contrary he expressed himself easily and fluently in official English : indeed, even in

[1] His influence on the improvement of police work, for example, was considerable. In 1922 a new policy had been instituted, of which the chief architect was Sir Arthur Dixon, to make the Home Office an effective centre of information and guidance in police affairs. Anderson placed the full weight of his authority behind this new departure, with the gratifying result that, largely owing to the deep impression which he made at all conferences and meetings concerned with police administration, excellent relations were established between the Home Office and the local police authorities and their Chief Constables.

ordinary conversation, he often spoke like an official minute. When he was telling a Private Secretary how to answer a letter, he would produce without hesitation a flow of orotund sentences which required no polishing. Many a Private Secretary has wished that he could ring the bell for a shorthand-writer, so that the letter could be produced in Anderson's own words — which he knew he would himself find difficulty in reproducing after he had gone out of the room. But despite this facility, John deliberately refrained from writing on files. He had none of the normal Civil Servant's passion for 'improving' a draft. If it was good enough to serve its purpose, he let it go : if it was sadly wrong he sent for the man concerned and told him how to rewrite it. In the main, no doubt, this was due to considered economy of effort — a deliberate decision to refrain from wasting his time and energies on minutiae. In part, however, it was due to a canny reluctance to become committed — perhaps too soon — to a particular formulation of a point of view. Later, certainly, when he was a Minister he would deliberately refrain from writing anything himself for fear that, through pride of authorship, he would be tempted to defend a particular form of words for too long and thus leave himself with too little room to manœuvre for a compromise in subsequent discussion.

In much of the work of the Home Office there was less scope than in some other Departments for the formulation of general policy by written memoranda. In many Departments the administrative staff deal mainly with large questions of general policy. But in the Home Office they are concerned mainly with case work, and the important points of principle tend to arise in the handling of individual cases — *e.g.* on petitions from prisoners or criminal lunatics, applications from foreigners for leave to remain in the country, etc. The more important of these cases go high in the hierarchy ; and the contribution of senior officials, being spread among a large number of individual case files, is perhaps more difficult to assess than it is in a Department where they are mainly concerned with matters of more general policy.

Anderson himself could get through a considerable volume of work in a comparatively short space of time because of his great capacity for scanning all the relative information and picking out the vital points of importance, and because he had outstanding powers of concentration. Though he was deliberate of speech, his mind was exceptionally quick, and when considering a problem he turned upon it the full power of his intellect, never letting his attention relax until he had reached a decision. He did not work overtime himself and discouraged it in his subordinates ; as he once told the Royal Commission on the Civil Service : 'A man cannot work very long hours if he thinks really hard'. His own capacity to work 'really hard' was one of the many indications of his rigorously disciplined mind and character. His control over his feelings was as firm as his thought and in times of stress, when many decisions had to be taken in haste, he was as composed as in times of absolute normality. There was indeed about him an almost Olympian equanimity. He was never irritable or impatient ; never seemed depressed or exhilarated.

Despite the mass of paper-work in the Home Office, Anderson never became immersed in it. By modern standards his office hours were not long. They were, however, very regular. It would be true that in those years one might have set one's watch by him. He arrived at the office punctually at 10.15 a.m. : he went punctually to lunch at 1.15 p.m. and returned at 2.45 p.m. And he left at 6.15 p.m. He never took official files away from the office to work on them at home. He carried, not an official dispatch case, but a small attaché case — which may often have contained Blue Books (he was reputed never to read anything else) but never files.

It was once said of Anderson that he was 'considerate to his subordinates and overbearing to his superiors'. There is some truth in this epigram, though the word 'overbearing' is perhaps misleading. He was never domineering or dictatorial, though his capacity to present concisely in a few short sentences the course which he was advising was sometimes overpowering. 'His mental powers gave him a giant's strength but he did not use it like a giant', one of his contemporaries, Sir Alexander Maxwell, has written of him, continuing : 'Moreover, in his relations with Ministers he had a sympathetic understanding of any difficulties which might make the Minister hesitate to accept his advice ; and he was so often able to suggest means of mitigating or circumventing such difficulties that the Minister was usually more likely to welcome the resourcefulness of his adviser than to resent his pressure'.[1]

Yet in his discussions with Ministers, as in all his dealings, Anderson was resolute and intrepid — and at times adamant. When the first Labour Government came into power in January 1923 pressure was brought upon them to inaugurate their first term of office by an act of clemency in reinstating or compensating those former members of the Police Force, some 2400 of them, who had been dismissed for participating in the Police Strike of 1919. Anderson obdurately withstood this view on the ground that such action would be prejudicial to the discipline and efficiency of the police forces of the country, and such was the strength of his argument that the Cabinet, on the advice of the Home Secretary, decided against reinstatement of the strikers.[2]

Nor would he allow himself to be stampeded by Ministerial exuberance into a display of emotion which he did not feel. Sir William Joynson-Hicks, on becoming Home Secretary in November 1924, paid a visit to his Permanent Under-Secretary on the morning of assuming office. With his usual ebullience he burst into the room, rubbing his hands. 'Well, Anderson,' he said, 'isn't this splendid ? I hope you're glad to see me here.' Standing with his feet in the fireplace and his back to the grate, John pulled his glasses down upon the bridge of his nose and, staring over them, replied : 'I have been brought up in a profession which has taught me that it is wrong to

---

[1] Letter from Sir Alexander Maxwell, G.C.B., to the author, July 23, 1959.
[2] Mr. Arthur Henderson, the Home Secretary, did, however, appoint a Committee under the chairmanship of Sir William Mackenzie (later Lord Amulree) in May of 1924 to report on the matter of reinstatement as a whole. The Committee rendered its report in November of the same year (Cmd. 2297) and by a majority vote decided that the men concerned should not be reinstated or reappointed. The minority opinion favoured the view that they should be reinstated as vacancies arose or, failing this, that Police Authorities should be at liberty to give them employment as police officers. It was the unanimous opinion of the Committee that the Police Authorities should be authorized at their discretion to apply the whole or part of the rateable deduction which had been made from the pay of the dismissed strikers in such a manner as they thought fit for the benefit of their wives and children and for this purpose the necessary legislation should be enacted. Mr. Baldwin's Government adopted the view of the majority report of the Committee on the first of these points and Parliament passed the Police Pensions Act in 1926 to meet the second. As a result some £10,000 was paid out in the Metropolitan Police Force and about twice as much in the provincial forces. When a further attempt was made in 1929 to demand reinstatement or pensions for the dismissed strikers, the then Home Secretary, Mr. Clynes, again on the advice of Sir John Anderson, refused to go further than the action taken to implement the Mackenzie Report.

give expression to emotions either of pleasure or sorrow on occasions such as this'. 'Jix' was nonplussed at this reception, but he later came to rely increasingly on John's counsel and advice. Indeed Anderson's ministerial chiefs always respected his great wisdom and his dauntless courage, recognizing in him, as one of them expressed it, 'a grand man to go tiger shooting with'.

When he first came to the Home Office in 1922 senior officials were expecting that they would be called upon to instruct their new chief, but in a very short time they were coming to him for advice on any difficult problem as if drawn by the magnet of his wisdom. A visitor to his room would be received by John seated in his desk chair, leaning back and looking over his spectacles, one leg crossed over the other. He would listen to what was said with grave interest and in complete silence until a point had been reached, not necessarily at which the visitor had finished the exposition of his views, but at which John Anderson had reached a conclusion. He would then interrupt the speaker with an upraised hand and deliver himself of his opinion — and his visitor never went away empty-handed. He welcomed argument and despised sycophants and 'yes-men'. If an argument contrary to his views were put to him he would give it every consideration before accepting or rejecting it. On the other hand, he did not suffer fools gladly and it was noticeable that fools were reticent about their foolishness when in his presence.

Yet to the subordinate staff of the Home Office he was a remote figure. He never tried to get on friendly terms with them ; as Head of the Department he was essentially aloof. It is not known that he ever entertained his colleagues at his private house, and it was rarely that he asked them to lunch at his Club.

His methods of controlling the official work of the Department reflected the same sort of attitude. It was unusual for him to hold meetings of senior officials within the Department. His consultations were more usually bilateral — with the head of the division concerned. Partly no doubt this was due to the organization of the office, which left little scope or need for co-ordination between different divisions. But it also seemed to be his natural way of working — and it helped to earn him the nickname 'Jehovah'. With Blackwell he was on more intimate terms, perhaps because he felt obliged to treat him as an equal ; but for all other members of the staff — even those in senior positions — he was always very much the Head of the Office. There were no Christian names. Certainly there was no easy familiarity with juniors.

As has already been said, Anderson was more interested in the art of administration than in the subjects which he administered. It is, however, also true to say that he was more interested in the art of administration than in the management of the people who worked under him. Perhaps this was a factor of his aloofness, as Head of the Office, but it is certainly true that he showed little interest in what is now called 'man-management'. Nor did he trouble to make changes in the structure of the Department. For the greater part of his time, its organization remained as he found it. Then, shortly before his translation to Bengal, he persuaded the Treasury to authorize the creation of several higher posts at the level of what was then called Principal Assistant Secretary and is now called Under-Secretary. This was felt in some quarters to be a last-minute recognition of earlier failure to look after the interests of his staff in the way that a Permanent Secretary nowadays would be expected to do.

But, though John might appear to many to be aloof, pontifical and Olympian, there was also about him a genuine kindness and humanity which prompted him to acts of quiet consideration. 'My wife and I will never forget', writes one who worked closely with him, 'that when I was dangerously ill with typhoid he found time on Christmas Eve to send her a most kindly letter of sympathy and encouragement.' [1]

He was also possessed of a golden simplicity. One morning, in his early years at the Home Office, he arrived in his room carrying a heavy suitcase and summoned his Private Secretary, Frank Newsam. [2]

'My father and mother are in London', he announced, 'and are coming here this morning.' (Somehow it was not easy to believe that John had a father and mother ; he was so splendidly 'Roman' that no-one would have been surprised to learn that he had sprung fully armed from the head of Jove!) 'They have never seen me in

[1] Sir Harold Scott, G.C.V.O., K.C.B., K.B.E., *Your Obedient Servant* (1959), p. 64.
[2] Later Sir Frank Newsam, G.C.B., K.B.E., who himself served as Permanent Under-Secretary at the Home Office, 1948–1957.

my G.C.B. regalia, so I am going to put it on for them, and you must help me dress.' The delight of David and Janet Anderson at being received by their son in the full dress of a Privy Counsellor with the mantle and collar of the Order of the Bath was boundless. This was not the act of a pompous man — nor even of one motivated by vanity.

(ii)

Anderson's concern with the problems of Ireland did not end when he vacated his room in Dublin Castle. He was intimately concerned with the circumstances which attended the setting up of the new régimes in Dublin and in Belfast and with their subsequent tormented relationship.

The threat of war in the Near East, culminating in the Chanak Incident of September 1922, had ousted Ireland from the pressing consideration of the British Cabinet and the consequent collapse of Mr. Lloyd George's Coalition Government in October was the cause of a further delay. The Bill establishing the new Irish Free State Constitution did not receive the approval of Parliament until the brief premiership of Mr. Bonar Law. It received the Royal Assent on December 6.

Various problems now arose. The establishment of the Free State had purported to give Dominion status to Ireland as a whole, but Article 12 of the Anglo-Irish Treaty of December 1921 had reserved to Northern Ireland the right to vote itself out of the Free State by means of an Address presented to the King by both Houses of the Northern Parliament. This secession was instantly forthcoming and new legislation by the Imperial Parliament at Westminster was therefore necessary to accomplish the changes requisite in the Government of Northern Ireland. These included the establishment of a Privy Council of Northern Ireland and the authorization of a Great Seal.

The Home Office became the governmental link between Belfast and London and John Anderson thus found himself back again in the field of Irish politics. There were many problems affecting the internal affairs of Northern Ireland in addition to issues such as the Boundary Question, which arose between her and the Irish Free State, and in all these John's good judgment and wise counsel, coupled with his first-hand experience of Irish affairs, played an important part.

The position at the outset was not an easy one. Ulster was still suspicious of the Imperial Government and there were occasions when charges of bad faith passed between Dublin, Belfast and London. Moreover, the curious constitutional arrangement whereby the United Kingdom Government retained jurisdiction over various specified matters in Northern Ireland necessitated frequent consultation and co-operation between the two Governments — at departmental as well as at ministerial level. The whole basis for the future good feeling and smooth relations between Belfast and London depended upon the precedents established in the early days, and the fact that these were successfully maintained owes much to the personal relationship which existed between the first Prime Minister of Northern Ireland, Sir James Craig (later Viscount Craigavon) and John Anderson.

Craig, though Irish born, had been educated at Merchiston Castle School, Edinburgh, and this itself was a bond between the two men. The Ulster leader, who had succeeded Sir Edward Carson in this rôle, had met Anderson on many occasions during the last troublesome years and had found in him a character and a personality which he could trust and admire. Anderson, for his part, discovered beneath the intransigent patriotism of the Ulsterman a core of common sense and integrity. In the many difficult circumstances with which they both had now to contend, the mutual confidence engendered in the past was a vital factor in maintaining good relations between their two countries ; and, when trouble was looming on the horizon, the magnetic force of John Anderson's calm judgment not infrequently drew James Craig to the Home Office for advice and friendly consultation.

Of all the outstanding issues existing between the Free State and the Government of Northern Ireland, that which constituted the chief obstacle to better relations between them was the Boundary Question. Under the Anglo-Irish Treaty of 1921 provision had been made for a tripartite Commission to establish the boundary between Northern and Southern Ireland. But, in view of the persistent refusal of the Belfast Government to appoint a member, the Imperial Parliament passed legislation transferring to itself the power of appointment originally vested in the Government of Northern Ireland. The Commission, as constituted in 1924, consisted of Professor John McNeill for the Free State, Mr. J. R. Fisher for Ulster and Mr. Justice Feetham, a judge of the High Court of the Union of South Africa and an original member of Lord Milner's 'Kindergarten', as Chairman.

The Commission pursued its investigation *in situ* and completed its report by the end of October 1925. This report has never been made public, but on November 7 an inspired forecast of its findings appeared in the *Morning Post*, from which it appeared that strips of land in Fermanagh and Armagh, each about twenty miles in length, were to be transferred to the Free State, and a tract of land in Donegal, inhabited chiefly by Protestants and Unionists, was to be awarded to the North. These were the only territorial changes but they pleased nobody. An immediate crisis followed. Sir James Craig and Mr. William Cosgrave, who had succeeded Arthur Griffith as head of the Free State Government, met with Mr. Baldwin at 10 Downing Street on November 26 and by common consent it was agreed that, as the *Morning Post*'s forecast of the Report of the Boundary Commission was less acceptable to both of them than the existing boundary, the Commission's Report should be jettisoned, since, under the provisions of the Treaty of 1921, publication of its findings would give them the effect of law. It was further agreed that new legislation should be enacted by all interested parties to retain the existing Boundary.[1]

This tripartite meeting was followed by a full-dress conference which began at Chequers on November 27 and at which John Anderson was the principal adviser to the Imperial Government representatives. Final agreement was reached on December 3, by which the three governments 'being united in amity' and 'being resolved mutually to aid one another in a spirit of neighbourly comradeship', reached accord on the Boundary issue in the following legalistic formula :

The powers conferred by the proviso to Article XII of the said Articles of Agreement [the Anglo-Irish Treaty of 1921] on the Commission therein mentioned are hereby revoked, and the

[1] St. John Ervine, *Craigavon, Ulsterman* (1949), pp. 500-508.

extent of Northern Ireland for the purposes of the Government of Ireland Act, 1920, and of the said Articles of Agreement should be such as was fixed by sub-section (2) of Section 1 of that Act.

Thus was the bogy of the Irish Boundary, at least temporarily, laid to rest, but what was far more important was the understanding engendered at this meeting between Sir James Craig and William Cosgrave. It was deep and believably sincere, and hopes were born for the inauguration of a true spirit of co-operation between the two Irish Governments. 'Unhappily for their country', an Irish historian has sorrowfully written, 'Mr. Cosgrave and Sir James Craig never saw each other again, nor was this hopeful augury followed up by a single meeting of their Cabinets. They did not hold apart on any punctilio, and probably the dead weight of extremism on both sides, of Orangemen in the North and Republicans in the South, made them averse from a policy of conciliation which would have been fruitful for the country but which might have been politically fatal to both.' [1]

(iii)

When in the summer of 1924 Mr. Ramsay MacDonald's Government decided to appoint a Royal Commission to enquire into the scheme of National Health Insurance established by the Acts of 1911–1912 and to recommend any alterations or extensions which might be thought desirable, it was natural, and indeed inevitable, that John Anderson should be appointed a member. Amongst the other Commissioners was Professor Alexander Gray, now an eminent academic figure at the University of Aberdeen, and another former colleague of Anderson's in the old days of the Insurance Commission was Sir Alfred Watson, now Government Actuary. Though the Chairman was Lord Lawrence of Kingsgate it was clear from the start that the predominating figure on the Commission was John Anderson, and his fellow Commissioners were deeply impressed by the working of his mind in the examination of the long series of expert witnesses from Approved Societies, Insurance Committees, medical men, and representatives of the Government departments concerned. His questioning was pene-

[1] Donal O'Sullivan, *The Irish Free State and its Senate* (1940), p. 180.

trating without being intimidating. With his thorough first-hand experience of the points at issue he got to the root of the matter with waste of neither words nor time.

Anderson's sense of proportion was equally displayed in the range and balance of his contribution to the framing of the recommendations of the Commission's report, in which he took a major part. 'He had an open mind for improvements, and at the same time, a steady recognition of what the 1911 Act had achieved during its fifteen years' run', writes one who served as Assistant Secretary to the Commission. 'The big changes in the scheme came later, namely the separation of the money from the medical benefits, the latter going to the new Health Services, the former taking its place in a money insurance scheme for the whole country in place of the original four Insurance Commissions. It is interesting to note that a hint of the medical separation appears in the Report of the Commission, though, it was felt by Sir John Anderson and others of the drafting Committee, too soon to offer any specific recommendation of such a drastic character. This illustrates the combination of adventure and caution in his administrative make up.'[1]

When the Commission reached the end of its labours in February 1926 it was not successful in arriving at entirely unanimous conclusions. In addition to the Majority Report, there was the report of a minority who favoured the abolition of the Approved Societies and the transfer of the administration of the cash benefits and of the medical benefits to the local health authorities. Even the Majority Report was the subject of a reservation by Alexander Gray and another of the Commissioners, and herein lies an interesting comparison. The Majority Report reflects throughout the clear, grave, almost lapidary, style of John Anderson, but the reservation is clearly Gray's. In it there is lightness of touch, almost a gaiety, which is unusual in the reports of Royal Commissions.[2]

(iv)

The problems of National Health Insurance and of Ulster were matters which related to John Anderson's past, but there was

---

[1] Letter from Sir James Peck, C.B., to the author, June 3, 1959.
[2] *Report of the Royal Commission on National Health Insurance*, Cmd. 2596, 1928.

another of his early activities in the Home Office which had an interesting connection with his future.

British Governments of varying political complexions have been frequently criticized for their neglect of national defences and none more so than those of Mr. Baldwin. It is therefore of no little interest to find action of an exploratory nature being undertaken in this field at a time when the man in the street was under the optimistic, if misguided, belief that the international barometer was set fair for international peace and understanding. The era inaugurated by the Dawes Plan, which was to solve the vexed question of German reparation payments, found its natural corollary in the negotiations for a Western Pact of Security, which ultimately found fulfilment in the Locarno Agreement of October 1925. It was confidently believed that a new age of peace and plenty had opened, but it was very proper that provision for preparedness should not be relaxed.

Early in 1924 the Committee of Imperial Defence appointed a sub-committee to enquire into the question of Air Raid Precautions, to which Mr. Stanley Baldwin appointed Sir John Anderson as Chairman. The work of the sub-committee hung fire during the brief premiership of Mr. MacDonald, but when the Conservatives returned to power in November 1924 they began an intensified study of the question. The report which the sub-committee presented in July 1925 was largely the work of their Chairman and, considering the spirit of the times, it was extremely far-sighted. In making their recommendations the sub-committee emphasized that these could be no more than palliatives. Adequate protection for the civilian population from aerial attack could only be secured by the vigorous prosecution of an active offensive campaign which would carry the war into the enemy's country and subject his people to conditions even more trying than those which the people of Britain would be called upon to endure. In short, the best means of defence was attack or, as Clausewitz once wrote of political warfare, the best means of waging it is to capture the enemy's capital! The sub-committee's primary recommendation was that the education of the general public to a full and lively realization of the whole significance of aerial attack was a matter of vital importance. Towards this end, a proclamation should be prepared for issue immediately on the outbreak of hostilities warning the people of the conditions likely to be encountered and exhorting them to meet these conditions with courage and endurance. On the practical side the report recommended the institution of a system of warnings and of 'black outs' and the provision of shelters. Preparation of plans for the evacuation of refugees, mainly women and children, from London was also advocated, and for the maintenance of vital services and for the movement of certain Government departments not directly concerned with the active prosecution of the war, if and when necessary, to alternative accommodation in other parts of the country. The institution of anti-gas measures and decontamination was also urged.

The interest of this report lies, first in its prescience and, secondly, in the fact that, with only minor revisions, it remained the basic document on the subject until some twelve years later when the question of Air Raid Precautions again became John Anderson's concern in circumstances at once more pragmatic and more momentous.

John's interest — both personal and official — in this problem of A.R.P. continued throughout his term as Permanent Under-Secretary. The plans evolved in 1925 were periodically revised and brought up to date in the light of later information, and Anderson did not hide from Ministers the importance of civil defence nor the horrors with which it would have to contend. During the second Labour Government of 1929–1931, the Home Secretary, Mr. J. R. Clynes, arranged for a meeting of Ministers to discuss the matter and invited John Anderson to address them. Among those present was Mr. Herbert Morrison, then Minister of Transport, who has written :

> Anderson, in his slow impressive manner, was called on to explain the purpose of the meeting. He painted a gloomy picture of destruction and the problems arising as regards communications, sanitation, fire, rescue, supplies and so on — a glimpse of a situation which was unhappily to become real within ten years. Considering the paucity of facts about air attack at the time, Sir John had produced a pretty clear résumé of the possible situation.
>
> Problems like that did not intimidate him, for he was a man

H

of great moral and physical courage. . . . One of the great
public servants of our time.[1]

(v)

But important though these activities of Anderson's were, the
major event, both in the life of the country and in his own personal
career, during his nine years at the Home Office was, of course, the
General Strike ; those nine tremendous days in May 1926 which, as
Mr. Duff Cooper has written : 'divided the people into two camps,
threatened the survival of parliamentary government, and brought
the country nearer to revolution than it has ever been'.[2]

The threat of a general strike had been recognized as endemic
in the industrial life of Britain ever since labour had become an
organized force. It was the ultimate weapon which the trade
unions, acting in concert, could use to enforce their terms upon the
Government of the country. Much canvassed and discussed in the
trade union world during the stormy periods of the nineteenth
century, it had latterly come to be regarded as a somewhat academic
issue. But, with the upsurging of the school of 'Direct Action' in
national and international labour circles as a result of the First
World War, it again came to the fore. From the beginning of
1919 onwards successive British Governments had regarded as
inevitable some trial of strength with organized labour in which the
weapon of the general strike would be employed, and it was almost
equally certain that both the *casus belli* and the *casus foederis* would
emerge from the coal-mining industry. Preparations for meeting
such an emergency were accordingly put in hand.

The years immediately following the war were — apart from
the brief immediate post-war boom — a period of economic
depression and industrial unrest. One result was the appearance in
power of the Triple Alliance of the Miners', Railwaymen's and
Transport Workers' Unions, which, though actually formed in
1914, did not emerge as a force until 1919. In this year the other

---

[1] Lord Morrison of Lambeth, *Herbert Morrison, an autobiography* (1960), p. 206.

[2] Viscount Norwich, *Old Men Forget* (1953), p. 147. It is of interest to note
that Mr. J. H. Thomas in his autobiography is at great pains to emphasize 'that the
General Strike of 1926 was not called with any idea of revolution. . . . It was
simply a gesture of sympathy with the miners' (*My Story* (1937), p. 96).

two unions threatened to strike in sympathy with the miners' demands for higher wages and shorter hours. The strike on this occasion was postponed pending the appointment by the Government of a Royal Commission under the chairmanship of Mr. Justice Sankey, to examine the whole condition of the coal industry.

Contrary to the expectations of many, the Report of the Sankey Commission proved highly favourable to the demands of the miners. It recommended increases in pay and a seven, instead of an eight, hour day, and by a majority composed of the Chairman and the six miners' representatives, it urged the nationalization of the mines.[1] Though Mr. Bonar Law, on behalf of the Coalition Government, expressed their intention of carrying out the Sankey Report 'in the spirit and in the letter', when it came to the House of Commons, the Prime Minister, Mr. Lloyd George, though conceding the increase in wages and the shorter hours, flatly rejected the idea of nationalization as impracticable.

The strength of the Triple Alliance had not been tried in 1919 but it was put to the test two years later when, in April 1921, the coal-owners announced sweeping wage reductions and posted lock-out notices at all collieries. The leaders of the Triple Alliance promptly called for a strike of railway and transport workers in support of the miners, to begin on April 12. This was the first instance of a combined effort for 'Direct Action' and the Government were well prepared to meet it. An Emergency Powers Act had been passed through Parliament in 1920 with a view to just such a contingency and, by virtue of its provisions, forceful action was taken. A state of emergency was declared, reservists were called to the colours, machine-guns were mounted at the pit-heads and troops in battle order were sent into many industrial areas. The strike duly began, but three days later it was called off through the joint efforts of Mr. J. H. Thomas of the National Union of Railwaymen and Mr. Frank Hodges of the Miners' Federation, under circumstances which engendered bitter, undying enmity and dissension in the trade union movement as a whole. Faced with the firm action of the Government, the Triple Alliance had crumbled. This was 'Black Friday', April 15, 1921.

The sequel came just four years later — and under very different

[1] *Report of the Sankey Commission on the Coal Industry — 1919,* Cmd. 359-361.

circumstances. In the summer of 1925 the mine-owners again announced a new and drastic wage structure which envisaged a considerable cut in pay all round and the abolition of the minimum wage altogether. On this occasion, both in organization and in personalities, the forces of labour were in a far stronger position than in 1921. The collapse of the Triple Alliance — which, after 'Black Friday', had become known as the 'Cripple Alliance' — had resulted in the rise of the General Council of the Trades Union Congress and in place of the pliant personality of Frank Hodges, the Secretary of the Miners' Federation was Arthur James Cook, who was, he said, proud to be a follower of Lenin.

Equally, on the Governmental side, the progressive Conservatism of Stanley Baldwin lacked that belligerency which had characterized the erstwhile radical, David Lloyd George. Mr. Baldwin desired above all things to avoid a show-down with organized labour, partly because he believed that the Government should not interfere with industry, partly because he cared deeply for the preservation of industrial peace while agreement by negotiation was possible in any form; and partly because of the simple fact, which years later he communicated to his biographer Mr. G. M. Young : 'We were not ready'.[1]

Negotiations between mine-owners and miners dragged on throughout July with tentative efforts at mediation on the part of the Government. The suggestion of a subsidy to the industry was advanced but was emphatically declined by the Minister of Labour, Sir Arthur Steel-Maitland, who declared 'quite openly and categorically that I do not think the coal industry ought to look for a subsidy to carry on'. A Court of Inquiry was appointed and reported on July 29 strongly in favour of a fixed minimum wage, adding that there was considerable room for improvement in the fields of management, organization and development in the industry. Their findings were flatly rejected by the coal-owners and on the same day the General Council of the Trades Union Congress placed an embargo upon the movement of coal as from July 31, the day on which the owners' notices terminated. On this day too, King George V noted in his diary : 'I fear a strike now is inevitable at the end of the week. It will play the devil in the country.'[2]

---

[1] G. M. Young, *Stanley Baldwin* (1952), p. 99.   [2] Nicolson (*op. cit.*), p. 415.

But His Majesty's fears were not realized — at least not then. Mr. Baldwin, in a personal interjection into the negotiations, bought time in the name of the Cabinet. In the face of complete intransigence on the part of both owners and miners, the Government gave way. They would, the Prime Minister informed both parties, grant a subsidy of £23 million to the coal industry until May 1, 1926 ; in the meantime there would be no wage reductions, the owners would withdraw their notices, and another Royal Commission would make a further full inquiry into the condition of the industry. 'So, thank God, there will be no strike now. I am much relieved', the King recorded. This was 'Red Friday', July 31, 1925.

There was little doubt in the minds of the Government, the coal-owners or the miners that all that had been achieved was an armistice and not a settlement, and that the final show-down would come inevitably in nine months' time when the Government subsidy expired. All possible advantage, therefore, must be taken of this breathing space.

Now, when Mr. Baldwin told Mr. G. M. Young that the major cause of his surrender in July 1925 was because 'We were not ready', his statement merits examination, more especially in respect of its connection with John Anderson.

To meet the threatened emergency of a coal strike in 1919 the Government had worked out an elaborate supply and transport system under the control of the then Minister of Transport, Sir Eric Geddes. Its efficiency had not been fully tested at the time but in the following year the Emergency Powers Act had still further strengthened the hand of the Government, and it was on the basis of its provisions that Mr. Lloyd George had so effectively challenged the Triple Alliance in 1921. Again no major test of strength had followed. Thereafter the machinery had been allowed to fall into a sad state of disrepair. But, in July 1923, Mr. Baldwin had ordered John Anderson to report on the state of the organization.[1] As a result of his findings the task of revision had been entrusted to Mr. J. C. C. Davidson, Chancellor of the Duchy of Lancaster, but before much progress could be made the Conservative Government fell, to be succeeded by the first Labour Administration. In handing over to his successor, Mr. Josiah Wedgwood, Mr. Davidson had

[1] Young (*op. cit.*), p. 119.

begged him not to destroy what had already been done and indeed to carry on the good work. Faced almost immediately with a railway strike, the Labour Government were shocked at the inadequacy of the existing arrangements for meeting the emergency and an *ad hoc* system was quickly improvised. Fortunately the strike collapsed within a few days and again no test of strength was made ; but again, once the emergency had passed, governmental interest slackened and when, in November 1924, the Conservatives again returned to power and Mr. Wedgwood transferred his responsibilities to Mr. Davidson, he is said to have done so with the remark : 'I haven't destroyed any of your plans ; in fact I haven't done a bloody thing about them'.[1]

Nevertheless some progress had been made. The Civil Service planners had continued their work throughout the interim of the Labour Government and shortly after the Conservatives had taken office, the new Home Secretary, Sir William Joynson-Hicks, presented the results of their deliberations to the Cabinet.[2] The plan evolved was an excellent one but it was a skeleton which required governmental action to give it flesh and blood. For various reasons this action was not forthcoming and the plan remained in draft form until the humiliation of 'Red Friday' taught the Government a lesson.

This then is the explanation of Mr. Baldwin's statement 'We were not ready'. The plans were there but no action had been taken to make them operative.

All this changed on the morrow of 'Red Friday'. The immediate necessity of having a plan, not in embryonic form but ready for immediate operation, was at last realized by all and the only question at issue was how it was to be operated and by whom. Mr. Churchill, then Chancellor of the Exchequer, was in favour of recalling Sir Eric Geddes from retirement and placing him at the head of a widely publicized organization, but such a proposal did not commend itself to Mr. Baldwin. The Prime Minister preferred — and wisely — that the whole thing should be carried on as quietly as possible under the control of a small committee, to the chairmanship of which he appointed John Anderson.

The choice of Anderson for this position was eminently sound.

[1] Julian Symons, *The General Strike* (1957), p. 24.   [2] Young (*op. cit.*), p. 119.

'His mind was logical, orderly and clear; his capacity as an organizer immense; his temperament impatient of rhetoric . . . his expression of opinion brisk to the point of curtness, with none of the hesitations and dubieties attributed (perhaps inaccurately) to Civil Servants, a man, certainly, eager to take rather than to avoid responsibility, and for that reason, as well as others, congenial to Baldwin.'[1] John had played little part in drawing up the plans for preparing the emergency system of transport and supply. These had been prepared on an inter-departmental basis in which the Home Office had been only one of many. But he was essentially the man who, given the requisite authority, could give them the necessary efficient operation. In the short space of time at his disposal he forged a powerful and effective weapon.

The plan was that each Government department should be responsible for some clearly defined field of action. The Board of Trade would accumulate stocks of food, coal and fuel, and arrange for local distribution; the Ministry of Transport would undertake distribution at a distance and also ensure electrical supply; the Home Office would see to the maintenance of law and order; the Ministry of Labour would occupy itself with the task of conciliation. Recruitment of volunteers was left to voluntary organizations under governmental supervision, and there was provision for publicity.

The country was mapped out into ten areas, with a separate scheme for Scotland, each with a Civil Commissioner, who was in most cases a junior minister. To each was attached an Inspector of the Ministry of Health as Staff Officer, to maintain liaison with the eighty-eight Voluntary Service Committees under local notables and to co-ordinate local services and local branches of national services. The Commissioners were authorized, in case of violence, to exercise all the powers of the Government for the maintenance of order and the protection of loyal subjects.[2]

The whole scheme was placed under the general direction of a Cabinet Committee, of which the Home Secretary was chairman, and the executive action was in the hands of John Anderson's Emergency Committee, on which fourteen Government departments were represented. The preliminary organization was carried out by Anderson's Committee, which met only once a week, and

[1] Symons (*op. cit.*), p. 25.   [2] Young (*op. cit.*), p. 119.

so quickly was the work done that, when the final moment came, none of the leaders of organized labour appear to have had any idea of the extent or thoroughness of the preparations.

Slowly the weeks drew on towards the moment of final testing. On March 11, 1926, the Royal Commission set up by Mr. Baldwin, under the chairmanship of Sir Herbert Samuel, presented its Report. It was unanimous. Many recommendations were made for the reorganization of the coal industry, among them, not nationalization of the mines but State ownership of the royalties accruing from them. The Commission was not in favour of extending the seven hour day for underground work and proposed a small reduction of wages, less drastic than that demanded by the owners in 1925. Above all they were strongly opposed to the continuance of the subsidy which 'should stop at its authorized term, and should never be repeated'.[1]

The Report was accepted by the Government after a fortnight's delay but Arthur James Cook, on behalf of the Miners' Federation, while accepting the recommendation regarding reorganization, stubbornly refused to accept or consider a reduction of wages. He at once began to exercise pressure on Arthur Pugh, Chairman of the Trades Union Congress, to enlist support for a general strike in sympathy with the miners.

On the afternoon of Saturday, May 1, the day on which the Government subsidy came to an end, the T.U.C. decided to call a general stoppage of work to begin at midnight on May 3. On May 2 the Cabinet insisted that a complete withdrawal of all strike notices must be a preliminary condition to any negotiation as to any consideration of the continuance of the subsidy — a contingency with which they were apparently still toying. There was a tendency of willingness on the part of the T.U.C. leaders to urge the miners to accept these conditions and a brief moment of optimism prevailed. At 11 p.m. on that Sunday night, however, word reached the Cabinet that some compositors and printers had refused to set up the leading article for the morrow's *Daily Mail*. Feeling that these were tactics of putting a pistol to the head of the Cabinet, Mr. Baldwin demanded that the T.U.C. should publicly repudiate the action of the *Daily Mail* employees and should issue immediate and

[1] *Report of the Samuel Commission for the Coal Industry*, 1926, Cmd. 2600.

unconditional withdrawal of notices for a general strike. These demands were handed personally by Mr. Baldwin to Mr. Thomas and Mr. Pugh at 12.45 a.m. on the morning of May 3. The T.U.C. could not contemplate so abject a surrender and the strike was therefore declared on the morning of Tuesday, May 4.

This was the moment of emergency for which John Anderson had been preparing over the past nine months. He had laboured diligently to foresee all possible contingencies and had himself given attention to many important details. To his intense satisfaction the machine, which others had devised but to which he had given power, functioned with smooth efficiency, save for the inevitable minor setbacks attendant upon the human element.[1]

Anderson, himself, was the dominating force at every level.

I was a member of the Cabinet Committee that met each day at the Home Office to deal with the crisis [writes Lord Temple-wood]. In the Chair sat Joynson-Hicks, the very embodiment of a Victorian Home Secretary, frock-coated, eloquent, determined to rise to an historic occasion. On one side of him were Churchill and Birkenhead, no less conscious of the magnitude of the crisis, and bent upon bringing it to an end by bold and dramatic action. On the other side was John Anderson, the Permanent Under-Secretary of the Home Office, an outstanding Civil Servant as yet unknown beyond Whitehall, but already showing the solid qualities of imperturbable resolution and sound judgment that were afterwards to distinguish his great career. From the first meeting of the Committee it was evident that he very well understood what should be done, and that, if left to himself, he intended to do it.[2]

---

[1] Among the many important decisions taken at this time was that of maintaining an adequate supply of electricity for the London docks. This was assured by an order from the Admiralty stationing six submarines in the Pool of London for the purpose of generating supply. Credit for this idea has frequently been given to John Anderson, whereas Sir William Joynson-Hicks's biographer claims it for the Home Secretary (see H. A. Taylor, *Jix — Viscount Brentford* (1933), p. 199). In point of fact neither was responsible. The idea came from Mr. E. T. Williams, at that time Assistant Director of Electrical Engineering in the Admiralty, who was subsequently commended by Their Lordships for his 'imagination in initiating this scheme'. Action on the suggestion could not have been taken without the authority and knowledge of both the Home Secretary and John Anderson, but neither of them gave it birth.

[2] Viscount Templewood, *Nine Troubled Years* (1954), p. 31. In view of this tribute, it is perhaps of interest to note that no mention of John Anderson is made in Sir William Joynson-Hicks's biography.

Indeed, John was completely master of the situation and, as previously in his career, he was ready to assert his views against those of the highest. On one occasion in the early days of the strike, a report was received that pickets had attempted to prevent supplies of paper from reaching the offices of the Government newspaper, *The British Gazette*, housed temporarily in the *Morning Post* building in Aldwych. Perhaps with memories of Sidney Street in mind, Mr. Winston Churchill urged that a detachment of Foot Guards, armed with ball cartridge, be dispatched to the docks to ensure freedom of passage for the supplies. Without referring to the Chair, John Anderson said clearly : 'I would beg the Chancellor of the Exchequer to stop talking nonsense.' Mr. Churchill stopped.

On another occasion someone on the Ministerial Committee urged that in view of the crucial need by London hospitals of certain medical supplies these should be conveyed in police vans. This plausible proposal was generally well received and was about to be given approval when Anderson killed it with one of his very rare orations. What he said, in effect, was this :

> This proposal would impose a very small burden on the police, but it would involve the contravention of a very big principle — the principle that in a dispute the police do not help either side. How is public order being maintained to-day? Think of the mining villages of Yorkshire and Durham. In any such village there may be scores of miners and only one policeman. The miners are idle and many of them feel bitter. Street meetings are being held and angry speeches made. Yet there is no rioting, no violence against persons, no wrecking of property. Why not? I can tell you one cause. When at any such meeting tempers are rising and things are beginning to look ugly, the one policeman intervenes, and says 'Now then, Bill, that's about enough ; time you went home to the missus.' And the meeting breaks up, because it is recognized that the police officer is not trying to help the 'bosses', but is only doing his job of keeping the peace. Any impairment of the reputation of the police for impartiality is calculated to impair their power to maintain order.

This speech, which so impressed one who heard it that he was able to reproduce the essence of it more than twenty years later,[1]

[1] Sir Alexander Maxwell, July 23, 1959.

is significant partly because it marks a complete departure from Anderson's usual style of utterance which, as a result no doubt of his anxiety to avoid all exaggeration and tendentious expression, was starkly devoid of anything which could remotely be called colourful, and partly because it illustrates so vividly his remarkable ability to see any problem in its full perspective, avoiding the often obvious solution for one which, though perhaps less easily perceptible, became apparent on consideration as pre-eminently the right one.

There is no doubt that in these nine stirring May days of 1926 John Anderson was seen at his best and in his most favourable element — a man in a crisis. His room in the Home Office became the focal point for co-ordination of all activities and to him came not only representatives of Government Departments but also those of Railway and Port Authorities and of many business organizations, all of whom were glad to bring him their problems — because they both valued his advice and respected his decisive methods of getting anything done which needed to be done. Knowing what had been decided at the Cabinet Committee, he was able to go direct to the salient points with each member of his own Emergency Committee and to secure the necessary action with the least possible lapse of time. 'I am sure', remarked one of his colleagues later, 'that he would have devised schemes for marshalling the whole community, from babes to octogenarians, had the Strike not petered out.'

But the strike did peter out, as much because of the effective functioning of the Government's system for the maintenance of supply and transport as of the cold logic with which Sir John Simon declared it to be unconstitutional.[1] On May 12 Mr. Pugh came to Downing Street and informed the Prime Minister of the Trades Union Congress decision to call off the General Strike unconditionally. The threat to the nation had passed and the thanks of the Government were conveyed to John Anderson by the Prime Minister.

The Cabinet desire to place on record [wrote Mr. Baldwin], their appreciation of the remarkable success which has attended

---

[1] The efficiency of the governmental machine may be judged from two instances. By May 10 more than 3600 trains were running, and at the end of the strike it was found that the milk pool in Hyde Park, which covered the metropolitan area of London, had actually shown a profit of £73,000.

the efforts of all those concerned in the organization and maintenance of the arrangements for safeguarding the essential services
of the country during the recent industrial crisis.

I have great pleasure in conveying to you personally the warm
thanks of the Cabinet for the services rendered by you on this
occasion. . . .

(vi)

When at the beginning of 1922 John Anderson returned from
Dublin to London he was faced with something more than the
resumption of his normal career as a Civil Servant. He had to
rebuild his own home life. The constant cares of his two years in
Ireland had anaesthetized his mind to the sorrow of Chrissie's death,
but he had now to face life in England without her and to make a
home for his two children.

Whether the loss of Chrissie accentuated John's 'serious side'
and whether, had she lived, her lively spirit would have staved off
that preternatural gravity which now overtook him, it is of course
impossible to say. But the presumption is that this might well have
been the case. Had John enjoyed the intimacy of anyone who could
tease him as Chrissie had teased him, or had made him laugh at
himself as she could do, it is more than probable that he would not
have earned so young the nickname of 'Jehovah', nor the undeserved
reputation for inhumanity.

This is in no way to disparage the devoted and zealous contribution which Nellie Mackenzie made to John's domestic world. For
twenty years she controlled his household and she 'mothered' his
children through a difficult period. Yet in temperament Nellie
differed greatly from Chrissie. She lacked her sister's lightness of
touch and gaiety of manner, and her natural shyness placed her in
considerable awe of John ; moreover, deeply devoted as she was
to him, she was not his wife, and was therefore debarred from
taking those wifely liberties which his disposition needed ; nor was
she able to fill the aching void in his heart.

Anderson's first step in his new life as a widower was to sell the
house in which he and Chrissie had been living at the time of her
death. He bought another and rather larger one called 'Leighlands'
in Grange Road, his fourth house in Sutton. The house had

pleasant grounds and here he 'cultivated his garden' with great
interest and developed his immense horticultural knowledge. He
made a pond and stocked it with goldfish, of which he became
extremely fond, and was persuaded to install a few hives, with the
result that he rapidly became deeply versed in the mysteries of bee-
culture.

There was a distracting moment also when John learned to drive
a motor-car. He was not a natural automobilist, his idea of driving
being to proceed rather slowly in the middle of the road with his
hand firmly clamped on the horn if any other vehicle approached
him. For some time he gave up driving altogether, to everybody's
relief, but later in life he resumed this activity, becoming a competent and reliable driver.

There were occasional dinner-parties too in Sutton at which he
was apt to cast a somewhat dampening influence. He had no small
talk and did not respond easily to the give-and-take of dinner-table
conversation. There were heavy silences until a topic arose in which
he was interested, at which point he would deliver a dissertation so
comprehensive that no one felt capable of contributing anything
further. On one such festive occasion the talk turned upon the
subject of methylated spirit, and a lady seated next to John, who had
suffered severely from his lack of response, remarked almost hysteri-
cally that the colour was an odd one to choose and she wondered
who had thought of it. 'I did', said Sir John Anderson, suddenly
breaking silence — the conversation then languished.

Gradually his week-end life assumed its former pattern. There
being no Presbyterian congregation in Sutton, the Andersons worshipped at the Congregational Church of the Rev. Stanley Shrub-
sole, where John was a fairly regular attendant and contributed
generously to the church funds. The Minister and his wife were
among his intimate friends and remained so till his death.

His friendship with the Patersons and the Jamiesons was also a
source of great happiness to him at this time. With the latter he
played golf and bridge, and he and 'Jimmie' Jamieson played many
games of billiards in the evenings. With them also he would go off
for week-ends to Cliftonville, where they would play golf on the
North Foreland course and watch the dancing after dinner. John
despised ballroom dancing. The rhythmic melody of the waltz,

the more barbaric allure of the foxtrot, the zest of the Charleston struck no responsive chord within him. But suddenly he became fascinated by the tango. Why this particular dance attracted him to the extent of performance is unknown. Perhaps it was some Latin American enticement long suppressed in his subconscious mind; perhaps it was 'the divine music of mathematics' which beguiled him. But, whatever the motivation, he appealed to Ruby Jamieson for her aid and together they solemnly made the round of the ballroom, she counting 'one-two-three-four-*dip*; one-two-three-four-*dip*', and he following her instruction with immense gravity, concentrating firmly on the matter in hand until he had attained at least adequate achievement. It was a sight which many of his colleagues in Whitehall would have given much to have seen.

Now too, the education of his children began to concern him. Mary was a pupil at Sutton High School and would later go to school in Switzerland. Alastair, on the other hand, having spent four years as a weekly boarder at Homefield School, entered Malvern College in the winter term of 1924. Here he laid the foundation of a fine athletic record which he later followed at Pembroke College, Cambridge, where he distinguished himself in the Inter-Varsity Relay Races and Hurdles. At Malvern, where he came under the influence of his housemaster, that remarkable figure Mr. W. W. Lowe, Alastair became a School Prefect and won his 1st XI Football colours. He showed an inclination towards following his father's early preference for a scientific career and became in due course a member of the Science Sixth, in preparation for a pre-medical course at Cambridge.[1]

In the summer term of 1928, to the intense satisfaction of the Headmaster, Mr. F. S. Preston, John Anderson consented to appear as the central figure at the Malvern Speech Day. It must be confessed that he went as a most reluctant speaker. 'I have been roped in to distribute the prizes this year', he wrote to his father on June 20, 'and that means a short address to a rather difficult mixed audience. I should have been glad to get out of it but it cannot be helped.' Nor, when he came to speak, did he hesitate to express the same

---

[1] Alastair Anderson, now Viscount Waverley, having studied at the universities of Cambridge and Frankfurt-am-Main and at St. Thomas's Hospital, became a qualified doctor and a Fellow of the Royal College of Physicians. He is now Consultant Physician to the Reading Group of Hospitals.

sentiments to his audience. 'If it had rested with me to determine the sort of gathering to which I might address remarks on any subject', he declared, 'you would not have been my first choice. I can tell you quite frankly, and without the slightest disrespect to anybody, that you are about the last audience I would have chosen at any time or in any circumstances.' He explained this somewhat uncompromising statement by analysing the audience itself : 'Boys, senior schoolboys, whose critical faculties were probably now in their most intolerant phase ; parents, presumably proud parents, with their thoughts centred, very properly on such an occasion, mainly on their offspring ; and school-masters, who, I am sure, are frankly bored with the whole business — but here I am, and I am going through with it.'

Those of us who have appeared on school platforms under similar circumstances will fully share John Anderson's sentiments, but one ventures to think that few among us have had the courage to express them thus forthrightly.

The speech which followed was of admirable value and his audience was receptive, especially of his jokes. Among these was the story of the boy who thought Anne Boleyn was the name of an electric iron because he had read that 'Henry VIII pressed his suit with Anne Boleyn'. This went over very well. An added touch of the unusual was the presence of Alastair Anderson in the front row with his head swathed in a turban of bandages as a result of injuries received while keeping wicket.

The pith of John's remarks was an exhortation to his hearers in the consideration of their education, to steer their course between learning too little and too much. 'In what you do acquire', he told them, 'get your facts right ; but for goodness' sake don't suppose that the mere accumulation of facts is going to be your supreme educational achievement.'[1] This advice is of interest as coming from a man possessing one of the most encyclopaedic brains in the country.

It cannot be said that John Anderson was an easy parent. His Presbyterian conscience and his deep sense of service and duty conflicted in some respects with his sincere affection for his children and his real desire to make up to them in some degree for the loss of

[1] *The Malvernian*, July 1928.

their mother by fulfilling certain functions of both parents. In view of the fact that the family was now domiciled in England, he had decided that his son should attend an English public school and an English university ; though it is greatly to be doubted whether the education which Alastair received at Malvern and Cambridge was in any way superior to that which his father had acquired at George Watson's and Edinburgh University. Never having himself experienced the least difficulty in studying or in application to study, it was not easy for John to realize that Alastair was not cast wholly in the same mould as himself ; that in his son's make-up there were not only his own genes but also those of Chrissie, whose gaiety and humour the boy had inherited, along with a certain lightness of approach to life, in addition to his father's good looks and native intelligence. Alastair was not a natural scholar ; he was a natural athlete. Work and application to study were difficult for him in a way in which they had never been for John. Because he was personable and animated and an athletic star, Alastair was subject to distractions which the more dour temperament of his father had never encountered. Moreover, living at home throughout the whole period of his academic career, John had had little opportunity and no inclination to indulge in the usual minor peccadilloes of university life and these, too, he could not understand.

With Mary his relations were easier ; it pleased him to help her with her lessons, exercising his phenomenal memory by repeating long passages from Virgil and Horace, and then translating them for her.

He played coach to Alastair also, but there the relationship was again more complex since, perhaps because of his own amazing grasp of scientific subjects, he could never, for example, comprehend his son's difficulties in mastering organic chemistry when preparing for his Cambridge examinations. 'I could understand your finding inorganic chemistry difficult but organic is so easy', he once remarked. Nevertheless, he applied himself to the task with characteristic determination. Having obtained past examination questions, he would devote his evenings to them after his return from the Home Office, demonstrating the problems on the blackboard in Mary's schoolroom, and to such good effect that, under his coaching, Alastair passed his tests quite comfortably.

ALASTAIR

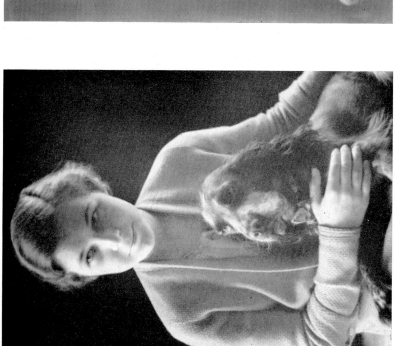

MARY

But the age-old father-and-son conflict persisted between them, and it was not until some years later that John and Alastair Anderson came to appreciate each other's true worth and to enjoy the full depth of parental and filial affection and admiration.

(vii)

The nine days of the General Strike and the months of preparation which went before them placed the final seal upon John Anderson's pre-eminence among the senior hierarchs of the Civil Service. His great qualities had always been recognized but the national crisis had brought them into sharper relief and, in addition, to the notice of a larger audience. Though he was still virtually unknown in the country as a whole, in Downing Street and Westminster and Whitehall his name had become one with which to conjure.

He was one of the small group of men, which at that time included Sir Maurice Hankey, Secretary to the Cabinet, Sir Warren Fisher, Head of the Treasury, and Sir Robert Vansittart, Permanent Under-Secretary of the Foreign Office, upon whose shoulders rests the responsibility for the continuous smooth functioning of the great machine of government. Cabinets come and go ; Ministers rise and fall ; personalities soar into the political firmament and either remain in orbit or collapse like damp squibs, but the great work of governing the country, as distinct from ruling it, remains the eternal anonymous task of the Civil Service, and in this sphere John Anderson was among the giants.

There is no doubt that he enjoyed his years at the Home Office. He was proud of the Civil Service and proud of his position in it, and in his pride there was a little harmless vanity which he occasionally indulged ; as, for example, in the exercise of his right as an Irish Privy Counsellor to sit on the steps of the Throne when listening to debates in the House of Lords, a privilege which his other senior colleagues did not share. His horizon, too, was broadening in other ways. He had been elected to Brooks's in 1923 and he used it as an alternative to the Reform Club, finding in its atmosphere a certain difference of approach and expression in the discussion of matters of the day. But, as time passed, he showed himself increasingly less interested in Home Office affairs and more concerned

I

with the wider world of Whitehall. It is probably true that, in his official contacts, he was closer to people outside the Office — such as Fisher, Hankey and Vansittart, with whom he was on Christian name terms — than with those within it.

With his reputation as an administrator and organizer it was not, therefore, surprising that Anderson should be called to the consideration of problems lying outside the strict province of the Home Office. Even in his early days he had been appointed Chairman of a Committee of Permanent Heads of Departments, which prepared three reports to the Cabinet on the extended scheme of social insurance. It was these reports, in the drafting of which he had taken a considerable hand, that became the basis of the Widows, Orphans and Old Age Contributory Pensions Act of 1925, thus extending the great scheme of social insurance legislation which Mr. Lloyd George had envisaged twelve years earlier. Now, when the Labour Party returned to power in June 1929 to find itself faced with the imperative necessity of solving the problem of unemployment, it was to Anderson that they turned for advice and guidance. Mr. Ramsay MacDonald confided this Herculean labour to the Lord Privy Seal, Mr. J. H. Thomas, who became virtually 'Minister of Unemployment', and to him he assigned as colleagues Mr. George Lansbury, First Commissioner of Works, and Sir Oswald Mosley, Chancellor of the Duchy of Lancaster — in the light of subsequent events, a somewhat oddly assorted couple. Anderson was seconded to lead a team of Civil Servants collected from other Departments and placed at Mr. Thomas's disposal. While still remaining in control of the Home Office *de jure*, he was content to leave a large measure of the supervision of the Office to Frank Newsam, now Principal Private Secretary to the Secretary of State.

The 'Ministry of Unemployment' was doomed to failure from the beginning. In the first place, Mr. Thomas was no Hercules and, in the second, all the forces of world events were ranged against him. The premonitory rumblings of the economic depression, which had already been heard in the Antipodes, were destined to burst into full eruption with the New York Stock Market crash of October 1929, which in its turn caused seismic repercussions to resound throughout the world. Such measures for the alleviation of Britain's unemployment problem as Mr. Thomas and his colleagues were able to devise crumbled almost as soon as they were evolved and his brief term of office as 'Minister of Unemployment' was memorable more for his monumental quarrel with Sir Oswald Mosley than for any measure of success. The circumstances of this major disagreement and of Mosley's subsequent resignation have been told in Mr. Thomas's memoirs and in Mr. Lansbury's biography.[1] Mr. Thomas pays warm tribute to the assistance which he was given in his labours by the Civil Service generally ; but, whereas he singles out for individual praise Sir Maurice Hankey and Sir Horace Wilson, the Chief Economic Adviser to the Cabinet, no mention or acknowledgment is made of the principal Civil Service adviser, Sir John Anderson, nor does any mention of him occur in the book.

With the collapse of the 'Ministry of Unemployment' in 1930, Anderson became Chairman of an inter-departmental committee, charged with developing the schemes originated by Mr. Thomas and his colleagues and with devising others thought to be likely to increase employment. Once again he took command and ranged far and wide over the economic field ; but not even his great abilities and inventive genius were proof against the greater potency of the storm which was shaking the economic structure of the country to its foundations, and which manifested itself in a growing loss of confidence throughout the business community. When the Labour Administration fell in August 1931, to be succeeded by the National Government, John was relieved of his thankless task.

It was now that the question of his future began to concern him. He was forty-nine years old and had held his present position for nearly ten years ; another eleven years must elapse before he became due for retirement. He could go no higher in his profession and no Permanent Under-Secretary had remained at the Home Office for twenty years, though his predecessor, Sir Edward Troup, had occupied the post for fourteen. If the truth must be told, he was perhaps a little bored with Whitehall.

Once again, however, Destiny was about to take a hand in his affairs. All unbeknown to him, discussions were in progress at the

[1] J. H. Thomas (*op. cit.*), pp. 167-176 ; Raymond Postgate, *The Life of George Lansbury* (1951), pp. 252-258.

India Office which were to affect him mightily and to result in his embarking upon a wholly new career. In the autumn of 1931 the British Government were faced with the necessity of finding a successor to Sir Stanley Jackson as Governor of Bengal, and it was this problem which was exercising the minds of the Secretary of State for India, Sir Samuel Hoare, and his Permanent Under-Secretary, Sir Findlater Stewart. It was their personal opinion that of all available candidates John Anderson stood head and shoulders above the others, and Hoare had twice seen his abilities at first hand, once when he was in Dublin Castle and again during the General Strike. 'No man was more experienced in problems of administrative efficiency', he later wrote in his memoirs. 'Stewart and I at once thought of him when the end of Stanley Jackson's term of office made a vacancy in the Governorship of Bengal. Would he be ready to leave a safe and distinguished career in the Home Civil Service for the risks of a temporary Governorship in the most disturbed province of India? Would the Home Secretary and the Treasury make it possible for him if he wished to go to Bengal?'[1]

To obtain the answers to these questions Sir Samuel Hoare tackled the Cabinet where he encountered no opposition, and Sir Findlater Stewart was deputed to sound out John Anderson. In the covert parlance of the Civil Service he asked John if he would like to be 'considered for the succession in Bengal'. John took it very calmly, but at once reminded Stewart that he had had his share of standing up to terrorism when he had been in Ireland. Nevertheless he said he would give the matter consideration. After much cogitation he accepted and his reasons for so doing — or at least some of them — are set out in a letter written to his father on November 21, 1931.

> I have been asked to become Governor of Bengal. Naturally the suggestion of so radical a change in my course of life gave me food for thought. At first blush I must say the idea was not very attractive. India is a long way off & affairs there are not in a very happy state. On the other hand the position is one of considerable eminence to which no Civil Servant either of the Home or Indian Services has ever before been appointed. It was therefore

[1] Templewood (*op. cit.*), p. 82.

no small compliment to have been approached & I had to consider whether, as I was thought to be the right man, I ought not to consent.

I reached the climax of my career here ten years ago. There is no post in the home service I would rather have than my present one. On the other hand, I don't very much fancy doing the same job for twenty years after having had so much variety earlier in my service. Again, Alastair & Mary have reached an age when I can go away without feeling that their interests might be prejudiced & you are still young enough & vigorous enough to make light of the five years for which the appointment runs.

The long & short of it is that I have decided to accept. . . . As I have said, the appointment is for five years but in the ordinary course I would return for a couple of months at the end of two years. The salary is large — all told something like £20,000, — but, of course, expenses are correspondingly heavy.

There was one reason, however, for his acceptance which John Anderson did not mention to his father and which he only confided to his son. He went up to see Alastair at Cambridge and, in his rooms in Pembroke, broke the news of his going to Bengal. It was common knowledge that terrorism was rampant in the province and that numerous attempts had been made on the lives of officials of the Provincial Government — some with fatal results. These considerations were in Alastair's mind as he said : 'Won't it be pretty dangerous, father?' 'Yes, my boy, it will,' was the reply, 'but the Police will take care of me.' He went on to say that he was proud to have been asked because it was, apart from anything else, an historic appointment which had been held by both Clive and Warren Hastings. And then he added what was certainly one of the compelling reasons for his acceptance. There were risks certainly, he said, but he was willing to accept them because, unlike the majority of his contemporaries, he had not served in the War. Though he did not mention it on this occasion that 'white feather' may well have been in his mind.

The appointment to Bengal offered John an escape from the monotonous security of the Civil Service, a chance to exercise his great abilities in a new field, and an opportunity to lay for ever that pale ghost of cowardice evoked by the flighty act of a thoughtless hoyden seventeen years before.

V

Governor of Bengal

1932–1937

(i)

THE India into whose service John Anderson was now called stood at a climacteric of her constitutional development. In international and national affairs the position of the Indian Empire was contradictory and anomalous. In company with the British Dominions, India had been a signatory of the Treaties of Peace at Paris in 1919 at the conclusion of the First World War and had thus become automatically a charter member of the League of Nations. Yet her legal status fell considerably short of the requirement stated in the preamble to the Covenant : namely that membership of the League could only be enjoyed by 'completely self-governing States, Dominions or Colonies' — and this India certainly was not.

Indian nationalism had drunk deeply of the heady wine of 'self-determination', purveyed with indiscriminate irresponsibility by both President Wilson and Lenin, and as a result the youth of the country had become infected with hopes and hatreds to a greater degree than had been known before. Neither the Imperial Government nor the Government of India was unaware of the fact that the time was now ripe for a further step towards Indian self-government on the basis of Dominion status and both realized that the magnificent response of the peoples of India to the service of the King-Emperor during the First World War merited some major measure of reward. It was in partial recognition of these services that India had been accorded equality with the British Dominions as a signatory of the Peace Treaties, but promises of further advance in responsible government had also been made in the course of the war.

These promises were fulfilled in the Government of India Act of 1919 which was based, in the main, on recommendations of the Viceroy, Lord Chelmsford, and the Secretary of State for India, Mr. Edwin Montagu. The Montagu–Chelmsford reforms and the resultant Indian Constitution established a central legislature for British India, with 70 per cent of its members elected by an extended franchise. The Executive, however, remained under the ultimate control of the Viceroy, as Governor-General, who was responsible to the Imperial Government alone, and the Viceroy was empowered in case of emergency to override the vote of the elective assembly. In the provinces the unique innovation of 'dyarchy' was introduced. Certain Departments, such as education and public works, were 'transferred' to Ministers responsible to the provincial legislatures ; others, such as internal order, revenue and finance, though subject to Budget discussion and interrogation in the Legislature, were administered by virtually irremovable Members of the Governor's Executive Council, and ultimately 'reserved' to the Governor-General, who remained in such matters responsible to the Government in London. A Chamber of Princes was established in Delhi for the discussion of matters of common interest.

The Montagu–Chelmsford reforms might well have marked the beginning of a new and felicitous state in Anglo-Indian relations had it not been for the almost simultaneous passage of the Rowlatt Acts against sedition, which provided that those accused of political crimes could be tried without a jury. Although these Acts were never actually put into force the very fact of their existence on the Statute Book, coupled with the unhappy Amritsar shootings of April 13, 1919, in which 379 people were killed and 1200 wounded, caused a deep and lasting resentment throughout India. Not least unfortunate was the effect made upon Mahatma Gandhi, leader of the Congress Party. 'From that moment', writes Sir Harold Nicolson, 'Mr. Gandhi decided that there was little more to be secured from co-operation. By applying the simple axiom of *Bhagavad Gita* and *Sesame and Lilies* to what until then had been a riot of emotional conceptions, he succeeded within a few years in transforming an intellectual agitation into a mass revolutionary movement.' [1] The campaign of non-co-operation and civil disobedience which followed, marked the beginnings of bitter agitation

[1] Nicolson (*op. cit.*), p. 503.

not unlike that preceding the final conclusion of the Anglo-Irish Treaty of 1921.

An important provision of the Government of India Act of 1919 had been that, when ten years had elapsed, a Commission should be appointed to enquire into the working and efficacy of the new Constitution and to report whether the time had come for the introduction of any further reforms. In the autumn of 1927 the British Government decided to anticipate the statutory date and appointed Sir John Simon as Chairman of a Commission of Enquiry composed of representatives of all shades of British political opinion. Since no Indian was included on the Commission, Mr. Gandhi called for its boycott by all good nationalists. Sir John Simon and his colleagues nevertheless proceeded to India, conducted their investigations and returned to England to write their report. The first volume, published on June 10, 1930, was one of the few Blue Books to be a best-seller [1] — 17,000 copies were bought in under a week. Brilliantly written, it brought before the eyes of many English men and women who had never before thought about India the vivid picture of that vast sub-continent, with its beauty and its riches and its dignity, its complicated problems and the difficulties and dangers inherent in them. Even to-day, thirty years later, it is as readable as a good novel.

The second volume of the Simon Report, which was published a fortnight later and proved less appealing to the general reading public,[2] contained the Commission's conclusions and recommendations, which were unanimous. Of these the most important were first, the abolition of the system of 'dyarchy' in the Provinces [3] and the transfer to Provincial Ministers of the charge of all departments,

---

[1] *Report of the Indian Statutory Commission*, vol. i, Cmd. 3568 of 1930.
[2] *Ibid.* vol. ii, Cmd. 3569 of 1930.
[3] The system of dyarchy had been a constant target for Nationalist criticism in India. In 1924 the Viceroy, Lord Reading, had appointed a Commission of Enquiry under Sir Alexander Muddiman to advise upon any defects in the working of the Act of 1919 or any amendment compatible with its general working and purpose. The Commission presented majority and minority reports in December 1924 (Cmd. 2360, 1925). The majority found that the experiment of dyarchy had not had a sufficient period for a fair trial of its effects to be made and concluded that 'except by some form of dualism, it was not possible to afford an equally valuable training towards responsible government in India and still to safeguard those conditions upon which government depends'. The minority report found that dyarchy had broken down, that transitional measures were inappropriate and that steps should be taken at once to establish a permanent constitution.

leaving to the Governors, however, the power to veto ministerial decisions in extreme emergency ; secondly, the envisaging, as an ultimate aim, of the distant possibility of an All-Indian Federation of self-governing Provinces on the analogy of Canada, to comprise not British India only but also the Indian States ; and, thirdly, the advice that the new Constitution of India should be flexible and capable of development.

The Report of the Simon Commission was one of the many proposals considered by the First Indian Round Table Conference which was opened by King George V in the Royal Gallery of the House of Lords on November 13, 1930. The Conference was composed of both British and Indian representatives of all political views, with the important omission of the Congress Party, which had followed Mr. Gandhi's orders to boycott it. It adjourned in January 1931, having accepted three main principles, namely, that the future development of India must be on a federal basis ; that certain safeguards concerning defence and financial stability must be retained by the Viceroy, and that, subject to these reservations, responsibility must be placed in Indian hands.

It was generally realized, however, that no real progress could be made towards Indian self-government while the state of deadlock prevailed between Mr. Gandhi and the Government of India. In an effort to resolve this impasse the Viceroy, Lord Irwin (later Lord Halifax), took his courageous and now historic decision to enter into direct negotiations with the Indian Congress leader. Summoning Mr. Gandhi to Delhi in early February 1931, Lord Irwin conducted with him a series of conversations which, although they ranged over a prodigious congeries of issues and appeared to be interminable, nevertheless resulted in the Delhi Pact of March 7, 1931. By this agreement Mr. Gandhi not only accepted the three basic principles adopted by the First Round Table Conference but also called off the civil disobedience campaign and even accepted an invitation to the Second Round Table Conference which was due to convene in London in September.

This hardy experiment of Lord Irwin's, despite its success, was not universally acclaimed in England. Whereas King George, by the hand of his Private Secretary, congratulated the Viceroy on 'the patience and forbearance you have shown. . . . His Majesty feels that you deserve the very greatest credit for bringing about this temporary truce with Gandhi and with Congress',[1] Mr. Winston Churchill thought otherwise. He expressed his disapproval in characteristically uncompromising language, deprecating 'the nauseating and humiliating spectacle of this one-time Inner Temple lawyer, now seditious fakir, striding half-naked up the steps of the Viceroy's Palace, there to negotiate and to parley on equal terms with the representative of the King-Emperor'.

The high hopes for the success of the Second Round Table Conference, which had been built on the presence of Mr. Gandhi, were doomed to frustration. The Conference broke down in December 1931, largely because of the dissension arising between the Indians themselves. Mr. Gandhi returned to India resolved to start his civil disobedience campaign all over again and, in 1933, the British Government announced the appointment of a Select Committee of both Houses of Parliament, presided over by Lord Linlithgow, to consider the application of the principles foreshadowed by the First Conference. From their deliberations emerged the Government of India Act of 1935.

(ii)

This, then, was the over-all picture of Indian constitutional development at the time of John Anderson's appointment to the Presidency of Bengal. For the greater part of his period of office as Governor he ruled his province under the powers of the Montagu-Chelmsford Act of 1919, but it was his destiny to introduce to Bengal the greatly increased measures of self-government contained in the Act of 1935.

An area of 77,500 square miles with a population of nearly sixty million (of whom 33 million were Muslims and 25 million Hindus), Bengal had been fated to be the Cinderella among the provinces of the Indian Empire. When Lord Curzon, as Viceroy, effected the celebrated first partition in 1905, transferring the predominantly Muslim districts to a new province styled Eastern Bengal and Assam, he gave deep offence to Hindu sentiment, and indeed the new impetus of revolutionary nationalism in India as a

[1] Nicolson (*op. cit.*), p. 507.

whole may be said to date from this event. The partition was rescinded in 1912, when Bihar and Orissa were detached from Bengal and formed into a separate province, and Delhi replaced Calcutta as the capital of India.[1] Discontent, however, persisted and Bengal remained a hotbed of terrorism.

Moreover the Province was unfavourably placed financially. Thanks to the Permanent Settlement of 1793,[2] the chief source of income, the land revenue, was almost completely inelastic and under the terms of the Meston Award of 1919, which had accompanied the Montagu-Chelmsford Reforms, Bengal enjoyed no share of the large sums that the Government of India collected in Calcutta from income tax, super tax and the jute export duty. Her annual contribution of 63 lakhs of rupees (approximately £472,500 stg.) to the Central Government imposed a crippling burden upon the finances of the Presidency.

The Governorship of the Presidency had been no bed of roses for many years past, a fact well realized by all. A popular line in one of the excellent amateur pantomimes produced annually in Calcutta put the position in a nutshell, when the Wicked Fairy concluded her evil spell with the words:

> I now pronounce the direst curse of all
> May you become the Governor of Bengal.

It is clear, therefore, that the task which John Anderson had assumed was no light burden and that the future held for him a formidable challenge not only to his physical and moral courage but also to his sagacity and genius for administration.

Although he was the first member of either the Home or Indian Civil Service to be appointed Governor of one of the Presidencies

---

[1] Bengal was destined to suffer a second and much more drastic partition as a result of Sir Cyril Radcliffe's Award of 1947, which was followed by the most hideous massacres.

[2] The Permanent Settlement of Bengal was introduced by Lord Cornwallis in 1793. Its main feature was that the British East India Company as sovereign authority, and the *zemindars* (the farmers of revenue) were recognized as having a joint interest in the share of the produce from the land. The *zemindars* became landlords instead of tax collectors and the revenue payable to the Government by them was fixed at the sum then assessed as the cash revenue of each estate. In effect it meant that the land revenue in Bengal was collected not from the tenants but from the landlords, and one of the primary objects of the Settlement was to safeguard the punctual receipt of such revenue and to secure its collection in the easiest and cheapest manner possible.

in India, the announcement of his appointment on November 24, 1931, passed almost without comment in the British press. *The Times*, the *Morning Post* and the *Daily Telegraph* reported it as a news item only, and even that usually astute commentator 'Peterborough' failed to find it worthy of a paragraph. The explanation doubtless lies in the fact that while his reputation had been long established in Whitehall and Westminster, he was still virtually unknown outside this sphere. His work in Ireland and at the Home Office at the time of the General Strike had naturally been cloaked in the anonymity of the Civil Servant. The public had never heard of him. In fact, he was not 'news'.

What is more surprising is that the Viceroy had never heard of him either. When his name was mentioned to Lord Willingdon as a possible Governor of Bengal, His Excellency confessed his complete ignorance and turned for guidance to his Military Secretary, Colonel Hastings Ismay—known to his many friends as 'Pug' [1] —who had served for five years in Whitehall with the Committee of Imperial Defence. 'Pug' was under no illusions as to John's suitability. With a fine disregard of the fact that Lord Willingdon had himself previously governed Bombay and Madras, he replied instantly : 'Grab him quickly, sir. He has an incomparably better brain than any governor that England has sent to India for the last twenty-five years.'

In general the reaction in Bengal to Anderson's prospective advent was favourable, if guarded. 'Calcutta has received the news of Sir John Anderson's appointment as Governor very well on the whole', wrote one singularly acute observer on the day following the announcement. 'Indian opinion will be disappointed at the appointment of an "official"—they prefer a "home" politician who will generally be more ignorant of conditions here and less uncompromising than an official may be expected to be. It is rather a blow that he is a widower and that his daughter is too young to be much use as a hostess. *Per contra*, it is a matter of undisguised satisfaction to the large population of Scottish origin in Calcutta (in the big commercial offices, jute mills, etc.) and will also be welcomed in Northern Bengal (on the tea estates) that he is a Scot. The Civil Service to a man will welcome an official . . . indeed

[1] General the Rt. Hon. Lord Ismay, K.G., G.C.B., C.H., D.S.O.

one Member of Council said to me, "Now what we want to do is to get his appointment ante-dated".'

It was inevitable that John's career in Ireland should cause comment, favourable in some cases, adverse in others. 'Sir John Anderson comes directly from the Home Office in London where for nine years he has been Permanent Under-Secretary', the responsible *Statesman* noted, 'but he has had a varied experience in Colonial Administration, in various departments of Government at home, and, perhaps, most notably of all, as Under-Secretary to the Lord-Lieutenant of Ireland in the troublesome days of 1920. He has the reputation amongst all who know him of being a brilliant administrator, a man of courage and one with a tremendous capacity both for work and for the direction of the work of others. If he maintains his past reputation he is likely to be felt as a force in Bengal.'[1] Not unnaturally, those opposed to strong government emphasized his past reputation and experience in Ireland in an adverse light. For example, the *Amrita Bazaar Patrika*, a prominent newspaper in Calcutta, denounced the appointment, alleging that he had been specially chosen to lead Bengal into servile submission.[2]

As the time drew on for Anderson's departure from England the news from Bengal grew steadily worse. Terrorism was rife. Police officers and district magistrates were murdered in the course of their duties and a Judge had been shot dead in his court-room. On February 6, 1932, came word that John's predecessor in Bengal, Sir Stanley Jackson, had narrowly escaped death at the hands of a girl assassin as he delivered his Convocation Address in the University of Calcutta.

A few weeks after this latter outrage John Anderson was received by the King at Buckingham Palace to kiss hands on his appointment and to be invested as a Knight Grand Commander of the Order of the Indian Empire. This event was recorded by the King with characteristic brevity :

> Sir John Anderson (new Governor Bengal) came to luncheon & I gave him the G.C.I.E.[3]

In effect, however, this laconic entry does less than justice to His Majesty's deep interest in the problems which Anderson was about

---

[1] *The Statesman*, November 24, 1931.
[2] *Amrita Bazaar Patrika*, November 24, 1931.
[3] *Royal Archives*, King George V's Diary, March 3, 1932.

to confront. In the course of their luncheon discussion the King displayed his own considerable knowledge of Indian affairs and finally posed the question : 'What is *wrong* with Bengal ? I want you to find out as soon as you can and let me have a personal memorandum on the whole subject when you have had time to look round.'

John sailed from England in s.s. *Ranpura* on March 10, 1932, accompanied by his friend William Paterson. 'I hope you will both keep well while I am away', he had written to his father and his sister Katie on the previous evening, '& that I shall see little change in either of you when I come back in two years' time.' He carried with him the prayers and good wishes of many friends. One of them wrote : 'We would pray for the protecting hand of God upon him in this post of peril and of power. Granted that, we are confident that what human wisdom and commensurate patience and prudence can achieve, will be achieved ; and that, as in the past, this strong man will find a way out where the politician has faltered and failed.'[1]

(iii)

John Anderson arrived in his Presidency on March 29, 1932. Punctually at seven o'clock that morning his train drew in to the Howrah Station, Calcutta. The *Ranpura* had reached Bombay at dawn on Sunday, March 27, and, after being entertained by the Governor, Sir Frederick Sykes, Anderson and his party left that evening on their long railway journey across India. His first impression was one of intense heat. 'The weather was decidedly hot', he wrote to his father. 'At one place we stopped — Raipore in the Central Provinces — the temperature was said to be 104° in the shade & it got hotter after that ; but we were able to keep the temperature down in the saloon by having fans playing on blocks of ice . . . it [the heat] does not worry me, at least it has not done so as yet.'

As he stood upon the station platform at Calcutta a Governor's salute of seventeen guns was fired from Fort William, and a guard of honour at the salute awaited his inspection backed by a line of officials attentive for his greeting. His new official life had begun

[1] *The Watsonian*, vol. xxviii, No. 1, December 1931.

and for the next five years, except when he was on leave in England, he was to know little of the blessed relief of solitude ; indeed, save in the privacy of his bedroom, he was scarcely ever to be alone.

The immediate reactions of his staff upon seeing him were not wholly favourable. His official Private Secretary [1] recorded in his diary : 'When Sir John Anderson first descended from the train at Howrah I thought he looked very solemn and my heart sank. I feared he was a real sober-sides and that my letters to him at Aden and Bombay might have seemed flippant and be disapproved. I took heart, however, when he thanked me for them and took much more heart when, on the drive from Howrah, he was quite genial and jokey.'

There were not many people in the streets to see the new Governor pass by. It was early for the Europeans — and all the Europeans who were 'anybody' were waiting, in their capacity as 'somebody', to greet him at Government House. Moreover he security precautions of the police kept the ordinary Indian public at a discreet distance. Anderson noted this but made no comment until later. But there were bursts of cheering at various points along the route and at each of these the Governor duly 'uncovered' in acknowledgment. After several of these occasions he turned with a disarming smile to Tyson and Sir Robert Reid [2] who were in the carriage with him and said : 'Am I doing all right ? After all, I've got to do this for the next five years and I don't want to make the pace too hot at the start.' The ice was well broken after that!

Arrived at Government House, Anderson went through the ceremony of taking the oath with no shadow of hesitation and with great dignity, and this, together with his general bearing and demeanour at the official reception which followed, made an excellent impression on the large and distinguished gathering of Europeans and Indians on the steps of Government House and in the Throne Room.

It was characteristic of him that as soon as he went to his study at 9.30, his first question was, 'When is my first engagement?'

---

[1] Sir John Tyson, K.C.I.E., C.S.I., C.B.E., Private Secretary to the Governor of Bengal, 1930–1935.
[2] Sir Robert Reid, K.C.S.I., K.C.I.E., Chief Secretary to the Government of Bengal, 1932–1934.

On being told that from 10.30 onwards he would be receiving the seven members of his Government one by one, he said he would change and go round the Government House garden at 9.45 — and this on a hot mid-March morning. His Military Secretary, accustomed to a Governor of less energetic habits, was startled but hastened to act as cicerone.

It did not take long for his staff to realize that in Anderson they had found a strong chief with a genius for administration, a capacity for getting through a great deal of work in a surprisingly short space of time, and one who demanded the utmost from his subordinates, while himself simultaneously giving of his own brilliant best. They welcomed the discovery. He settled to his new work with amazing speed and adaptability and within a week gave evidence that he was well in the saddle with a firm grip of the reins. His Private Secretary noted, 'The way he conducted his first Cabinet meeting greatly impressed both Members and Ministers.[1] He is taking to files like a duck to water. The local flies are finding few opportunities of using him as a landing ground. But I think he will be ruthless when occasion demands. . . . He is going to do us very well in Bengal, if he gets half a chance, and he will be very popular too as soon as he is known.'

John had done a good deal of thinking on the voyage out from England and had arrived in India with a very clear idea of what his first objectives were to be. Within the first few weeks of his arrival he had found that many of his original theories were confirmed, though some required modification. While adhering to his general precept that the art of administration was much the same the world over, he was wise enough to recognize that the problems with which he now had to contend were entirely different from those which he had faced in his past career. 'Anyone who says that the conditions here are like Ireland is talking through his hat as I always maintained', he wrote to his father, and he set out to tackle his immediate issues *ab initio*. His initial task was to fulfil his promise to supply King George with an answer to His Majesty's query, 'What is *wrong* with Bengal?' and to this he addressed himself with his habitual concentration and energy of mind.

----

[1] The Cabinet of the Governor of Bengal was composed of four members of the Executive Council and three Ministers.

GOVERNOR OF BENGAL

After six weeks of intensive study he felt himself qualified to reply to his Sovereign's question, and accordingly, on June 10, he sent a seventeen-page memorandum to the King from Government House, Darjeeling.[1] In this he outlined, in a style free from hyperbole yet vivid and compelling, the situation with which he and his Government were faced and the policy which he proposed to adopt in dealing with it. 'That these problems are of the utmost gravity', he wrote, 'and are likely, unless radical measures are taken, to become more and more intractable and to lead before long to such a collapse as would render the grant of further autonomous powers a sheer mockery, I venture to assert with complete confidence and with all the emphasis I can command.'

The problems which Anderson examined in his memorandum were the suppression of terrorism and finance, and it was his purpose to establish their inter-connection. To do this he proceeded to demonstrate how financial stringency in the past had reacted upon administration and had brought about conditions highly favourable to the growth of the terrorist menace.

> Repressive measures alone will never destroy terrorism [he wrote to the King]. They are essential : but, to achieve the desired result, they must be accompanied by measures of quite another kind — measures which in present circumstances the Local Government are not in a position to take. It is essential to create an atmosphere in which the germs of terrorism, now so widely disseminated and, as the grim experience of this Province bears witness, so tenacious of life, cannot readily survive. Not only must the political aspiration of the people of Bengal be satisfied by the fulfilment of pledges already given, but the Government must be placed in a position to develop a constructive policy deliberately calculated to enlist in increasing measure the interest, support and co-operation of the masses.

The vital factor in the solution of this problem was that of finance, and Anderson went on to show how unavoidable but fatal parsimony over the years had increasingly hampered the administration of Bengal. The cost of the police force had been cut down whenever the threat of terrorism showed a transitory abatement and a large part of it was consequently operating on an *ad hoc* basis.

[1] *Royal Archives*, G.V., P. 1154/61.

K

Prison administration had been starved, the jails were in many cases obsolete and ill-equipped and the staff often inefficient.

In the field of education conditions were also partly to blame for the spread of revolutionary doctrines ; one reason being that the primary teachers received miserable salaries (half what they were paid in the province of Madras and one-sixth of those in the province of Bombay), and only 12 per cent of them were fully trained, as distinct from 71 per cent in Madras and 75 per cent in the Punjab. School buildings and equipment were defective and the operation of the Primary Education Act of 1930 had had to be suspended through lack of funds. Secondary education was perhaps even worse both as regards the standing of the teachers and the quality of the instruction given. The Government could not insist upon a proper standard in Calcutta University unless it could recoup the University for the loss of income from examination fees which would result from the withdrawal of recognition from institutes operating under unsatisfactory management and the fixing of a proper matriculation standard ; but here again financial conditions were an insuperable obstacle.

Although considerable sums had been spent on the Public Health Services these were still deficient. Districts which seventy-five years before had been health resorts were now malarial. 'Portions of Central Bengal are fast becoming derelict.' Little had been accomplished in irrigation and land drainage, and waterways were decaying. 'The people of Bengal see great constructive developments being undertaken in other provinces, believing, not without justification, that Bengal had indirectly paid for much of this development outside her borders.'

Anderson went on to explain that this highly unsatisfactory state of affairs was not all the fault of the Bengal Government, despite the fact that it had become fashionable in Delhi and in Whitehall to disparage the provincial administration.

> The partition and re-partition of the territory in 1905 and 1912 must have tended to throw the administrative machine out of gear. Then came the successive waves of terrorism not only entailing the loss of valuable officers but throwing a heavy, and at times an intolerable, burden upon those officers to whom it would normally fall to guide the policy of the Province on sound

constructive lines. Superimposed is the abnormal economic depression. . . . To my mind the surprising thing is, not that the standard of administration has sagged down, but that it should have been so well maintained in spite of the vicious circle in which the Local Government has been trapped.

Again finance was the clue. There had been no extravagance in departmental expenditure. 'On all sides I find evidence of proposals, desirable in themselves and in some cases urgent, being held back by the Departments interested from a recognition of the desperate condition of provincial finances.'

Anderson then put his finger on the nub of the situation. In revenue Bengal differed from most other provinces in that nearly the whole of her area was governed by the Permanent Settlement of 1793, and her land revenues were almost entirely inelastic. But this total revenue *of* Bengal by no means represented the revenue *derived from* Bengal. A total of Rs.23,87,44,000 collected in the province, made up of income tax, super tax and the jute export duty, all flowed automatically into the coffers of the Government of India, whereas, in the opinion of the Governor, the whole of the jute tax and a large proportion of the income and super taxes should undoubtedly have come to Bengal.

'Bengal's problems are not Bengal's alone. If the terrorist menace is not overcome the mischief will inevitably spread and other provinces will find themselves also confronted by the same problems. So long as there is a running sore in Bengal, India cannot be healthy.' Nor should Bengal have been compelled to sue to the Government of India *in forma pauperis*. This was not only undesirable but unnecessary. The province paid her quota to the Central Government through the medium of import duties, income tax and super tax, all of which were justified and well adapted to the purposes of a federal organization, though in respect of income tax and super tax the share contributed might be considered as over-generous. But the retention of the jute export duty by the Central Government was, in Anderson's opinion, wholly indefensible. When the duty was originally imposed during the First World War the jute trade was booming. Bengal had a virtual monopoly and powerful arguments might well have been adduced in support of making the duty a source of revenue to the Central Government.

By 1932 a great change had taken place. The jute trade was declining. The catastrophic fall in the prices of raw jute and jute manufactures, consequent upon the onset of the world-wide depression which began in America in 1929, was still seemingly unchecked. Moreover, substitutes had made their appearance — paper bags for cement, straw bags for grain, cheap cotton bags which could be used seven or eight times against three or four at the most in the case of a jute bag. The cultivator suffered severely, gaining the barest livelihood, since the duty fell in great measure, if not entirely, upon him.

> To retain the duty for the Central Exchequer [Anderson wrote, in concluding his argument] is merely to tax Bengal for the benefit of the other units in the Federation. Such a position would be intolerable, even apart from the special considerations brought to notice in this memorandum. It is now [1931–1932] at the rate of about Rs.3,10,00.000. The addition of this sum to the annual income of this Province would transform the whole situation. In my considered judgment it is called for no less as a matter of bare justice than as a matter of political expediency. Without such relief the reforms are, in my opinion, doomed so far as Bengal is concerned and I cannot but think that a complete breakdown in Bengal would spell disaster to India. Once the decision is taken to remove this long-standing grievance, we can make an appeal for co-operation to which I am certain there will be an immediate and widespread response.

King George could not have received a more complete or cogent answer to his question 'What is *wrong* with Bengal?' and he was highly appreciative.

> The King read your memorandum of June 10 with intense interest and wishes me to thank you for giving him such full information of all the difficulties which confront you [wrote his Private Secretary, Sir Clive Wigram, on July 13]. You have indeed many problems to solve, but His Majesty is confident that you will succeed . . .
> Your description of the inadequate finances of Bengal to render all the departmental services adequate and efficient gave The King an idea of the causes which have helped to keep alive the revolutionary organizations. We are now suffering from the

lack of foresight of our ancestors in fixing the Permanent Settlement, which presumably cannot now be altered.

Will the Central Government be generous and remit any of their revenues especially the Jute Export Duty ? The report of the Federal Finance Committee rather shows that there is not so much milk in the coconut as the Indian Representatives at the Round Table Conference expected, as their share of the swag when they administered the Central Government.

It will be interesting to hear whether you get your way.[1]

(iv)

John Anderson had every intention of succeeding. Indeed, by no means the least important point of his memorandum to King George, written within six weeks of first setting foot in India, was that, apart from containing a clear and blistering appraisal of the situation, it also constituted the ultimate objective of Anderson's ambition for Bengal and the blueprint of the measures which he proposed to employ for the attainment of that ambition. He knew his own mind exactly, and what he planned to do was to build a new Bengal with terrorism not only crushed and broken but with its roots and confederate circumstances destroyed through the reorganization of her finances and the consequently improved administration of the Province. In short, *mens sana in corpore sano*.

Anderson's first task, however, was to restore the morale of his own 'official family'. As he had written to King George, it had been customary for the Government of India and the India Office in London to disparage the Bengal Administration and this had had the inevitable effect of producing a state of frustration and *malaise* among the provincial officials themselves. His immediate predecessor, Sir Stanley Jackson, a man of infinite charm and a great gentleman, but more distinguished as a first-class amateur cricketer than for his proconsular qualities, had done little to alleviate this baffling sense of defeatism, but from the very beginning of his period of office John inspired his subordinates with an ever-increasing degree of hope and confidence. Twelve years before he had been faced with a similar situation in Dublin Castle. Then, as now, he had assumed charge of a governmental machine in a state of almost

[1] *Royal Archives*, G.V., P. 1154/62.

chronic disrepair. Then, as now, he had restored its efficiency by the inspiration of his own personality and example.

In an amazingly short space of time his personal staff, his Ministers and the Members of his Executive Council learned that in 'His Excellency our Governor' they had a man of iron will, determined — even ruthless — but not inhuman ; a man of great personal and moral courage and wide vision, who had a policy for Bengal which he was resolved to carry through. They responded at once to such leadership and the Governor's influence and inspiration spread from the top to the most outlying districts of the Province. It was soon patent to all that a new spirit was abroad in Bengal. Frustration vanished ; men took fresh heart to face and conquer the problems which before had seemed insuperable.

In unofficial circles also both Europeans and Indians felt Anderson's influence. The businessmen of Calcutta, who had been dubious at the outset at the appointment of a Civil Servant as Governor soon revised their opinions. Their hopes for a restoration of law and order and sound finance and, in consequence, of good commercial conditions, rose again and they became enthusiastic in their support of what shortly became known as 'the Anderson Policy'.

In the execution of this policy Anderson was not, of course, acting alone, and of this he was fully conscious. He was particularly fortunate in the personalities of his Chief Secretary, Sir Robert Reid, and the Political and Finance Members of his Council, Sir William Prentice and Sir John Woodhead. Moreover, there had been no lack of men with original and constructive ideas in the Secretariat and Departments of the Bengal Government and in the Districts. But it was John Anderson's contribution to build up the conditions under which they could work more effectively, to select and to encourage. Over the whole field of government he had original and striking ideas to offer, both in design and procedure, and he was not averse, when occasion demanded, from cutting the Gordian knot of detail.

The suppression of terrorism, then at its height in the Province, was Anderson's first and most demanding task. He tackled it with characteristic courage and foresight, first with the resources of the Bengal administration alone and later, as confidence in the Government of Bengal was restored, with the co-operation of the Home Department of the Government of India and the Army. While continuing and intensifying the existing punitive measures and strengthening the forces deployed against the terrorists, he also acted to remove the *ad hoc* method of approach to the problem against which he had inveighed in his memorandum to King George. In the course of his first session of the Provincial Legislature he persuaded his Government — having first obtained the approval of the Government of India — to put through a Bill consolidating and placing on a permanent basis much of the anti-terrorist legislation which had hitherto consisted of Executive Ordinances of a limited duration. The passage by the Legislature of this Bengal Criminal Law Amendment Act of 1932 gave powerful proof to the Province as a whole — to the restive Europeans and, above all, to the terrorists themselves — that the Government were in earnest. There was to be no more 'cat and mouse' treatment. They meant to crush terrorism permanently.

As a further measure Anderson adapted and greatly extended the system of 'collective fines' imposed upon those disaffected areas where terrorist offenders had been sheltered and supported. The proceeds of such fines were in some cases appropriated for the recruiting or posting of additional police in the area concerned and in others to some other constructive purpose. Chittagong was one of the first districts to which these punitive measures were applied and in a speech in reply to addresses presented on the occasion of his first visit there on August 16, 1932, John Anderson defended the principle in eloquent terms. Some of the petitioners, notably those of the Islam Association, had expressed disapproval of terrorism with which, it was said, they had nothing to do, and the Governor took this as his point of attack :

> Let me say at once that of no one of you can it be said that 'you have nothing to do with terrorism'. Believe me, gentlemen, you have everything to do with terrorism : it is *your* liberty that is at stake — your liberty to speak, to vote and, within the limits of the law, to live as you like. It is your liberty that is at stake and your battle that Government are fighting. . . . You cannot stand aside as though you could remain unaffected by the result of this struggle. . . . Ordinances and legislation arming

the Executive with special powers are the necessary reply to the challenge of the terrorist. They are directed solely against those who break the law and it is almost a truism to say that they are not intended to hamper those who merely wish to pursue their legitimate business and to proceed in peace 'on their lawful occasions'. . . . If for the present the peaceful public have unfortunately to submit in some degree to restriction and inconvenience, whose fault is it? You had certainly no restrictions until the terrorists brought them upon you. And is it not far better that you should suffer temporary inconvenience, which I have been told repeatedly has been very little felt by the bulk of the inhabitants and has been made the occasion for very few complaints, than that you should live out your lives under the constant menace of an unseen foe who knows no law. . . . The quickest and most effective method of getting rid of the Ordinances in Chittagong and elsewhere is to unite with Government for the suppression of the evil which the Ordinances are designed to combat. To the extent to which Government may be denied the support of the general public in this matter, their task is rendered harder — but the obligation which rests upon Government is not thereby weakened.

Anderson also seized upon this occasion to make a moving appeal designed to stir the civic consciences of his hearers and to enlist their co-operation in the fight against terrorism :

Can you be blind to the fact that your young men, just when they are reaching the age of service to themselves, their families and their country, are being seduced to paths of violence ? Can you be indifferent to the damage which is being caused to the economic interests of the country ? Have you considered what will be the position of an autonomous Government if the tradition has been established that, where a Government is unpopular, violence may legitimately be employed by those who disapprove of its policy against its agents and against those who publicly support it in the Press or on the platform ? And it is the fate, remember, of all Governments, even the most democratic, to incur unpopularity from time to time. Can you be indifferent — you who look to Government for financial support for so many of your schemes of local improvement — can you be indifferent to the strain imposed on the finances of Government in fighting this menace ? Have you thought ahead and pictured the position of the autonomous Government shortly to be established, dependent as it will be on its own credit and with no other resources to draw upon than those which a final and irrevocable financial settlement will have left to it ? How far will those resources go and what will that credit be worth if the vices of terrorism have not been completely expelled ?

He went on to tell them that he and his Government were deeply sympathetic with them in their dilemma and the tragedy of their position. While asserting that unemployment was not the root cause of the terrorist movement, he admitted that it did constitute one of the fields of recruitment and that the fear of unemployment predisposed the minds of young men to the morbid and fanatical outlook which the terrorist leaders sought to induce. The problem of unemployment could only be solved by the close co-operation of the best elements in the community with Government and he pledged the willingness of Government to take their share in such a compact. But, he added, their capacity to do so 'must be gravely impaired so long as they are pre-occupied and their funds are locked up in fighting the terrorist menace'.

This speech of Anderson's — only one of many similar speeches which he made at this time in different parts of his Province — is indicative of his approach to the serious problem of terrorism. He was determined to destroy this cancerous affliction of the body politic; in so doing he realized that its permanent eradication could only be accomplished if the decent and law-abiding element in Bengal were awakened to the fact that this was not just a fight between Government and lawless, irresponsible factions, but a great battle between the forces of right and wrong in which there could be no neutrality and in which each must bear his part.

John's anxiety, from the first day he arrived at Calcutta, was to belie the story which, derived from his Irish record, had gained circulation and credence before his arrival, that he intended to be a 'Black and Tan' Governor. It was not his wish to pursue, or to appear to be pursuing, a purely repressive course of action. He felt strongly that a firm rule must go hand in hand with a constructive policy both for the Province as a whole and especially for those who were already, or who were prone to become, the dupes of the terrorist leaders.

One of his early measures in this vein, after consultation with the recently appointed G.O.C. Eastern Command, Major-General Sir Norman Macmillan, was to reinforce considerably the number of regular troops in Bengal. The purpose of this was not so much to overawe the populace as 'to show the flag', to inspire both Service morale and public confidence, and to make it clear beyond doubt that no attempt at organized violence on a large scale could hope to succeed. Few Bengalis then living, except those in Calcutta, Darjeeling or Dacca, could ever have seen troops and certainly no-one had had experience of their use to reinforce the civil administration without impinging on its functions.

At the same time a close liaison was established between the police resources of Bengal and Military Intelligence with highly beneficial results. The Garrison Commander, Major-General George Lindsay, a man devoted, apart from his military career, to the happiness and welfare of young people, chose as his Intelligence Officers to be posted to the various Districts, young officers who had a ready understanding of the deeper meaning of the terrorist movement. Many of the schoolboy recruits to the movement had first been lured into its meshes as much by boredom, the love of adventure and the lack of healthy counter-attractions as by the glamour of the patriotic aims attributed to the movement and the possibility of being called upon to make the supreme sacrifice of a martyr's death. With the strong support of John Anderson and of his Minister of Education, Aziz-ul-Huq, a warm-hearted Muslim, General Lindsay inaugurated through the medium of his picked Intelligence Officers — one of whom was destined to become Sir John Hunt, the conqueror of Everest — a campaign in the schools and colleges of the rural areas to provide the Bengali youngster with an alternative outlet for his natural youthful enthusiasm. By the introduction of competitive games, physical training, folk dancing, scouting and the like, it was sought, and with considerable success, to scotch the recruitment of terrorism at its source by giving the Bengali boy a healthier physique and a healthier outlook on life — or, as someone described it, to make him the kind of young man who, though he might not agree with you, would punch you on the nose instead of stabbing you in the back!

Successful though the campaign against terrorism was destined to be, this success was 'not attained by sudden flight'. It was a gradual process marked by a shocking, if slowly dwindling, number of bloody murders. Within six weeks of Anderson's arrival in the Province, the District Magistrate of Midnapore fell a victim to the assassins who had killed his predecessor ; shortly thereafter two attempts were made on the life of Sir Alfred Watson, editor of *The Statesman*, to be followed by a bomb attack on the railway station at Pahartali and an abortive attack on a number of Europeans at a cricket match there. In September 1933 a third District Magistrate was murdered at Midnapore.

But, despite these incidents, there was clear evidence that the movement was languishing in face of Anderson's firm measures and constructive policy. The young Bengalis no longer fell so easily to the blandishments of the terrorist leaders and many of the leaders themselves had been captured. In desperation they plotted a final *coup* — the life of the Governor himself.

(v)

From the earliest moments of his arrival in Bengal John Anderson had been conscious of the danger which threatened him personally. If he had had any illusions on this score beforehand, the security precautions which surrounded him as he left Howrah Station must have dispelled them, and the attack upon his predecessor only a few weeks before was still fresh in the public memory.

John had, of course, been under constant threat of murder during his time in Dublin, but there was a difference. Conditions in Ireland had been those of tacitly recognized warfare and the precautions for safety were in accordance, though all too often insufficient. There he had driven in an armoured car with armed escorts very much in evidence and he himself had carried a revolver. Here in Bengal the situation was very different. Though the threat of danger was even greater, the precautions against it had necessarily to be less obvious. The Provincial Government was not at war but yet had to deal with a group of dangerous fanatics. It behoved the King's Representative to show himself publicly, to drive through the streets not in an armoured car but in a normal Rolls and at times in an open carriage, thereby presenting a good target for any miscreant with a pistol and, although the security measures were of the most comprehensive possible, they could in no way be considered one hundred per cent effective.

It was John Anderson's rule of conduct to meet danger with courage. Adapting himself to the situation with apparent equanimity, he accepted the occupational hazards of his position with a remarkable combination of physical and moral dauntlessness. He took no unnecessary risks but he did not hesitate to move about freely, completely unperturbed and undeflected by the personal perils involved.

This imperturbable courage was not without its effect on Europeans and Bengalis alike and was remarkable to visitors from Britain, even those who were least in sympathy with British policy. The late Ellen Wilkinson who, as a Labour Member of Parliament, was on intimate terms with a number of the leaders of the Indian National Congress Party, was once in a private discussion group in the House of Commons at which someone made a critical remark about Anderson. She at once sprang to his defence, instancing her own personal experience of his courageous conduct and the impression which it had made upon her Congress friends. 'Of course we are enemies of the British Administration', they had told her, 'but, while some young hothead may always be out of our control, we shall do our utmost to see that nothing happens to the Governor. We admire his courage and we appreciate the compliment to ourselves of his going about so freely and fearlessly among our people.'

This fearlessness was not long to go untested. However truthful the protestation of admiration by the Congress leaders might be, they were evidently quite incapable of controlling the leaders of the terrorist movement. A plot to blow up the Governor's train as he journeyed from Calcutta to Darjeeling was unmasked and successfully averted, but on another occasion the Governor was fired on as he drove through the streets and his chauffeur wounded. And the police were aware of further conspiracies hatched against his life.

In the spring of 1934 the terrorist leaders were determined to make an all-out effort to kill John Anderson during his period of residence in the hill-country. The master brain of the plot was a fanatical terrorist who had established himself in a respectable Hindu family near Dacca as a tutor to the son and daughter of the house. He had seduced the girl and had got the boy completely under his control, persuading him, with another young Bengali, to assassinate the Governor at the race meeting at Lebong on May 9.

Police intelligence had got wind of the plot but could not discover the time and place of the attempt. They were gravely apprehensive that it would be made when the Governor opened the annual flower show at Darjeeling on May 8, and were duly thankful when this event, in which John passed through dense crowds on foot, passed off without untoward incident.

On the following day John, accompanied by his daughter Mary and Nellie Mackenzie, drove in semi-state to the Lebong racecourse for the Spring Meeting at which the chief event was the Governor's Cup. The course was a small one. There was an open stand for spectators, raised in tiers, with the Governor's Box to the left of it close to the winning-post. The crowd was dense, for the Governor's Cup was always a popular event, and anyone could get into the public enclosure on payment of 5s. As the race finished many Indians surged across the course to the front of the stand, among them the two assassins. The Governor stood up to see the winner of his Cup led in, presenting an easy target, and at that moment the first assassin, resting his arm on the rail of the stand, fired at him at a range of approximately 3½ feet. Tandy Green, the starter, had seen the boy's movement and had grappled with him just too late, but they went to the ground together and Mr. Green wrested the revolver from him. The bullet had missed the Governor and, passing between him and Nellie Mackenzie, wounded in the ankle an Anglo-Indian girl standing at the back of the box.

Almost simultaneously the second assassin fired at what seemed to be almost point-blank range but his shot also went wide of the mark and his revolver jammed before he could fire again. He was overpowered by the Raja of Barwari with the plucky assistance of the Rani of Nazarganj.

John Anderson owed his life to a number of fortuitous causes. First, the courageous intervention of Tandy Green, who later received the Medal for Gallantry of the Order of the British Empire; secondly, the extreme nervousness of the assassins and the inefficiency of their weapons; and, thirdly, the prompt action of his immediate entourage. John was standing up as the first shot was fired and his A.D.C., Captain Pat Sykes of the 60th Rifles, pulled him down so forcibly that he missed his footing on a loose piece of carpet and fell full-length on the floor of the box, where a second A.D.C., Captain Teddy Worrall, sat on his lap. Meanwhile Colonel Reginald Woods and the Governor's special bodyguard, Sergeant Coombes, made a shield of their bodies above him.[1]

The episode was over in a matter of minutes and John's first reaction was, not unnaturally, one of irritation. 'I have spoken about that piece of carpet before. Most undignified', he remarked, as he rose to his feet. Then he came forward to the front of the box, coolly lit a cigar, and directed that the next race should be run. Both during and after the whole affair there is unanimous witness to his complete calm and courage.[2]

Meanwhile pandemonium had broken out. Both assassins had been seized and pretty roughly handled before being taken in charge by the police. Moreover the hill-men were furious at this violation of their code of honour and hospitality by down-country Hindus. Several Bengalis who tried to run away — including an entirely innocent Deputy Magistrate on leave from Bihar — were set upon by the Nepalis with their *kukris* and suffered considerable injury. Indeed there would have been wholesale lynchings had not the local regiment made a prompt appearance, with fixed bayonets and ball ammunition, and restored some semblance of order.

It is not without interest that John did not see fit to send his father a reassuring telegram nor indeed to write to him any account of the attempted assassination. No letter to David Anderson exists between May 2 and May 16, in the latter of which John makes but passing reference to 'the trial of the two miscreants of last week'. It was therefore from the B.B.C. that the seventy-nine-year-old

[1] Sergeant Coombes had recently succeeded Sergeant Jock Adams, who had been personal shadow and bodyguard to the Governor since his arrival in Bengal, and who had met a tragic death during a tiger hunt in Jalpaiguni District in which a wounded tigress charged the elephant on which he was riding and, knocking him off the pad, seriously mauled him before Anderson's eyes. Adams later died in hospital, greatly to John's distress.

[2] Anderson was far from ungrateful, however, to those whose prompt actions had saved his life. He thanked his A.D.C.s warmly and at once recommended Mr. Tandy Green for a decoration, while to Colonel Woods he wrote on the following day : 'I have a pretty clear recollection of the sequence of events & one thing that I recollect vividly is that when the second assailant was being tackled you came over & stood in front of me. I know you were deliberately acting as a shield & it is difficult to find words to express what I feel about such action. I realized what you did & now offer my grateful thanks.'

gentleman in Edinburgh learned of his son's escape and it would appear that he may have made mild protest against this neglect, for on May 22, John wrote to him, with no comment and indeed without much contrition : 'I am sorry you had the shock of hearing the news of the Lebong affair on the wireless. I hope the announcement was not too crudely worded.'

The repercussion of the attempt on Anderson's life was both widespread and momentous. Congratulations on his escape poured in from all quarters, from the most exalted to the lowliest. 'I am profoundly thankful at providential escape from dastardly attempt on your life' telegraphed King George V, and the Viceroy expressed similar sentiments. 'We have had over 1000 letters and over 500 telegrams & they have not yet stopped coming in', John wrote to his father on June 6. 'I had a telegram yesterday from Lhasa where the news apparently had just been received.'

The occasion, however, was not only one for congratulation and rejoicing. It had a deeper significance than that. It marked the turning point in the reaction of the general public of Bengal against the hideous menace of terrorism, and this reaction found practical and constructive expression in the Anti-terrorist Conference held in Calcutta Town Hall in September 1934. This gathering was a great tribute to the work which Anderson had set himself to do and a clear indication of the esteem and respect in which he was held, for it placed popular opinion squarely behind the Government in their anti-terrorist policy. In point of fact, the Lebong affair was almost the last overt act of terrorism to be committed during Anderson's Governorship. He had won his great battle.

It had, moreover, a very happy sequel. Both the would-be assassins were condemned to death, attempted murder having previously been made a capital offence by special anti-terrorist legislation. They were sentenced by the criminal court to be hanged, and this sentence was sustained by the Court of Appeal. Anderson, however, commuted their sentences to imprisonment for life and they were duly sent to serve them in the Cellular Jail in the penal settlement of the Andaman Islands. Here they came under the benign influence of Canon Cyril Pearson[1] the All-India chaplain of

[1] Canon C. G. Pearson, now of Guildford Cathedral, was an Honorary Canon of Calcutta Cathedral and Examining Chaplain to the Bishop of Calcutta.

Toc H, who, in the course of his ministration, formed the opinion that, whereas the older boy was a convinced revolutionary, the younger, a foolish lad of seventeen, had been led away by the evil doctrines of his tutor and was not beyond redemption. He reported his findings to Anderson whom he had known well in Darjeeling and Calcutta. In the course of a tour of the Andamans in February 1937, the Governor visited the jail and talked with the boy, finding him much as Canon Pearson had reported.

Later in that year, on the eve of the Governor's final departure from Bengal, Canon Pearson, who was also returning home, asked if the boy might be paroled to him on a suspended sentence, to be trained for a career in England. Anderson agreed, authorizing a grant for the boy's education, but he added with a wry smile, 'Don't put him on my boat'. The boy was apprenticed as an electrical engineer, and on the outbreak of war promptly joined the Royal Air Force. In November 1942 he wrote the following letter to his benefactor whom he had once tried to murder.

DEAR SIR JOHN,

I hope you will excuse me for taking the liberty of writing to you but I do feel that it would be my first duty to thank you for your kindness you have shown to me.

With your permission Sir, I would like to introduce myself first as you may not remember me.

In 1937 you granted me reprieve and permitted me to come to England under the guardianship of the Rev. C. G. Pearson.

Mr. Pearson has always treated me like his own son and given me every opportunity of study and education which I could never have dreamed of and I am pleased to say that I have obtained my Diploma in Engineering from Faraday House College.

I have also been granted complete pardon by the Government of Bengal.

I would like to say this, Sir, that it was indeed a generous and kindly gesture on your part to grant me this opportunity and trusting me fully. If it hadn't been for you I would perhaps have been quite in a different world, and I am indeed indebted to you for my very existence.

I have now completed my study and you may be pleased to hear that I am joining the R.A.F. as a pilot and I hope I shall prove myself successful.

I do appreciate your kindness and I thank you most sincerely for all you have done for me and I do mean it.

With kindest regards and good wishes

Yours sincerely,

At the close of the war the boy married a Jewish girl and in the course of a few years both became members of the Christian Faith.

(vi)

With the battle against terrorism won, there still remained the problem of the *détenus*, that considerable category of prisoners who were detained without trial under Bengal legislation of 1925 because of their strongly suspected terrorist activities. They constituted both a political and a security problem, for the Indian Congress leaders were constantly agitating for their release and, indeed, it had become customary on previous occasions when terrorism had been brought under control to discharge them from protective custody. Such a policy of appeasement and clemency had proved gravely mistaken, for within a short time of their release terrorist activity broke out again and it was found that the liberated *détenus* had been responsible for its revival.

There had also been a tendency in the Bengal Government to pamper these persons because they were merely held in preventive custody. Such infamous characters as the late Bose brothers, one of whom collaborated notoriously with the Japanese forces during the Second World War, were in the habit of taking out expensive life insurance policies in expectation of arrest and both the Provincial Government and the Government of India had considered themselves bound to maintain the cost of the premiums.

John Anderson was determined that this mistaken leniency towards the *détenus* should not be repeated. As to the insurance policies, he ruled that 'a life insurance policy is an improvement of a man's estate ; the Government is under no obligation to improve the estate of a *détenu*', and under his persuasion the law officers in Calcutta and in Delhi agreed that the holders of such policies should be forced to accept their surrender value, thereby simultaneously discouraging the practice and saving the Province the cost of the premiums.

L

With regard to the problem of *détenus* as a whole, Anderson recognized that to keep them in custody indefinitely was no solution and that means must be found to give them the opportunity of re-establishing themselves as decent members of society. Taking advantage of the situation created in 1935, when the forces of law and order had got the upper hand and public opinion against terrorism had gained considerable impetus, he announced in a speech to the Legislative Council of Bengal on August 28 a scheme for the training of carefully selected *détenus* in agriculture and manufacture and for their release at the end of this training period.

This wise act, which received great public support, was in consonance with Anderson's determination to show that repressive methods must go hand in hand with ameliorative measures. It was widely welcomed and increased both the esteem in which he was held personally and the public confidence in his general policy.

(vii)

But, as John had written to King George V in 1932, the crux of the situation in Bengal was the problem of finance, and he took the opportunity of repeating publicly the warning which he had conveyed to his Sovereign on this point. 'I have never made any secret of my view', he told his Legislative Council on February 11, 1935, 'that without adequate financial provision any scheme of Provincial Autonomy must fail and fail disastrously.'

When he arrived in Bengal the Province was passing through an acute economic depression. The prices of agricultural products, particularly jute and rice, had fallen to a very low ebb with serious repercussions on the whole economy of Bengal. The population — predominantly agricultural — was hard hit and found it increasingly difficult to meet its dues. Rents were falling heavily in arrear and dues to money-lenders went unpaid. The financial position of the Government, which had never been easy, had worsened gravely. In spite of every economy there was a deficit of about 2 crores ($£1\frac{1}{2}$ million) and, owing to public dissatisfaction with the Meston Award and its unfair apportionment of the jute export duty, there was little hope that the Legislature would sanction new taxation.

In tackling this thorny situation, Anderson was particularly fortunate in having at his side so wise a counsellor as the Finance Member of his Council, Sir John Woodhead, and that in Delhi he had to deal with that sagacious and understanding person Sir James Grigg, ('P.J.', of the caustic tongue and kindly heart), an old colleague from Whitehall,[1] whose appointment as Finance Member of the Viceroy's Council he had warmly supported. The wise and honest collaboration of these three men in their search for a fair and viable solution to the financial problems of Bengal and their subsequent success was an outstanding example of the integrity of British rule in India.

John's first outstanding financial success in his battle for the revision of the Meston Award was achieved in 1934–1935 when the Bengal Presidency was assured, as from the date from which the new constitutional provisions would operate, of a grant equivalent to half the net proceeds of the jute export duty. With this measure of success Anderson was far from satisfied. 'Our claim', he told the Legislative Council on February 11, 1935, 'goes far beyond that and the final adjudication upon our claim, which we have no intention of abating, has still to come.'

Nevertheless what he had already achieved undoubtedly added to Anderson's prestige, and it also enabled the Provincial Government to gain the assent of the Legislature to certain taxation proposals. The final full measure of success came as a result of negotiations with Sir Otto Niemeyer, who had been entrusted with the task of framing the new financial arrangements under the Government of India Act of 1935. The two main constituents in the Niemeyer Plan were the assignment of only half the provincial income tax receipts to the Government of India and the remission — in some cases, of part, in others of the whole — of the provincial debts to the Central Government. This second provision was accompanied by an arrangement whereby the provinces were for the future to borrow in the open market rather than from the Central Government.[2]

In the case of Bengal this meant that, in addition to the acquisition

---

[1] The Rt. Hon. Sir James Grigg, K.C.B., K.C.S.I., later joined John Anderson in Mr. Churchill's Cabinet as Secretary of State for War (1942–1945). It is believed that they are the only senior Civil Servants who, on entering politics, achieved Cabinet rank, though Sir Arthur Salter held briefly the office of Chancellor of the Duchy of Lancaster in Mr. Churchill's Caretaker Government of 1945.

[2] Sir James Grigg, *Prejudice and Judgement* (1948), p. 295.

of statutory title to half the proceeds of the Central Government's export duty on jute grown in Bengal and to half the income tax collected in the province, Bengal's debt of 8 crores (£6 million) to the Government of India was cancelled. Anderson's initial aim had been attained.

The degree to which John Anderson played a personal part both in Delhi and in Whitehall, in this extraordinary financial triumph, may be judged from the fact that when he and Grigg had returned to England, it was the latter's successor as Finance Member on the Viceroy's Council, Sir Jeremy Raisman, who declared : 'Now that John Anderson has gone, the days when Bengal can bamboozle the Government of India are over'.

(viii)

In every respect John Anderson's years in Bengal were the watershed of his life, both personal and official. In the realm of politics they marked his translation from a great and respected Civil Servant to a public figure of some eminence, from being recognized by the few as an administrative genius to being hailed by the many as a proconsular statesman. His success in Bengal made him a man marked for even greater opportunities of public service on his return to England.

If this were true of John's public career the change in his private life was even more accentuated. One of the salient characteristics of the life of a Civil Servant is its anonymity and this he had left behind him for ever. As an Indian Governor, and particularly as a Presidency Governor,[1] he had at one step mounted a pedestal on which he must remain isolated throughout his term of office, with rare contacts with his equals — other provincial Governors — and his one 'superior', the Viceroy. He lived in regal state. In addition to a large personal staff he had 'exclusive rights' to a mounted bodyguard of about seventy, a band, a team of six gorgeously caparisoned *chaprassis*, four Government Houses (Calcutta, Darjeeling, Barrackpore and Dacca) and about 120 servants who

---

[1] The Presidencies of Bengal, Bombay and Madras were the oldest units of Government in British India, dating from the rule of the British East India Company. Robert Clive was appointed first Governor of Bengal in 1758.

followed him to most of these various residences. A fleet of cars and two special trains on broad and narrow gauge were at his disposal, as well as a steam yacht and a houseboat for river travel. For reasons of dignity, as well as of security, he was practically never alone during his waking hours. An armed sentry was posted outside his bedroom door ; an A.D.C. with a loaded pistol was in close attendance ; and a plain-clothes sergeant of police, a crack marksman, hovered near. Always, as he was kept constantly in mind, he was the King's Representative. The National Anthem greeted his arrival at a theatre or cinema ; he passed through all doorways and entered all vehicles first, unless his partner was the wife of the Viceroy. The life of a Presidency Governor — restricted by a fierce protocol enforced by his Military Secretary — was not only, and inevitably, a very lonely life, it was also very unlike the life of Whitehall and of Sutton.

That John was lonely there is little doubt, though there is scant evidence of this in his letters to his father. At various times he had the companionship of his daughter Mary and of his sister-in-law Nellie Mackenzie, but the one was too young and the other too shy by nature to be of much help to him. Alastair visited him on several occasions and he wrote with pride of his son's medical prowess to his own father in Edinburgh. There were visits, too, from his old friends, the Patersons, 'Jimmie' Jamieson, Geoffrey Russell and his brother-in-law, Frederick Ellison, who had married another of the Mackenzie sisters, and he was delighted to renew his friendship with Charles Lyall Philip, with whom he had made that memorable bicycle tour through France and Switzerland in 1900, and who was now a member of the Board of Inland Revenue in the neighbouring Province of Bihar and Orissa.

More and more, however, he was dependent upon the company of his A.D.C.s and in their companionship he encountered a new factor in human relationships. These young men, with their social background and military training, their natural aplomb and effortless ease of manner, were a new phenomenon which both interested and pleased him. They opened up a world of comparative youth with which he had hitherto been unfamiliar. Though he was a stern taskmaster who would rebuke a lapse of duty or a piece of mistaken information, his relations with them when off duty were very friendly and informal and they found him unresentful of an occasional and discreet 'leg-pull' of the sort at which an accomplished A.D.C. is adept. In many ways they 'humanized' him.

Now, too, in that strange procession of semi-official guests which pass self-invited through every Government House and Embassy, came types of a social world which John had never met before. They included that redoubtable traveller and hostess, Mrs. Ronnie Greville, with whom he was to form a fast friendship, and in whose house at Polesden Lacey he was to spend his second honeymoon. These, too, broadened his horizon and had a marked effect upon his later life.

But perhaps the most broadening experience which John endured in this strange new world in which he found himself was his encounter with that formidable lady the Marchioness of Willingdon — known throughout European society in India as the 'Purple Empress'. The Viceroy was a man of great suavity and courtliness of manner and Anderson's relations with him were always of the best. Lady Willingdon, however, though capable of great kindness, was of an imperious character and their first meeting was strangely unpropitious. It occurred some six weeks after John's arrival in India during his first official visit to the Viceroy at Simla.

John liked to wear a buttonhole and, though warned of Her Excellency's antipathy to such floral adornment, he did not see fit to remove the rose he was wearing on his arrival at Viceregal Lodge. Lady Willingdon reacted in character. She went straight up to him and, plucking the flower from his coat, remarked : 'Oh, I can't let Your Excellency of Bengal wear so faded a buttonhole in my house', and so saying, she pitched it into the fire. John smiled : 'I was well warned', he replied. 'I was told that you would not approve of it.' Quite unabashed, Lady Willingdon said : 'Oh, so someone has been giving away my little foibles. It's quite true. I don't like buttonholes.' To this John retorted : 'Ah, so now the truth is coming out. It's buttonholes you object to, not my poor little rose.'

Some eighteen months later there was a repeat performance. On this occasion John was meeting Her Excellency on a visit to Calcutta and he greeted her at Howrah Station wearing an orchid. Lady Willingdon snatched it from him, threw it on the platform and stamped on it, saying, 'I don't like buttonholes'. This time John did not smile. No flicker of emotion showed in his face and he proceeded with the established ceremonial of welcoming the wife of the Viceroy to his Province.

There were other incidents. John's taste in hats was not impeccable. His grey top hat was reminiscent of the Gaiety at its Edwardian best, whereas his silk hat evoked memories of a Kirk elder of the Victorian era ; but his topee, furnished by a tropical outfitter in London, was pure Kipling or, at best, of the most fruity Curzon vintage, and it was to this that Lady Willingdon took a dislike. She chose the moment of a visit by John to Belvederes — the Viceroy's Calcutta residence — to present him, in the presence of the Viceroy and in front of their staff and his, with a topee of a more up-to-date pattern, saying that she could not bear the sight of his any longer. John accepted the gift with complete imperturbability, but insisted that it should be autographed on the lining both by its august donor and by the Viceroy.

In these curious ebullitions of almost schoolboy humour the balance of the honours lay in John's favour. Lady Willingdon must have recognized in his unruffled calm an element which she could not hope to subdue, and she respected him accordingly. She subsequently developed a great affection for him. John's greatest victory was, however, his gentlest, displaying a delicate courtesy which could not be surpassed. He was aware that Lord Willingdon had not received a G.C.B. and he therefore took meticulous care never to appear in the Viceroy's presence wearing his own. He contented himself on these occasions with his G.C.I.E., of which Order the Viceroy was *ex officio* Grand Master.

The effect of regal splendour and isolation upon one of John Anderson's natural dignity and solemnity of manner was, not unnaturally, to throw into strong relief his lack of lightness of touch on purely social occasions. Official dinner-parties at Government House were a great trial to him. Never a master of small-talk — and indeed somewhat contemptuous of this form of frivolity — he would sit silently between his dinner-partners, thus reducing some to the verge of tears or inducing in others a ceaseless flow of hysterical chatter. He was unmoved by the one and intolerant of the other. Or he would himself deliver a pronouncement that completely exhausted the subject. In the drawing-room, after dinner, there was the ordeal of having people brought up to him for conversation and this he found particularly trying. 'I can scarcely keep from yawning in their faces', he wrote to his father. Alas, there was no prescribed time limit to these conversations. The decision to bring them to a close was entirely with the Governor, and the A.D.C.s, knowing his frame of mind, would watch anxiously for the sign for the next guest to be presented. Unfortunately John had no regular method of transmitting this signal. It might be a finger tapping, or a hand gently waving over the side of an armchair, or a nod of the head, or even just a look. If, as occasionally happened, the signal were missed or passed unrecognized, the reaction was violent and there followed an obvious indication that he must be relieved of the present incubus, which not infrequently occasioned acute embarrassment to the guest concerned.

Among those who were accustomed to the gay courtliness of the Viceroy and remembered the urbanity of Sir Stanley Jackson, it was not unnatural that such conduct gave rise to revival of the nickname 'Pompous John' and to reference to the Governor's 'howdah manner'. Yet John was really more socially inhibited than pompous. He lacked the mellowing influence of feminine companionship and the domestic discipline of married life. Had Chrissie lived it is not improbable that, given confederate circumstances, she would have blossomed forth as a successful hostess and she would certainly have taken occasion to puncture the balloon of John's gravity.

Nor was John Anderson, though he had a 'good conceit of himself', consciously vain for his own dignity. He had, however, a very lively sense of the respect due to his position as the King's Representative and sometimes this became somewhat exaggerated — even with those whom he knew most intimately. It is said that when so old a friend and colleague as P. J. Grigg — ever unceremonious — addressed him at an official occasion by his Whitehall term of endearment 'Jonathan', His Excellency of Bengal replied frigidly : 'You forget yourself, Sir James'.

When off duty, however, the trappings of his official dignity fell from him and he could take a joke against himself. Sailing up to Barrackpore on the occasion of his fiftieth birthday he was delighted when his staff produced a large birthday cake as a surprise. 'But there are no candles', he jocularly complained, to which one of the wives present replied gaily, 'Have a heart, sir, you'd need a bigger cake.' There was a moment's silence, but John laughed heartily and frequently repeated the story.

(ix)

The life of the Governor of Bengal moved daily and yearly upon the rails of long-established routine. It began at 7.30 when the A.D.C. on duty waited upon him in riding clothes and together they would drive from Government House to the Maidan for a ride in the cool of the morning. Most of the *élite* of Calcutta would be similarly employed on their polo ponies and the young 'box-wallahs' would also be at exercise with their chargers from the Calcutta Light Horse. John's expertise as a horseman was not great. He had, in fact, not mounted a horse since those lurid days in Dublin when with Mark Sturgis he had ridden Dickie Wyndham-Quin's ponies in the guarded seclusion of the grounds of Viceregal Lodge. He acquitted himself competently, however, upon a massive beast, well up to his weight, which on official occasions drew the open state landau. Accompanied by a mounted police escort, he would make two or three rounds of the racecourse and it was noted that, whereas he would urge his mount to a canter, he was less co-operative when the horse broke into a gallop. Meanwhile the A.D.C. was striving madly to keep the prescribed half-length behind him and finding it not too easy when riding a horse normally accustomed to trotting in line ahead of the Governor's mount in the state carriage!

Back at Government House to bath and dress, the Governor would proceed to the breakfast room, again escorted by the A.D.C., now in undress uniform. He would be engaged in his office until lunch-time when he would proceed, always under escort, to the Throne Room where the other A.D.C.s would be assembled with such guests as had been invited to luncheon. Thereafter he would play a round of golf or two or three games of billiards with his A.D.C.s, and the young men discovered that, whereas John was tolerant of being beaten by a better player, he greatly resented defeat by a successful fluke!

Billiards or golf over, John would retire again to his office and work with his Private Secretary until 'collected' at 7.45 to dress for dinner. At small 'black tie' dinner-parties, after a few introductions had been made, host and guests would move 'informally' into the dining-room to the strains of 'The Roast Beef of Old England' played by the Governor's band. Bridge or billiards would follow until the Governor gave the signal to retire.

Formal dinner-parties, with as many as 110 present, were very glittering affairs : women in their best gowns and jewels, men in tails or uniform with orders and decorations, the personal staff in blue tail-coats with yellow facings, looking rather like members of the Beaufort Hunt. Often as many as half of the guests would be Indians and their costumes would create an even more brilliant effect, the men's jewels outshining those of the European ladies. The Governor would 'make the round', speaking a word to each guest, and would then lead the procession with musical honours from the Throne Room to the Great Marble Hall, where Indian servants in gorgeous liveries of scarlet and gold and white cotton gloves stood behind each chair. After the Loyal Toast, drunk to the National Anthem, the ladies would withdraw, to be followed in due course by the men, and there would ensue the 'ordeal of the drawing-room'. The signal to leave would be given about half-past ten, after which the Governor would retire thankfully to bed, or, if pressure of business were great, for a further session in his office. Such was the ordinary day in the life of a Presidency Governor in Calcutta, a day hedged about with formality and circumstance.

The year was divided into a regular sequence. Once the hot weather began in April the whole establishment moved to Darjeeling, the hill station, and remained there until the beginning of the rains early in June. The Governor then returned to Calcutta and it was soon time for the annual visit to Dacca, in fulfilment of a promise made to Eastern Bengal when partition was annulled in 1912 that an official visit of at least one month would be made each year to the former capital of Eastern Bengal and Assam. There the Governor held a minor court, and a microcosm of the Calcutta social and civil functions was enacted. Thereafter a return was made to Darjeeling until the cold weather began, when the Governor and the seat of Government moved down to Calcutta until the spring.

A form of relaxation during the spells at Calcutta were the week-end visits by river to Barrackpore which took place whenever John could manage it during the cold weather. Government House there was particularly attractive — well situated and built in the early eighteenth-century manner much affected by the rich indigo planters of Bengal. Lord Mornington, later Marquess of Wellesley, and brother of the Duke of Wellington, a great dispenser of the East India Company's revenues, had planned during his Governor-Generalship a grandiose scheme for linking the Government House at Calcutta with that at Barrackpore by an avenue straight across country, a distance of some fourteen miles. This, however, had proved too much even for the long-suffering Board of Directors, and the conqueror of Tippoo Sahib had had to abandon his project, but this did not prevent him from subsidizing the building of a church belonging to the Danish colony so that from Barrackpore he could enjoy an 'English view'.

These rural amenities John inherited and much of his day was spent in enjoying the prospect provided by the profligate munificence of his great predecessor. There was an enormous banyan tree, too, under which breakfast and lunch were served, while the *koels* (a type of Indian cuckoo) disported themselves with brash fearlessness in the branches above. The grounds had been landscaped to some extent and were ablaze with huge beds of cannas and golden mohur trees, while a charming neo-classical temple stood in delightful anomaly amid these oriental surroundings.

John played golf on Sunday afternoons and rode on the race-course in the early morning and he may, or may not, have known that the popularity of race meetings at Barrackpore in the days before the First World War derived from the initiative and ability of that picturesque personage, Brigadier Ormonde de l'Épée Winter, who had been his Director of Military Intelligence in Dublin. He looked forward to his Barrackpore week-ends as a welcome and well-earned relief from his protocol-ridden existence in Calcutta.

Interrelated with these fixed peregrinations were the visits which the Governor made to the twenty-six Districts of his Presidency, in all of which he was expected to show himself at least once during his term of office. Normally these journeys were made by special train but, by its very nature, much of Bengal — and particularly the eastern part of the Province — is only accessible by river, especially at the end of the monsoon when vast volumes of water are carried down to the *sundarbands* from the great rivers of Bengal and Assam. Thus much of John's travelling was done by river barge, and when a new one was supplied to him he named it after his daughter, the *Mary Anderson*. The advantage of this mode of travel lay in the fact that while the *Mary Anderson* was being towed up or down stream the Governor and his party were able to relax in a manner that the train did not permit. However, whether on station platform or river landing-stage, there were the concomitant cere-monies of red carpets, meetings and greetings, and lengthy tea-parties with Indian gentlemen who entertained His Excellency their Governor with whisky and soda, lemonade and sweet cakes.

In these District visits John was seen at his best. His ever active mind took a deep interest in all he saw and his terrifying brain and memory made him a formidable person to encounter. He would ask all manner of discerning questions. One who served on his staff has written :

> What was being done about the Curse of Bengal ? — the water hyacinth which was laying a stranglehold on the waterways and irrigation systems, silting them up and producing an increase in malaria and a decrease in the drainage of the country. How were the roads ? What was the progress of the jute harvest ? Was the police force effective ? What was being done in the District to beat terrorism ? How was unemployment ? He had a penetrating grasp of the local situation and it was little use trying to hoodwink him ; when he really wanted information he was determined to get it. In this connection I derived some caustic amusement when it came to a visit to some technical or scientific establishment, possibly a jute mill or some similar place. I used to watch with interest the deployment of the opposing forces — the airy chitter-chatter of the manager, and Sir John's growing interest — the skirmish had only begun. Presently the main forces would be [en]joined and Sir John would really get down to questioning. The manager would then deploy his heavier forces but, about this moment, Sir John would unmask his batteries and roll up the opposition horse, foot and guns, by some highly technical and thoroughly pertinent question of which he

had complete scientific grasp and deeper knowledge than his unfortunate opponent. It was only then that it would be revealed to his adversary that he had a first-class scientific training and, had he not chosen to embark on administration, would have had a brilliant future in the scientific world.[1]

One of the more fascinating of his journeys was that which he made to Sikkim, a protected Indian state situated on the northern borders of Bengal and adjoining Nepal. Of this journey John wrote the following vivid account to his father, and the letter is of interest as a very fair example of those which he found time to write home to Scotland every other week with unfailing regularity throughout his period in India, and indeed during many years of his life.

Changu, Sikkim
10th October, 1932

MY DEAR FATHER,

Here I am three days journey into Sikkim & 12,600 ft. above sea level. There are just 4 of us, myself, my Private Secretary, my Physician (!) & an honorary Aide de Camp called Laden La who is a Thibetan by birth & therefore particularly useful on such a trip as this, but we have a cavalcade of no less than 40 ponies & mules for of course we have to carry all supplies bedding &c. with us & there are the servants (9 in number) & the small escort which considerations of dignity rather than safety demand.

We went by motor cars direct from Darjeeling to Gangtok the capital of Sikkim. It is of course only a village — indeed there are only just over 100,000 people in the whole of Sikkim though it extends to over 2800 square miles. A mile and a half out of Gangtok we were met by a ceremonial escort — the most barbaric affair you ever saw. We had to get out & take tea in a gorgeous shamiana (ceremonial tent). Then we got on ponies & formed a procession. First came a band in bright blue short coats striped kilts & white trousers playing weird instruments & making weirder music, the drums strapped on men's backs — then the armed escort in bright red coats with small basket work hats topped by peacock plumes — then, on ponies, about a dozen lamas (Buddhist priests) in magnificent silk robes with high scarlet hats except the Chief Lama who wore a yellow lacquered hat shaped like a muffin dish — then about a dozen Kazis (local

---

[1] Brigadier J. A. Hopwood, C.B.E., D.S.O., to the author, October 20, 1959.

noblemen) also in gorgeous raiment — then me on a pony led by a syce in a scarlet robe trimmed with leopard skin, the other members of the party bringing up the rear. The Maharaja insisted on our spending 2 days in Gangtok & on our being his guests for the whole of our tour. He has certainly done us extraordinarily well. He gave a big dinner party the night before we left which all the local notables attended — some had come a 5 days journey to be there. After dinner we had a display of Thibetan dancing mostly stamping of feet & weird noises. Before I left the Maharaja loaded me with gifts — quite literally — for we had to wire specially for a baby Austin to take them back to Darjeeling. There were 2 rugs, a carved table, 2 chaddars (Sikkimese robes), a short sword silver mounted, a bow & quiver of 9 arrows & a silver mounted vessel in which the native drink called Marwa is brewed.

Gangtok is 5800 feet above sea level & we have come up here in two stages through very beautiful scenery. Unfortunately the weather today has been misty but we have seen some fine precipices & waterfalls & the vegetation is very fine. The hills or rather mountains are all forest clad & though it is past the season for wild flowers we passed some very fine clumps of blue primulas, mixed with a pale mauve thelictrum & some sort of bright yellow flower. The blue poppies are all over. The forest is mostly rhododendron & silver fir above 9000 feet. Tomorrow we are going to the top of the Natu La (14,400 ft) which is one of the passes leading from Sikkim into Thibet. We shall actually enter Thibet — just to say we have been there — & shall then turn & make our way back by another route. If all goes well we shall be back in Darjeeling by the 19th. The pony I am riding is a historic beast for it once belonged to that mysterious personage the Dalai Lama. The Maharaja of Sikkim has lent it to me for the journey.

I have written so much about myself that there is barely room — or time — left for other matter. You will just be finishing your holiday & I hope you have found it both enjoyable & beneficial. I have not had your usual fortnightly letter — it will probably arrive tomorrow — so have not heard from you since you went to Seamill.

> With love to you both
> Your affectionate son
> (Sgd) JOHN ANDERSON.

(x)

John Anderson was not a religious man in the sense that religion played a dominant part in his life, as it did, for example, with Lord Halifax. Nevertheless, as with all good Scots, 'the fear of God was in him' and it was in sincere humility that, on March 26, 1933, he accepted ordination as an Elder of the Church of Scotland in St. Andrew's Church, Calcutta, where he became a member of the congregation of the Reverend Robert E. Lee. He worshipped also in the Anglican Cathedral but, whereas he necessarily went there in state as Governor, his attendance at St. Andrew's, and at St. Columba's in Darjeeling, was made with as little ceremony as possible. At his first session meeting all rose to greet him on his entry, but he hastened to rectify this by saying : 'I come here not as Governor of Bengal but as an Elder of the Church of Scotland.'

'He was faithful in the sacred duties he had voluntarily accepted', writes Mr. Lee. 'At a time when his every appearance in public involved exceptional risk he attended church services very frequently. . . . At celebrations of the Sacrament of the Lord's Supper he took his allotted part among the other Elders with complete self effacement.'[1] On these occasions John sat at the Communion Table and distributed the elements to the congregation. It so happened that the first person to whom he handed the Bread was an old Nepali woman. This act caught the imagination of the non-Christian Bengalis and their newspapers noted the fact that the Governor had first served an Indian woman before going on to the British worshippers.

John's contribution to religious matters was not, however, restricted to the Church of Scotland. When, in 1935, the Mother-General of the Community of St. Mary the Virgin (the Wantage Sisters) was visiting India in connection with the possible foundation of an Anglican College, she sought and obtained his active cooperation for her project. That this wonderful woman, whose manifest saintliness was combined with great charm and humour, was the sister of Sir Samuel Hoare who had played a considerable part in persuading John to go to Bengal, may well have accounted in some degree for the measure of the assistance that he gave her.

[1] Letter from the late Rev. Robert E. Lee to the author, July 8, 1959.

She was greatly impressed by him. 'Sir John is a Presbyterian elder', she wrote in one of her vivid letters to the Community, '[He] is one of the wisest men I have ever met.' And somewhat later : 'He is a man of iron, and if the college is launched, it will be due to him'.

In the event the project for the college did not materialize, but — so far as the evidence goes — John did much in its interests both in Delhi and elsewhere. The fact, however, that at the moment when he was formidably engaged in the matter of constitutional reforms, he should exert himself thus strenuously on its behalf is in itself indicative of his capacity and willingness to serve his God, his friends, and India wherever an opportunity was presented.

It was to the missionary zeal of the Church of Scotland that John Anderson owed what was perhaps the closest friendship which he formed during the Indian phase of his career. In the first year of his governorship he became acquainted with the Rev. Dr. John Graham,[1] who, together with his wife, had dedicated their lives to the work of the St. Andrew's Colonial Homes which they had founded at Kalimpong at the beginning of the century. The object of this most deserving enterprise — which was a sort of 'Dr. Barnardo's' for the Anglo-Indian community — was to offer some solution for the problems connected with the education of the children of the Anglo-Indians and domiciled European communities, and in the thirty-odd years of their existence the Kalimpong Homes had built up a justifiably high reputation for their achievement in educating and training their five hundred Anglo-Indian boys and girls in useful occupations for later life. In addition to a high standard of scholarship, the children were taught such practical attributes as bakery and the cultivation of fruit, flowers and vegetables, which not only met the requirements of the Homes but provided a surplus for sale in Calcutta.

When Anderson first visited the Kalimpong Homes in 1932 he was immediately struck with the remarkable character of the place, its founder and his work. As he later explained :

---

[1] The Very Rev. John Anderson Graham, C.I.E., V.D., F.R.G.S. (1861–1942), having served in the Home Civil Service in Edinburgh from 1877 to 1882, was ordained in 1889 and went out to India as a missionary in 1898. He founded the Kalimpong Homes in 1900. He was elected Moderator of the General Assembly of the Church of Scotland for the year 1931–1932.

I do not exaggerate when I say it was a revelation to me of the spirit of happiness and service that animates the life of the Homes. I understood more quickly and more thoroughly than any description can convey the force of their appeal. . . . For this is more than an Institution ; it is a living witness to the power of love and faith. The Homes as an educational centre have been recognized as an asset of irreplaceable value to the poorest among the Anglo-Indian community. . . . Whoever may be the direct beneficiaries of work such as this, India and humanity must be richer in consequence.[1]

John's interest was also caught by the other work which Dr. Graham had been able to do among the local hill peoples through the Church of Scotland Guild Mission which he had also founded for instruction in medical, educational, industrial and agricultural work.

To John there was something instantly appealing about this brother Scot who had given himself selflessly and wholeheartedly to the betterment of social conditions in India. A close affinity — amounting to sincere affection — grew up between them, and Anderson would come to Kalimpong as often as his official duties would permit. In the natural simplicity of the Graham home he would throw off his gubernatorial trappings and become relaxed and approachable. Here was the atmosphere of his childhood, the sound and simple Scottish upbringing with its tremendous emphasis on education and hard work. This tradition Anderson and Graham had in common ; the one from George Watson's, the other from Glasgow High School. They talked the same language, shared the same ideals and standards — and the same mutual love of oatcakes! In all his days in India John was probably happiest at Kalimpong.

Nor did his interest in the Homes and his devotion to his friend cease with his return to England. The Kalimpong Homes were ever close to his heart. He became a member of the London Committee and Hon. President of the Scottish Committee, and was responsible for raising a considerable sum of money for the continuance of the work. His friendship with Graham was maintained until the latter's death in 1942.

[1] Farewell speech of Sir John Anderson on September 24, 1937, at the 37th Anniversary of the founding of the Kalimpong Homes.

M

(xi)

Meantime in Westminster the constitutional development of the Indian Empire had been carried a step further along the road to complete self-government within the Commonwealth. In March 1933 a White Paper had been issued by His Majesty's Government summarizing their decisions taken in the light of the Round Table Conferences and setting forth their general proposals for an Indian Constitution.[1] These they referred a month later to a Joint Committee of both Houses of Parliament, under the chairmanship of the Marquess of Linlithgow, charged 'to consider the future government of India' and to draft legislation accordingly. This formidable task was undertaken with conscientious thoroughness,[2] and the Bill which resulted from the Committee's deliberations and was introduced into the House of Commons on December 12, 1934, was a model of careful, detailed and effective drafting, but its failure to mention dominion status in the preamble displayed a lack of vision which certain contemporary critics did not hesitate to stigmatize as 'a profound error'.[3] 'As an essay in constitution-making it has not been surpassed in modern times', Professor Mansergh has written. 'As a piece of constructive statesmanship it lacked boldness of conception and imaginative insight'.[4]

Both the tempo and the principle of the Bill were sharply criticized by the Labour Party who, in an amendment moved by Mr. Attlee on February 6, 1935, advocated the explicit recognition of India's right to dominion status and provision for its attainment. From the other side of the House Mr. Winston Churchill attacked it vehemently as 'a gigantic quilt of jumbled crochet work, a monstrous monument of shame built by pigmies'. Nevertheless, the Bill was ultimately passed by both Houses of Parliament and received the Royal Assent on August 4, 1935.

John Anderson had followed with intense interest the progress of the Bill from its inception in the Joint Committee to its consummation in the House of Lords. He considered its provisions

---

[1] *Proposals for Indian Constitutional Reform* (Cmd. 4268, 1933).
[2] *Report of the Joint Committee on Indian Constitutional Reform* (London, 1934).
[3] Professor A. Berriedale Keith, *Letters on Imperial Relations* (London, 1935), p. 347.
[4] Professor Nicholas Mansergh, *Survey of British Commonwealth Affairs ; Problems of External Policy 1931–1939* (Oxford, 1952), p. 248.

adequate and in any case inevitable, and he deprecated the more intransigent type of criticism which, to him, savoured only of irreconcilable unreality.

Mr. Winston Churchill seems to be pursuing a vigorous campaign against the National Government on the Indian policy [he wrote to his father from Calcutta]. It is too late to propose any substantial changes now. Faith is deeply pledged & to withhold what has been offered will only lead to widespread disorders here. It is a pity when things are going reasonably well to throw so many apples of discord about.

The Government of India Act of 1935 contemplated a Federation of British-Indian provinces and Indian States, with Burma as a separate political entity. In the case of the provinces, accession to the Federation was automatic, but in the case of the States it was voluntary, dependent upon the desire of the Princes. The Central Government was to comprise a Council of Ministers responsible to a Legislature composed of two Chambers, which would be in full charge of all matters except Defence and External Affairs. These two 'reserved' subjects were to be administered by the Viceroy, aided by Councillors appointed by himself.

Within the provinces complete self-government was accorded to the provincial governments, with certain provisions in the case of deadlock or breakdown. In the case of Bengal this meant that the Cabinet, composed of Ministers appointed by the Governor, and having full charge of all Government departments, was responsible to the Provincial Legislature. This was bi-cameral. The Legislative Council, consisting of some 65 members, was elected for nine years ; it was not subject to dissolution but a third of its members retired every third year. The Lower House, the Legislative Assembly, comprised some 250 members elected for a maximum statutory period of five years, but was liable to dissolution at any time.

The head of the provincial administration was the Governor, 'aided and advised' by a Council of Ministers. In principle, the relations of the Governor to his Cabinet were the same as those in any other system of cabinet government, that is to say, the Ministers were jointly and severally responsible for all the work of the Government. Under the Act, however, the Governor was invested with certain special powers, unique in constitutional history. These were his 'discretionary' and 'individual judgment' powers and his 'special responsibilities', in respect of which he was under the superintendence of the Viceroy and Governor-General — or, in effect, the control of Parliament, for the Constitution contemplated no uncontrolled or irresponsible power. His 'discretionary' powers corresponded in the main to prerogative or other powers normally vested in the Head of State, or powers necessary to 'hold the ropes' during a formative period ; Ministers had no constitutional right to tender advice as to their exercise but the Governor was encouraged progressively to consult Ministers before reaching decisions ; in matters subject to the 'individual judgment' of the Governor, Ministers had the right and duty to tender formal advice, and to the extent that he departed from it, the Governor was responsible through the Governor-General to the Secretary of State.

To provide against a complete breakdown of Cabinet Government, the Governor — in practice with the ultimate sanction of the Secretary of State — was empowered to suspend by Proclamation the operation of 'Parliamentary' and 'Cabinet' Government and to take upon himself the administration of the Province, if at any time he was satisfied that a situation had arisen in which the government of the Province could not be carried on in accordance with the stipulations of the Act.

Although the Government of India Act had become law in August 1935 its provisions did not become operative in respect of the Provincial Governments until April 1, 1937. By this time John Anderson's original term of office of five years would have terminated. It was no surprise, however, to the Bengal Government, nor to the Province as a whole, when it became known that, at the urgent request of the Secretary of State and of the Viceroy, he had agreed to accept a six months' extension in order to launch the Bengal ship of state on an even keel upon the uncharted waters of autonomy. The news that his hand was to be upon the helm at this momentous time of the transfer of power in the Province was hailed with relief and satisfaction by Europeans and Indians alike, for his reputation stood higher at that moment than that of any other of the King's representatives in India.

Indeed there was a determined effort in certain quarters to retain John Anderson's services for India for an even longer period and in an even more exalted sphere. Sir James Grigg, for example, was convinced that Anderson should be appointed Viceroy and wrote forcefully in this vein to Mr. Neville Chamberlain, then Chancellor of the Exchequer, when John was going on home leave in the summer of 1934 :

> I hope that you will have long private talks with him for in my view he is the ablest man we have got out here and he is so sane. And, if I may be so bold, may I beg that you will do your utmost to get him the succession to Willingdon ? Unless you have a man who is at once able, courageous and informed you may easily get a shambles out here in the next few years, and I can think of nobody who satisfies all these criteria but our Jonathan — and he has made a stupendous position for himself in Bengal.

'P. J.' followed up this appeal with similar letters to Mr. Baldwin, then Lord President of the Council, to Mr. Tom Jones, Deputy Secretary to the Cabinet, and to Sir Findlater Stewart, the Permanent Under-Secretary of the India Office. At the same time a *ballon d'essai* to the same effect was flown by the editor of *The Scotsman*. In reporting the Lebong outrage that newspaper made the following comment : 'His [Anderson's] colleagues in the Civil Service believe that if and when the system of Government foreshadowed in the Indian White Paper is established, he is likely to be the first Viceroy, as being one of the few living men who have the administrative capacity which that office will demand'.[1] This intelligence was duly reported to John by his father and drew from him a reply full of sceptical common sense. 'I wouldn't worry if I were you about what the newspapers say', he wrote. '*The Scotsman* won't have the appointment of the next Viceroy & anyway I think there is a distinguished Marquess in view.'

This proved to be entirely correct. Though there is reason to believe that serious consideration was given to these suggestions, in the event, when Mr. Baldwin became Prime Minister in 1935, he offered to Lord Linlithgow the choice of the Viceroyalty or the post of Secretary of State for India and, when he chose the former, gave the latter appointment to the Marquess of Zetland.

The elections for the provincial legislatures under the Act of 1935 were held early in 1937. The Congress Party of Mr. Gandhi

[1] *The Scotsman*, May 9, 1934.

gained a clear majority in eight out of the eleven Provinces. Bengal was one of three Provinces in which they were in a minority. Here the Krishak Praja Party won a large number of seats and its leader, Fazlul Huq, a veteran Bengal politician, succeeded in forming a coalition ministry, despite the refusal of the Congress Party members to co-operate.

Few states in the natal processes of self-government could have been blessed with a more beneficent amalgam of midwife-cum-wet-nurse than Bengal had in John Anderson. From his great experience in Whitehall and as a Presidency Governor he knew to a nicety the vital importance of the true relationship between Civil Servants and Ministers and between the executive and the legislative branches of Government. This wisdom he continued to impart successfully to the three organisms concerned, so that both the birth pangs and the teething troubles of autonomy in Bengal were rendered as painless as possible.

Much of the initial work of preparation for the transfer of power fell upon the Governor's personal office which was in process of transformation into a small recognized Secretariat. Among those who worked closely under Anderson, with great efficiency, were his Private Secretary, Mr. L. G. Pinnell,[1] who under the new Act became Secretary to the Governor and to his Cabinet, and his Legal Remembrancer, Mr. James Roxburgh,[2] whose invaluable contributions the Governor was the first to recognize with gratitude. But ever and anon problems would present themselves which required recourse to his superior knowledge and pragmatic wisdom.

One such conundrum, for which there seemed no easy answer, was the allocation of departmental responsibilities. Under the old system it had been possible to divide up the work between Members of Council or between Ministers with a certain amount of flexibility. In the future, however, it was possible to foresee that Ministers might well like to arrange the work to suit their own convenience which, in its turn, might result in the division of responsibility of various departments between several of them. For

---

[1] Mr. Leonard George Pinnell, C.I.E., Private Secretary to the Governor of Bengal, 1935–1937 ; Secretary to the Governor, 1937–1939 ; Domestic Bursar of St. John's College, Oxford, 1953–1960.

[2] Sir James Roxburgh, C.I.E., Legal Remembrancer to the Government of Bengal, 1937–1939 ; Puisne Judge, High Court, Calcutta, 1939–1952.

this problem it was difficult to provide a solution by rule and the point was referred to John. His answer was prompt and simple, born of his own experience. The Departments were the permanent structure of Government and the permanent repository of records ; Ministers would change but the Departments remained static. Therefore, he ruled : 'Allot each subject firmly to a Department and give Departments to Ministers'. And it was so.

Anderson was at great pains to inculcate the principles of departmental integrity into the new body politic of Bengal. This he did both in private conversations with Ministers and Civil Servants and in the course of public addresses. One such occasion was a Rotary Club luncheon in Calcutta at which he seized upon the Rotarian motto of 'Service before Self' to deliver a homily on the Public Service.[1]

It was not, he assured his audience, that he considered the traditions of the Indian Civil Service to be intrinsically inferior to those of their counterpart in Whitehall, but they had grown up under conditions which had now to be profoundly modified by the advent of responsible government. There were many who hoped to see the traditions of Public Service in India develop upon lines similar to those of the British Civil Service, which had worked under conditions of responsible government for many generations, and he therefore developed, from his own wide experience, a series of precepts which, without so stating, he offered as a moral and a model to the Civil Service of Bengal. They might well be quoted as a textbook.

> The first thing is that the Civil Servant has nothing to do with politics. He must have no obvious political affiliations. He is entitled as an individual to his own political views. He has a vote and can use it as he likes. But he is not entitled to make a parade of any particular political faith. Here I must digress : I must try to make clear what I conceive to be the difference between policy and politics. To do that I must be forgiven if I make some reference to the functions of Ministers. Now, Ministers have two capacities. In the first place they are servants of the State, charged with a duty not to one party but to all parties and entitled in carrying out that duty constitutionally to the full resources, moral

---

[1] Speech at a luncheon of the Rotary Club of Calcutta, August 10, 1937.

and material, that the State can provide. In that capacity they are paid salaries and in that capacity have to formulate and put into execution administrative policies for which they take responsibility to the Legislature. Now once they have taken responsibility to the Legislature and are carrying out the administrative policy, they are not politicians but Ministers of the Crown. On the other side of the picture they have another capacity. They come into office as the leaders of political parties ; to get themselves into office and to keep themselves there they need all the machinery of party propaganda and party organization, and that implies party connexions, party emblems and party programmes. That is politics.

With that side of the picture the Civil Servant has nothing whatsoever to do, but with the other side of the picture, with Ministers in their capacity as servants of the State, putting into force administrative policy for which they are responsible, the Civil Servant has everything to do. That then is what I mean when I say that a Civil Servant can make no parade of his political faith. Most Civil Servants at Home avoid political meetings altogether and for a Civil Servant to go no further even than to occupy a seat on a party platform would certainly be regarded as of very doubtful propriety. It is only by rigid avoidance of party connexion that a Civil Servant can give that unquestioning and unquestionable loyalty which every lawful Government is entitled to expect from him in the formulation and the carrying out of its administrative policy. On the other hand, it is sometimes said that the Civil Servant has nothing to do with policy. That is not true ; but before we go any further we must stop for a moment to see the source from which servants of the Crown derive their authority. . . .

At Home in my experience, the relation between a Minister and his senior departmental advisers is of a very close and intimate character. The Civil Servant is the recipient of many confidences, and I have never known such confidence abused. If the Minister feels he can tell his departmental adviser frankly what his own difficulties are — difficulties with his political opponents and with his party colleagues — the adviser will be in a position to apply far more intelligently and helpfully the departmental experience which it is his main function to contribute. It is upon the effectiveness of the partnership established between the Minister, irrespective of party, and his chief permanent advisers, that the practical results attained very largely depend. This applies not only in administration but also in the transaction of Parliamentary business. No head of a department can perform his duties adequately unless he is thoroughly familiar with Parliamentary forms and procedure.

That is broadly the position at Home. I realise well that the conditions cannot be exactly reproduced here. A tradition has to be built up by degrees and apart from everything else there is an element of lack of continuity here which does not exist at Home where every department contains senior officers of 20 to 30 years' experience of responsible work in the same department. But at this juncture when all is new there ought to be in the minds of all concerned some conscious ideals to which to work in the relations established between Ministers and their officials. For that reason I have thought it might be of interest to Rotarians whose primary concern is service, as well as to others whom these remarks may reach, to have these few first-hand impressions of the system as it works in one of the oldest democracies in the world.

Anderson had not waited for the new Government of India Act to come into force to develop along the lines of a Cabinet the weekly Joint Meetings of his Members of Council and Ministers at which all matters, whether 'Reserved' or 'Transferred' were freely discussed. Not without misgivings on the part of his colleagues, he had introduced a system of 'Cabinet Minutes' before 1935. These were originally his personal records but they became more and more valuable and by the time Cabinet Government became an accomplished fact they were accepted as an integral part of the procedure.

It was, perhaps, in dealing with his Cabinet that John made his greatest personal contribution to the working of the new Constitution. He developed the method, followed thereafter by all subsequent Governors, of presiding in person at all meetings. In addition to his own wide grasp of the fundamentals of Cabinet Government, he exercised great patience and persuasiveness. He was always completely prepared on all subjects under discussion and usually came to a Cabinet meeting with his mind made up as to what under the circumstances was the wisest course for the Government to adopt — or possibly with a compromise solution ready on an issue on which the Cabinet were divided. Yet he was never dictatorial or even overbearing in his manner. After allowing full discussion, he generally managed to steer his Ministers round to his own point of view while leaving them with the satisfactory belief that the solution had been of their own finding. This he did by seeking to attach any new idea of his own to something already advanced by some Cabinet member, as an adaptation of that point or a mere extension of it.

He had learned, too, that in all but matters affecting India his Ministers had a surprising veneration for the wisdom of Whitehall and he played upon it accordingly. When discussion upon some specific subject reached a point of threatened deadlock John would intervene with : 'Of course I know that circumstances are quite different here, but we did have a problem comparable in some ways with this in Whitehall — I remember Joynson-Hicks was at the Home Office — and the way it was tackled at that time by the Cabinet was this. . . . I wonder whether a similar approach here might not be fruitful.' This gambit rarely failed to have a beneficial effect upon his Indian colleagues.

Indeed he soon learned to weigh and assess their minds with great accuracy. There was occasion when it had to be decided whether a certain Bill, which was sure to be bitterly fought, should be introduced into the Legislature at the start of the session, before tempers had got frayed, or towards the end, when Members had become jaded and were anxious for a prompt dispatch of business. As was his custom, John asked each Cabinet Member for his opinion, and one — the 'lightweight' of the Cabinet — gave his view in favour of bringing in the measure later rather than earlier because that would allow time for 'manipulation'. '"Manipulation" ?' commented the Governor majestically, yet with a twinkle in his eye. 'Surely you meant that it would give time for the essential virtue and wisdom of the Government's proposal to penetrate and be appreciated ?' 'Oh, yes, Your Excellency, that is exactly what I meant. . . .' But there was a general laugh because all present knew that he really *had* meant 'manipulation'.

Both in Cabinet and at his weekly discussions with Ministers, Departmental Secretaries and Heads of Departments, John provided an increasingly unifying influence. His Ministers grew to value his complete grasp of the administration and also his phenomenal memory which provided a living and up-to-date liaison machinery in all fields of government. More and more he became the centre of gravity, with Ministers — and others — coming to him for advice and to try out their ideas at the earliest stage. And this was the Governor whose advent had been awaited with trepidation and foreboding.

It was not only in personal contacts that John Anderson pressed home the essential principles and responsibilities of self-government. In the many public addresses which he made during his last year of office, he let no opportunity escape him of emphasizing the nature and gravity of the obligations of Government involved in the achievement of autonomy.

(xii)

The days drew on towards the time when John Anderson's work in Bengal would be ended. A happy and fruitful personal relationship between Calcutta and Delhi closed with the departure of Lord Willingdon.

I hate the thought of breaking our association in India [wrote the retiring Viceroy], for it has been good in every way & I feel some reflected glory in the splendid way you've pulled your Province together, & are going on from strength to strength in yr. economic legislation. Go on & prosper ; I wish I cld. help you to see it through. But I rejoice in the feeling that our association has ripened into the best of friendship & I look forward to our seeing much of each other at home when you have completed a great proconsulship.

With the new Viceroy, Lord Linlithgow, John was unable to establish the same affinity of mind. There were inevitable difficulties in respect of the introduction of the new constitutional reforms. John felt that the Viceroy was not wholly appreciative of the new status of the Province *vis-à-vis* the Central Government. The Viceroy found the Governor of Bengal perhaps unnecessarily assertive. Their interviews were apt to result in tension and after one of them John remarked to P. J. Grigg with some asperity : 'Your Viceroy appears imperfectly to apprehend that the new Constitution is in force and that the Provinces have certain privileges'.

Anderson could indeed look back upon a record of unqualified and almost unparalleled success. The gloomy picture of his Presidency which he had reported to King George V in 1932 had been all but completely dissipated in the ensuing five years. Terrorism had been virtually stamped out, both in the root and in the branch. A bankrupt Province had once again become financially solvent and healthy and now enjoyed a budget surplus. But this was not all. In other areas of the economic and social field his contributions had been very great. He had been responsible for the campaign against the menace of the water hyacinth, which threatened to clog most of the waterways of Bengal. He had successfully brought about the regulation of jute production through voluntary restriction. He had established a panel of enquiry to deal with the problem of the indebtedness of the rural population and had fathered the legislation for scaling down the accumulated debts of the agriculturists. To his energetic support had been due the introduction of compulsory primary education in the Province. Finally, it was his great experience of government, his clear-headedness, his integrity of character and the reputation which he had earned throughout the Presidency as a sympathetic administrator, devoted to the interests of Bengal, that had made him so ideal a pilot in the early days of provincial autonomy. Well and truly might he say :
Si monumentum requiris circumspice.

That Anderson's great achievements were recognized and appreciated became clearly apparent as the time drew on for his departure. He was hailed by the newspapers and in addresses of farewell as 'The Builder of a Better Bengal' and Europeans and Bengalis alike deplored his going. Nor was it only the departure of a great public figure that saddened them. John had certainly made for himself a permanent place in the history of Bengal but he had also won the lasting regard of all communities. Those Indians who had feared his coming as a portent of a 'Black and Tan' counter-terror now mourned the leaving of a sagacious and understanding friend. Those Europeans who had sniggered at 'Pompous John' now openly regretted the loss of the 'best Governor since Ronaldshay'.[1] Indeed the British community in Calcutta had rarely

[1] The Marquess of Zetland, then Lord Ronaldshay, was Governor of Bengal, 1917–1922.

evinced such emotion as was displayed on various public occasions during these final months. Especially moving were the farewell scenes at the St. Andrew's Day Dinner in November 1936 and at the Armistice Day Dinner a year later. On both occasions the vast audiences repeatedly sang 'Will ye no come back again?' and cheered and cheered again. More intimate, and even more significant, was a dinner given in his honour by the Bengal branch of the Indian Civil Service at Barrackpore ten days before he left Calcutta for the last time. There were about eighty present from all over the Province, which meant that every officer who could get away from his post to attend had done so. It was a tribute never before paid to any departing Governor.

John was deeply touched by the obvious sincerity of the sentiments expressed in regard to himself and his achievements, but he was under no illusion about the feelings of other and less friendly sections of the community. 'I do not wish you to be misled', he wrote to his father on November 16, 1937. 'People of widely different views are vieing with each other in showing me kindness but I expect that the more extreme Nationalist press will be more or less abusive. In a sense that is a compliment for I certainly have not served their ends.'[1]

His own farewell to the people of Bengal was made in a broadcast on Sunday November 21. In it he gave a final admonition to the newly autonomous Province and a message of hope for the future:

> . . . I believe that, looking forward, there are solid grounds for optimism. The financial position of the province has been re-established : terrorism has been brought under control, and lines of economic development for the future have been sketched out. Still more, there have been signs that men of influence in the province have begun to realise the waste and futility of barren introspection and embittered controversy : I can think of nothing better for the future of Bengal than that such a realisation should spread and should result in a determined effort to carry on the

[1] John was quite right. On the morning of November 25, 1937, the virulently Nationalist paper *Advance* made the following comment : 'It must be confessed Sir John Anderson's régime has been altogether barren of substantial results. All the five years of his rule he thought, and earnestly thought, of terrorism. He can point to not one administrative act which the people will feel inclined to remember with gratitude. . . . If Bengal is not sorry to part with him to-day, Bengal is not at all to blame. A humdrum rule has come to an end.'

political life of the country in an atmosphere all the more stimulating because it will be free from rancour. I believe that if a determined effort is made on the part of those who are in a position to command respect and following — if a determined effort is made by such men to build the future of Bengal on sound lines, there is no reason why their efforts should not be fully successful. I am aware, perhaps more fully than most, of obstacles in the way of real progress — obstacles that might at any time become formidable ; but those obstacles are there to be met and overcome. The greatest possible obstacle would be a recrudescence, not necessarily of terrorist acts, but of that state of mind in which terrorist acts are possible or probable. I fervently hope that the policy which the Government of Bengal are pursuing as regards terrorism may evoke the kind of response that is essential if that policy is ultimately to be successful. And here may I say that nothing that has happened in the last few days has been prompted so far as I am concerned by any desire on my part to see a particular stage reached before I leave Bengal : I am profoundly thankful that it has been found possible in my time to go as far as my Ministers have now gone, but I would ask you to believe that I myself regard the measures they are taking as part of a deliberate and consistent policy to be put into practice as and when responsible men with a full sense of their responsibility judge the time appropriate.

May I express the hope that feelings of communal bitterness, all too prominent of late, may with the passage of time and with a greater appreciation of realities be allayed. I would ask the Hindu community to remember that Bengal is no less the country of the Moslems than of the Hindus : that Moslems are in a numerical majority and that they have in fact, for reasons into which I am not concerned to enter, lacked in the past advantages which their Hindu fellow countrymen have enjoyed. I would ask the Moslems to remember that the province needs, and cannot afford to dispense with, the services which the Hindu community with their ability, their long traditions of association with the administration and their advanced culture are eminently qualified to render.

. . . . .

In six days' time the Governorship of Bengal will rest upon my successor, Lord Brabourne. Parting as I do, with many regrets, from the province with whose affairs I have been so intimately bound up, I cannot but say quite simply how glad I was when I learnt some months ago that it is Lord Brabourne who is to succeed me. I shall never forget Bengal, its problems or the many friends I am leaving behind, and I shall always pray that Divine Providence may vouchsafe to her in rich measure those blessings of tranquillity and prosperity which we all so ardently desire.

Goodbye.

John's last public act as Governor of Bengal was one of clemency and it was one which had its parallel at an earlier moment in his career. A few months before, in his reply to the farewell addresses presented at Dacca (July 20, 1937) he had made his only public reference to his service in Ireland :

I have never talked about my work in Ireland. What I did or refrained from doing is a matter in which I was answerable not to public opinion but to the British Cabinet and I would not say what I am about to say even now were it not that by so doing I may remove misapprehensions and thereby serve a public interest. With this in mind I think there is one disclosure which after a lapse of 16 years may be made without impropriety. When in 1921 in pursuance of a treaty the British Government were about to transfer to Irish Ministers responsibility for what is now the Irish Free State there were many Irish prisoners still in gaol as a result of the preceding conflict. As the principal adviser of Cabinet Ministers in such matters I had to consider the situation and with full knowledge of all the facts and circumstances and after weighing up possible consequences and reactions with the greatest care, I recommended the release of those prisoners. That course, as a matter of fact, was followed. Whether it was right or not is not now in question and I must ask you not to draw any analogy as regards the present situation from this personal reminiscence. The facts and circumstances were so different from those of Bengal that no practical inference can be drawn for us — except this, an inference which you may perhaps be good enough to draw, that I do not approach and never have approached such questions with any bias in favour of keeping people in custody merely for the sake of doing so.

It was characteristic of Anderson that he should wait until the last months of his rule in Bengal to reply to — or indeed to give any evidence that he had even taken cognizance of — the copious references, some of a very lurid character, to his Irish career. It was even more characteristic that he should now do so with some constructive thought in mind. For, though he had warned his audience in Dacca to draw no inferences from the reminiscence which he had related, the sequel to his remarks occurred on the day of his leaving Calcutta. Among the last decisions of his Cabinet, made at his instigation and suggestion, was one authorizing the release of certain classes of convicts before the expiry of their sentences, as a measure of clemency. 'The Ministry are confident', ran the official statement, 'that no more appropriate moment could be chosen to announce their decision than the occasion of the departure of His Excellency, Sir John Anderson.'

John left the Howrah Station, Calcutta, on the morning of November 23. He journeyed across India to Bombay, where he stayed with the Governor, Sir Roger Lumley (now Lord Scarbrough), until, on the afternoon of the 26th, he sailed for England in the P. & O. liner *Comorin*, accompanied by Dr. Jamieson and another friend who had been paying him a visit. 'I am looking forward to a thoroughly lazy fortnight on board ship with books and congenial company', he wrote to his father.

As the shores of India receded and the liner's prow headed towards the westering sun, it seemed that across the ocean a voice was singing new words to an old song:

> John Anderson, my jo, John,
>   When we were first acquent,
>   The Province was a cauldron
>   Of seething discontent.
>   You came, and saw and conquered;
>   To thank you as you go,
>   Here's blessings on your massive brow,
>   John Anderson, my jo.[1]

[1] These lines, by H. S. Vere Hodge, appeared in *Punch* on December 29, 1937, and were reprinted in *The Watsonian*, vol. xxiv, No. 2, April 1938. They are printed here by the courtesy and with the permission of *Punch*.

VI

Back Bencher

February–November 1938

(i)

THE return of John Anderson to England on December 11, 1937, was something of a triumph. His appointment as Governor of Bengal in November 1931 had occasioned only the veriest ripple of publicity and his departure in the following March had gone unheralded, but the return of the 'Builder of Better Bengal' was a very different affair. *The Times*, which on the date of his leaving Calcutta had printed a turnover article by its special correspondent recording the achievements of his Governorship,[1] accorded him a 'leader' on his arrival, eulogizing his work in the Province which had shown that

> in addition to the qualities of efficiency, industry and integrity that are traditionally associated with the Civil Service, he is blessed with exceptional constructive powers, and not least with a liberal mind. He will now, no doubt, wish to retire for a while into private life, but it is hoped that the great qualities which he has displayed in Bengal will be used again in the service of his country.[2]

On the same day encomiums were published from the Viceroy, from the Secretary of State for India and from Lord Willingdon. John was greeted at Victoria Station by a group of officials and friends and some of those prevented from attending his reception sent him glowing letters of congratulation. 'How glad I am that Stewart and I pressed you to go to Bengal', wrote Sir Samuel Hoare, now Home Secretary, 'and how wise you were in making the courageous decision to accept the appointment.'

---

[1] *The Times*, November 24, 1937. [2] *Ibid.*, December 11, 1937.

Now, too, came high honours from his Sovereign. On December 15, John was appointed a Knight Grand Commander of the Order of the Star of India and received the insignia of this decoration at the hands of King George VI in private audience at Buckingham Palace on the same day.[1]   Two weeks later the New Year's Honours List contained the announcement of his appointment as a Privy Counsellor of the United Kingdom.[2] 'You have done marvellously, Jonathan', Sir Maurice Hankey wrote to him on this occasion, 'and no honour would really be too much for your work during the past five years.'

In his essentially modest and humble way — that inner self which disclosed itself at just the right moments in his life — John was delighted with his new honours and more particularly with his Privy Counsellorship. 'To be a member of the Privy Council (of the United Kingdom) is quite a nice thing to be', he wrote to his father. 'It is very sparingly given outside political circles.'

The prognostication of the editor of *The Times* that John would now desire some measure of retirement into private life was indeed wholly correct, since for five years he had laboured like a Trojan for the good of Bengal and with manifest success. The strain, however, had been very great, even for a man of his physique and mentality. In addition to the cares of office and the burden of affairs of State there had been, at least during the early years of his Governorship, the almost constant threat of physical danger. These factors had taken their inevitable toll and he felt himself to be a very tired man.

There was, moreover, the question of his personal affairs. Never a rich man, he was now faced with the problem of how to make a living. His annual salary as Governor of Bengal had been approximately £114,000 (with a £25,000 sumptuary allowance and a contract grant of some £100,000, intended to cover the wages of his staff and establishment) and though he had made it a condition of acceptance that he should be permitted to remit home from his pay

---

[1] It is to be regretted that the King was not keeping a diary at this period of his life since it would almost certainly have contained a full, and possibly a pungent, record of their conversation. King George VI was a far more human and illuminating — and a less meteorological — chronicler than his father, but he did not begin a regular day-to-day diary until the outbreak of the Second World War.

[2] John Anderson was sworn of the Privy Council at Buckingham Palace on February 24, 1938.

a sum of £1800, this together with his pension rights as a former Civil Servant was his only asset,[1] and he was now rising fifty-six years old.

It was a combination of these reasons which had prompted John to refuse the urgent requests of Lord Zetland that he should consent to a further extension of his governorship, and also a further demand made upon his public service.

On October 24, 1937, he had received a personal and secret letter from the Prime Minister, Mr. Neville Chamberlain, offering him the High Commissionership of Palestine. This would have entailed exchanging one 'hot spot' for another, almost literally going from the frying-pan into the fire, for the state of affairs in Palestine was much the same as that of Bengal in 1932, and the activities of terrorists were rife. John was no physical coward — his record in Ireland and in Bengal was eloquent witness to this — but he felt that he was being asked unreasonably to take on a further heavy burden without sufficient regard to the strain that Bengal had already imposed on his physical and mental resources. He had no hesitation, therefore, in cabling his refusal of the offer. On October 25 he set out his reasons for this decision in a secret and personal letter to Mr. Chamberlain from Darjeeling :

MY DEAR PRIME MINISTER,

I received your letter of 15th Oct. yesterday & as requested have sent you my reply by cable. It may be desirable to add a word of explanation.

I was able to give you my answer at once because the most important considerations involved were precisely those that I had already had to weigh when I was pressed by Zetland to undertake a longer period of service here. If I could possibly have accepted that suggestion I would have done so. But after most earnest consideration I felt compelled to say No.

The plain truth is that the wear & tear entailed by this job has been very great & I have been conscious for some time past of the need for a really prolonged period of recuperation if I am not to go prematurely on to the scrap heap. The arguments against

---

[1] Anderson was awarded a pension of £1200 a year, with an additional lump sum allowance of £3248. Of these amounts £975 of the annual pension and £2369 of the lump sum were recoverable from the United Kingdom Government and the balance from the Government of India.

my undertaking an exacting *new* job without having had an adequate rest seem to me stronger than in the case of an extension in a job I already know.

These considerations are so compelling that I need not dwell on any other aspect of the matter that might on closer examination have presented difficulty. But there is one point I might just mention as its bearing is general. I had to break my service in order to come to India & as soon as may be after I return home I must see about re-establishing myself on a permanent or quasi-permanent footing. This is dictated not by choice but by sheer necessity.

It has made me very unhappy to have to say 'No' to any request of yours especially as the matter is put to me on public grounds but I venture to hope that in the circumstances I shall be acquitted of any lack of public spirit.

Yours sincerely,
JOHN ANDERSON.

Anderson was now actively concerned for his future. Nellie Mackenzie and his daughter Mary, who had preceded him to England, had rented a furnished house north of Hyde Park, 11 Chepstow Villas. The rent was nine guineas a week — a surprisingly small sum by modern standards and even then considerably less than current rates of rentals — but even this John considered excessive. 'It is more expensive than I could afford for very long', he wrote to his father on December 19, 'though well below prevailing rates in London, but it will give us time to look round for something permanent.'

He need not have been too anxious on the score of unemployment, however. Already, before he left Calcutta, he had received, through Sir Warren Fisher at the Treasury, an approach from the Midland Bank offering him a directorship with an indication that his acceptance might well carry with it the reversion of the Chairmanship of the Board, the existing incumbent, the Rt. Hon. Reginald McKenna, being then seventy-four years old and contemplating retirement. This, John replied, would be very welcome after his return home.

There were also numerous other concerns which were desirous of acquiring the benefit of John's wisdom and experience in the direction of their affairs. During the first months after his arrival in England he received, and accepted, in quick succession invitations to join the boards of Vickers Ltd., Imperial Chemical Industries (I.C.I.) and the Employers Liability Assurance Corporation. He seemed to be well launched upon a business career. Nor was this the only prospect which opened before him.

(ii)

On November 9, 1937, James Ramsay MacDonald died suddenly at sea in the course of a holiday voyage to South America ; thereby simultaneously concluding a stormy and spectacular career and creating a vacancy in the parliamentary representation of the Scottish Universities.[1]

The Unionist Party of Scotland, who had accepted Mr. MacDonald for the University Seat with some reserve, were now anxious to acquire a candidate for the by-election who would be more in accordance with their previous traditions. The day for nominations drew on and the Party were still without a nominee, for there was no agreement on the names hitherto suggested, none of whom was considered a strong enough personality to hold the seat.

It was at this moment that in conversation in the House of Commons, one of the remaining members for the Scottish Universities, Sir John Graham Kerr,[2] confided the woes and difficulties of the Party to his colleague from Cambridge University, Mr. Kenneth Pickthorn.[3] Pickthorn replied that his university was intending to give an honorary degree to John Anderson at the forthcoming Congregation and suggested his name as a possible solution for the dilemma of the Scottish Unionists. Sir John Graham Kerr jumped at the idea and at once communicated it to the Unionist Association.

[1] Having been defeated in the Seaham Constituency in the General Election of November 1935, Mr. Ramsay MacDonald had been adopted as the National Government candidate for the Scottish Universities when a vacancy occurred on the appointment of Colonel John Buchan, Lord Tweedsmuir, as Governor-General of Canada. Mr. MacDonald was elected in January 1936.

[2] Sir John Graham Kerr, an eminent anthropologist, who had been Professor of Zoology at Glasgow University, represented the Scottish Universities from 1935 until the abolition of the university seats in 1950. He died in 1957.

[3] Sir Kenneth Pickthorn represented Cambridge University in Parliament from 1935 to 1950, and has subsequently sat for the Carlton Division of Nottinghamshire. He was created a baronet in 1959.

A hasty telephone conversation with Katie Anderson established the fact that her brother was on his way home and thus to John on board the P. & O. liner *Comorin* there came the following cablegram :

> Would you be prepared to stand as Unionist Candidate, that is as the official National Government candidate, for the parliamentary representation of the Scottish Universities if unanimously invited ? Please radio reply.

To this invitation John replied that while he found it attractive, he feared it might be inconsistent with his existing provisional commitments. He said that, if time permitted, he would like to reconsider the matter after consultations in London on his arrival. If, however, the Association required an immediate answer, he would be compelled to say 'No'. The Association agreed to await his return.

John's temporizing reply did doubtless stem from his desire to make sure of certain business connections in London, but it also had other causes. Though he found the offer of a seat in Parliament attractive, it was a new idea to him and he required time to consider whether he really wished to enter upon a political career. Certainly he would never have sought election in an ordinary constituency, for he would not have lent himself to the rough and tumble of an election campaign. But the university seats were contested by a postal vote, so that this particular objection did not arise. On the other hand, however, though he had imbibed much of his father's Gladstonian Liberalism, John had never been a party man and had no desire now to adopt a party label. Moreover — and this was a matter of fundamental conviction with him — he believed deeply and sincerely that a former member of the Civil Service should not on any account become an adherent of any one political party ; if an ex-Civil Servant entered Parliament at all, it must be as an Independent Member. This remained a basic principle throughout his political career and was to affect it materially at its close.[1]

When Anderson arrived in London on December 11, he had still not made up his mind to accept the invitation of the Scottish Unionists, though he was not unmindful of the honour thus done

[1] See below pp. 340–353.

him. He placed his objections before his would-be supporters, but they were undeterred by his dislike of being a party candidate and urged him to stand. 'I am being pressed to become a candidate for the Scottish Universities constituency in succession to Ramsay MacDonald', he wrote to his father on December 19. 'I have refused to accept any party label but still they seem to want me. I'll have to decide within the next few days. I doubt if it is a safe seat & do not relish spending some hundreds of pounds if I am to be beaten in the end by some freak.'

On the following day Sir John Graham Kerr invited John to talk over the whole situation at the House of Commons.

It is a great relief to me to know that you have not absolutely turned the matter down [he wrote]. Personally I feel that the old Party labels have really ceased to have any meaning so far as fundamental principles go. The only division that really holds is into pro-government and anti-government and even this division depends hardly at all upon theoretical views but almost entirely upon the personnel of the party leaders — upon the question whether one believes in the one group — Chamberlain, Hoare, Simon, Eden, & so on, or in the other, Atlee [sic], Morrison, Cripps & so on.

These arguments, together with the strong desire expressed by Sir Samuel Hoare and others that he consent to stand, eventually caused John to make up his mind in favour of acceptance — but on his own terms — and on Christmas Day he wrote to his father :

I have told the Scottish organization that I am prepared to stand as a Nat. Govt. candidate without any party label & if that is accepted the matter will go forward. It will be a new departure both for me & for the constituency & we shall see what comes of it.

The Scottish Unionists were in no doubt as to their decision and the formal announcement of John's adoption was made on January 4, 1938.[1] 'I can hardly visualize myself as a Parliamentary Candidate but the proposal does not seem to have been taken amiss', he

---

[1] The announcement was accompanied by letters of commendation and endorsement from the leaders of the National Government and the Prime Minister for the Conservatives, Sir John Simon for the Liberal National Party and Mr. Malcolm MacDonald for the National Labour Party.

wrote to his father. In reporting the announcement, the *Glasgow Herald* took occasion to make some editorial comment upon the constitution of the University seats in general which, now that they have unhappily ceased to exist, it is of some interest to recall :

> Perhaps it is true that, in some respects, the whole idea of University representation in Parliament is on its trial just now. There are of course many things to be said in its favour. University graduates are, or should be, an élite. They represent interests and a point of view which may not easily find expression through other constituencies. But, above all, the University seats can give a place in Parliament to men who stand a little apart from the rough and tumble of party politics but have something very valuable to contribute to the nation's councils. Some University constituencies have recently emphasised their consciousness of this fact by electing candidates who had no party allegiance. But it is right that the National Government should be given the help of M.P.s who belong to the fine tradition which has produced such Parliamentary figures as Lord Tweedsmuir. Sir John Anderson can certainly add something to such a tradition. In spite of his past achievements he is still young enough to have a considerable career before him in politics, and if the Scottish graduates elect him — as one can scarcely doubt that they will — they are not likely to regret their choice.[1]

Thus, within less than a month of his return to England from Bengal, John had embarked upon a career which was to lead him to even greater heights than those which he had hitherto attained. But his appearance in the political arena came as a surprise to some of his friends, certain of whom had expected to see him created a peer rather than become a candidate.

> I was at first rather surprised to think of you as a Parliamentarian [wrote Alexander Gray], and indeed visualised you as in another place rather than in the House of Commons. But the real objection to going into the H. of C. is that normally one has to say that one is a Conservative or a Labourite, or a Mosleyite or something ; from which source springs all hypocrisy and humbug. But if you can get in without a label, then may the Lord bless you ; also I shall begin to change my opinion of the University-constituency question.

[1] *Glasgow Herald*, January 4, 1938.

For an electorate which exercised its suffrage by a postal vote the election address of a candidate played an even more important part than in a contest which involves a campaign and an eventual pilgrimage to the ballot box. John was fully aware of this and, in drafting the address which he dispatched from London on January 28 to the graduates of the Universities of St. Andrews, Glasgow, Aberdeen and Edinburgh, he was at great pains to make his position abundantly clear. He began it with a declaration of his political faith.

I am not a Party man. Having for more than thirty years, as a matter of duty, studiously avoided any Party affiliation, I could not now, without a tinge of hypocrisy, assume any Party label even if I did not feel that by doing so I should be, to a considerable extent, undermining the basis of the only claim I can legitimately make to the confidence of any electorate — that of a public servant. But I present myself as a convinced supporter of the National Government. I feel that in present circumstances, and probably for many years to come, the affairs of the country can best be conducted by a Government which combines in itself strong elements from each of the main Parties. I feel that to-day it is the men who count, even more than the policies to which they stand committed, so long as they pursue courses calculated to unite rather than divide the various classes and sections in the community. I feel that a National Government is the type of Government not only best fitted to enable our country to play the part she ought to play in world affairs, but also most likely to bring to a satisfactory solution the many domestic problems which now confront us. I therefore come forward as a declared supporter of the National Government, claiming for myself, however, that degree of independence to which, in my opinion, any University representative is entitled in matters in respect of which he may possess special knowledge.

My past experience compels me to look upon Parliamentary Government as essentially a practical affair. When it comes down to serious business there is, I have found, little room for fads and fancies or for those political nostrums that merely make a transient and meretricious appeal. Through six years of residence abroad I have endeavoured to keep in touch with at least the main lines of development in public affairs at home; I could not pretend now to pronounce a competent opinion on many of the questions at present before the public. I will make it my business, if returned, to bring myself up to date without delay, but there are two matters put to me in the course of meetings that I have recently attended in regard to which I think the electors might fairly expect me to make my position clear at this stage.

I have been asked, first, — What is my attitude towards Socialism? I think I can answer that question best by a paraphrase of words used by a great Statesman nearly a half a century ago. 'I prefer the moderate forms of Socialism practised by the great majority of supporters of the National Government to the more extreme forms advocated in other quarters.'

Then I have been asked a more difficult question — What is my attitude towards Scottish Nationalism? Without any desire to hurl myself wantonly into an arena of controversy, I think I must answer that question and at somewhat greater length. Some minority communities have need of a Nationalist Movement to keep alive a spirit that would otherwise be stifled or decay. That is emphatically not the case in Scotland. The essential features of Scottish national character and feeling are not thirled to Scotland. I can testify from personal experience that the flame of Scottish sentiment burns as brightly in remote places of the world where Scotsmen foregather as it does at home. Scotsmen, who have for centuries played so large a part in great matters, have no need to take a parochial view of their own affairs. That there are disadvantages and inconveniences attendant upon the existing arrangements for the conduct of Scottish parliamentary and executive business I am well aware; and, if a practicable remedy can be found, it should be applied. But it serves no purpose merely to state a principle. The matter must be tested and the crucial test comes in the settlement of details. Remembering always that the distribution of financial resources is the rock upon which most schemes of devolution have crashed, I declare my readiness to support any considered plan which would result in Scottish interests being better served than they are at present, provided always that it is a plan which involves neither prejudice to the wider interests to whose advancement Scotsmen have contributed so much in the past, nor risk of creating new divisions and cleavages within Scotland itself.[1]

---

[1] This reference to Scottish Nationalism was considered far from satisfactory by the more fanatically enthusiastic stalwarts of that cause and John Anderson was subject to considerable criticism from this quarter, on the grounds that he was

The united request of the Unionist Associations of the Scottish Universities is one to which no Scotsman could willingly turn a deaf ear, and I shall be happy and proud if the electors think fit to place me in a position to repay something of what I owe to a Scottish upbringing, a Scottish school, and a Scottish University. If I am so fortunate as to be elected, I undertake to use my best endeavours to justify the confidence reposed in me.

John steadfastly refused to recognize in the issue of his address that he had in any way descended to the level of election canvassing. This he felt was beneath him ; it was a part of that vulgar side of party politics for which he had neither liking nor affinity. What he had done, in his own mind at any rate, was to make known his political credo which the graduates of the Scottish Universities could either take or leave as they saw fit. 'So you are soliciting my suffrage, Anderson', a recipient of the address, a former colleague of John's in the Civil Service, whom he had particularly disliked, said to him in the Reform Club. 'I am not seeking your vote, I have simply stated my position' was the somewhat ponderous but nevertheless strictly truthful reply.

Though both the Labour and the Liberal parties had decided not to put forward candidates, it was soon apparent that John was not

thought to represent Imperial, to the effacement of Scottish, interests. One young man, then full of fiery intolerance, now a sedate schoolmaster, composed yet another parody of 'John Anderson, my Jo' which appeared in the *Scots Independent* of Glasgow. I am indebted for permission to reprint it to the kindness of the author, J. A. Russell, J.P., Ph.D., M.A.

'John Anderson, our foe, John,
  When history first acquents,
You'd thinned the Bengal "jungle",
  And pined for Parliament's ;

Our Universities you won :
  For Scotia's welfare ? No !
For England, Empire, A.R.P.,
  John Anderson, our foe !

John Anderson, our foe, John,
  Our plight might gar you swither,
'Twas no' a cantie [happy] nicht, yon,
  We had wi' ane anither ;

Aye, ye had best be warned, John,
  You'll stir us like a blow,
Gin you efface what freedom's left,
  John Anderson, our foe !'

to be returned unopposed. The Scottish Nationalists nominated Mr. A. Dewar Gibb, Professor of Law in Glasgow University; in addition, Dr. Frances Melville, formerly Mistress of Queen Margaret College, Glasgow, put up as an Independent, and the eminent biologist Sir Peter Chalmers Mitchell came forward as an Independent Progressive. 'Probably this is just as well', John wrote to his father, 'as the opposition vote would have been more formidable if concentrated in one person.'

Much engaged though he was with public affairs, Anderson gave himself the pleasure of going up to Cambridge on January 26, to see his son take his degrees. It was a source of great pride for him that Alastair was now launched upon his medical career. 'He took the M.A. as well as the M.B. and B.Chir. so he is now a full member of the University', John wrote to David Anderson. 'He has now started on his appointment at St. Thomas's & I gather is going to be pretty closely tied.'

The date for the announcement of the result of the poll had been fixed by the Principal of Edinburgh University for Monday, February 28, as late as the law allowed, and as the day drew on John kept his father abreast of what news he had:

> I get little indication of how the election is going [he wrote on February 6]. My address went out on the 2nd & so far as I can judge has not provoked much controversy. I have had a few letters as a result, mostly appreciative but some critical. A few of the critics appear to think that I ought to have dealt more or less exhaustively with all the main topics of the day! Dr. Frances Melville will, I think, do better than any of my other opponents & I hope mainly at their expense. I have joined Walton Heath Golf Club & played my first game there yesterday. I had Lord & Lady Willingdon & Lord Justice Scott with me & we had quite an exciting foursome in which Lady W. & I were victorious.

> Everyone says the election result should be beyond doubt [he wrote again on February 17], but of course no one knows. The counting of the votes starts on Monday & by Tuesday we should have a pretty good idea of the ultimate result. I expect to travel north on Saturday the 26th & to return on the night of Tuesday the 1st. I would leave on Friday night but I have to dine with the Duke & Duchess of Abercorn that evening & as Queen Mary

is to be there I can't rush away. I hope to take my seat — if there is one to take — on the 2nd & to get off to Switzerland on the 3rd. It will not be a long holiday for I must be back in London on the evening of the 18th of March for a Watsonian Club Dinner at which I am to be the principal guest.

In the event the prophets of easy victory were justified in their confidence. John won handsomely. When the final figures of the election result were announced on the night of February 28, they were as follows :

ANDERSON	. .	14,042
MELVILLE	. .	5,618
GIBB	. . .	5,246
MITCHELL	. .	3,864

In accordance with his plans he took his seat in the House of Commons on the afternoon of March 2.

On the following day he left, with his daughter Mary and Nellie Mackenzie, for Switzerland, his first real holiday for many years. 'We had perfect weather throughout & all enjoyed the change & I think benefited by it', he reported to his father on his return.

John made his maiden speech in the House of Commons on Wednesday, June 1, and it was characteristic of him that he prepared it with meticulous care and even with some trepidation.

It is for me, at least, a very important occasion & I must know exactly what I am going to say so I have put it all in writing [he wrote in his letter home, on May 29]. I expect to speak for not more than 25 minutes. One cannot, of course, read a speech in the House of Commons & I don't know whether I shall be equal to the effort of memory required, but I must try.

The occasion was, appropriately enough, a debate in Committee of Supply for the vote of £5,693,400 for the charges which would arise in connection with the Air Raid Precautionary Services which had been authorized under the A.R.P. Act of 1937.[1] It was a subject with which John had been closely identified some fourteen years before and with which he was to be intimately associated in the near future. He began by recalling his early connections with Air Raid Precautions and passed to a eulogy of the British genius

---

[1] See below, p. 198.

for improvisation, supported with reminiscences drawn from his own experience in the National Insurance Commission and the Ministry of Shipping.

> I am well aware [he said] that there are many people who are inclined to say that we with our go-as-you-please methods can be at best but a poor match for countries which have at their disposal a close-knit organization, held by authority at every point in an inflexible grip, organizations of whose mechanical efficiency the world has recently had conspicuous and spectacular illustrations. I respectfully decline to accept that view. The elephant is a cumbrous and ungainly creature, and to all appearances singularly ill adapted to the performance of tasks requiring delicacy or precision, but I have reason to know that he can take one through obstacles and extricate one from situations with which the most highly developed type of mechanical transport would be quite unable to cope. [Laughter.]
>
> I think that in this country we shall probably never achieve the degree of mechanical efficiency that is possible, for example, in Germany. It does not follow that we should try and copy German methods. To attempt to do so would be, in my opinion, a profound mistake. Leaders in Germany aim, no doubt from their point of view rightly, at developing the special aptitudes, I might say the idiosyncrasies, of the German people. We must do the same, *mutatis mutandis*. Mechanical precision is not everything; it may even be a positive disadvantage in dealing with conditions which cannot be precisely foreseen. But if we are to set up, as I believe we can in this country, an organization equal to the requirements, the very exacting requirements, of the case, we must, I suggest, consider with great care the peculiar disabilities to which in this matter we are subject.

He went on to outline the kind of organization which he felt to be necessary, 'a hierarchy of officials working in full collaboration with local authorities, voluntary bodies, and a vast number of individuals giving voluntary service', all of whom would be fervently hoping that the results of their labours would come to naught, and that the emergency against which they were preparing would never arise. To overcome this initial disadvantage it was necessary to establish in the minds of the people that an effective organization could be brought into being without any sacrifice of the principles upon which the national life was based, and to convince them that the creation of such an organization was in itself a guarantee that the dire calamity envisaged would never befall them.

Decisions of policy are essential, and they should not be delayed. But granted those conditions, the composure with which our people always face grave emergencies when they have confidence in their leaders and themselves will, I believe, serve to rule out the hazard of the knock-out blow which is the most tempting inducement that we at present offer to any potential enemy.

John concluded with a moving enunciation of his basic beliefs regarding the major issues which were confronting the British people.

Putting out of account altogether for the moment any thought of armed conflict, there have entered into direct competition before the eyes of the world to-day two rival ideologies — fundamentally different. For those who believe in free institutions and in individual liberty, it must be a task of supreme importance to prove that in the pursuit of all worthy aims in life a system based upon those principles can at least hold its own against any rival. [Cheers.] From this point of view, as it seems to me, the potentialities of such an organization as we are considering this afternoon can be regarded as providing a crucial test. If we fail in this higher task I do not think we shall turn to some rival system. I feel pretty sure we should fail there too. We shall at best, I suggest, sag down into senility as a nation, having nothing that we or our children or our grandchildren can contemplate with pride, except what Disraeli called the 'golden promise of deceptive youth'. That, surely, is not to be our fate. It will not be, I suggest, if we approach our present tasks, formidable as they are, late in the day as it may be, in the spirit of :

'One who never turned his back but
marched breast forward,
Never doubted clouds would break,
Never dreamed, though right were
worsted, wrong would triumph,
Held we fall to rise, are baffled to fight better,
Sleep to wake.' [1] [Cheers.]

[1] *House of Commons Debates*, June 1, 1938. Cols. 2109-2115.

It is unusual to quote Browning in the House of Commons,[1] but there were other aspects of John's maiden speech which marked it as outstanding ; its practical common sense, coupled with its imaginative vision and its confident, and confidence-inspiring, belief. He was accorded the customary courtesy of the House to the maiden venture of a new Member, and Miss Megan Lloyd George, who followed him, declared that Anderson's remarks had made her wish that he had never left the Home Office. The press reported him fully and *The Times* described the speech as 'a notable contribution'. 'My speech went well, I think', he wrote to his father on the following day. 'The House listened very attentively & *The Times* published it in full & makes quite a complimentary reference in a Leader. I am glad it is over. Lloyd George & Churchill both sat through it.' For some, however, the speech seemed rather ponderous and, although the analogy about the elephants in the jungle caused laughter, it also drew from Mr. Churchill the comment of : 'Elephantine platitudes'.

Apart from his formal introduction into the House and his maiden speech, John's arrival on the Back Benches passed almost unnoticed. He chose, more often than not, a seat literally on the back bench, out of the public eye and the centre of debate about the Table. Here, as was his wont, he observed and absorbed the atmosphere and customs of the House until he had developed a comprehensive knowledge of Parliamentary Procedure, which later stood him in good stead when he became a Minister. He was a regular frequenter of the Smoking Room, that innermost sanctum of the House of Commons where almost as much history has been made as on the floor of the Chamber, and gradually his fellow Members came to realize that behind his austere, reserved, 'proconsular' demeanour, John was approachable, kindly and helpful, ready to make available his great experience of men and affairs and his encyclopaedic knowledge to any colleague who had a serious end to pursue, though he was disinclined to unbend to the merely superficial or conversational enquirers. It was not long before he was 'John' or 'Jonathan' to many members, and later both friends and foes spoke of him as 'Jehovah', with differing implication.

---

[1] Anderson's quotation was from *Summum Bonum* (*Asolando*).

(iii)

John Anderson's career in the House of Commons was very nearly terminated before it had well begun.

For some time there had been criticism in public and in Parliament of the management of Imperial Airways and on November 30, 1937, Mr. Chamberlain's Government had appointed a Committee under the Chairmanship of Lord Cadman to enquire into the organization and working of this corporation. The Cadman Report was published on March 8, 1938 — while John was on holiday in Switzerland — and among its primary recommendations was the appointment of a full-time Chairman of Imperial Airways in succession to Sir George Beharrell who, being also Chairman of the Dunlop Rubber Company, had only been on a part-time basis. In accepting the report the Government were naturally anxious to secure a chairman 'whose very appointment would give quietus to the agitation and so take the matter off their agenda'.[1]

John was tentatively approached by the board of Imperial Airways soon after his return from Switzerland with regard to his acceptance of this new position, to which some fairly drastic conditions were attached. It would be necessary, he was informed, in the opinion of the Prime Minister that he should resign all his other directorships and that, while remaining for the present in the House of Commons, he should announce his intention not to stand for re-election at the end of the current Parliament.

Such a decision was for him a very serious matter. His income from directors' fees was about £5000 a year but, though the salary offered as Chairman of I.A. was in the neighbourhood of twice that sum,[2] there was a decided degree of insecurity of tenure inherent in the position. He was, therefore, unwilling to sacrifice all his other

---

[1] Lord Reith, *Into the Wind* (1949), p. 307.

[2] Exhaustive researches have failed to elicit the exact figure of the salary offered to John Anderson on this occasion. However, Lord Reith, who was ultimately appointed to the Chairmanship of I.A., states in his memoirs (p. 314) that, when asked by Sir George Beharrell what salary would be required, 'I said that I was getting £10,000 from the B.B.C. and would not require any increase on that. He [Beharrell] "thought they might be able to go to that figure but no more".' On page 329, Lord Reith goes on to say that he was informed by Sir George Beharrell that 'the board had accepted my conditions'. It is to be presumed, therefore, that the salary offered to John Anderson was not in excess of the same figure.

sources of income. He agreed to give up Vickers and I.C.I. and his insurance company altogether and to resign temporarily from the Midland Bank, but he sought some assurance of the possibility of returning to the board of the Bank in the event of his finding Imperial Airways not to his liking — or that he was not to theirs.

The Midland Bank was prepared to go a considerable way to meet John in this matter but not altogether as far as he would have liked, and it was in a somewhat disgruntled frame of mind that he went to a meeting with the Prime Minister in the first half of April shortly before Easter. It is to be believed that Mr. Chamberlain also was in no easy mood and was not prepared to listen to Anderson's objections. The interview was inconclusive. John agreed to go away and think the matter out in consultation with his friends, and as a result he sent to the Prime Minister on April 28 the following memorandum :

> The Airways appointment was not of my seeking, and did not fit in at all with the plans I had previously mapped out for myself. I was prepared, however, to take the appointment and give my whole heart to it on certain conditions :—
>
> (a) That in the opinion of those most competent to judge, I should be serving the public interest.
> (b) That I could feel assured of the goodwill of all concerned — including the main critics of Imperial Airways.
> (c) That the appointment would not involve abandonment of obligations recently undertaken, except so far as those might be clearly incompatible — as, for example, in the case of my Directorship of Vickers. I would not, of course, undertake any fresh obligations.
>
> I had hoped that it would have been possible to put the whole matter to those whose misgivings led to the recent enquiry, and that, given goodwill, it would not be thought unreasonable to leave the question of outside obligations on the footing that if I was the sort of person that those who favoured my appointment must believe me to be, I could safely be trusted to give up any activity that, in practice, was found to conflict with my paramount obligation to Imperial Airways.
>
> I clearly must accept the view of the Prime Minister (which I know others share), that in the actual circumstances of the case

it is inexpedient that the Chairman of Imperial Airways should hold outside Directorships.

In deliberating with a few of my more intimate friends whether I should be justified, having regard to my family obligations, in making the sacrifice entailed, I have come to this crux, from which I can see no way of escape — that the considerations which are held to weigh so heavily against outside Directorships of any kind, must apply with even greater force to my continuing, even for a limited period, to sit in the House of Commons. I cannot let my constituents down, either by resigning my seat before a General Election, or by neglecting their interests in the meantime. The sacrifice therefore, if made, would probably be made in vain.

(Intd) J. A.

The interpretation placed by Mr. Chamberlain on this paper appears to have been that John was prepared to acquiesce, subject to his reservation about the interests of his constituents, and the Prime Minister hastened to reassure him that he could certainly retain his seat for the life of the current Parliament which had another two and a half years to run before its statutory limitation.

Two days later, however, John sent in a second memorandum (April 30). He had thought over the matter again and had decided not only to safeguard his position still further but to make it clear beyond peradventure. He therefore wrote to the Prime Minister :

I can arrange that other interests (paid or unpaid) shall not, for the next two years, claim more than four hours a week at the outside. For the same period I will, in practice, confine my Parliamentary activities to occasions when Scottish business, or other business of special interest to my constituents, is being transacted. I will resign Vickers as incompatible.

Subject to those conditions I am willing to accept the Chairmanship of Imperial Airways for a period of two years in the first instance ; but I will do so only :—

(a) If H. M. G. are willing to make it clear in Parliament that I have yielded to an urgent representation that I should be serving the public interest by so doing, and

(b) If the main critics can be got to indicate their entire satisfaction with the arrangement.

My position in the House would be impossible if constant sniping were to go on. On the other hand, given goodwill, personal contacts in the House might be an advantage.

(Intd) J. A.

It would seem that in wishing to obtain a clear-cut statement on the part of the Government that he was accepting the Chairmanship of Imperial Airways at their instance, John was planning to insure his position in Parliament and to silence in advance those sharpshooters who might snipe at him. In short, he was not going to subject himself to what he regarded as irresponsible criticism and he made the acceptance of the Chairmanship thus conditional.

This course of action, however, did not commend itself to Mr. Chamberlain. The Prime Minister was not prepared to accord this proposal the dignity of a Government offer when it was no more than an offer from the Board of Imperial Airways made with the Government's support and goodwill ; nor was he disposed to arrange that somebody should go round the House of Commons explaining the situation on John's behalf and silencing criticism in advance. In all this John Anderson had made a poor impression upon the Prime Minister, who decided to advise Imperial Airways to look elsewhere for a Chairman. Their choice eventually fell upon Sir John Reith.

This episode in John's career illustrates the extreme caution which characterized his every action. He would never scruple or haggle over a duty which he recognized, and which should appear to be recognized by others, as being in the service of the State. He was certainly no moral coward and there were many instances in his past career which were eloquent proof of his contempt for, and immunity to, criticism. In this case, it is highly probable that he feared not the critics themselves nor their potential strictures of himself but the degree to which they might hamper him in the execution of an important task.

The financial aspect of the case is also of interest. Like many a man who has made his way in life by his own unaided efforts, John was obsessed with a strong sense of the necessity for financial security. Apart from what he had saved he could depend only upon his pension as a Civil Servant. It was imperative to him that he should have anchors to leeward as a precaution against disaster, and this he had already made clear to Mr. Chamberlain some six months before in refusing the position of High Commissioner for Palestine. If Imperial Airways, with the approval of His Majesty's Government, desired his services he had at least a right to expect that he should not suffer in giving these services to them and that as many obstacles as possible to the effective discharge of his duties should be removed in advance. Had the matter been represented to him, at the instance of the Prime Minister, as a matter of national urgency John's strong sense of public duty would have been touched and quickened, but since Mr. Chamberlain was apparently unprepared to give it this appearance, John was entirely happy, and perhaps not a little relieved, to remain with his directorships and as a private member of the House of Commons — though Fate was not to leave him long thus undisturbed — and, as will be seen later, there were other factors coincidental with these negotiations which may have influenced his final decision.[1]

(iv)

The international situation to which John Anderson returned from Bengal was very different from that which had prevailed at the time of his departure five years earlier. When he sailed from England in March 1932 conditions in Europe were more or less quiescent ; Hitler and the Nazi Party were considered only as a potential threat to the domestic political situation in Germany and public attention and anxiety were more closely focused on the Asiatic scene, where the provocative policy of Japan had begun to manifest itself in aggression against China and in defiance of the League of Nations.

When John returned to England in December 1937, although the measure of Japanese aggression had increased, the whole European situation had suffered a grave deterioration. Hitler had been in power for four years, had completed his domination of the German people and had torn up the Treaty of Versailles and the Pact of Locarno. Italy had conquered Ethiopia and had resorted to the use of poison gas in the process, and both she and Germany had joined Japan in leaving the League of Nations and in forming a

[1] See below, pp. 199-201.

triple alliance of their own. A civil war of a savage nature in Spain had provided the world with its first example of heavy bombing at Guernica. On every hand the edifice of peace was crumbling despite the desperate efforts of British and French statesmen to shore up the cracks by means of concession and appeasement.

Nor was this all. The first four months of Anderson's residence in England after his return had witnessed a serious increase in the tempo of events. On February 20, 1938, Mr. Anthony Eden, unable to concur further in Mr. Chamberlain's policy of appeasement, had resigned as Foreign Secretary, to be succeeded by Lord Halifax. Less than a month later Hitler flung down another challenge to the Powers in his annexation of Austria on March 12, and, even as Mr. Chamberlain and John Anderson were discussing the Chairmanship of Imperial Airways, the Führer had entered upon the first stages of his plans for aggression against his next victim, Czechoslovakia.

Anderson had followed with great interest the course of events from afar and had occasionally commented upon them in his letters to his father from Bengal, but since his return to England and his entry into politics he had been deeply concerned with their development. His interest naturally centred upon the problem of civil defence with which he had been so actively associated during his years at the Home Office. The Anderson Committee of 1924 [1] had laid sound foundations upon which others had built in the years which followed. A Committee under the chairmanship of Sir Warren Fisher had carried the planning for Air Raid Precautions a stage further in the light of modern developments and of the increased scale of potential attack which became evident with the progress of the Spanish civil war, and, as a result of their consideration in July 1937 of the Fisher Committee's report, Mr. Chamberlain's Government had introduced an A.R.P. Bill into the House of Commons in November to give effect to its recommendations. The Bill received the Royal Assent on December 22, and came into force on January 1, 1938.

The new Act did not itself enter into details of the schemes which it authorized and, as the Home Secretary, Sir Samuel Hoare, remarked during the debate : 'As soon as the Bill has passed we

[1] See above, p. 96.

have to start a new chapter in which the Government and the local authorities and the citizens in this country will all co-operate to make a much more comprehensive plan of air raid precautions than anything that we have contemplated during the last few years.'[1]

The evolution of so comprehensive a plan, however, required time — a commodity of which the Western Powers, if they had only realized it, were in desperately short supply — and of this John Anderson was himself only too well aware. 'It will be another year at least before our defence preparations are anything like adequate', he wrote to his father on April 26, 1938. It can have been no source of surprise — though of some gratification — to him, therefore, to be invited by Sir Samuel Hoare to take some important part in the new organization.

The first approach was made in personal conversation on April 25 at the Home Secretary's house in Chester Square and John, though, as ever, 'canny', was sufficiently forthcoming for Hoare to follow up two days later with a definite proposal :

27th April, 1938

DEAR ANDERSON,

I am writing in continuation of the talk that we had at Chester Square on Monday evening. I gathered from it, I hope rightly, that you were not disinclined to help with the very difficult problems of A.R.P. If this is so, could I persuade you to make an Inquiry into the question of evacuation ? Hitherto, the question has been mainly considered by Departmental experts and Staff Officers. I have, however, had the feeling that however excellent may be technical views, the problem is to a large extent political. This being so, I am very anxious to have it surveyed from a broader angle. Supposing that you were kind enough to undertake the investigation, I would of course put at your disposal the experts of the A.R.P. Department and I am inclined to think that it might be useful to associate with you two members of the back bench A.R.P. Committees presided over by Simmonds[2] and Haden Guest.[3] I am most anxious to keep these Committees

[1] *House of Commons Debates*, November 15, 1937. Col. 43.
[2] Sir Oliver Simmonds, Conservative Member of Parliament for the Duddeston Division of Birmingham, 1931–1945 ; President of the Air Raid Protection Institute.
[3] Dr. Leslie Haden Guest sat as a Labour Member of Parliament for North Southwark, 1923–1927, and North Islington, 1937–1945. He was created a Baron in 1950.

on a basis of co-operation rather than to allow them to drift into opposition. It seems to me therefore that from the parliamentary point of view there would be a considerable advantage in bringing them into the Inquiry. If, however, you would prefer not to have their representatives, I would of course agree with your view.

Eady [1] also suggests adding to the Inquiry Game [2] and Gater,[3] the very able Clerk of the L.C.C. I am rather inclined to leave these two as experts whose opinions you would obtain during the investigation. There is a good deal to be said for keeping the investigation either to you alone or to a small parliamentary body. I should indeed be glad if you were able to accept this invitation.

Yours ever

(Sgd) SAMUEL HOARE.

If you would like to talk over the question, I am always at your disposition.

It is of interest to revert briefly here to the matter of the Chairmanship of Imperial Airways. John Anderson would have received Hoare's letter on April 28, the day on which he wrote his first memorandum to the Prime Minister.[4] He was at that moment, therefore, considering the (to him) somewhat unalluring prospect of accepting the chairmanship, resigning his directorships and losing his seat at the end of the current Parliament. It is very probable that the work involved in Sir Samuel Hoare's proposal would have seemed at once more attractive and of more immediate national importance. He certainly could not do both jobs, for the emphasis had been laid on the need for a whole-time Chairman of I.A. It may well be, therefore, that Hoare's suggestion, which was apparently made without the knowledge of the Prime Minister and in ignorance of the I.A. negotiations in which Anderson was engaged, may have influenced John in the composition of his second memorandum to Mr. Chamberlain of April 30,[5] as a result of which

---

[1] Sir Wilfrid Eady, G.C.M.G., K.C.B., K.B.E. Deputy Under-Secretary of State, Home Office, in charge of Air Raid Precautions, 1938–1940.

[2] Air Vice-Marshal Sir Philip Game, G.C.B., G.C.V.O., G.B.E., K.C.M.G., Governor of New South Wales, 1930–1935 ; Commissioner of Metropolitan Police, 1935–1945.

[3] Sir George Gater, G.C.M.G., K.C.B., D.S.O. Clerk of the London County Council, 1933–1939 ; Permanent Under-Secretary for the Colonies, 1939–1947, and Permanent Secretary to the Ministry of Home Security, 1939–1942.

[4] See above, p. 194.   [5] See above, p. 195.

the Prime Minister decided to advise Imperial Airways to look elsewhere for a Chairman. That there was doubt in John's mind in considering the Home Secretary's letter is indicated by the fact that he marked it in pencil 'Pending 29/4/38'.

In the event he accepted the task which Sir Samuel Hoare had offered him, preferring not to conduct the enquiry alone but to be associated with other prominent back benchers whose interest and experience would be of value. The appointment of the Committee was announced on May 24, and point was given to the announcement by the fact that it was made on the morrow of the first Czech Crisis of May 21, when, as a result of rumoured German troop concentration on the Czechoslovak frontier, the British, French and Soviet Governments made strong representations in Berlin.

In addition to John, the Committee consisted of Sir Percy Harris, Liberal M.P. for South-West Bethnal Green; Lieut.-Colonel George Doland, Conservative M.P. for Balham and Tooting; and Dr. Haden Guest; with Mr. Alexander Johnston of the Home Office as Secretary.[1] Their terms of reference were stated to be the consideration of 'various aspects of the problem of transferring persons from areas which are likely to be exposed to continuous air attack, including the plans said to be in contemplation in other countries', and to prepare plans accordingly.

John threw himself into this new work with all the wealth of his great energy and powers of concentration. He drove himself and he drove his Committee, for to him at least it was apparent that time was of the essence. 'My work on Air Raid Precautions is taking up a great deal of my time here', he wrote to his father on July 4. 'We hope to make our first report before the Parliamentary recess starts at the end of this month'; and again, on August 1, 'I've been hard at it. I was determined that the Report of my Committee on Evacuation should be presented before Parliament adjourned & we just managed it.'

They were certainly not idle. In the space of eight weeks the Committee held twenty-five meetings and examined fifty-seven independent witnesses, as well as representatives from twenty-six

---

[1] Now Sir Alexander Johnston, G.C.B., K.B.E., Chairman of the Board of Inland Revenue.

governmental and private organizations. Nor did this exhaust their activities.

One member of the Committee had persistently urged that they should all make a survey flight over London. John thought but little of the idea but, when the issue was forced, he accepted it. The two other members of the Committee 'contracted out', saying that when they had agreed to serve they had not considered it necessary to go up in an aeroplane. Whereupon John said that he and his persistent colleague and the Secretary would go. On the appointed day they met at the airfield and John, still with the aura of the Governor of Bengal about him, enquired for the Air Council plane. He was shown an aircraft almost completely dismantled in a corner of the field and it was indicated to him that their flight was to be made in an elderly machine of uncertain appearance. In this they embarked with some trepidation and John in a royal temper. Scarcely were they airborne when John's colleague, who had been so enthusiastic an instigator of the excursion, succumbed to air-sickness and demanded to be put down. 'No', replied John Anderson grimly. 'You have persistently asked for this flight and you shall have it.' They proceeded with their aerial survey and, in due course, returned to earth, John's colleague in a state of semi-collapse. Impassively John Anderson remarked : 'Our Secretary at least seems to have benefited by his breath of fresh air.'

'I forgot to mention that, as you may have seen in the papers or heard on the wireless, I went up in an aeroplane with another member of the Committee on Saturday to have a look at London & especially some of the congested areas from the air', was John's comment to his father on this incident. 'It was very interesting — particularly to see the amount of open space even in the slums.'

The report which the Anderson Committee submitted to the Home Secretary on July 26 was a clear-cut basic document.[1] Their main conclusion was that, in the event of war, the evacuation of the *bouches inutiles* from the densely populated industrial areas was highly desirable, and that arrangements should be made for their accommodation in safer parts of the country. As a corollary to this, however, they were of the opinion that, since a wholesale evacuation of the main industrial centres in this country would

[1] *Report of Committee on Evacuation*, 1938. Cmd. 5837.

cripple the nation's war effort, there must be some clear guidance from the Government as to who should stay and who should go. They indicated the advisability of compiling a national register in time of peace to aid in such a decision.

In presenting the Anderson Report to Parliament Sir Samuel Hoare declared that the Government accepted its main principles and laid particular emphasis upon its five main points. First, that except in so far as it might be necessary for military or other special reasons to require persons to leave some limited area, evacuation should not be compulsory ; secondly, that, in order to support the national war effort and the supply of essential civilian needs, production in the large industrial towns must be maintained, but that it was desirable to provide organized evacuation facilities for substantial numbers of persons from certain industrial areas ; thirdly, that arrangements for the reception of evacuees should be mainly on the basis of compulsory billeting in private houses, special care being taken to avoid unnecessary hardship either to the evacuees or to their hosts ; fourthly, that the initial cost of evacuation should be borne by the Government but that those evacuees who could afford to contribute something towards the cost of their maintenance should be expected to do so ; and fifthly, that, in cases where parents wished to send their children away but could not make their own arrangements for so doing, special arrangements should be made for schoolchildren to be moved out in groups from their schools in charge of their teachers.[1]

'Here, at last', the official historian has written, 'after many years of study and postponed Ministerial decision, were the firm outlines of the scheme which became effective in September 1939. There were still many details to be settled, and a vast amount of operational planning to be done, but the basic principles were now firmly established.'[2]

The Anderson Report concluded with the warning : 'The whole issue in any future war may well turn on the manner in which the problem of evacuation from densely populated industrial areas is handled . . . the task appears to us to be one of great urgency.'

[1] *House of Commons Debates*, July 28, 1938. Col. 3283.
[2] Professor Richard M. Titmuss, *Problems of Social Policy*, History of the Second World War, United Kingdom Civil Service (1950), p. 28.

It was in this impelling spirit of conscious need for urgency that John had conducted the whole of the business of the Committee. They had skimped nothing ; they had explored all possible sources of information, but both he and they had been painfully and terribly aware, with an eye to the steady deterioration of the European situation, that the grains of sand might well be running out in the glass.

And were they not justified ? In the two months which elapsed between the appointment of the Anderson Committee and the presentation of their Report, it had become patent to all but the wilfully myopic that Hitler had major designs of aggression upon Czechoslovakia. Yet at the same moment that Sir Samuel Hoare was presenting the Committee's Report to Parliament, Mr. Chamberlain was dispatching Lord Runciman's Mission to Prague in an attempt to wring from the unfortunate President Beneš a further measure of concession which, it was fondly hoped, would satisfy the Führer's claims. The hopes and expectations reposed in the success of the Runciman Mission exercised a paralysing influence upon Whitehall, upon which descended a curious *malaise* of inactivity in the face of manifestly approaching peril.

It was not until the Runciman Mission had failed and the German Chancellor had trumpeted abroad his intention to occupy the Sudetenland by force, that Mr. Chamberlain awoke to the full seriousness of the situation and resorted to his now famous series of personal negotiations with Hitler. It was not until the date of the Prime Minister's flight to Berchtesgaden on September 15, that the Report of the Anderson Committee was submitted to the Committee of Imperial Defence.

Even when considered and adopted the Report remained a secret document. It had originally been intended that it should be published immediately and that John on September 15 should broadcast for the B.B.C. on its recommendations. He interrupted his summer holiday at Grantown-on-Spey, where he had gone with Alastair and Mary, to return to London for this purpose, but on his arrival on the 14th he received a letter from Broadcasting House returning his script with the information that the Home Office had cancelled the broadcast. This was a part of the general policy of the Government not to alarm the British people unduly. It was in direct contradiction to the principle of the Report that its success depended on the overwhelming support of public opinion. The Report was not published until October 27 when Mr. Chamberlain's achievement at Munich was deemed to have brought 'Peace with honour'.

Full-time planners for the evacuation were only appointed on the very eve of the Munich Crisis. Of the three senior officials appointed to run the evacuation section of the Home Office, one did not start work until September 5, the second on the 12th and the third on the 23rd. In the two months between the completion of the Anderson Report and the Munich Crisis, overworked permanent staffs at the Home Office did their *ad hoc* best to translate the principles of the Report into concrete planning. Such plans were inevitably incomplete and it was perhaps as well that they were never put to the test.[1] In effect they very nearly were, for the Home Secretary had given instructions for them to be put into operation on September 30 and had then left for a week-end at Cromer. Home Office officials had to intercept him *en route* in order to obtain cancellation of the order.

In the meanwhile John had been recalled to temporary active duty in his old Department, the Home Office. The Munich Crisis had found Britain completely unorganized for war on the home front and, in default of any other plan, it was decided by the Cabinet to fall back upon that same Civilian Emergency Organization which John Anderson had operated with such conspicuous success and efficiency at the time of the General Strike. Bearing in mind the lessons of the past, the C.E.O. had been kept in being and now lay ready to hand. The urgency prevailing, however, 'allowed of no more than modernization of the chief features of this scheme and their incorporation, under the title of "Civil Defence Emergency Scheme Y", in the internal mechanism of official action to be taken in transforming the nation from a state of peace into a state of war'.[2] Under 'Scheme Y' Regional Commissioners were appointed with the responsibility for passive defence if war broke out. Their actual powers were only defined in brief general terms. They were to act as the representatives of His Majesty's Government in their

[1] Titmuss (*op. cit.*), p. 29.
[2] Terence H. O'Brien, *Civil Defence*, History of the Second World War, United Kingdom Civil Service (1955), p. 154.

regions and their functions were chiefly to operate as chairmen of regional committees, with responsibility mainly for co-ordination. The description applied by one of them to himself as 'the head of a breakdown gang ready to ensure the smooth working of the administrative machine during abnormal conditions' reflected accurately enough the spirit in which the organization was set up.[1]

'Scheme Y' became nominally operative on September 15 and under it John Anderson was appointed Commissioner for the London and Home Counties (No. 5) Region, so that instead of broadcasting to the nation on the recommendations of the Report of his Committee, he found himself installed in New Scotland Yard, with Sir Harold Scott, later Commissioner of Metropolitan Police, as his Principal Officer and Sir George Gater as Chief A.R.P. Officer. His area covered the Metropolitan Police District, the City of London, and the remainder of the counties of Essex, Hertfordshire, Surrey and Kent.

The return of Mr. Chamberlain from Godesberg on September 24, baffled in his efforts to deter Hitler from his intention to invade Czechoslovakia, caused the immediate intensification of defence measures. A week of feverish activity followed. John and his officers wrestled desperately with problems for which a solution should have been found much earlier but which had been tacitly ignored in the general reluctance to think of war as a possibility and by local refusal or inability to incur expenditure. Now, under the threat of imminent peril, everything had to be done at the last minute.

> Cellars and basements were requisitioned as air raid shelters [writes Sir Harold Scott], trenches were dug in the parks, schoolchildren and hospital patients were evacuated and volunteers fitted gas-masks to endless queues of people.[2] The A.R.P. services were suddenly besieged by applicants for duty, and training officers did their best to meet the sudden change of public mood from apathy to enthusiasm. . . . If air attack had come in that autumn of 1938 it would have found us very unprepared.[3]

[1] Terence H. O'Brien, *Civil Defence*, History of the Second World War, United Kingdom Civil Service (1955), p. 157.

[2] For example, 1200 nursery children and 3100 physically defective children were evacuated by the L.C.C. on September 28 (Titmuss (*op. cit.*), p. 29, f.n. 4).

[3] Scott (*op. cit.*), pp. 106-107.

On September 30, however, Mr. Chamberlain flew back from Munich and on his arrival at Heston waved his sheet of notepaper with Hitler's assurance that the agreement signed was 'symbolic of the desire of our two peoples never to go to war with one another again'. It was 'peace with honour', it was 'peace for our time'. The London Region came to an end and John Anderson wrote sorrowfully to his father : 'We can only trust that we shall not have to face the like again . . . a big national effort is called for if we are to avoid humiliation and possibly worse in the future.'

(v)

The first nine months of John Anderson's resumed residence in England — that is to say, from his arrival in mid-December 1937 to the Munich Crisis in mid-September 1938 — had been full of event and movement, of alarums and excursions. High honours had been bestowed on him. He had successfully fought a by-election and had made his maiden speech in the House of Commons. There had been the affair of the Imperial Airways Chairmanship, to be followed by two months' intensive labour on the Evacuation Committee. Over and above these events the storm-clouds of the international situation had gathered and darkened, culminating for John in the two weeks' feverish activity as Regional Commissioner for London. It had certainly not been a quiescent period.

In addition to being plunged into the world of politics and affairs of State, John had also led an active social life. There were dinners and banquets at which he was either the guest of honour or a principal speaker. He played golf with the Willingdons and dined with the Abercorns. Those great and tireless London hostesses, Lady Colefax, Lady Cunard and Mrs. Ronnie Greville, were delighted to entertain the 'Tiger of Bengal', and he was a not infrequent guest at week-end house parties.

All these things John chronicled for his father, to whom he wrote as sedulously from London as he had from India, and whom he visited in Edinburgh as often as his busy life permitted.

The train got in twenty minutes late on Sunday morning [he wrote on June 16, after a visit to Edinburgh]. I had to leave again after two hours to spend a couple of days with Lady Byng [1] at her house at Thorpe, near Clacton-on-Sea. The other guests were Queen Mary, Princess Alice & her husband, Lord Athlone, Sir Reginald Poole (Senior partner in George Lewis & Co., Solicitors) & a young man called Hodgson who used to be Private-Secretary to the present King when he was Duke of York. We were therefore quite a small party & it was an interesting experience. I sat next the Queen at dinner on Sunday & at lunch on Monday. Everything was entirely informal. . . . The Queen was in good spirits and made herself most agreeable.

Despite this fascinating whirl of social life, John's heart was turning more and more towards the idea of a house in the country. The house in Bayswater was not really to his liking and, though he rode in the Park with his daughter Mary, this was far from being his favourite form of exercise. Moreover, though he was not by nature essentially a countryman, he longed for a garden where his great horticultural interests and knowledge could find expression.

I expect to have a little more free time now [he wrote to his father in August, after the completion of his Evacuation Report] & shall have to occupy it in trying to find a permanent abode. It is not going to be very easy to get just what I want. I must be in London for the greater part of the week ; at the same time I feel the want of fresh air and a garden. So it may mean a small service flat & a house 15 or 20 miles out — that is to say, if I can afford it.

With Mary and Nellie Mackenzie, and Alastair when he could spare time from his work at St. Thomas's, John employed his brief leisure that summer in house hunting. His natural inclination was towards the North Downs and he had nearly purchased a property there when, 'quite by accident' — as he wrote to his father — 'I learnt of a project for a by-pass road which is cut right across the immediate foreground'. When the Andersons left for their summer holiday at Grantown-on-Spey at the beginning of September their search was still unrequited. That holiday was interrupted by the Munich Crisis and it was not until early in October that the quest could be resumed. Finally John's choice settled upon a

[1] The widow of Field-Marshal Viscount Byng of Vimy, G.C.B., G.C.M.G., who had been Governor-General of Canada, 1921–1926, and Commissioner of Metropolitan Police, 1928–1931, while John Anderson had been Permanent Under-Secretary at the Home Office.

property of some ten acres called 'Picket Wood', adjacent to the little town of Merstham in Surrey. The negotiations of sale were completed by the beginning of December and the Anderson *ménage* took possession early in the new year.

'Picket Wood' itself was a big rambling comfortable house built in 1911. Along its south front ran a terrace from which the ground sloped sharply. There were a summer-house and flower beds, a large rose garden bordered with yew hedges and a pleasant lawn. Roses draped the balustrade of the terrace and wistaria mantled one end of the house. On the wooded slope some magnificent beeches, one at least over two hundred years old, gave dignity and beauty, and in the front of the house stood a noble ash tree. From the terrace and the windows on the south side a magnificent view unrolled across woods, farm lands and meadows to the North Downs.

John was delighted with it and his pleasure increased with the approach of spring. 'I am sure that the place is going to suit our requirements even better than I had thought', he wrote to his father in February; and, three months later : 'There has been much progress in vegetation & most of the trees are now in full leaf. The ash, of which we have a few large specimens, is the main exception. The daffodils are practically finished & tulips are now coming on. I heard a nightingale from my bedroom window the other night. There are quite a lot round here, I believe, & no doubt as the weather grows warmer we may hear more of them.'

But, even as John Anderson became master of 'Picket Wood', a further turn of the wheel of Fate had opened up for him a new field of service to the country — he had joined the Cabinet.

P

VII

Cabinet Minister : Civil Defence
1938–1940

(i)

'YOU have everything in your own hands now — for a
time — and you can do anything you like. Use that time
well, for it won't last', had been Lord Baldwin's advice
to Mr. Chamberlain in congratulating him on his return from
Munich,[1] and it is true that, in certain respects, the Prime Minister
took this advice to heart. He had received other wise counsel as
well. Driving back to London from Heston on that great and
exalted afternoon of September 30, Lord Halifax had made two
important suggestions to Mr. Chamberlain — one negative, the
other positive ; first, that, if pressed by the Conservative Central
Office to exploit his present overwhelming popularity to have a
'snap' General Election, he should refuse ; and secondly, that he
should now take the action he had intended to take should war have
come and reconstitute his Cabinet as a truly National Government
by bringing into it such outstanding Conservative figures as Mr.
Winston Churchill, Mr. Anthony Eden and Lord Cranborne, and
also Leaders of the Labour and Liberal Parties if they would consent
to join.[2]

The Prime Minister accepted the first of these points of guidance
at once, but postponed decision on the other until he had had time
for further thought. In effect he was faced at once with the first
grave difficulty in interpreting his Munich Policy which, while it
was claimed to have achieved 'Peace for our time', also contained
a pledge of rearming and overhauling the national defences. To
bring the 'Warmongers' of the Conservative Party into his Govern-

---

[1] Sir Keith Feiling, *The Life of Neville Chamberlain* (1946), p. 382.
[2] The Earl of Halifax, *Fulness of Days* (1957), pp. 199–200.

ment might, he thought, be tantamount to indicating that he doubted the good faith of Adolf Hitler's signature on the Anglo-German Declaration of Friendship, and he felt little enthusiasm in contemplating the inclusion of Labour and Liberal colleagues.

Mr. Chamberlain discussed this grave issue with King George VI on October 19 and the record of their conversation shows that they agreed that 'as regards reconstruction of the Cabinet on a broader basis, the Opposition might help in producing armaments, but would criticize the P.M.'s foreign policy as being a paradox to [the] rearmament programme. The Opposition would be kept fully informed, in confidence, of what policy the Government were pursuing.' [1] As a result, the only effort made by the Prime Minister to broaden his Cabinet on a national basis was to invite the veteran Liberal leader Lord Samuel on October 25 to become Lord Privy Seal. The offer was declined. [2]

The Prime Minister did make some Cabinet changes, however. His close friend Lord Stanhope became First Lord of the Admiralty in the place of Mr. Duff Cooper who had resigned in protest over the Munich Agreement and, as Mr. Chamberlain considered Lord Hailsham's health was too frail for him to continue as Lord President of the Council, he asked him to resign to make room for Lord Runciman. [3] Neither of these appointments was held by the country at large to have enhanced the Cabinet's distinction. The spell of Munich was already beginning to wear a little thin and popular anxiety about civil defence generally had been aroused during the crisis. The demand was voiced that someone of authority and experience should be placed in control of this vital aspect of the national defence, and this became intensified after the considerable alarm occasioned by the statement of a prominent A.R.P. official towards the end of October : 'We are not prepared ; we have hardly begun to prepare ; we do not know how all the failures that occurred during the crisis can be avoided next time'.

This public demand became rapidly identified with the name of John Anderson, and his appointment began to be canvassed both in public and private. In the course of a seven-point minute to Sir

[1] Sir John Wheeler-Bennett, *King George VI, His Life and Reign* (1958), p. 358.
[2] *Memoirs of the Rt. Hon. Viscount Samuel* (1943), pp. 278-279.
[3] Feiling (*op. cit.*), p. 386.

Warren Fisher, that inveterate chronicler and gossip Tom Jones, formerly Deputy Secretary of the Cabinet, wrote as follows :

> 5. Can't you make use in Cabinet of Chatfield [1] and John Anderson ? It is the executive that needs strengthening.
> 6. If Anderson took Inskip's job, could P. J. Grigg take Arthur Robinson's ? [2]
>
> *Pro patria.*
>
> A. R.   born 1874
> P. J. G.   ,,   1890.[3]

Within the Cabinet itself Sir Samuel Hoare and others urged the Prime Minister to appoint John Anderson to the still vacant office of Lord Privy Seal, which Lord Samuel had refused, with special authority over Civil Defence.

Meantime the Report of the Anderson Committee on Evacuation was published on October 27 and was on the whole well received by the press, the general impression being fairly epitomized by *The Economist*, which stated : 'The Committee have done a good job of work, but it ought scarcely to have taken two years for the Government to find itself in agreement with its many and sincere critics who urged the need for evacuation plans long ago.' [4] The popular reaction to the publication of the Anderson Report was to quicken the growing belief that John Anderson should be called upon to implement it.

It cannot have been easy for Mr. Chamberlain to entertain this idea. His relations with Anderson hitherto had not been of the most halcyon. He had been irked at John's refusal to go as High Commissioner to Palestine and the episode of the Chairmanship of Imperial Airways was not six months old. Nor had John made any secret of his view that Munich was more of a humiliation than a triumph, though he voted with the Government in the historic divisions of October 6. But something had manifestly to be done

---

[1] Admiral of the Fleet Lord Chatfield had been First Sea Lord and Chief of the Naval Staff from 1933 to 1938. He entered the Cabinet in 1939 as Minister for Co-ordination of Defence, in succession to Sir Thomas Inskip (who had held the office since 1936), with a seat in the War Cabinet later.

[2] Sir Arthur Robinson, G.C.B., C.B.E. (1874–1950), was Chairman of the Supply Board of the Committee of Imperial Defence and Secretary of the Ministry of Supply.

[3] Thomas Jones, C.H., *A Diary with Letters, 1931–1950* (1954), pp. 412–413.

[4] *The Economist*, October 29, 1938.

about A.R.P. and Anderson was clearly the man to do it. Any real reluctance which the Prime Minister may have felt was finally overborne and by October 30 Tom Jones could write to Abraham Flexner, the Director of the Institute for Advanced Study at Princeton University : 'The likelihood is that John Anderson will be made Lord Privy Seal and given the job to organize voluntary service against air attack'.[1]

It is a not uninteresting commentary on the security surrounding Cabinet appointments at this time that someone outside the official circles — even one so intimately informed as Tom Jones — should be (a) in possession of the knowledge of John's pending entry into the Government and (b), writing from Blickling, Lord Lothian's house in Norfolk, should pass on this information to a citizen of a foreign country, however well disposed to Britain that individual might be. For, on October 30 — the date of 'T.J.'s' letter to Dr. Flexner — John Anderson was himself writing to his father :

. . . there is, I fear, a definite prospect of my being invited to enter the Cabinet. The matter is, of course, most strictly confidential until the public announcement appears — perhaps early next week — but approach has been made to me & I thought you should know now what is in the wind as there will probably be no interval after the matter becomes definite before it is announced. The idea seems to be that I should be Lord Privy Seal, with special responsibility for Civil Defence & national voluntary organizations.

It is rather a depressing prospect & knocks all my own plans for my future edgeways but in these critical times I could not bring myself — with a long record of public service behind me — to refuse to answer a call from the head of the Government.

Well, there it is. I shall have to make the best of things. On the other hand it may not come off after all, in which case I can go on my way rejoicing.

My directorships will, of course, all have to be given up & the future will have to take care of itself.

The matter did, in fact, become definite within the next twenty-four hours and Mr. Chamberlain informed his Cabinet colleagues on October 31 that he had invited John Anderson to become Lord

---

[1] Jones (*op. cit.*), p. 418.

Privy Seal and to assume the far-reaching duties of supervising the A.R.P. Department of the Home Office, together with the planning of a system of national voluntary service. He would preside over a committee of Ministers whose Departments were 'specially concerned with the Home Front' which was to plan and co-ordinate all civil defence measures, and also over a committee of the Permanent Heads of these Departments. In the event of war the new Ministerial Committee would be merged in a 'Standing Council of Home Security'.[1] In explaining these new arrangements to the House of Commons next day, the Prime Minister said that A.R.P. had 'assumed such gigantic proportions and developed such complexity' that it was now too great a burden for the Home Office, and he called the new Minister, John Anderson, the 'Minister for Civilian Defence'.[2]

The announcement was well received by the press and the editor of *The Times* gave expression to the general satisfaction :

> Sir John Anderson is not in his first youth, and his appointment does not affect the basis of the Government from the party point of view but there will be no jealousy or criticism that he should find himself in the Cabinet at this early stage of his parliamentary life and in charge of a task of which the whole country recognizes the magnitude. He may be a newcomer to the House of Commons, but he is not strange to public administration. . . . Whitehall, no less than Ireland and India, can testify to both his capacity for organization and to his steadiness and courage. That he will need all these qualities is not to be doubted by anyone who realizes the intense anxiety of the whole country for the kind of civilian organization which the recent crisis found so essential to a sense of security at home, and therefore to firm handling abroad, and so largely lacking hitherto.[3]

The task which Anderson was now called upon to perform was a very necessary, but far from easy, one. It required a degree of blended tact and ruthlessness which he was well equipped to provide, and his administrative mind was quick to perceive the essentials of the situation. Much criticism has been levelled against the authorities for the confusion in Civil Defence which existed at the time of

[1] O'Brien (*op. cit.*), pp. 166-167.
[2] *House of Commons Debates*, November 1, 1938. Cols. 83-85.
[3] *The Times*, November 1, 1938.

Munich. Some of these strictures are justified but there were certain difficulties inherent in the situation which must be understood if it is to be fully appreciated. Civil Defence represented a new departure in the life of Britain and neither the British people nor the functional organism of the country adapt themselves easily to innovations in time of peace, though in war-time they are assimilated with remarkable ease and celerity.

The organizational dilemma of Civil Defence was one of planning for war in time of peace. It was, in fact, a generic term for certain activities which in war are carried on by a number of civil Departments. Then, on the outbreak of hostilities, the Ministry of Transport, the Ministry of Local Government and the Public Assistance Board become jointly responsible for evacuation ; hospitals and ambulances become the responsibility of the Ministry of Health ; the maintenance of public utilities rests with the Ministries of Transport and Power ; and many of these responsibilities are exercised separately in respect of Scotland. In time of peace, however, it is natural that these Departments should be preoccupied with their normal day-to-day duties and both Ministers and senior officials become inevitably immersed in the complexities of current problems. Planning for hypothetical wartime conditions is apt, therefore, to lag behind.

Yet because executive responsibility was dispersed through a number of Departments the need for co-ordination became the more imperative, and this was recognized in the early thirties when the Air Raid Precautions Department was constituted as a branch of the Home Office, with the duty of making a study of the 'passive' defence of the civilian population against air attack and preparing plans accordingly. This was a step in the right direction but, because of the dispersed responsibility in time of war, the A.R.P. Department was in effect making plans which would have to be executed by others whose knowledge and experience had not been tapped in their formulation.

When Anderson assumed ministerial charge of Civil Defence in November 1938, this situation was already giving rise to a good deal of friction. Under the impact of the prolonged crisis of that summer, with its close proximity to war, the Departments concerned were becoming increasingly interested in the tasks which would fall to them in the event of hostilities. As a result of this newborn interest they expressed scepticism about the assumptions on which the A.R.P. Department had been working and were critical of many of the features of the plans proposed. Anderson saw at once the necessity for bringing the Departments concerned into active participation in these wartime preparations. No further advantage could be gained by the continuance of the A.R.P. Department as the sole planning agency. The time had come for dividing up these responsibilities between those Departments which would ultimately become answerable for the operation of the plans prepared. Now, after Munich, they could be trusted not to neglect or delay the fulfilment of the work already begun and would bring to its completion the full benefit of their knowledge and experience.

To this end, therefore, he took certain immediate decisions. The A.R.P. Department was directed to confine itself to the functions for which they would have executive responsibility in time of war — the organization of the Wardens and Rescue Services, the Air Raid Warning System and the Blackout — while the other Departments assumed the planning for their own wartime responsibility. There remained the problem of co-ordination. His long years in Whitehall had taught Jonathan that whatever might be achieved by 'overlords' at the ministerial level no Department could succeed, at the official level, in co-ordinating the work of other Departments. He therefore wisely decided to have a small but separate staff to help him with this delicate task, and that the A.R.P. Department, though he was its Minister, would stand in exactly the same relation to this body as did the other Departments concerned.

In assembling this 'civil general staff', John made full use of his intimate knowledge of Whitehall personalities. He chose as his chief of staff Sir Thomas Gardiner,[1] the Director-General of the Post Office, whom he had known since they were undergraduates together at Edinburgh University, and who possessed wide departmental experience of how to run a large dispersed executive organization. Gardiner was well known and well trusted by his equals in Whitehall, and respected, and sometimes feared, by his subordinates.

John also selected from among the younger generation two men

---

[1] Sir Thomas Robert Gardiner, G.C.B., G.B.E., Director-General of the Post Office, 1936–1945, seconded as Secretary of Ministry of Home Security, 1939–1940.

whom he had marked out, when Head of the Home Office, as possessing both ability and promise — Norman Brook and Alexander Johnston. Brook [1] was to remain with him until in the spring of 1943 he was appointed Deputy Secretary (Civil) of the War Cabinet. Johnston, who had already served with Anderson on the Evacuation Committee, brought to him now the detailed knowledge of Civil Defence which he had gained in the Planning Section of the A.R.P. Department.

His general staff also helped John with the National Service side of his duties — the recruitment of volunteers for all the varied forms of civilian war service which were then being planned. For this work he borrowed a Principal Secretary from the Ministry of Education — R. S. Wood [2] — who soon proved to be a tower of strength in planning the recruiting campaign and organizing both speakers and speeches at meetings throughout the country, and also E. W. Barltrop [3] from the Ministry of Labour.

It was now that a voice from his past in Dublin Castle sounded again in John's ear. The picturesque figure of Andy Cope emerged from retirement and offered his voluntary services to his old chief. He was allowed to come and see what he could find to do, and at once threw himself with unorganized enthusiasm into the work of arranging recruiting meetings. Arriving on a cold November day, he literally took off his coat and set to work in his shirt sleeves to demonstrate his keenness for the task.

For Anderson it was a novel experience to be dealing with Ministers as colleagues and equals. He had to learn a new technique, and he was a little time in learning it. At first his manner was somewhat stiff and didactic. Accustomed by his earlier experience to give advice (and to expect it to be accepted) he had a tendency to deal too exhaustively with the subject in hand : every aspect was covered, and every sentence was finished. In these early days there

[1] Rt. Hon. Sir Norman Brook, G.C.B., Secretary to the Cabinet since 1947, Joint Permanent Secretary of the Treasury and Head of the Civil Service since 1956.

[2] Sir Robert Stanford Wood, K.B.E., C.B., served as Principal Assistant Secretary at the Ministry of Education, 1936–1940, and Deputy Secretary, 1940–1946. In 1946 he was appointed Principal of University College, Southampton, and became the first Vice-Chancellor of Southampton University in 1952.

[3] Mr. Ernest William Barltrop, C.M.G., C.B.E., D.S.O., became Regional Controller successively for Birmingham and Leeds and in 1947 was appointed Labour Adviser to the Secretary of State for the Colonies.

were even some occasions when he had recourse to an admonitory wagging of the forefinger. This attitude, if it had been continued, would have been resented. His colleagues would certainly not have liked to feel that they were being lectured by this apparently omniscient man. But, as the weeks passed and he settled into his new surroundings, his manner became more relaxed and easy and he acquired a lighter touch. Moreover, as his ability and performance became increasingly apparent to his colleagues, their respect for him grew. Among the small group of Ministers concerned with Civil Defence, with whom his personal contacts were at this stage more constant and intimate, there soon developed feelings of real affection for the new Lord Privy Seal. Among this group he came to be known, fondly, as 'The Seal'; and his room at the Home Office, in which they met at increasingly frequent intervals to discuss their problems, was known among them as 'The Tank'. As time went on, the younger members of this group — men like Euan Wallace and Malcolm MacDonald — turned increasingly to him for advice on their Ministerial problems. They came to know that they could always rely on him for a patient hearing of their difficulties and, at the end, wise and disinterested counsel. These were the foundations on which he built, as the years went on, the position of weight and influence among Ministers which enabled him, in the middle years of the war, to discharge with such outstanding success the co-ordinating rôle which he exercised as Lord President.

A.R.P. received its extended charter in the Civil Defence Bill, which conferred considerably greater peacetime powers upon both the Government and the local authorities. The Bill was introduced by Anderson into the House of Commons on March 23, 1939, and, as a result of the 'agonizing reappraisal' which followed Hitler's occupation of Prague on March 16, its passage through both Houses of Parliament was greatly accelerated. It received the Royal Assent on July 13.

John had piloted the Bill through the House of Commons with notable skill and felicity, and in its later stages he was indefatigable.

In the last three days I have spent no less than 22 hours on the front bench & have made dozens of speeches short & long — he wrote to his father on June 15 — but as the upshot is that I have got my bill through with great good will & also my Estimates, I suppose I should not complain.

Both Professor Titmuss and Mr. Terence O'Brien, in their invaluable and important volumes of the Official History which have proved of such great assistance to the present writer, have provided detailed studies of the problems and workings of the Civil Defence Organization and of its impact upon the social policy of the country. It is no part of the task of John Anderson's biographer to attempt to duplicate their highly skilled work, and indeed any such attempt would be both presumptuous and futile. The following section of this chapter gives some examples of those aspects with which Anderson was more personally associated, though it will be generally admitted that his remarkable personality, his administrative ability and his all-pervading initiative dominated the whole.

(ii)

On the morrow of Munich, His Majesty's Government decided to issue an appeal to the people of Britain for voluntary national service in time of need, and a booklet was prepared for circulation in the New Year to every home in the United Kingdom, giving details of the various forms that such service might take. This was entirely in consonance with Anderson's views. As long ago as 1925, when he had been chairman of the interdepartmental Committee on Air Raid Precautions he had recognized in his report the necessity of a widespread public appeal[1] and the same chord had been repeated in the report of the Anderson Committee of 1938.[2]

The actual decision had been taken before John joined the Cabinet but his advice as Lord Privy Seal was sought on a later development of the plan, namely a personal broadcast by King George VI as the inauguration of this new effort to arouse fresh interest and initiative in national service. He gave his unqualified approval of the idea, which received the full agreement of the Sovereign, the Government and of the leaders of the Labour and

[1] See above, p. 96. [2] See above, pp. 204-205.

Liberal Parties. The date of the broadcast had been set and the text of the King's speech prepared when differing counsel was tendered by the Governor of the Bank of England, Sir Montagu Norman, and by the Chief Press Liaison Officer of the Government, Mr. George Steward, both of whom expressed alarm at the idea of the King's broadcast. It was feared that so momentous a statement by the Sovereign would be interpreted in the country as a whole and in the world at large as meaning that war was imminent, and the Governor of the Bank went so far as to say that it might lead to a slump on the Stock Exchange. Neither the Prime Minister nor his colleagues, including John Anderson, shared these views but they felt that they could not take the responsibility of advising the King to ignore them. They therefore tendered the advice that a broadcast by the King should not be made and that the drive for national service should be launched by the Prime Minister instead, a course which was eventually followed.[1]

Again, it was at this time that John established those relations with Ernest Bevin which were to become close and personal when later they both served as members of Mr. Churchill's War Cabinet. More than a dozen years earlier they had been on opposite sides at the time of the General Strike, when Bevin played a notable part in the General Council of the T.U.C. and Anderson was in control of the Government organization for the maintenance of supplies. But this old enmity held no place in the minds of either man when the life and safety of the nation were threatened by a foreign enemy. They now collaborated with a sincerity and mutual respect characteristic of the innate greatness of them both.

Bevin had taken the initiative during the winter of 1938-1939 in preparing plans for wartime organization in the four key industries of the docks, road haulage, demolition, milling and provender. It was due to his persuasive advice that the joint councils of the flour milling and provender industries agreed in July 1939 to set up a Civilian Defence Committee which, by means of fifteen area committees, made provision for air raid precautions, for the

[1] Wheeler-Bennett (*op. cit.*), p. 359.

pooling and transfer of labour and the continued production of flour and foodstuffs in an emergency. John Anderson welcomed this voluntary initiative, gave it his full support and went on to appoint Mr. Bevin as Chairman of the Civil Defence Committee for the Constructional Industry, with a brief to work out the industry's own proposals for demolition work.[1]

When the activities of the 'Black and Tans' have been forgotten — save perhaps in Ireland — and when the memories of the terror in Bengal have passed into the limbo of history, John Anderson will be remembered by his countrymen for the association of his name with the 'Anderson Shelter'. For the better part of six years millions of citizens of the United Kingdom lived with one of these structures at the bottom of their gardens and of these millions very many owed their lives to his forethought in providing them. Though he was the progenitor of the shelter, he was not, in fact, the only Anderson connected with it, but it was his vision, his inspiration and his initiative which brought it into being.

From his first contact with the problems of Air Raid Precautions some thirteen years before, John had been concerned for the protection from bombing of the small householder, 'the little man', and as early as that time he had been revolving in his mind the possibilities of providing by mass production a small domestic shelter to which families could go when attack was imminent without having to herd together with strangers in deep or other communal shelters. The vital prerequisites of such a structure were, in his view, that it must be strong and it must be cheap. Even before he joined the Cabinet John had begun his campaign for such a shelter and had advocated the accumulation by the Government of a great store of material which could be handled readily by people without technical knowledge or skill when the emergency came. His vision was of 'something like a glorified Meccano', which could be erected either in a trench in the garden or in a passage or scullery of a small house.

When he became a Minister of the Crown John pursued this

---

[1] Alan Bullock, *The Life and Times of Ernest Bevin*, vol. i (1960), p. 635.

idea vigorously, but he soon realized that an idea was no good unless it could be shown to be practical, and immediately his mind turned to the skilled engineering brain of his old friend William Paterson. To his dismay he discovered that Paterson was in America but was expected back in London on November 10, 1938. John was on the platform as the boat train pulled in to Waterloo Station. As they drove to Paterson's house he explained the problem, which at once fired the engineer's inventive genius. He recognized immediately both the possibilities and the immediacy of the matter and before they separated that evening Paterson had narrowed the field of potential designs to two : either 'a wigwam construction', really a tripod with steel plates, or 'the elephant arch'. Before deciding finally he asked for a day or two for reflection. John gladly consented. The only specifications which he made were that the material should be capable of being rapidly produced, that it should be of such dimension that two able-bodied adults could easily erect it, and that the cost should not exceed £2 per person sheltered.

Paterson was as good as his word. Within a week of his initial talk with John, he and his co-director, Mr. Oscar Carl Kerrison, had drawn up a blueprint based on the principle of the 'elephant arch'. Within two weeks a model had been constructed in their workshop in Kingsway, and this they proudly took to John Anderson. John was ever a pragmatist. He promptly jumped on the model with both feet. It withstood this no mean test without yielding. John then turned the model over to the President of the Institution of Civil Engineers, who submitted both it and its design to three of his expert colleagues, Mr. David Anderson, Mr. Bertram Lawrence Hurst and the late Sir Henry Jupp. Their report was favourable in every way for use out of doors but they jettisoned John's idea that it might be used indoors, putting before him a grisly picture of what might happen if the building collapsed, a fire broke out, and people inside the shelter were roasted. The plans were therefore approved for outdoor use only.[1] The patent filed by Mr. Paterson and Mr. Kerrison was generously presented by them to the nation.

[1] Some years later, when wartime experience had been gained, an indoor shelter was brought into use by John Anderson's successor at the Home Office, Mr. Herbert Morrison.

Such is the story of the birth of the Anderson Shelter,[1] and it is a remarkable example of the speed with which such things can be done, given the will and the necessary means and initiative. John Anderson became 'Minister of Civilian Defence' on November 1, 1938 ; he placed the problem before William Paterson on the night of November 10 ; Paterson and Kerrison filed their patent on December 1, and the experts of the Institution of Civil Engineers presented their report on December 22. There followed an inevitable interval while the tooling-up process in factories was in progress, but by the end of February 1939 the first shelter had been installed and by the outbreak of war (September 1939) delivery had been made of nearly 1,500,000 free 'Andersons', which were estimated to offer shelter to some 6,000,000 persons, while the rate of production had reached 50,000 a week ; and before air attacks came upon the country in any strength the estimated number of those sheltered was 12,000,000.

John Anderson was greatly and justifiably proud of his association with the shelter which bore his name and which played so vital and personal a part in the protection of millions of his countrymen. He fully realized and keenly appreciated the part which William Paterson had played in the project and was himself always generous in his attribution and praise in this respect. Yet he was apt to resent this line being taken by others, and an incident occurred after the war which caused, at least temporarily, a *refroidissement* between himself and his other old friend, Alexander Gray, after William Paterson's death. The occasion was the presentation in December 1956 on behalf of Lady Paterson and her late husband to his old school, Heriot Watt College, Edinburgh, of a portrait of James Watt, attributed to Raeburn. It was a small private gathering of not more than twenty people, and it was essentially a 'Paterson occasion'. Gray, who had been asked to make the speech of presentation, very properly thought fit, in his own words, 'to offer up incense to William Paterson', and in so doing half jocularly used the words : 'The outer world almost got to know him [Paterson]

---

[1] At a dinner given in the Hall of the Worshipful Society of Apothecaries on June 23, 1952, to commemorate the Jubilee of the founding of the Paterson Engineering Company, John Anderson gave an entertaining account of the development of the plans for the shelter. The present writer has used this, but is also greatly indebted to Mr. O. C. Kerrison for additional information.

when in the war he invented the "Anderson Shelter" ; for, as you know, it is of the essence of the scientist that he leave the credit and the name to the politician'. John was deeply wounded by this remark when he heard of it and afterwards wrote to Gray expressing his disapproval.

He was also sensitive to any reference to the 'Anderson Shelter' which might, however unintentionally, detract from its initial purpose. I well recall, as his biographer, the first occasion on which I met him. I had been on Government service in the United States during the period of the 'Phoney War' and my first experience of England under wartime conditions was on my return after Dunkirk. My ship docked at Liverpool and in the course of my journey to London I was struck by the number of 'Anderson Shelters' which had been installed in the back gardens of the houses along the railway, and also by the fact that the Englishman, with his innate love of gardening and his genius for improvisation, had discovered that this structure, half covered with earth, afforded an ideal means of growing vegetable marrows. These plants, with promise of an excellent crop, decorated the majority of the shelters. Shortly after my arrival in London I found myself sitting next to Sir John Anderson at luncheon. Greatly impressed, I endeavoured to introduce conversational topics which I thought might interest him : the state of public opinion in America ; one's experiences in crossing the Atlantic in wartime, etc., all of which failed to elicit any but the most monosyllabic though courteous replies. Finally, in desperation, I told him about the vegetable marrows. His interest quickened perceptibly but he was still barren of utterance until, some minutes later, he remarked : 'I had not intended the shelters for the cultivation of vegetables.'

(iii)

If John Anderson's appearance as a back bencher in the House of Commons had gone virtually unnoticed, there was considerable speculation as to how he would shape on the Front Bench. It is fair to say that he never really understood the House of Commons. He naturally regarded all men, and, in particular, men in public positions, such as Members of Parliament, as being rational in their words and actions, and the House of Commons as a rational assembly. When this did not seem to him to be so, it distressed him and even offended his sense of propriety. 'I am shocked at their irresponsibility', he once remarked.

The House soon learned that from John Anderson as a Minister they could expect no flights of oratory. His own formidable capacity for extracting the last ounce of information from any document before him acted in reverse in the preparation and delivery of his speeches. It was clearly his duty, he thought, to give honourable Members the maximum of information that security and other circumstances permitted, and there was also much concerning Civil Defence on which, in his view, Parliament should be informed. This made for somewhat lengthy speeches in his earlier days, and though these read well in Hansard and kept the record right, they were often unappreciated by his hearers, and particularly those of the Opposition. 'Don't talk to us as though we were a lot of niggers', one Labour Member once shouted across the floor of the House, but John was unperturbed. He had a duty to perform and he performed it in the manner which seemed to him best.

He had a good diction and his voice carried well without effort ; he spoke in measured terms, which some felt to be pontifical, and with a grammatical correctness achieved by few — his speeches required little correction in the Hansard Room. Standing erect at the Dispatch Box, with his papers on top and a hand on either side, he was almost entirely free of gesture, save occasionally for a mild, minatory wagging of a forefinger to emphasize a particularly important point.

When it came to exchanges in debate the Government soon found that in Anderson they had a sound, if not a spectacular bat, and one who could quietly and always politely punish the Opposition bowling when occasion demanded. At Question Time, moreover, it was discovered that he was playing on a wicket he knew well. As a senior Civil Servant he had drafted too many answers to awkward 'P.Q.s' to be caught out and he could assume a rock-like demeanour against which supplementary questions beat in vain.

Yet it was in the handling of Questions that John's lack of understanding of the House also manifested itself. He lacked lightness of touch in dealing with questioners and had no capacity for

Q

repartee. Though he took immense pains with his answers, he had not the technique of the experienced Parliamentarians who, as often as not, reply to the man and not the question and, if possible, reduce the answer to 'No, sir', or 'Yes, sir'. John would answer a sensible question from an obscure or unpopular M.P. in accordance with its content while giving short shrift to a more irrational question from a skilful and popular Member like James Maxton.

But though John did not understand the House, the House understood him, regarding him with immense respect and having a very real appreciation of his remarkable qualities. They realized that almost invariably he was right, and proved by events to *be* right, even though his inflexibility of approach was a liability from a purely political point of view. The more the House saw of John the more they liked him. Here was someone who was solidly dependable and never ruffled ; a man of basic integrity and great parts ; a man, moreover, whose length and accuracy of memory became so legendary that one Member was heard to enquire whether he sported elephants as 'supporters' to his crest.

(iv)

Hitler's final revelation of his duplicity in occupying the remnant of Czechoslovakia on March 15, 1939, caused events throughout Europe, and especially in Britain, to move with an ever-increasing acceleration. The diplomatic revolution wrought by Mr. Chamberlain in belated recognition of the Führer's villainy was remarkable and far-reaching in results. Whereas a year before the Prime Minister had, with great definiteness, refused to commit Britain to automatic action in support of France, he now gave exactly that undertaking to Poland, and, by the middle of April 1939, Britain found that her European obligations extended from the North Sea to the Black Sea and the Aegean. Within this vast expanse were half a dozen States, any one of whom, should they be menaced by Nazi aggression and elect to resist, could automatically plunge Britain and France into war.

The 'Peace Bloc against Aggression' had developed piecemeal as the tempo of events dictated rather than in accordance with any carefully prepared and co-ordinated plan and it soon became apparent that a drastic revision of policy on the home front was necessary to meet the far-flung obligations which Britain had suddenly assumed abroad. On April 27, for the second time in our national history and the first in time of peace, a Bill for compulsory national service was introduced into the House of Commons. It was opposed by the Labour and Liberal Parties who, by persistent obstruction in debate and in committee, delayed the final division on its Third Reading until May 18 — by which time the international situation had deteriorated still further.

The early summer months brought no improvement, though a sinister calm, an ominous quiet, seemed to have settled over Europe. Over and above their efforts to place Britain's own defences in order the chief task of Mr. Chamberlain and his Cabinet colleagues was the essential necessity of making Hitler understand that never again could he count upon a repetition of the Munich Agreement ; of convincing him that, though Britain and France had no desire to provoke war and were anxious to settle all outstanding questions with Germany by free and peaceful negotiations, they were, nevertheless, no longer susceptible to blackmail and were prepared to meet force with force. The difficulty lay in conveying to the Führer the fact that when, for example, Lord Halifax declared at a dinner of the Royal Institute for International Affairs on June 29 : 'Our immediate task is . . . to resist aggression', he spoke for a country and a government who were in deadly earnest. If only, it was felt, Hitler could be persuaded of this fact he might well be deterred from embarking upon further acts of depredation.

An opportunity for conveying such a message in concrete form was presented on July 2, on the occasion of a review in Hyde Park of 20,000 representatives of the Civil Defence Forces — the fruits of seven months of John Anderson's labours. The King took the salute of the march past, attended by both the Prime Minister and John Anderson. Thereafter the parade was addressed by Mr. Chamberlain who also read a message from King George, which was later broadcast. In his message His Majesty spoke of 'the spirit of service which is everywhere present in the nation to-day, and which shows itself in a determination to make the country ready to meet any emergency, whatever the sacrifices or inconveniences entailed'.

Unfortunately the true inwardness of this message was lost upon Adolf Hitler, who persisted in the belief — founded on past experience — that Britain and France would, in the final analysis, find some formula for leaving the Poles in the lurch. In this sublime confidence he proceeded throughout the summer to bring intensified pressure upon Poland to accept his solution of the Danzig and Corridor issues, at the same time ensuring his position *vis-à-vis* the Western Powers by out-bidding them in Moscow.

In Britain there were many who, because they were in some measure deceived by the false calm which had descended on the Continent, or because they were the victims of their own wishful thinking, could not bring themselves to believe in the possibility of so insane a thing as war. Among these was David Anderson, John's father, who wrote in this strain to his son. But John was not for a moment deluded. 'I think most people would agree with you about the madness of war but it may be that we are in fact dealing with a madman', he replied with gentleness on August 14, and within ten days there came proof of what he had said. In the devious course of his evil lunacy Hitler signed his infamous pact of non-aggression with Stalin on August 23, and the world stood aghast at this irresponsible act which could but betoken war.

David Anderson sought to find some grounds for hope even in this event, and again he wrote to his son for enlightenment. John replied in prescient terms on August 29 : 'There is not I am afraid any background to the Russo-German pact such as you hoped. Just another betrayal is how we regard it. However, it may well prove a boomerang so far as Germany is concerned. I write this having just returned from the House of Commons. The spirit there is very good. I would not say myself that *all* hope must be abandoned, though undoubtedly peace hangs by a very slender thread.'

John wrote in full knowledge of the events of the last few days. The Prime Minister and his Government had reacted to the threat of the Moscow Pact in complete integrity. They had at once reaffirmed the guarantee to Poland and in proof of their sincerity had signed a formal treaty of alliance with her on August 25. They had done their best to keep their wavering French allies in line with this policy and on the evening of the 28th had conveyed to Hitler in writing the renewed assurance that Britain and France stood by their pledges to Poland.

Thereafter the Cabinet was in continual daily session. On the 30th came Hitler's temporizing reply accepting the principle of discussion with the Polish Government but demanding that such discussion must begin immediately in Berlin and that a special emissary equipped with plenary powers should be dispatched at once from Warsaw. On the following day it was clear that this was but a final act of bad faith in that Hitler had no intention of negotiating. The Cabinet decided to call up the Army Reserve and to begin the evacuation of women and children from London and other cities. By six o'clock on the morning of September 1, it was known that German troops had penetrated into Poland at at least three points, and in London the order went forth to mobilize the Fleet and the whole of the Army and Air Force.

The Cabinet met in momentous session at 4.30 on the afternoon of Saturday, September 2. Mussolini had advanced a proposal for a Five-Power Conference (Great Britain, France, Germany, Italy and Russia), with which the French Government were sympathetic, but it was agreed that the withdrawal of German troops from Poland must be made *conditio sine qua non* of such a meeting, and that an ultimatum to this effect should be delivered in Berlin. The French, it was said, desired to postpone such action for another 48 hours, but on the recommendation of the Secretary of State for War (Mr. Hore-Belisha) and the First Lord of the Admiralty (Lord Stanhope), with the strong support of the Chief of the Air Staff (Sir Cyril Newall), this counsel of hesitancy was rejected and the unanimous decision was reached to send an ultimatum at once which would expire at midnight September 2/3.

Hitherto the Cabinet had been united, but now a critical juncture occurred when there appeared to be a division of opinion. The Prime Minister was due to meet the House of Commons at six o'clock that same evening. It was a House packed and expectant, ready for news of imminent war, braced for the sacrifices thus entailed. It waited two hours for Mr. Chamberlain to appear, two hours in which the Prime Minister had been desperately — and unsuccessfully — endeavouring to keep the French Government in step with British policy. When he did arrive a little past eight o'clock he was understandably weary and was under the added inhibition of not being able to take the House fully into his confidence in respect of the difficulties he was encountering with the French. In consequence his statement was vague and indefinite. He made a deplorable impression on a House which was fully prepared for an announcement of automatic action in support of Poland. Members on both sides of the gangway were shocked, restive and resentful, scenting the possibility of a second Munich ; the Labour Party were particularly suspicious. It was in order to prevent a purely partisan speech from Arthur Greenwood, who rose to speak for the Opposition after the Prime Minister, that Leo Amery called across to him : 'Speak for England, Arthur', and the Deputy Leader of the Labour Party responded to the appeal with patriotism and statesmanship. Had he turned on the Government he would have had Tory support and he might have brought it down at a moment when it was vitally important to show that Britain spoke with one voice in a single cause. Instead, he spoke with great emotion of what was in the hearts of all present: 'An act of aggression took place thirty-eight hours ago. The moment that act of aggression took place one of the most important treaties of modern times automatically came into operation. . . . I wonder how long we are prepared to vacillate at a time when Britain and all that Britain stands for, and human civilization, are in peril.'[1]

It was on this note that the House adjourned, but many of Mr. Chamberlain's colleagues were aghast at the divergence of the statement which he had just made from their unanimous decision, taken earlier that afternoon, to send an immediate ultimatum to Berlin. A group of nine dissident Ministers, of whom John Anderson was one, met in Sir John Simon's room in the House of Commons.[2] They urged that the Cabinet should be called again in

[1] *House of Commons Debates*, September 2, 1939. Cols. 282-283.
[2] According to Lord Hore-Belisha, who has left a vivid account of these events in his diary, the Ministers were Sir John Simon, Chancellor of the Exchequer ; Mr. Hore-Belisha ; Mr. Walter Elliot, Minister of Health ; Lord De La Warr, Minister of Education ; Mr. Euan Wallace, Minister of Transport ; Sir John Anderson, Lord Privy Seal ; Hon. Oliver Stanley, President of the Board of Trade ; Mr. Leslie Burgin, Minister of Supply ; Sir Reginald Dorman-Smith, Minister of Agriculture ; and Mr. John Colville, Secretary of State for Scotland. (R. J. Minney, *The Private Papers of Hore-Belisha* (1960), pp. 224-228.)

immediate session and deputed the Chancellor to see the Prime Minister. Mr. Chamberlain, accompanied by Sir Kingsley Wood (then Secretary of State for Air), received his anxious colleagues in his room and Sir John Simon put their case to him very forcefully. The Prime Minister explained what had occurred in the interval between the last Cabinet Meeting and his statement in the House ; he told them of the difficulty he had encountered with the French in his efforts to persuade them to synchronize their ultimatum with that of Britain : Paris, he said, was still pressing for a postpone-ment ; and he apologized for not having had time to consult the Cabinet beforehand. His colleagues urged that a statement should be made forthwith, irrespective of the French, but Mr. Chamber-lain would give them no satisfaction on this point and withdrew to Downing Street. The Ministers met again in the Chancellor's room and drafted a letter to the Prime Minister repeating their points of argument. Having dispatched this by hand to No. 10, they then adjourned for dinner.

They met again at 10 o'clock and, as no word had come from Downing Street, John Simon and John Anderson were deputed to go over and see how the situation was developing. Shortly there-after Simon telephoned to say that a new statement by the Prime Minister was 'incubating'. A little later Anderson arrived with the news that the French had proved intransigent and that a British ultimatum would be delivered in Berlin at 8 o'clock the next morn-ing, September 3, to expire at 12 noon the same day. At a Cabinet meeting held at once at No. 10, it was agreed after some discussion that the time of expiry should be cut to eleven o'clock, and this was duly announced by the Prime Minister next day to a House of Commons which met for perhaps the first time in its history on a Sunday.

All Britain waited with bated breath that Sunday morning as the clocks ticked off the last hours, the last minutes, of peace. A faint hope remained with some that, even at this final moment, peace might, by some miracle, be preserved ; but the hope was very faint, and fated to be still-born. No answer was forthcoming from Berlin and it was with mingled relief and sorrow that the nation listened to Mr. Chamberlain's announcement at eleven o'clock that morning that Britain was at war.

(v)

In company with the majority of his countrymen, John Anderson found that the outbreak of war had a dislocating effect on both his private and his public life. His son Alastair, then twenty-eight years old, at once gave up his position at St. Thomas's Hospital and entered the Royal Air Force as a doctor, continuing in this service throughout the war. In due course also, his daughter Mary, then 24, joined the Auxiliary Territorial Service, which she subsequently made her career.

The family's domestic arrangements too had to be reorganized. John needed a base in London. He had disposed of the lease of the house in Chepstow Villas in October 1938 and, until his purchase of 'Picket Wood', had lived at his clubs. Merstham, however, was too far from London for anything but week-end use and he had, in any case, offered it for the use of evacuees — who, in the event, never arrived.

His problems were solved through the kindness of his old friends William Paterson and his wife, and he moved in with them in Stanhope Terrace, while Nellie Mackenzie and Mary continued to live at 'Picket Wood', keeping the house ready for his brief hurried visits and for Alastair's spasmodic spells of leave. 'It is quite impossible for me to live there [at Merstham]', John wrote to his father on September 14th. 'The most I can hope is to have 24 hours break in the week. The Patersons have very kindly given me accommodation in their London house which I can reach in 10 minutes by car & I also have a bed in the office in case of need.'

There were also changes in his position in the Government. According to pre-arranged plans, he and Sir Samuel Hoare changed places in the Cabinet at the outbreak of war and John achieved what was possibly his highest personal ambition, the office of Home Secretary, with which was combined the additional office of Minister of Home Security. His sense of satisfaction at becoming the ministerial head of the Government Department of which he had so long been the Permanent Under-Secretary was very great and he would gladly have continued in the post for the duration of the war.

With the state of war an actual and hideous reality, Mr. Chamberlain's first aim was to reorganize his Cabinet on the lines which Lord Halifax had unsuccessfully urged upon him after the Munich Agreement. He hoped now to achieve a government on a national basis and to this end he invited the co-operation not only of the dissident Tory leaders but also the leaders of the Labour and Liberal Parties. Mr. Churchill and Mr. Eden at once accepted — the one as First Lord of the Admiralty, the other as Secretary of State for the Dominions — but the Prime Minister's overtures to the Labour and Liberal Leaders were rejected, in each case with the same formula — that their parties could best serve the national cause from outside the Government. Disappointed, Mr. Chamberlain proceeded to form a War Cabinet of nine members, consisting of himself ; his former 'Inner Cabinet', Lord Halifax, Sir John Simon and Sir Samuel Hoare ; the three Service Ministers, Mr. Churchill, Mr. Hore-Belisha and Sir Kingsley Wood ; together with Admiral of the Fleet Lord Chatfield, Minister for Co-ordination of Defence, and Lord Hankey, Minister without Portfolio.

The exclusion of John Anderson from the War Cabinet may well have been understandable. It was essential to keep this body as small as possible and in the opinion of many — including King George VI — it was already too large. Nevertheless it seems curious to find the Lord Privy Seal and a Minister without Portfolio included while the man largely responsible for the efficient organization of Civil Defence on the Home Front, and an admitted genius of administration, remained outside. So at least it seemed to some of John's friends, if not to himself.

It is quite ridiculous that you are not a member of the Inner Cabinet [Sir Warren Fisher wrote to him on September 29]. The ablest man in the Govt. — & that Govt., as a whole, nothing more than a set of inexperienced mediocrities — left out is characteristic of the general incompetence. We shall win — but at what an unnecessary cost of suffering & loss, because of the hopeless inefficiency & lack of vision of Govt. over the years.[1]

---

[1] At least one member of the Government shared, to some extent, Sir Warren Fisher's anxiety as to its efficiency. 'Aren't we a very old team ?' Mr. Churchill wrote to the Prime Minister on September 2. 'I make out that the six you mentioned to me yesterday aggregate 386 years or an average of over 64 ! Only one year short of the Old Age Pension ! If, however, you added Sinclair (49) and Eden

It is exceedingly doubtful whether John Anderson was even remotely disturbed at his exclusion from the inner councils of the Government. He had more than a sufficiency of problems to occupy him, in addition to which his advice was continually in demand. 'Though not a member of the War Cabinet I attend its meetings regularly', he wrote to his father, '& that takes up a good deal of time.'

Like many of his Cabinet colleagues John was surprised and puzzled at the course of the opening stages of hostilities. The rapid conquest of Poland in September 1939 was followed by a period which came to be known as the 'Phoney War'; a period of in-activity — deceptive on the part of the enemy, wishful on that of the Allies — which gave rise to many false hopes and theories within the councils of Britain and France. John's views on the general trend of events may be gathered from the following extracts from his letters to his father :

September 20, 1939
I am no wiser than you are as to how this war may end but it is clear that we have got to see it through & I have a feeling that this unholy alliance with Russia will prove Hitler's undoing. I do not see that we need feel under any obligation to oust Russia from the parts of Poland she now occupies, which Poland in fact seized against the opinion of the Allies after the last war. How-ever, that is not an immediate problem.

October 14, 1939
Chamberlain's statement [of October 12 rejecting Hitler's peace offer of October 6] has carried the war into another phase & I don't think we shall hear anything more of peace proposals for some time. We now have to wait & see what Hitler & Co. are going to do. I don't profess to have any clear view.

Enemy aircraft attacked Rosyth and ships lying in the Firth of Forth on the afternoon of October 16th, some of the raiders being chased across Edinburgh to the Pentland Hills. John wrote :

(42) the average comes down to fifty-seven and a half.' (Winston S. Churchill, *The Gathering Storm* (1950), p. 361.) In the final count the aggregate age of Mr. Chamberlain's War Cabinet was 530 years, with an average of 58·8. The eldest member was the Prime Minister himself, aged 70, and the youngest, Mr. Hore-Belisha, aged 46.

October 27, 1939

I was naturally concerned to hear how you had fared during the air raid. It must have been — for some — quite a thrilling & perhaps rather alarming experience. One or two of the German machines seem to have passed over the town quite low & it is fortunate that there were no civilian casualties — at any rate of a serious character. On other occasions, & there may of course be many others, there may be a different tale to tell but the kind of defence we can put up should hearten everybody.[1]

November 19, 1939

The war, as you say, is going slowly. For us at any rate that is not a bad thing for we can use the lull to great advantage in many directions. It would seem as if Hitler & Co. had missed a good many opportunities but perhaps they have some surprise in store.

Had John Anderson, or anyone else in the Cabinet, but known it, Hitler had, on October 27, ordered the attack on the Low Countries to be made on November 12, and had only grudgingly agreed to its postponement for meteorological reasons. As it was, John was evidently in danger of sharing that 'Hitler-has-missed-the-bus' mentality which afflicted Mr. Chamberlain — and even Mr. Churchill.

The year closed for him with a happy and peaceful family Christmas at 'Picket Wood', with Nellie Mackenzie and Mary, for which Alastair was also able to get leave.

(vi)

The period of the 'Phoney War' was abruptly terminated on April 9, 1940, when Hitler made his long-prepared invasion of Denmark and Norway, and the Western Allies moved to the support of these new victims of Nazi aggression. The first popular reaction in Britain to the Scandinavian campaign was one of relief that the stalemate had been broken. It was not doubted that in an operation with a strongly naval flavour, and with Mr. Churchill at the Admiralty, the British would be more than a match for the

---

[1] In point of fact no siren warning was sounded in Edinburgh before this raid, which took place in broad daylight at 2.30 p.m. Questions were subsequently asked in both Houses of Parliament, to which the Prime Minister replied.

enemy, and expectations rose high. Within a month, however, despite the confident pronouncements of the Prime Minister and the First Lord of the Admiralty, it became unavoidably apparent that, except for a precarious Allied foothold at Narvik, all Norway was in the hands of the enemy and that, notwithstanding the gallantry of their forces, Britain and France had suffered a heavy defeat. The disastrous outcome of the campaign released in Parliament, and in the country as a whole, the pent-up dissatisfaction with the Chamberlain administration which had so long been latent. In time of war a government must be overwhelmingly strong to withstand failure, and after seven months of a war without movement the position of Mr. Chamberlain and his colleagues was too weak to survive disaster. Feeling ran high when the Prime Minister faced the House of Commons in the crucial two days' debate which opened on May 7, and when Mr. Herbert Morrison announced the intention of the Labour Party to divide on a motion of confidence it was felt on both sides of the House that the death-knell of the Chamberlain Government had sounded. The Government's majority fell to a comparative handful and the Prime Minister resigned on May 10.

John Anderson's reactions to these events were rather those of the great administrator, by nature rational and preferring continuity, than those of the politician, by nature inured to change and particularly in times of crisis, guided as much by emotion as by reason. He was shocked and dismayed at the prospect of the Government's downfall and expressed to his Parliamentary Secretary, Mr. William Mabane,[1] his conviction that so blatant an exhibition of divided opinion in the country would create political disorder at home and afford aid and comfort to the enemy. He could not bring himself to share the realization of many that, for better or for worse, the time had come for a showdown, nor their belief that thereafter the strange and indefinable instinct of Parliament on such occasions for doing the right thing would soon put matters back on an even keel.

John soon found out, and admitted, that he was wrong. He was not, however, at all sanguine about his chances of being asked

---

[1] Rt. Hon. Sir William Mabane, K.B.E., later Minister of State in the Foreign Office, 1945.

WAR CABINET, 1940

(*Standing*) Arthur Greenwood, Ernest Bevin, Lord Beaverbrook, Sir Kingsley Wood
(*Seated*) Sir John Anderson, The Prime Minister, C. R. Attlee, Anthony Eden

to continue in office and when summoned by the new Prime Minister to an interview at the Admiralty was not unmindful of the fact that Mr. Churchill would be likely to remember the differences which they had had at the time of the General Strike when John, as an official, had spoken quite sharply to him.[1] But the Prime Minister had no such picayune considerations. He was anxious to build as strong an administration as possible. John responded at once to the inspired and determined leadership of Mr. Churchill and willingly agreed to continue as Home Secretary and Minister of Home Security in the new Coalition Government which was formed on May 10-11.

Mr. Churchill's Government assumed its duties at the moment of Hitler's lightning attack upon the Low Countries and Northern France. The first days of its existence were marked by almost unrelieved disaster. Within three weeks the armies of Belgium and the Netherlands had capitulated and the British Expeditionary Force, crowned with new laurels but denuded of equipment, had been evacuated from Dunkirk; within six weeks French military resistance had ended with the signing of the Armistice agreement at Compiègne on June 22, and once again in her history Britain was threatened with invasion.

It was at this moment of crisis that John Anderson's great qualities shone out effulgent. His serene calm in every circumstance and the incisive clarity of his decisions on the most difficult and complex problems filled his subordinates with admiring wonder and inspired his colleagues with confidence. He approached the planning of arrangements in the event of a successful German invasion almost as if such an event presented a normal administrative problem, determining, on the one hand, the manner in which the civil authorities would function under the invader and, on the other, the extent to which others should occupy themselves in sabotaging their work.

Anderson's innate sense of justice, conduct and decorum was in great evidence in these days of stress and trial and in no issue were greater demands made upon it than in that of the internment of aliens. From his experience as Permanent Under-Secretary of the Home Office he was well aware of the policy of government in

[1] See above, p. 106.

respect of the admission of foreigners into Britain and of the machinery which had been established after the First World War for their registration and general supervision. On assuming office as Minister of Home Security at the outbreak of the Second World War, he had at once taken action, in conjunction with the Committee of Imperial Defence, to make the necessary revision in policy and methods which wartime conditions necessitated. His primary concern was to strike an even balance between ensuring the security of the realm and maintaining the basic rights of the private citizen which, while necessarily restricted in war-time, can never be done away with altogether. Above all, he was determined not to be stampeded into precipitate and oppressive measures by panic pressure from without.

The situation created by the problem of aliens in 1939 was essentially different from that which had existed in 1914, particularly with regard to those of German origin or nationality. In the First World War Germany was a country united in support of the Imperial Government and it might reasonably be assumed, therefore, that any German citizen was loyal to his country and ready to do anything he could do without undue risk to himself to serve his country's interests. Moreover, in 1914, because of the absence of any general control of immigration or residence, the Home Office had no idea of the number of aliens — let alone Germans — in the country; where they lived, what occupations they followed nor anything about their character or sentiments. As a result the public mind of Britain was thoroughly uneasy about enemies in their midst. The outbreak of war saw hostile demonstrations against Germans, or against persons or shops with German names, and an epidemic of spy mania forced the Government to arrest and intern many Germans and Austrians — some of them entirely innocent — for their own protection.

In 1939 none of these conditions obtained. Thanks to the measures introduced in 1919, immigration, particularly for more than a short stay, had been strictly controlled and aliens were only admitted if their entrance seemed likely to be in the national interest; the whereabouts, occupation and character of every alien resident were known to the police. Moreover the persecution by the Nazi régime since 1933 of numerous classes of German citizens on political and religious grounds had produced the result that most of those persons admitted to residence in the United Kingdom from Germany for the past six years were refugees from oppression and were in many cases willing and anxious to work, and even to fight, for the defeat of National Socialism.

It was felt, nevertheless, that some winnowing process was necessary, and one of John Anderson's first actions on the outbreak of war was to set up 122 special one-man tribunals, composed in most cases of County Court Judges or King's Counsel, to examine the cases of all Germans and Austrians over the age of sixteen resident in Britain in order to determine whether in the interests of national security they should be interned. It is a matter of interest, as Anderson informed the House of Commons, that of the 73,353 aliens who were thus examined 569 were interned, 6782 were exempted from internment but not from special restrictions applicable to enemy aliens, and 62,244 were exempted altogether. No fewer than 55,457 were classified as refugees from Nazi oppression.[1]

For the greater part of the 'Phoney War' period public opinion in Britain was contented, or at least quiescent, concerning the adequacy of these precautions, but by the spring of 1940 the rumblings of dissatisfaction could be heard in press and Parliament. John Anderson remained comparatively unmoved by these early premonitory symptoms.

> The newspapers are working up feeling about aliens [he wrote to his father on March 2] I shall have to do something about it or we may be stampeded into an unnecessarily oppressive policy. It is very easy in wartime to start a scare. [And again, on March 26] There has been a lot of fuss in the papers about aliens but I have seen no sign of real trouble in Parliament as yet. The Irish are, as you say, an even greater potential menace. But in wartime people are easily worked up & a spy scare can be started at any time as a 'stunt'.

The clamour in the press and in the House of Commons increased with the new phase of the war which opened with the Nazi invasion of Denmark and Norway, and to it were added representations from the Chiefs of Staff and the heads of the Service

---

[1] *House of Commons Debates*, March 1, 1940. Col. 2410.

Intelligence Departments. Anderson, however, still resisted their demands for a wholesale and indiscriminate internment of all aliens of enemy origin, a policy which he regarded as unjust, since it would inevitably involve the detention of many innocent persons. That he realized that he was only fighting a rearguard action is evident from his remark to his father on April 26 : 'I expect to be able to hold the position unless the war begins to go badly.'

But the war did begin to go badly. The invasion of Norway had added the word 'Quisling' [1] to the vocabulary of treachery and this, combined with the term 'Fifth Column',[2] produced an awesome formula of fear and menace, which intensified the pressure upon Anderson for the wholesale internment of all enemy aliens. 'Would it not be far better to intern all the lot and then pick out the good ones?' demanded Colonel Henry Burton, Conservative Member for Sudbury, in the House of Commons,[3] and for many people this was no longer a query. Public feeling became so strong that *The Times* spoke of 'hysterics' and the attacks by Conservative back-benchers upon the Home Secretary for his seeming inactivity and unawareness of danger became even sharper.

With the *Blitzkrieg* of May and June the pressure became irresistible. On the evening of the May 11 the military authorities came to John and, as he subsequently told the House of Commons, 'represented that, in view of the imminent risk of invasion, it was in their view of the utmost importance that every male alien between 16 and 70 should be removed forthwith from the coastal strip which in their view was the part of the country likely, if invasion took place, to be affected'.[4] This advice was, of course, eminently sound and, in accordance with it, John issued orders for the internment of some

---

[1] Vidkun Quisling (1887–1945) founded the Norwegian Nazi Party, the *Nasjonal Samling* in 1933, and in 1940 invited Hitler to occupy Norway. He was tried before a criminal court in Oslo and executed as a traitor on October 27, 1945.

[2] The phrase 'Fifth Column' has its origin during the Spanish civil war in the statement made by the Nationalist General Mola on the eve of his offensive against Madrid in October 1936, that he would launch four columns against Madrid but that it would be the fifth column of sympathizers within the city which would start the offensive. The statement would appear to have been made at a press conference or in a radio speech on October 1 or 2, since it was quoted by the Communist press in Madrid on the 3rd. However, Lord St. Oswald, then Reuter's correspondent with the Republican forces, has a claim to have used the phrase some weeks before General Mola. (Hugh Thomas, *The Spanish Civil War* (1961), p. 317, f.n.)

[3] *House of Commons Debates*, April 23, 1940. Col. 33.

[4] *House of Commons Debates*, August 22, 1940. Col. 1543.

3000 German and Austrian males resident in the sea-coast counties from Nairn to Hampshire.

The clamour for wholesale and indiscriminate internment, however, increased a hundredfold as refugees poured in from the Netherlands with appalling stories of the stratagems of the Fifth Column in their country. British correspondents working in Holland confirmed these accounts. On May 12 the *Observer* published a story from a Dutch source that *Reichsdeutsche*, living in the Netherlands and furnished with special passes, had awaited the parachutists of the *Luftwaffe*.[1] On the following day *The Times* and the *Daily Telegraph* reported that in The Hague over a hundred German citizens had been killed in street fighting in one day and on the 14th the *Daily Express* wrote that 'Poisoned chocolates and wine, spies disguised as priests and postmen and housemaids, every kind of trick to sap confidence and cause confusion has been used by the Nazis'.

The struggle in Belgium and in France gave rise to a whole series of similar reports and the effect upon the British public was understandably acute. The German menace drew ever nearer. 'We must expect in any case to be attacked here on the Dutch model before long', Mr. Churchill wrote to President Roosevelt,[2] and the demand for sterner measures grew louder. The national press had unanimously applauded John Anderson's earlier action but there was general approval of the view of the *Manchester Guardian* that 'no half measures will do'.[3] The Home Secretary's mail-bag was crowded with letters urging him to go further and he did so. On May 16 a further 3000 males, previously labelled as category B (absolute reliability uncertain), were rounded up and the *Daily Herald* proclaimed 'Country saved from Fifth Column Stab'.[4] Later in the month 3500 women were transferred with their children to the Isle of Man, and on June 21, 'after the fullest and most earnest consideration',[5] Anderson came to the decision to intern the whole

---

[1] Mr. van Kleffens, then Netherlands Foreign Minister, tells of German girls who had lived in Holland as servants being dropped by parachute along with parties of raiders for the purpose of guiding them to particular houses in The Hague. (*The Rape of the Netherlands* (1940), p. 161.)
[2] Churchill, *Their Finest Hour* (1949), p. 50.
[3] *Manchester Guardian*, May 13, 1940.
[4] *Daily Herald*, May 17, 1940.
[5] *House of Commons Debates*, August 22, 1940. Col. 1545.

R

of Group C, those refugees who had been previously labelled 'reliable'. A few committed suicide but most of them accepted their new adversity with resignation. Almost eight thousand were transferred to Canada and Australia. One of the transports, the *Arandora Star*, was torpedoed in the Atlantic with heavy loss of life. A group of interned German clergymen, exiled for their faith from their homes by National Socialism, arriving in Canada in another ship, the *Ettrick*, were assumed to be Nazi parachutists in disguise who had been dropped on Rotterdam during the frightful raid which almost destroyed the city, and they were treated as such. They and others were greeted with jeers of 'How's Hitler ?' and comments which were a good deal more thorough-going than that.[1] Such incidents, though deplorable, were unavoidable under the circumstances of peril with which Britain was then confronted. As Mr. Churchill told the House of Commons : 'I know there are a great many people affected by the orders which we have made who are the passionate enemies of Nazi Germany. I am very sorry for them, but we cannot, at the present time and under the present stress, draw all the distinctions which we should like to do.'[2]

There was, however, a further aspect of this particular problem of national security with which John Anderson had to contend. The treacherous action of Vidkun Quisling and his followers in Norway aroused very naturally the apprehensions of many as to the possibility of similar activities by British nationals under like circumstances. Various attempts to impede the war effort had in fact been made since the outbreak of hostilities by three main groups, the Communist Party, the Peace Pledge Union and the British Union of Fascists, all of whom had come under the surveillance of the authorities. Of these the British Union was considered the most dangerous. Its similarity to the Fascist and National Socialist régimes was obvious and striking, and its publicly avowed policy was to work for the overthrow of the existing democratic form of government and, when an electoral victory had placed a Fascist Government in power, to alter the whole parliamentary system by providing for the election of members on an occupational instead

[1] Alan Moorehead, *The Traitors* (1952), p. 77.
[2] *House of Commons Debates*, June 4, 1940. Col. 794.

of a geographical franchise ; in fact to establish the Corporate State on the totalitarian lines adopted in Italy and Germany.

At the outbreak of war, the Leader, Sir Oswald Mosley, had issued a message to his followers which, though it specifically bade them 'to do nothing to injure our country or to help any other power', nevertheless declared : 'This war is no quarrel of the British people ; this war is a quarrel of Jewish finance'. Thereafter, through its organ *Action*, the British Union had continued its anti-war propaganda by the circulation of many items calculated to undermine confidence in the Government, such as reports of increasing unemployment, alleged scandals in connection with evacuation, articles emphasizing Germany's invincibility and statements calculated to stir up hatred against the Jews.

Under the existing Defence Regulations the powers of the Home Secretary were restricted in dealing with such organizations and a demand arose both in the press and in Parliament for more stringent measures. Anderson received a parliamentary deputation on April 18 which urged that immediate steps should be taken to deal with anti-war propaganda and promising full support in the House of Commons if he felt it necessary to take new powers. Fortified by this support, he made a statement in the House on April 25 :

> I have for some time been carefully watching the activities of certain small groups of people, of whom some appear to be deliberately anxious to hinder the war effort. . . . The question what steps can properly be taken to check propaganda of a harmful kind was discussed when the Defence Regulations were debated on 31st October, and there was general agreement that every effort should be made, even in time of war, to avoid interference with the propagation of opinions held by small minorities. There is, however, a risk that the liberty allowed by our traditional principles may be abused by extremists of whom some are anxious to destroy that liberty, and I am at present considering whether some strengthening of the regulations is desirable for the purpose of checking activities specifically directed towards impeding the national war effort.[1]

Two weeks later, on May 9, Anderson announced in the House of Commons the amendments which the Government intended to

---

[1] *House of Commons Debates*, April 25, 1940. Col. 354.

make to the Defence Regulations and which were in fact promulgated as Orders in Council on the same day. Even in their amended state, however, the Regulations were only designed to deal with propaganda, and, with the swift and relentless passage of events, these were soon found to be inadequate to meet the new emergency.

The overrunning of Holland and Belgium resulted in reports reaching London of the traitorous activities of Anton Mussert and his Dutch Nazis and of the Rexist followers of Léon Degrelle, who seemed almost to out-quisling Quisling. The threat to national security in Britain seemed imminent. Public indignation was loudly voiced that the British Union of Fascists was still allowed to demonstrate in public and on May 19 a meeting addressed by Sir Oswald Mosley at Middleton was broken up by enraged artisans. Three days earlier John Anderson had been received in audience by King George VI, who had received reports on events in the Netherlands from Prince Bernhard and from the British Ambassador, Sir Nevile Bland, both of whom had recently escaped from The Hague. His Majesty impressed upon John the necessity for taking immediate action against political Fifth Columnists and other enemies of the State, both male and female.

The King's warning was enforced by many others from official quarters and was indeed entirely in accordance with John's own views. On May 22 a paragraph was added to Defence Regulation 18B by Order in Council giving the Home Secretary the power to intern persons who he had good reason to think were members of an organization in sympathy with the enemy. The same night Mosley and 35 other leading members of the British Union were arrested, to be joined a week later by a further 346 of his followers.[1]

A general announcement of these detentions was made by Mr. Churchill in the House of Commons on June 4. 'We have found it necessary', he said, 'to take measures of increasing stringency, not only against enemy aliens and suspicious characters of other nationalities, but also against British subjects who may become a danger or a nuisance should the war be transported to the United

---

[1] Among others detained at this time under Regulation 18B were Captain A. H. Maule Ramsay, R.N. (rtd.), Member of Parliament for Peebles and South Midlothian, and also members of an Anglo-German organization known as 'The Link', including Captain Barry Domville, R.N. (rtd.), a former Director of Naval Intelligence.

Kingdom. . . . Parliament has given us the powers to put down Fifth Column activities with a strong hand, and we shall use those powers, subject to the supervision and correction of the House, without the slightest hesitation until we are satisfied, and more than satisfied, that this malignancy in our midst has been effectively stamped out.'[1]

Anderson had, however, forgotten — or at any rate omitted (for he never 'forgot' anything) — to inform his Cabinet colleagues, or even the Prime Minister, of the widespread arrests which he had already made and Mr. Churchill was breathing fire and brimstone at what he considered to be John's undue dilatoriness. At length he could contain himself no longer and on June 28 he sent a characteristically peremptory minute : 'Let me see a list of the prominent persons you have arrested'.[2] John at once complied. At lunchtime on the 29th a dispatch rider braked his motor-bicycle with a flurry of gravel in the forecourt of Chequers and handed to the Private Secretary a letter from the Minister of Home Security. The Prime Minister seized it with avidity and began to read aloud to those at the luncheon table the list of detainees. To the huge delight of his children who were present, amongst the first three names were two of Mrs. Churchill's cousins! The Prime Minister was at first disposed to consider this a deliberate piece of impudence on the part of Anderson. 'He did it on purpose', he muttered. However, he was soon laughed out of this by his family and all others present, and later congratulated John on the efficiency of his action.

The lot of a Cabinet Minister is rarely easy and in time of war it is far from being a happy one ; of none is this more true than of the Home Secretary. Whereas John had been criticized for leniency in dealing with enemy aliens and some said that he acted only in response to pressure, this, of course, was just not true. From the first he had held steadily on a middle course refusing to be swayed by the wave of 'near-panic' which spread over the country, accompanied by an hysterical clamour for extreme action. He kept his head and, when the right moment came, he took firm but limited action. Similarly he maintained an equal degree of detachment when his next action was censured on grounds of illiberal

---

[1] *House of Commons Debates*, June 4, 1940. Cols. 794-795.
[2] Churchill, *Their Finest Hour*, p. 565.

tendencies and the House of Commons flew into a panic in the other direction.

Faced with the imminent and impending threat of invasion, the Government felt constrained to strengthen its judicial powers for dealing with such emergency conditions as might arise. On July 10 a Bill was introduced into the House of Commons authorizing the institution of special courts, analogous to courts martial, for the trial of civilian as well as military offenders in the event of invasion, and a week later John Anderson desired the House to pass the Bill through all its stages without delay as a matter of urgency. But the House would have none of it. Both Parliament and the country were thoroughly alarmed at what appeared to be an attempt on British freedom, and Anderson was much assailed. The prime rebuke came from the liberally minded *News Chronicle*, which observed courteously : 'Begging your pardon, Sir John, and with the greatest respect, we would remind you that you are no longer in Bengal'.[1]

Scenting in these 'special courts' a threat to the ancient and inherent right of a civilian to trial by jury, several members of the House of Commons attacked the measure on the ground that it contained no specific provisions as to the character and authority of the proposed courts and, though the Bill was accorded a second reading, this was only on the understanding that such provisions should be inserted. John then tabled a number of amendments of which the most important was one which stated explicitly that the proposed courts would not be courts martial. But the House was still not satisfied and, when the Committee stage was reached, a further amendment was proposed providing that the sentences of the courts, especially those which imposed the death penalty, should not be summary but should be subject to review. Anderson at first refused to accept this change, but the House was so insistent that he at length gave way and the Bill was then passed through its remaining stages, becoming law on August 1.

By the grace of God and the strong arm of the Royal Air Force it never became necessary for the provisions of this Act to be applied, but it is an interesting and salutary comment on history

---

[1] *News Chronicle*, July 17, 1940. This criticism of Anderson was in fact made under a misapprehension, and an apology was printed by the *News Chronicle* on July 25. Their onslaught had been intended for Mr. Duff Cooper!

that, even in moments of grave national peril, the House of Commons is still ready to fulfil its duties as the guardian of the citizen's rights and privileges.

To John Anderson this sequence of events was deeply disturbing. It was not that he wished to be lenient with the King's Enemies. He realized to the full the danger of leaving at large those who would give aid and succour to régimes in Germany and Italy to which he was, by all standards, fundamentally hostile, and he welcomed the opportunity presented by the additional powers granted to him to scotch their nefarious activities. But because he was a profoundly just and humane man he deplored conditions, however inevitable they might appear to be, in which the innocent suffered with the guilty, in which the basic rights of the citizen were abrogated, however temporarily, and as a result of which the political informer must necessarily flourish. Something of the depression which he felt at this time is evident in his letter to his father of June 15, 1940 :

> I am having, as you can imagine, a very strenuous time. . . . It is on the Home Office side that I am most pressed. There is a whispering campaign going on which puts the witch-hunts of the Middle Ages completely in the shade. Everyone tends now to look askance at his neighbour — very unfortunate, I think.

In view of these sentiments it is ironic to find that at this moment an American historian was recording in his diary (on July 23) : 'Now that Great Britain is fully as totalitarian as Germany, it may be asked : what is the difference between Sir John Anderson and Himmler ? Surely it is merely a matter of nationality.' [1]

(vii)

As the smoke-clouds of the Battle of France dispersed to disclose the rubble of defeat the world held its breath in anticipation of the

---

[1] Francis Neilson, *The Tragedy of Europe* (5 vols., Appleton, Wisconsin, 1940–1946), vol. i, p. 560. Time did not mitigate Mr. Neilson's curious impartiality. Five years later, on June 27, 1945, he was still unregenerate in his judgment. 'There were 1847 persons interned in Great Britain as political prisoners under Defence Regulation 18B. . . . Before the General Election is over we may hear from some of these men. They might tell us wherein lies the particular difference between the methods of Hitler and those of Churchill and Sir John Anderson' (vol. v, p. 423).

opening of the Battle of Britain. Where and how would Hitler strike at the island fortress ? It was agreed that in order to invade Britain successfully the Nazis must first secure command of the air and, secondly, mastery of the sea approaches from Europe, but there was speculation as to how Hitler would act, given these confederate conditions. Would he strike boldly across the Channel and attempt a landing in Kent or Sussex or Hampshire, or would he direct his attack upon the low-lying coasts of East Anglia ? Or might he indeed adopt both courses of action, making one of them a feint ?

Within the fortress the spirit of resistance was high. The capacity of the British people for illogical virtue in politics is only equalled by their absolute refusal to recognize defeat and their ability to deck their disasters with the laurels of victory. The feeling of elation and pride which swept through Britain after the evacuation of Dunkirk was enhanced rather than diminished by the knowledge that Britain now stood alone. A people which had lit the Armada beacons 'from Eddystone to Berwick bounds, from Lynn to Milford Bay', and had watched undismayed the twinkling camp fires of Napoleon's army at Boulogne, now responded worthily to Mr. Churchill's grim promise of 'blood, toil, tears and sweat'. There was no bravado, no vainglory, no return to the old-time 'jingoism' of the nineties, which Rudyard Kipling had deplored in his *Recessional*, for in June 1940 both 'reeking tube and iron shard' were woefully lacking. The Army had come back from the Continent with added glory but with little else. The Home Guard were armed in many cases with pikes and pick handles, and drilled with broomsticks. The spirit in which Britain 'stood alone' in 1940 was certainly one of pride, but of a pride tempered with dedication to a defence, if need be to the death, of the decencies of life and common behaviour and to a defiance of a rule of dishonour, treachery and brute force.

Feverish preparations were set on foot to withstand the coming onslaught, for none then doubted that an invasion of Britain would be attempted and none could say how soon. In point of fact, Hitler did hesitate before carrying the war across the Channel, hoping in view of the adverse fortunes of war that the British Government might be persuaded to treat for peace. Though on July 16 he gave to his High Command the order to prepare plans for the attack, in his speech to the Reichstag on July 19 he made 'a final appeal to common sense' and urged upon Britain the futility of continuing the struggle. It was only when these approaches had been rejected with contempt and defiance that the Führer gave the final orders to the Luftwaffe to prepare the way for the implementation of 'Operation Sea Lion'. In the meantime Britain waited and looked to her defences.

The assault from the air began gradually. The German Air Force had carried out small-scale raids before the armistice with France had been concluded ; since July 10 enemy aircraft had attacked various targets in force. The main battle, however, was not joined until August 13, when a full-scale attack began on Channel shipping and the south coast ports. On August 26 the enemy switched his attacks to fighter airfields in the south and south-east. On September 7 the onslaught on London began by day and by night, and night raids on the capital continued with varying intensity throughout the winter.

This was the moment for which John Anderson had prepared and organized as long ago as 1926. Then the planning had been theoretical and hypothetical ; but when, in November 1938, it had again come within his competence, it had assumed proportions of hideous potentiality. Now was the moment of testing when the services of A.R.P. and Civil Defence were to be tried in the ghastly furnace of the Blitz, the crucial trial which should prove whether this careful preparation and training had been all to some purpose or whether it had been in vain.

Beyond all peradventure the services which Anderson had created and inspired stood up magnificently to the gruelling demands now made upon them. Prodigies of gallantry, wonders of efficiency, miracles of improvisation were performed day and night by these organizations. Faults, weaknesses and omissions there inevitably were but these were met and accounted for in short order and in the main John could be justifiably proud of the services which his administrative ability and initiative had brought into being.

Yet it was at this very moment that he became enmeshed in the toils of a controversy which was to end in his temporary discomfiture and his translation to another sphere of office.

The Anderson Shelter proved the salvation of thousands of persons who were in their homes at the time of the raids. It was a marvel of engineering, a miracle of strength and simplicity, to which recognition was accorded by even the fiercest of the Government's critics. 'I have seen plenty of evidence of the way in which "Andersons" have behaved under bombing', wrote Mr. Ritchie Calder, one of the most virulent of John's assailants. 'I have seen them buckled into full circles and the people brought out unscathed. I have seen them poised on the lips of craters and those sheltering in them escape with a few bruises. People have told me how, with a bomb 20 feet away, sleeping children were jarred off the seats and were picked up still asleep, while the adults were merely jolted.'[1] John Anderson and William Paterson had wrought well and truly.

But the Anderson Shelter, admirable though it proved to be for the purpose for which it was devised, was not the answer to the problem of the safety of people in the mass, people whose homes had been destroyed by enemy action, people who were caught in raids away from their homes, people who lived in the densely populated districts of cities. This problem had faced the planners long before John Anderson became responsible for Civil Defence and he inherited the controversy which had arisen in consequence between those who advocated the building of 'deep shelters' and those who placed their confidence in a policy of dispersal and in surface shelters and strengthened basements.

As early as August 1938 an unofficial body of architects, surveyors and engineers had produced a plan for a system of tunnel shelters in St. Pancras for which it was claimed that it would give better bomb-proof protection at smaller cost than any other type of shelter. They received support from Professor J. B. S. Haldane who, in an article in the journal *Nature*, having stated that incendiary bombs had proved 'a negligible danger to life' during the Spanish civil war, went on to demonstrate mathematically that random bombing would cause just as many casualties if people were dispersed as if they were concentrated. In a book entitled *A.R.P.*, Professor Haldane strongly pressed for deep shelters.[2] The Communist Party, ever anxious to fish in troubled waters, initiated a

[1] Ritchie Calder, *The Lesson of London* (1941), p. 82.
[2] J. B. S. Haldane in *Nature*, October 1938, and *A.R.P.* (1938).

series of public meetings for the same purpose, which proved of no little embarrassment to the Government and, after the Munich Crisis, public opinion became so stirred on the subject that both the Labour and Liberal Parties joined in the general agitation.

The contrary view of the Civil Defence authorities was based on two factors, one practical, the other psychological. In the first place the introduction of a comprehensive deep shelter plan would make stupendous demands on money, materials and labour, and in the second, it was felt that an undue strain would be placed upon the morale and ability of the A.R.P. services if mass casualties were incurred in one spot, which would be the inevitable result of a direct hit on a deep shelter.[1]

When John Anderson assumed responsibility for Civil Defence in November 1938 he found the controversy at its height. A very strong feeling in favour of deep shelters existed throughout the country and was vigorously supported from various quarters in the House of Commons. In his statement to the House on December 21, outlining the shelter policy of the Government, Anderson said that, while immediate steps would be taken to provide the widest possible measure of protection for the civil population against the effect of splinters, blast and the fall of debris, the problem of the provision of heavily protected shelters remained for consideration.[2] To advise him on this point he convened an independent conference under the chairmanship of Lord Hailey to survey the whole issue.[3]

The Report of Lord Hailey and his colleagues was presented to Anderson on April 6, 1939.[4] After an exhaustive analysis of practical and technical issues they recommended that no attempt be made to provide deep shelters for the general public. In reaching this conclusion they paid less attention to the question of cost, which they regarded as of only relative importance, than to the immense diversion of labour and materials from other war preparations which

---

[1] O'Brien (*op. cit.*), pp. 190–192.
[2] *House of Commons Debates*, December 21, 1938. Cols. 2880–2892.
[3] The Hailey Conference consisted, in addition to the Chairman, of Mr. George Hicks, a prominent trade unionist and Member of Parliament ; two industrialists, Mr. F. J. Leathers and Sir Frederick Marquis (later Lord Leathers and Lord Woolton respectively) ; a lady doctor, Dame Louise McIlroy ; an accountant, Sir William McLintock ; an engineer, Sir Clement Hindley, and a scientist, Professor (later Sir) R. V. Southwell.
[4] *Report of the Lord Privy Seal's Conference on Air Raid Shelters*, Cmd. 6006 (1939).

a deep shelter programme would entail. In addition, they stressed the time factor involved, computing that it would take at least two years to build an adequate shelter protection for 160,000 persons. They reiterated the view that if a deep shelter failed to resist a direct hit, heavy casualties would occur with danger of confusion and panic, and added the further psychological argument that a deep shelter system would almost inevitably create a 'shelter mentality' which would interfere with essential war production. They therefore confirmed the general policy of the Government against deep shelters, while recommending that more strongly protected shelters should be furnished for certain vital industrial undertakings.

The Government accepted the findings of the Hailey Report and, on April 20, John Anderson informed the House of Commons that there would be no change in their general policy regarding the provision of deep shelters.[1] His statement was accorded a mixed reception and the controversy continued to smoulder, with occasional outbreaks of flame, for the next eighteen months, by which time it had ceased to be academic.

It is not to be doubted that Anderson was in full accord with the views of the Hailey Report and with the general policy of the Government. When he assumed the onerous responsibilities of Civil Defence in November 1938, he had been fully aware of the main difficulties which he would have to face. He had foreseen the demands which would arise from some quarters for a comprehensive deep shelter policy, from others for wholesale evacuation, and from yet others for 'business as usual'. He had anticipated, and had discussed with his subordinates, the inevitability of the press joining issue on all these matters. With his usual methodical thoroughness he had gone into the various aspects of popular protection with his experts and had reached the conclusion that casualties would be less and protection greater if people were dispersed than if they were congregated together. He considered the adoption of a deep shelter policy, though, ideally speaking, it had much to recommend it, impractical for the reasons which the Hailey Report later endorsed, and of these reasons he was most impressed by the psychological.

It seemed clear to John that if Hitler could force a 'shelter

[1] *House of Commons Debates*, April 20, 1939. Cols. 471-476.

mentality' upon the people of Britain he would have won a very considerable psychological victory, for any people who ducked underground every time the sirens wailed would inevitably lose its war. The enemy had but to keep the nation's head down long enough and often enough to convert them into a race of troglodytes and to slow vital production to a standstill. Moreover, he propounded the logical and unanswerable question : 'How deep is safe ?' Having adopted this view he was unshakable in maintaining it.

But with the coming of the Blitz to London in September 1940 the controversy on deep shelters blazed forth again amid the fiercer fires of the burning city. British and American journalists, reporting the effect of bombing and the plight of the homeless, vehemently attacked the Government for its lack of provision of communal protection. John was unmoved by the onslaught, but he was also opposed to a concurrent opinion among some of his Cabinet colleagues for the abolition of the air-raid siren warnings. These were sounded when enemy aircraft crossed the English coast, with the result that many factories stopped work for hours though no German planes were within miles of them, and the work of Government departments was also similarly disrupted. The loss to production was considerable and there were those in the Defence Committee of the Cabinet who favoured the abolition of the siren system altogether. This course of action Anderson strongly and successfully resisted, arguing that the population were entitled to such warning.[1]

But on the subject of deep shelters he remained adamant in the face of the newspaper demands and — perhaps ill-advisedly, for the workings of the popular press were remote from his understanding — he summoned a conference of editors. In no uncertain terms, he told them that a policy of deep shelters would not be adopted and virtually recommended them to drop their campaign. 'Is that the policy of the Government ?' one of his hearers enquired, and John replied in tones of thunder : 'Do you think I should have said what I have said were that not so ?'

From that moment he was doomed. The attacks in the press persisted and became more personal to him. As the force of the

[1] James Leasor, *War at the Top, based on the experiences of General Sir Leslie Hollis, K.C.B., K.B.E.* (1959), p. 109.

enemy's onslaught continued and the winter drew on, the demands for some mitigation of the Government's policy became irresistible.

> The simple fact was [as Ritchie Calder has written], that lots of people wanted communal shelters, preferably deep ones. They wanted the moral support of having others around them. They wanted even that 'fug' which caused doctors so much concern and the herd comfort, even though 'comfort' meant sleeping on stone platforms or between the rails of the Underground, or the tedious discomfort of standing in a queue for half the day for places in the shelters. Above all . . . they wanted to sleep with a sense of security, even though that security was often just an illusion. For there is no doubt that lots of popular shelters were no safer, and often less so, than the domestic shelters.[1]

For the people of London, in their search for communal shelters, simply occupied the Tube stations, in defiance of the established official policy that the underground railways were to be kept free for the movement of troops and other essential war services. In the severity of the Blitz people decided this issue for themselves by the simple device of buying a $1\frac{1}{2}$d. ticket and parking themselves on the platforms, and they queued up at midday to do so. Service men on leave kept places for their families at work. Unevacuated schoolchildren acted as 'proxies' for their relatives. Old people in bath-chairs, cripples on crutches, children in perambulators, and men and women of every age and condition queued up towards evening, oblivious of daylight siren warnings and even of dog-fights overhead. The station staffs had not the heart to turn them out into the raids and, once the occupation of the stations had really developed, they had not the means. The Government and the London Passenger Transport Board accepted the inevitable. They installed sanitation and water supplies and even ran canteen trains to help feed the shelterers. London had solved the issue of deep shelters for itself, and the Government later receded further from its original position by arranging for the basement shelters provided by City firms for the protection of their staffs by day to be available to the public at night.

There was no doubt, however, that popular confidence in John Anderson as Home Secretary and Minister of Home Security had been shaken as a result of the newspaper attacks made upon him, and the position of the Government as a whole was consequently weakened.[1] To meet this situation Mr. Churchill decided to use the opportunity presented by the retirement at the end of September of Mr. Neville Chamberlain, now a sick and failing man,[2] from the office of Lord President of the Council, to reorganize his Cabinet.

Sir John Anderson [he has written] had faced the Blitz of London with firm and competent management. By the early days of October the continuous attack on the largest city in the world was so fierce and raised so many problems of a social and political character in its vast harassed population that I thought it would be a help to have a long-trained Parliamentarian at the Home Office, which was now also the Ministry of Home Security. London was bearing the brunt. Herbert Morrison [then Minister of Supply] was a Londoner, versed in every aspect of Metropolitan administration. He had unrivalled experience of London government, having been leader of the County Council, and in many ways the principal figure in its affairs. At the same time I needed John Anderson, whose work at the Home Office had been excellent, as Lord President of the Council in the wider sphere of the Home Affairs Committee, to which an immense mass of business was transferred with great relief to the Cabinet.[3] . . .

It would be erroneous to say that John Anderson's translation from the Home Office to the Lord Presidency of the Council, with a seat in the War Cabinet, was in any sense a demotion, or that it was due solely to the public criticism which had arisen in regard to his shelter policy. Mr. Churchill's statement gives clearly the reasons which were in his mind for the changes of office of Anderson and Morrison and, of these, that which was most compelling was 'popular leadership'. Once the Blitz had started, the Civil Defence structure was no longer a problem of organization behind the scenes : it came under the fire of public and Parliamentary strictures. Thenceforward the main ministerial task was to defend it against these criticisms, to make people believe that it

---

[1] A characteristically vitriolic attack on Anderson was made by Mr. Aneurin Bevan in the House of Commons. *House of Commons Debates*, October 8, 1940. Cols. 348-350.   [2] Mr. Chamberlain died on November 9, 1940.
[3] Churchill, *Their Finest Hour*, p. 326.

was the best they could have and to rally public support. Now this was precisely the sort of thing that John could not do. He was not a popular orator nor one who could easily carry the House of Commons with him. His genius lay in organization and administration and the day for that had now passed in this particular contingency. Herbert Morrison, on the other hand, was in his element ; a Londoner born and bred, a Member for a London constituency, an experienced Parliamentarian and an expert in public presentation, he was 'a natural' for the job of handling the public phase into which Civil Defence had now passed. As much, indeed, of 'a natural' as was John for the complex variety of tasks which assailed him in the Lord President's office. This basically was the essential reason for the change.

> There are two reasons why Ministers are given new offices [wrote Lord Simon, who had had considerable experience in this field, to Anderson] (1) because they filled the old one so well, (2) because they filled the old one so badly. In your case it is reason (1). You have had a grilling time & the whole country ought to be grateful to you. But I am sorry for the change. . . .

Nevertheless, John Anderson had been superseded, for the first and last time in his career, and he felt it deeply. For though, in announcing the ministerial changes in the House of Commons on October 8, the Prime Minister was handsome in praise and gallant in defence — 'There is no better war horse in the Government. I am ashamed of the attacks which are made on him in ignorant and spiteful quarters' [1] — John was bitterly disappointed at being removed from the administration of a Government Department for which he had a great affection and where he believed he was serving to good purpose, even though he was immediately appointed to an office of higher seniority. 'I should like to have seen the job through, Bill', he said to William Mabane, with a rare display of emotion, on his last evening at the Home Office, and he expressed

---

[1] *House of Commons Debates*, October 8, 1940. Col. 294. *The Times* also acclaimed him editorially on October 9 : '. . . a given quantity of German explosive dropped on England now inflicts less than a tenth of the casualties it did in the last War. . . . This represents a remarkable success for the system of shelters ; and Sir John Anderson, in handing over the Ministry of Home Security, is entitled to claim that he has done most of what is possible to solve the problem of safety, though he leaves to Mr. Herbert Morrison a formidable task in solving those of comfort and health.'

MR. CHURCHILL, SIR JOHN ANDERSON AND MR. ATTLEE

similar, though more guarded sentiments, in a letter to his father
on October 3 :

> You will have seen what has happened. If I could have given
> you word in advance I would have done so. I am very sorry
> indeed to be leaving the Home Office even for the more exalted
> position of Lord President of the Council with a seat in the War
> Cabinet. I have been very happy where I am & would have
> liked to see the job through.
> I daresay it will be represented that I have been shunted. I
> don't think that is so. I shall still have in my position a general
> oversight of everything on what is called the home front. In
> addition I shall of course have a more direct share in the responsi-
> bility for the general conduct of the war — which I should have
> been glad to be spared! However in times like these I think one
> must just do what comes one's way & make the best of it.

John was not without his popular defenders, however, and
amongst them was A. P. Herbert, ever a champion of the oppressed.
In verses entitled 'Tough Boy' he expressed the admiration which
many in Britain felt for the services which a great man had given
to the nation :

> You will not mind, as many do,
> The foolish things the clever say :
> You saw the grim decisions through ;
> The sticky jobs all came your way.
>
> But millions, from your armoured nest
> Emerging safe, defiant, free,
> Will say 'John Anderson knew best :
> And we can be as tough as he'.[1]

---

[1] These verses originally appeared in the *Sunday Graphic* of October 20, 1940,
but were later included in a collection of poems by Sir Alan Herbert, entitled *Let us
be Glum* and published by Messrs. Methuen in 1941. I am indebted to both the
author and the publisher for their permission to reproduce them here.

VIII

Cabinet Minister : War Cabinet

1940–1945

(i)

IN the days when the Lords of the Council exercised a dominant power in the government of the country the office of Lord President was one of great personal influence; but, with the growth of Cabinet government and the consequent increase of the authority of the First Lord of the Treasury and Prime Minister, the ascendancy of the position of the Lord President diminished accordingly until it became one of the great sinecure offices of the Crown. This is not to say, however, that it became of no value. Indeed the contrary is the case. There is in Britain a deep-seated prejudice against the term 'Minister without Portfolio', which has a continental and 'un-English' flavour, yet the machinery of administration renders some such posts essential in every government. It therefore became customary to utilize the so-called 'sinecure offices' — the Lord President of the Council, the Lord Privy Seal, the Chancellor of the Duchy of Lancaster and the Paymaster-General — for this purpose. A Prime Minister was thus enabled to have within his Cabinet four persons, who might be members of either House of Parliament, and who, being unencumbered by departmental responsibilities, were free to devote their time to special problems or spheres of governmental activity or to be charged with wide co-ordinating functions. Of these offices that of the Lord President is the senior and the most important, ranking among the great offices of State.

Mr. Churchill's object in appointing John Anderson to this office was thus to free him from Parliamentary responsibilities, for which he was not best suited, while retaining for the service of the State his great administrative genius, his outstanding capacity for co-ordination and his very real ability to resolve any *ad hoc* problems which might arise on the Home Front, whether as a result of enemy action or of the clash of formidable personalities. This, as the Prime Minister wrote, 'lightened my own burden and enabled me to concentrate upon the military conduct of the war, in which my colleagues seemed increasingly disposed to give me latitude'.[1]

Never was a man of Anderson's talents more acutely needed in this capacity. Mr. Chamberlain's Government had never been entirely attuned to the conduct of modern war, a war of totality involving every citizen of the Kingdom as well as every fighting man, and requiring the harnessing of every medium of the nation's energy. When Mr. Churchill assumed the premiership Britain was still groping towards effective policies for the mobilization of men and machines, shipping and money, food and munitions. Good-will there was in plenty and much genius, but what appeared to be lacking was leadership, co-ordination and afflatus. Mr. Churchill provided these requirements for the nation as a whole and for the military conduct of the war in particular, but the fact that Britain began in 1941 to solve, in whole or in part, the vast problems of supply and thereafter moved rapidly to the peak of a great war effort was due in a very major degree to John Anderson.

In forming and reorganizing his all-party administration Mr. Churchill's one thought was to evolve as rapidly as possible and, if necessary, by means of trial and error, a governmental machine which would win the war. Though no aspect of this task was easy, the defence side of the problem presented fewer difficulties than that of supply. The Prime Minister was himself Minister of Defence and, with the Defence Committee of the Cabinet and the Chiefs of Staff Committee, he had ready to his hand a war-winning combination. On the civil side remedies for the early shortcomings of central direction and control were less easily come by. It was not Mr. Churchill's original intention to create in this sphere a Minister with the same degree of authority as the Minister of Defence on the military side, and he knew full well that he himself could only effectively discharge his functions as Minister of Defence because he was Prime Minister also. What he aimed at as a primary objective was to diminish to the lowest possible minimum the

[1] Churchill, *Their Finest Hour*, p. 326.

plethora of advisory committees with which the nation's war machine was encumbered and to replace them by some simpler form of co-ordination. 'Committees', he wrote at this time, 'which are advisers or consist of persons without administrative machines and departments at their disposal and without responsibility for making good any decisions to which they come, are an encumbrance from which I am sedulously endeavouring to free our system.'[1]

In accordance with this admirable principle the Prime Minister decided to essay a new experiment in government, that of entrusting specific powers of decision under important heads of policy to various members of the War Cabinet. Thus Mr. Attlee, as Lord Privy Seal, became Chairman of both the Food Policy Committee and the Home Policy Committee, and to Mr. Arthur Greenwood, Minister without Portfolio, were assigned the Economic Policy Committee and the Production Council. This method of co-ordination — to make the same War Cabinet Member chairman of two committees with a generous provision for overlapping membership — proved effective and economical of time ; but for even greater efficiency a new 'steering committee' was established, its function being to co-ordinate the work of the other civil committees and to ensure that no part of the field was left uncovered.[2]

It was this task of forwarding the plans for harnessing to the war machine the full economic resources of the nation which Mr. Churchill allotted to the Lord President, Sir John Anderson, to whom he gave the following directive :

> . . . it is essential that the larger issues of economic policy should be dealt with by your committee and primarily by you. This is in accordance with the drift of well informed public opinion. You should therefore not hesitate to take the initiative over the whole field. You should summon economists like Keynes to give their views to you personally. You should ask for any assistance or staff you require, utilizing of course the Statistical Department. Professor Lindemann and his branch will assist you in any way you wish, and will also act as liaison between

[1] Quoted by Sir Keith Hancock and Mrs. M. M. Gowing in *British War Economy* (1949), p. 218. To this great work of official history the reader is referred for details of the functions and achievements of the Lord President's Committee.

[2] During the time that Anderson was its chairman, the hard core of the Lord President's Committee consisted of Mr. Attlee, Mr. Bevin, Mr. Morrison, Sir Kingsley Wood and Sir Andrew Duncan.

you and me. I wish you to take the lead prominently and vigorously in this committee, and it should certainly meet once a week, if not more often.[1]

At first this seemed a somewhat lonely assignment. Anderson moved over to the Privy Council office, in the old Treasury building which had already been damaged by bombing and was in a dreary and draughty condition. He took with him, as Personal Assistant, Norman Brook, who had been his Private Secretary since he became a Minister, and who continued to serve him brilliantly. After the thronging responsibilities of the Home Office, there seemed at first to be little to do — save sit and read the telegrams and the Cabinet papers. Even his attendance at meetings of the War Cabinet, of which he was now for the first time a full member, provided little scope for Anderson's abounding energy in these early weeks before he found his feet in his new co-ordinating rôle. The contrast with his heavy executive responsibilities as Home Secretary was very marked. In those early days he did not take kindly to the rôle which Mr. Churchill himself subsequently described as 'that exalted brooding over the work done by others which may well be the lot of a Minister, however influential, who has no Department'. As Mr. Churchill went on to say : 'It is easier to give directions than advice, and more agreeable to have the right to act, even in a limited sphere, than the privilege to talk at large.'[2]

This mood, and the circumstances which provoked it, did not last for long. Other Ministers had already learned, through his work in Civil Defence, what wise advice Anderson could give on almost any problem of administration and how deft he was in resolving interdepartmental differences. It was not long before they began to turn to him for help, in problems of every sort and kind on what was coming to be known as 'the Home Front' ; and these were handled smoothly and effectively either at small meetings of Ministers which he held *ad hoc* or through the standing machinery of the Lord President's Committee. The Prime Minister himself increasingly relied on Anderson to handle on his behalf a widening range of problems outside the military and strategic area which he reserved to himself.

---

[1] Churchill, *The Grand Alliance* (1950), p. 102.
[2] Churchill, *The Gathering Storm*, p. 365.

The year 1941 was perhaps the most crucial of the war. For the first six months, until Hitler's invasion of the Soviet Union on June 22, Britain stood literally alone, and though, with the passage of the Lease-Lend Act in March, American economic aid became increasingly more accessible, it was not until Japanese treachery at Pearl Harbour made the United States an active belligerent that the full resources of that great country were thrown into the balance.

In the meantime crises of all kinds arose in Britain and were dealt with effectively by the Lord President's Committee. As Lord President, John had no Department and he made no attempt to build up a staff of his own, being able to call on the services of members of the War Cabinet Secretariat. Moreover, for the economic problems with which he now had to deal, he could draw on the galaxy of genius of the Economic Section of the War Cabinet, where shone such luminaries as John Jewkes, Lionel Robbins, James Meade and D. N. Chester.

Anderson's first impact upon the members of his Economic Section was very similar to that experienced in the past by his colleagues and subordinates in Dublin and in Calcutta. As he had found despondency in the Castle and in the Civil Service of Bengal so now he encountered it in Whitehall. Hitherto the economic conduct of the war had been largely devolved by the Cabinet upon a mass of special committees with various Ministers with ill-defined areas of responsibility in charge of them ; and the relationship of the Economic Section to these committees was nebulous in the extreme. They lived, in point of fact, for the most part in a state of endless frustration. Men of high professional eminence would spend weeks writing to order memoranda of no obvious immediate relevance and no clear destination as regards ministerial consumption. When finished, as often as not these memoranda would be rewritten at a higher level, presumably to fit them better for assimilation by Ministers who probably never saw them. The morale of the Section was consequently distressingly low. 'It was well nigh intolerable', writes one of its members, 'to have to sit around at this critical period of the war, watching the economic conduct thereof in chaos, and ourselves not able to do anything effective to remedy it.'

John Anderson's coming changed all that. It is true that in the earlier period the main responsibility for economic co-ordination had been gently edged towards the Lord President's Committee under Mr. Chamberlain who, whatever his faults as a leader, was at least a trained administrator and a Minister out of whom it was possible to get quick and clear-cut decisions. But it was not until Anderson's appointment that the position was defined and the machinery which was to serve so well and relieve the War Cabinet of all but the most important decisions in the economic sphere was definitely established. Some credit here must certainly go to the Prime Minister's advisers at the official level, who by then had learnt by bitter experience the need for this kind of co-ordinating body. But it was Anderson's personality and ability which gave it life and impulse. For although it was endowed by the Prime Minister's directive with most extensive powers, unless it had been run by someone of Anderson's grasp of administrative principle and capacity as a chairman, it might well have been a failure. The ministries whose policies had to be co-ordinated were powerful establishments, whose activities tended only too easily to be more like the activities of independent sovereign states than parts of an integrated whole. For a Minister without a ministry to bring them into a common plan and to school them, often almost without their knowing it, was something of a miracle, and it is to be doubted whether anyone else could have achieved it.

The effect on the Economic Section was instantaneous. At once their official work acquired purpose and meaning. Their main business became clear : to provide briefs for the Lord President on the various items coming as the agenda of the regular meetings of his Committee ; to provide secretaries for the various special committees and enquiries over which he presided and, in general, to keep him in touch with the current state of the economy and the problems which loomed ahead. This was a full-time job and overnight their lives became very strenuous. But they enjoyed working for John Anderson : he took what they did seriously, they felt they were playing their part.

Mr. John Jewkes [1] was then Director of the Section, and the

---

[1] John Jewkes, C.B.E., M.A., now Professor of Economic Organization in the University of Oxford.

first time he saw Anderson he was told : 'I will read what you send me and I am not necessarily a foe to long documents if you think it is important that I should read them.' This was shortly after Mr. Churchill had issued one of his more picturesque directives laying down that all minutes should be condensed to one sheet of paper. This put the members of the Section on their mettle : they took great pains to see that the Lord President got only what they thought was strictly necessary for him to read. But it was a great comfort to know that what they did was likely to be noticed ; and as, day after day, the papers that they had sent up the night before were returned with a big tick initialed 'J.A.' and the salient passages side-lined in the margin, they speedily began to feel that life in the public service in war-time was not so futile and unrewarding after all.

John Jewkes moved on to the Ministry of Aircraft Production, for which his services had been begged from the Lord President, and Professor Lionel Robbins [1] was appointed to succeed him. He reported to Anderson through Norman Brook, but Brook would take Robbins with him when there was anything of economic importance to discuss ; and Anderson welcomed the presence of other members of his Economic Section when their special qualifications bore on the subject. This was an education for them all. John had a deep respect for expert knowledge and treated his advisers on equal terms. But on application he was in a class by himself and, with his vast knowledge of the machinery of government and his massive sanity and practical wisdom, he was a man with whom, as the Germans say, you argue with the hat in the hand.

At this time, among Ministers, Anderson was one of the three most important in the conduct of the war, the others being the Prime Minister and Ernest Bevin. It was because John was economic co-ordinator at this critical stage that the Prime Minister was able to leave to him and his Committee the responsibility for the running of that side of the business of government — a task which, it is safe to say, Mr. Churchill would have found both tedious and unrewarding ; for it was one for which his own shining qualities were not conspicuously suited. Not that from time to time there

---

[1] Lord Robbins, C.B., Professor of Economics in the University of London (1929–1961).

THE LORD PRESIDENT

were not incursions from on high into these complicated matters ; but on the whole, the main business of civil and economic administration flowed on under the orderly review of the Lord President's Committee, leaving the War Cabinet free to concentrate on the higher issues of strategy and politics.

With the aid of its Economic Section, the Lord President's Committee met and overcame issues in the fields of prices and wages, compensation, the level of home consumption, the concentration of industry, and the supply of coal, rubber, petroleum and other materials. By the end of the year the main lines of economic policy had been clearly defined and established and the authority of the Committee had grown with its achievements. No problem in the sphere of home affairs and economic policy reached the War Cabinet before being first discussed by John Anderson and his colleagues, and as their willingness to take firm hold of this power and to produce results was recognized so were other burdens added to them.

In his rôle as co-ordinator and arbiter in differences between Departments, Anderson dealt with a wide variety of miscellaneous questions mainly, though not exclusively, on the Home Front. But his chief concern — the continuing theme of his work during these middle years of the war — was to stimulate and concert the measures needed to ensure that the country's economic resources were fully mobilized for war. And at the heart of this lay the work which he did from the end of 1941 onwards in planning, together with Ernest Bevin, the Minister of Labour, the allocation of the country's manpower.

As a result of the pre-war planning the Government had avoided some of the errors of the First War, when all the able-bodied young men were free to volunteer for service in the Armed Forces, where only too often those with special skills had no opportunity to deploy their abilities to the best advantage of the State. The system of 'reserved occupations' had ensured that, by and large, men would be kept or placed in the jobs, whether military or civilian, in which they could make their best contribution to the national cause. But, by the end of 1941, it had become plain that manpower would be the limiting factor in our war economy. There were not enough men and women in the country to do all the jobs that were needed in furtherance of the war effort. The nation faced, in fact, an over-all shortage of manpower. The demands of the Armed Forces and the munitions industries were insatiable ; and it was evident that, if these were left to absorb all the men and women they needed, other industries and services essential to the conduct of the war would break down. No system of priorities would suffice to meet this situation ; for, if the services of high priority were allowed to take all they needed, others would be left with nothing at all. It was clear that, as with scarce materials in the special area of war-production, so over the whole range of the war-economy it would be necessary to apply a system of allocation which would ensure that the limited number of men and women available would be apportioned in such a way that even the less important services, if they had to be maintained at all, would receive the bare minimum which they needed to keep themselves in operation.

In this situation the manpower allocations became the main governing factor in controlling the distribution of resources be-tween the various parts of the war effort. As in peace a Govern-ment determines, through its financial control, the direction and pace of its various policies ; so during the war it used the man-power control to modify the pattern of the nation's effort. The War Cabinet's annual review of the distribution of the nation's manpower was known, in fact, as the Manpower Budget. Through the manpower allocations the Government varied the emphasis to be given at different stages to different aspects of the nation's war effort. Thus, in the early years, men and women were drawn into the Armed Forces, munitions production and other 'essential' industries — first from the pool of unemployed and then, pro-gressively, by reducing the labour force employed in the less essential industries and services which ministered to civilian needs. By the middle of the war the country had been reduced to the level of a siege economy, with a vast proportion of its men and women in the Forces or in the factories supplying them. Then in the last phase the strategic decision was taken that the war in Europe might be won by the end of 1944, that weapons not available by then would not be used, and that men could now be drawn out from the munitions industries to build up the strength of the Forces for the final onslaught against the German fortress in Europe.

This broad planning was based on a mass of detailed work. The supervision of it all was shared between John Anderson and Ernest Bevin, in a fruitful partnership based on the mutual respect which they had first formed for one another in the desperate days of improvisation at the time of the Munich crisis.[1] Anderson, assisted by his small personal staff and by his advisers in the Economic Section, was responsible for framing the broad outline of the plan and for gaining its acceptance by the Ministers in charge of the Departments competing for the limited supplies of manpower. This required an enormous amount of patient sifting of facts and figures and preliminary negotiations between Departments, and in this sort of work John's clear head and massive judgment were seen at their best. Bevin, through the expanded organization of the Ministry of Labour with its regional framework spreading throughout the country, was responsible for the vast task of supplying the labour in accordance with the allocations. But he and his official advisers were also able to make a significant contribution towards the planning — by the exercise of their judgment, based on practical experience up and down the country, of the pace at which the expanding industries could absorb, and the contracting industries could release, labour.

So long as John Anderson was Lord President, the manpower allocations were considered by the Lord President's Committee before being submitted for final approval by the War Cabinet itself. It is proof of the personal contribution which Anderson made to this work that, when he became Chancellor of the Exchequer, these responsibilities were transferred to a Ministerial Manpower Committee under his chairmanship. In that capacity he continued to supervise the Government's manpower planning until the end of the war. He shares with Ernest Bevin the credit for a system of manpower allocation which throughout the war enabled the nation to make the fullest and best use of its men and women, whether for work at home or in the field, to a far greater degree than that achieved by any other country during this or any previous war.[2]

[1] See above, p. 220.
[2] A detailed account of this all-important aspect of the national war effort and of John Anderson's part in it is to be found in Mr. Henry Parker's book, *Manpower, a Study of War-time Policy and Administration* : History of the Second World War, United Kingdom Series (1957).

Early in 1942 the Home Policy Committee was abolished and its functions transferred to the aegis of the Lord President, who also became Chairman of the Food Policy Committee, and it was from the Lord President's Committee that there evolved the system of points rationing both of food and clothing. The difficulties of extending straight rationing were obvious : an entitlement to $\frac{1}{20}$ of a tin of preserved apricots would have been derisory, quite apart from the excruciating difficulties of administration. All sorts of plans were considered, most of which involved tying customers to particular shops. But eventually the problem was solved by the introduction of a sort of food money — points — which could be spent freely according to the point prices fixed to different goods by the Ministry of Food — a kind of substitute price system which preserved the maximum freedom for the customer, while ensuring orderly distribution. It would be difficult to give the credit for this striking innovation to any one person : it was essentially a co-operative effort whose origins were at quite a humble level. But there can be no doubt that much of the success of the movement in this direction was due to Anderson, who, the moment the scheme was explained to him, grasped the underlying theory and lent to what, to the more sedate spirits of Whitehall, was a fantastic and frivolous whimsy of the academic imagination, the solid weight of his authoritative support.

Anderson also brought to the Lord President's Committee the really terrifying magnitude of his own experience and knowledge. From the deep resources of his memory he would cull facts and precedents long forgotten in the Government Departments of their origin. For example, one Ministry, wishing to put up a proposal to the Committee, deputed one of their senior Civil Servants to make their case. He elected to preface his main remarks with an historical précis and began with the words : 'Under the scheme of 19— (naming a year fully a quarter of a century or more ago) the schedule of payments was based upon two categories.'

'Three', observed Sir John quietly.

Somewhat disconcerted by the interruption, which he was not sure if he had heard correctly, the official began again : 'Under the scheme of 19—, the schedule of payments was based upon two categories'.

'Three', repeated Sir John.

Now thoroughly rattled, the Ministry's spokesman said almost appealingly, 'Really, Lord President, there were only *two* categories under the scheme of 19—.'

'There were three', Sir John asserted, adding, 'I drafted the scheme of 19—.'

He was right on both counts, and there ensued what Mr. Punch would once have called 'collapse of stout party'.

John also expected his ministerial colleagues to be at least as well briefed as he was, and to some of them it seemed as if they had gone back to school, with the concomitant danger of being hauled over the coals if their 'homework' was not properly prepared. The Lord President insisted upon their ability to answer even the most abstruse questions in their own fields : 'How many wagons are immobilized south of the exchange points ?' he once demanded suddenly of the Minister of Transport. 'I'm afraid I have no idea, Lord President', was the reply, to which John responded magisterially : 'On future occasions you will come "arrrmed" with the necessary information.'

In addition to his work with his own Committee, Anderson was a member of the Defence and India Committees of the Cabinet and he was also invited to give personal consideration, before decision by the War Cabinet, to a great variety of special problems such as the heavy bomber programme and plans for the military occupation of Persia. So widely were his gifts recognized that when the question arose of incorporating the Royal Air Force Regiment into the Army it surprised nobody that John should be appointed chairman of the Committee formed for this purpose.[1] Moreover, from first to last, in whatever office he held, he was entrusted by the Prime Minister with the supervision of British activities in connection with the atom bomb.[2]

As part of the traditional duties of the office of Lord President John also exercised ministerial responsibility for a number of governmental scientific organizations, notably the Department of Scientific and Industrial Research, the Agricultural Research Council and the Medical Research Council, and it was his connection with

[1] Sir Arthur Bryant, *Triumph in the West* (1959), p. 194.
[2] See below, pp. 290-299.

the last of these which was the occasion of one of Mr. Churchill's happiest minutes. The War Cabinet had set up, in August 1942, a ministerial committee consisting of Sir Stafford Cripps, then Lord Privy Seal, and the three Service Ministers, to supervise the work of an expert body on the use made of psychologists and psychiatrists in the fighting services. By December Sir Stafford's interest in this work had waned and the Prime Minister desired Anderson to take over his duties. The Prime Minister's directive was both trenchant and lucid :

I am sure it would be sensible to restrict as much as possible the work of these gentlemen [he wrote to John] who are capable of doing an immense amount of harm with what may very easily degenerate into charlatanry. The tightest hand should be kept over them, and they should not be allowed to quarter themselves in large numbers upon the Fighting Services at the public expense. There are no doubt easily recognizable cases which may benefit from treatment of this kind, but it is very wrong to disturb large numbers of healthy, normal men and women by asking the kind of questions in which the psychiatrists specialize. There are quite enough hangers-on and camp-followers already.[1]

It would be both untrue and unjust to John Anderson's colleagues on the Lord President's Committee to attribute its phenomenal rise and authority on the Home Front to his personality alone, but few will deny the truth of the official historian's judgment that 'just as the collaboration between Mr. Churchill and the Chiefs of Staff gave the Defence Committee its own special character, so also did the Lord President's Committee take its stamp from the personality and endowments of Sir John Anderson and the manner of his collaboration with his civilian advisers'.[2]

John's years in this high office were the high-water mark of his Ministerial career. Neither before nor later did he achieve such undoubted pre-eminence nor such an outstandingly felicitous outlet for his tremendous attributes. 'His extremely wide knowledge, his great administrative experience, the powers of analysis and clarity of mind which would have made him an outstanding judge', writes one who worked with him at this time, 'these were just the

[1] Churchill, *The Hinge of Fate* (1951), p. 815.
[2] Hancock and Gowing (*op. cit.*), p. 223.

qualities required in one whose job it was to judge between conflicting advice and interests, to secure acquiescence in policies which, though in the national interest, were difficult for certain departments and to see that departmental Ministers did not get out of step.'

His unique position in the life of the country was recognized and appreciated not only by his colleagues and subordinates, but by those foreign observers with whom he was thrown into contact. The American Ambassador, John Winant, wrote of him at this time:

> His ability in integrating the skill of the expert, whether scientist, engineer or economist, without disturbing the efficiency of routine controls, permitted the maximum contribution by the expert, and the full authoritative drive of officials responsible for purely administrative activities. There was no duplication or waste of brains or energy in the functioning of his over-all planning. Mr. Churchill referred to him as the 'Home Front Prime Minister'. He was tough and hard-working, patient and sagacious. Nor did he give the impression of being endowed with more than average ability — a nice trait in a man who can afford it.[1]

John's nickname throughout Whitehall was 'Jehovah', in kindly tribute to his Olympian calm 'and a recognition . . . even in jest that here was someone built on lines distinctly grander in scale than those of everyday men'.[2] 'Here we all are — Jehovah's witnesses', Mr. Attlee once remarked to a Committee that was waiting for John,[3] and in that calm lay both his strength and also a certain weakness. His imperturbability seemed sometimes to be carried to the point of unwillingness to think ahead ; his analytical and administrative cogency to be matched by a lack of creative power ; his fairness and balance to arise to some extent from a lack of excitement or any feeling of involvement.

It was indeed this very quality of detachment — which unfriendly critics did not hesitate to term 'lack of imagination' — that accounted for John's least successful performance in the House of Commons. The occasion was the initial statement in February

---

[1] John Gilbert Winant, *A Letter from Grosvenor Square* (1947), p. 153.
[2] Rt. Hon. Walter Elliot, M.P., in *The Scotsman*, January 6, 1958.
[3] C. R. Attlee, *As it Happened* (London, 1954), p. 128.

1943 of the Government's intentions regarding the Beveridge Plan, and the circumstances were unusual. A stage had been reached in the course of the war when public opinion, both in Britain and in America, had become diverted towards problems of post-war reconstruction, and in the previous year the British Government had entrusted to Sir William Beveridge the task of preparing a plan for the improvement and extension of the existing measures for social insurance. The outcome of his efforts was awaited with considerable interest on both sides of the Atlantic, for there still lurked in America certain impressions that Britain remained at heart a reactionary country, one at least of whose war aims was to make the future safe for the privileged few. In Britain itself, and among the troops overseas, attention was focused on the Beveridge Report, and the Government's reaction to it, as an indication of what reliance could be placed upon the promises for a 'better world' and 'equality of opportunity' which had been offered with a certain glib profusion.

In November 1942 the Beveridge Report was published. It proposed a comprehensive scheme of insurance available for the entire population of the United Kingdom and giving title to a whole range of benefits. Interlocked with this plan were to be a complete and full medical service for all, children's allowances, a new method of dealing with industrial injuries, and training schemes for the unemployed. The whole was to be administered by a Ministry of Social Security as a unified scheme.[1]

The recommendations contained in the Report constituted a full and abundant fulfilment of the most optimistic hopes which had been entertained for the betterment of social conditions after the war ; the question, however, remained — what did the Government intend to do about it ? As weeks, and even months, went past without a statement of these intentions, doubts began to arise about the Government's sincerity in their professed desires for a better world, and doubts grew into suspicion when an order issued by the Secretary of State for War forbade the circulation among troops of a résumé of the report composed by Sir William Beveridge himself.

In order to draw the Government into the open, Mr. Arthur

[1] *Report by Sir William Beveridge on Social Insurance and Allied Services*, Cmd. 6404.

Greenwood (now no longer in the Cabinet), introduced a motion in the House of Commons on February 16, 1943, welcoming the recommendations of the Beveridge Report and inviting the Government to state their plans for bringing them to fruition. To John Anderson fell the task of making this statement. He was indeed an obvious choice, for as Lord President of the Council he was ministerially responsible for the Home Front, both present and future, and his whole background of experience in the field of national insurance seemingly made him a most appropriate spokesman. The moment was an important one. The attention of America was centred on the Front Bench that day and the Labour Party as a whole looked to John to dispel the anxieties and distrust engendered by the Government's long delay.

Both were lamentably disappointed. Anderson announced at the outset that the Government could not accept the Beveridge Plan in its entirety nor could they take immediate steps to make it operative. While the general lines of development of the social services laid down in the report were those which Ministers wished to follow, not all the main features of the Plan commended themselves equally to the Government. Furthermore, in view of the uncertainties of financial and world conditions after the war, the Government could not undertake any definite commitments at this stage. None the less, draft legislation would be prepared as soon as possible, on the assumption that employment would be maintained at a level sufficient for the purposes of the Plan — an assumption which, he pointed out, was at present entirely incapable of proof.[1]

Anderson's statement, with its very guarded and seemingly lukewarm acceptance of the main features of the Beveridge Plan, was heard with great impatience by Labour members and he was subjected to frequent interruptions. They were especially annoyed at his insistence upon no final commitments. While it was recognized that he spoke for the Government as a whole, a Government which contained eminent leaders of the Labour Party, it was also felt that his manner of address showed little personal enthusiasm for the recommendations of the Report, and it was generally felt that he had not risen to the full possibilities of the moment.

[1] *House of Commons Debates*, February 16, 1943. Cols. 1655-1678.

T

Disappointment was voiced on all sides. The Labour Party decided to table an amendment expressing its dissatisfaction with the Government's statement and calling for an early implementation of the Report. Some forty Conservatives agreed to call for the setting up forthwith of the proposed Ministry of Social Security and a Liberal amendment demanded legislation at the earliest possible moment.

The Government remained unmoved in the face of these expostulations and indeed further fuel was added to fires of exasperation on the following day (February 17) by the Chancellor of the Exchequer, Sir Kingsley Wood, who made the realization of the Beveridge Plan seem even more remote and problematical than had John Anderson. The Labour Party, disregarding the appeals of Mr. Attlee and Mr. Bevin to the contrary, remained determined to press their amendment to a division. A spirited defence of the Government by Mr. Herbert Morrison in the House on February 19 — a defence in which he declared that, far from being dilatory, the Government had made extraordinary dispatch, thanks chiefly to the energy and industry of the Lord President — went some considerable way to meeting criticism. Mr. Morrison drew attention to the fact, which John had failed to do, that the Government had already published pretty specifically their provisional conclusion about the main points of the Report and had in reality committed themselves to a whole series of items in it, but these commitments were necessarily dependent upon financial considerations. Instead of dwelling upon what the Government could *not* do, as John had done, Mr. Morrison emphasized what they *had* done, which he represented as substantially accepting the Report. He could not understand, he said, the idea entertained by some people that the Government had almost rejected the Beveridge Plan. This was a complete illusion. The necessary machinery for framing legislation was already in operation and the necessary Bills would be placed before Parliament as soon as possible.

Mr. Morrison's fighting defence did much to redeem the day and he succeeded in removing the bad impression created by John Anderson and the Chancellor of the Exchequer upon Conservative and Liberal members, who withdrew their amendments. With his fellow-members of the Labour Party he was less successful, however. They remained obdurate, refusing to be pacified, and pressed their amendment to a division. Ninety-seven of them voted in support of it, while only two non-official Labour members supported the Government. The Labour amendment was lost by 335 votes against 119 in favour.

The whole affair was a remarkable example of the difference between the amateur and the professional in Parliamentary technique. What Mr. Morrison had said was not very different in essence from the content of John's statement, but his manner of saying it was one which, at least to some extent, reassured the House, whereas John's passionless periods had merely antagonized it.

It was perhaps his very qualities of detachment which prevented the development of any degree of intimacy between John Anderson and Mr. Churchill. The Prime Minister was fully and generously cognizant of the great services which John was performing and of the immense burden of responsibility which he was carrying on the Home Front, thereby relieving the Prime Minister himself. When he and Mr. Attlee were absent from the country simultaneously, Mr. Churchill had no qualms about leaving the conduct of affairs in John's hands, calling him 'the automatic pilot',[1] and in due course he was to name him to the King as second in succession to himself.[2]

Mr. Churchill treated John with respect but as a friendly power of equal status rather than a satellite ; a friendly power with whom it was difficult, if not well nigh impossible, for him to get on intimate terms. John never became a crony of the Prime Minister.

Nevertheless, there was virtually no office, either at home or abroad, which Mr. Churchill did not consider John Anderson capable of filling. In the spring of 1943 the choice of a new Viceroy of India, in succession to the Marquess of Linlithgow, greatly exercised the Government. The Prime Minister proposed the name of Mr. Eden to the King and when, for very good reasons, His Majesty counselled against this,[3] his choice fell upon John Anderson. An excellent Viceroy he would have made in war or in peace, and no member of the Government was better versed than he in Indian problems. But the arguments which had been adduced by King George against the appointment of Anthony Eden — namely that

---

[1] Attlee (*op. cit.*), p. 128.   [2] See below, pp. 316-317.
[3] Wheeler-Bennett (*op. cit.*), pp. 700-702.

he could not be spared from the direction of foreign affairs — were equally cogent in the case of John Anderson's indispensability on the Home Front, and the possibility of his being removed from this sphere filled many with dismay. The great wisdom and experience of General Smuts saved the day. 'Don't let Churchill send Anderson away', he conjured Mr Attlee. 'Every War Cabinet needs a man to run the machine. Milner did it in the First World War, and Anderson does it in this.' Attlee was in complete agreement. Together they made representations to the Prime Minister and there was no more talk of sending John to India.[1]

(ii)

On the sixth of October 1941, John Anderson wrote one of his regular dutiful letters to his father. Having dealt with the weather (it had improved), the fruit crop at 'Picket Wood' (they had not had 20 lb. of apples from the whole garden) and the autumnal glories of the dahlias, chrysanthemums and Michaelmas daisies, he came — on the third page — to the meat of his letter :

> I don't usually have much news. I have this week, however, one item that will surprise you & may perhaps startle you. I have decided — not in any undue haste — to marry again. The lady is a widow — aged 45 — whose husband died five years ago. He was in the diplomatic service. Her name is Mrs. Ralph Wigram. I expect we shall be married very quietly within the next two months.

The name of Mrs. Wigram apparently meant nothing at all to David Anderson and he seems to have said so, for on October 22 his son replied, with a touch of asperity :

> I am sorry you had so little information about Mrs. Wigram's circumstances. There was a good deal about her in the London papers & I thought, wrongly as it seems, that you would have seen similar reports.

The lady who had now become the object of John's affections had indeed a most interesting background and her life to date had been full of incident and success.

[1] Attlee (*op. cit.*), p. 128, and *House of Lords Debates*, January 28, 1958. Col. 221.

In 1880 her father, John Edward Courtenay Bodley, then a young Oxford graduate, had become Private Secretary to Sir Charles Dilke, then Under-Secretary of State for Foreign Affairs in Mr. Gladstone's Government and later President of the Local Government Board. Bodley was destined to play an important part in the life of this brilliant and erratic statesman *manqué*, serving him with devotion and only parting from him after the unfortunate circumstances which terminated Dilke's official career some five years later.[1]

Thereafter Bodley adopted a career of letters. He lived much in Paris and in 1898 published a major standard work on the political history of modern France — a work which many thought comparable to Lord Bryce's *American Commonwealth* — which placed him in the forefront of historians of his day. Four years previously he had married Evelyn Frances Bell (whom he divorced in 1908) and by her had four children, three sons and a daughter, whose existence he, curiously enough, omitted to acknowledge in his entry in *Who's Who*.[2]

His daughter, born in 1896, had for one of her godmothers that great and splendid relic of the Second Empire, Princess Mathilde Bonaparte, daughter of King Jerome of Westphalia and niece of the Emperor Napoleon I. So strongly Bonapartist was Bodley in his sympathies that his first intention was to have his child christened Laetitia Ramolino, after Napoleon's mother. From this fate, however, she was rescued by the Marquess of Dufferin and Ava, then British Ambassador in Paris. As his wife was the other godmother, he insisted on the child being given the name of Ava.

Ava Bodley grew up in the fascinating atmosphere of her father's wide circle of friends in France and England. From her earliest years she was accustomed to the society of politicians, artists and writers, and at the age of four she was painted — albeit very reluctantly — by the great Ernest Hébert, then nearing the end of

---

[1] The circumstances of the relationship of Dilke and Bodley, and of Bodley's conviction that Joseph Chamberlain had purposely encompassed Dilke's downfall — a belief that Dilke himself did not share — are related by Mr. Roy Jenkins in his admirable book, *Sir Charles Dilke, a Victorian Tragedy* (1958). See also Sir Shane Leslie's *Memoir of John Edward Courtenay Bodley* (1930).

[2] Bodley married again in 1920, five years before his death, and had two sons by his second wife. This fact is also omitted from *Who's Who*.

his life.[1] Pretty and witty and highly intelligent, she derived the full benefit from her upbringing.

After the close of the First World War Ava became a bright figure in the mad gaiety which gripped London and Paris. She had many admirers but it was not until 1924 that she fell seriously in love with a man five years older than herself. In the autumn of this year she had gone to Algiers to look after an ailing brother. There she met Ralph Follet Wigram, then First Secretary at the British Embassy in Paris, who was spending a belated leave in North Africa.

It was a whirlwind courtship. They were married in February of the following year and there opened before Ava the happy vista of a brilliant diplomatic and social career.[2] They were eminently suited to one another. 'Wigs' was marked for success, and Ava, with her remarkable facility for bringing people together and making them talk and her connoisseur's knowledge of food and wine, was designed by Fate and Nature to be a great hostess. But it seemed that, at the outset at any rate, Fate was against her. Her father died in May 1925. In the following year Ralph Wigram was stricken with infantile paralysis and, in 1929, Ava gave birth to a son who, from his earliest days until his death some twenty years later, was an incurable invalid due to a maldelivery. Ava withstood this wave of misfortune with great fortitude. It was her determination and loyalty as much as his own gallantry that brought Ralph Wigram back to active service, albeit lamed for life, and her loving devotion to her son Charley was deep and abiding throughout his life.

Wigram's return to duty and the subsequent years of his life were not only a supreme triumph of mind over matter but also of great benefit to British diplomacy. Though young in years and

---

[1] 'Your old painter, M. Hébert, died yesterday in his ninety-second year', Bodley wrote to his daughter on November 6, 1908. 'I hope the original of his most beautiful painting will live as long. It will be a most interesting reminiscence for you, in years to come, to say that you had your portrait painted by a great French artist, who was born when Napoleon was still alive, at the request of the Princess Mathilde, who was the niece of the Emperor' (Leslie (*op. cit.*), pp. 416-417).

[2] 'Now that you are embarking on a new road my prayer is that it may be as happy and as interesting as the old one which we trod together', her father wrote to Ava on the eve of her marriage. 'My life, of which we shared so much, is behind me ; while you have before you a career which I trust will be full of blessing' (Leslie (*op. cit.*), p. 430).

comparatively junior in service, no secretary in the diplomatic service of any country ever established such a position as 'Wigs' made for himself in the Paris Embassy and in the Foreign Office, whither he was transferred in 1933.[1] From the earliest days of Hitler's rise to power in Germany he recognized the threat to world peace inherent in National Socialism. His prodigious memory, his indefatigable industry and his high courage — undeterred by physical disability — enabled him to foresee and foretell almost every move in Central Europe during these fateful years and, though his warnings went unheeded in the highest councils of government, they received recognition and concurrence from such of his seniors in the Office as Robert Vansittart, 'Moley' Sargent, Ronnie Campbell and George Clark.

Those few Conservative leaders who could read the writing on the wall also esteemed the opinions of this young rising star of the Foreign Office. 'He was charming and fearless, and his convictions, based upon profound knowledge and study, dominated his being', wrote Mr. Churchill. 'He saw as clearly as I did, but with more certain information, the awful peril which was closing in upon us. This drew us together.' Indeed, the help which Ralph Wigram gave to Mr. Churchill in fortifying his opinion about the Nazi Movement was very great, and he never failed to give full and frank information to the great leader who was temporarily in the wilderness.

In all these activities Ava was a perfect helpmate. She shared 'Wigs's' fears and hopes with a passionate sincerity and she played an important part in his valiant efforts to gain a wider recognition for his views. Their house in Lord North Street became a rallying point and meeting-place for those who favoured some strong action to stop the Nazi menace while there was time, before the new German rearmament was completed.

The opportunity for such action seemed to have arrived in March of 1936 when Hitler reoccupied the demilitarized zone of the Rhineland and thereby violated both the Treaty of Versailles

[1] On Ralph Wigram's death on the last day of 1936, at the age of forty-six, the tributes paid to him in *The Times* were exceptional for so young a man but not exaggerated. Warm praise was also given to him by Mr. Churchill in the first volume of his war memoirs (*The Gathering Storm*, p. 73) and by Sir Robert Bruce Lockhart in his *Your England* (1955), p. 191.

and the Locarno Agreement. Wigram was indefatigable at this moment. With Lord Halifax he accompanied Mr. Eden to Paris for conferences with the French Government and, when M. Flandin came to London for the meeting of the League Council, 'Wigs' spared no effort to achieve a formula whereby Britain and France might meet the Nazi challenge with force and courage. He failed. The Western Powers submitted to Hitler's seizure of the Rhineland with no more than a spirited display of finger-shaking. This was the more tragic since it was suspected at the time — and the suspicion has since been confirmed as a fact — that the German High Command were far from being in agreement with the Führer's policy at this moment and had wrung from him the concession that the German troops should be withdrawn from the Rhineland in the event of serious military opposition by France and Britain.

This failure of the Western Powers to grasp what was virtually their last opportunity to defeat Hitler without becoming involved in a major war, was a mortal blow to Ralph Wigram, a blow from which he never recovered.

After the French delegation had left [Ava wrote to Winston Churchill] Ralph came back and sat down in a corner of the room where he had never sat before, and said to me : 'War is now *inevitable*, and it will be the most terrible war there has ever been. I don't think I shall see it but you will, wait now for the bombs on this little house.' I was frightened at these words, and he went on, 'All my work these many years has been no use. I am a failure. I have failed to make the people here realize what is at stake. I am not strong enough, I suppose, I have not been able to make them understand. Winston has always, always understood, and he is strong and will go on to the end.'

'Wigs's' premonition that he would not see the outbreak of the war whose inevitability he divined so clearly was fulfilled. By the close of 1936 he was dead, and, in Winston Churchill's words, 'His untimely death was an irreparable loss to the Foreign Office, and played its part in the miserable decline of our fortunes'.[1]

I admired always so much his courage, integrity of purpose — high comprehending vision [Mr. Churchill wrote to Ava]. He

---

[1] Churchill, *The Gathering Storm*, p. 178.

was one of those — how few — who guard the life of Britain. Now he is gone — and on the eve of this fateful year. Indeed it is a blow to England and to all the best that England means. . . . You shielded that bright steady flame that burned in the broken lamp. But for you it would long ago have been extinguished, and its light would not have guided us thus far upon our journey.

Ava Wigram was thus left a widow at the age of forty. She had loved Ralph dearly and she mourned him deeply. She divided her time between the care of her invalid son, Charley, who lived with his nanny in Sussex, and the little house in Lord North Street which 'Wigs' had loved so much. Here she received her wide and varied circle of friends. Lord Lothian was a frequent visitor; General Smuts, the Duke of Alba, and R. B. Bennett were often to be found there, with Walter Elliot and 'Shakes' Morrison, Oliver Lyttelton and 'Crinks' Johnstone — to name only a few — and also the younger and rising Conservatives — Harold Macmillan, 'Rab' and Sydney Butler, Euan Wallace, and Brendan Bracken. Ava, with her insatiable interest in men and affairs, became an irresistible magnet for those whom she wished to see.

It was in these last years between the wars, those early years of Ava's widowhood, that John Anderson returned in triumph from India. The 'Tiger of Bengal' soon became a social lion in London and in this *monde* it was inevitable that he and Ava should meet; it was perhaps appropriate that they should have been introduced by the Aga Khan. The initial impact seems to have produced no favourable impression upon either of them. They met intermittently during the next few years and these meetings presumably proved more auspicious. It was not, however, until the period of the 'phoney war' that John displayed any active interest in Ava and then only obliquely.

The occasion was a theatre party after which John drove Ava and another lady home from the Dorchester. It was a perfect evening of full moonlight, made the more lovely because the 'black-out' had diminished street-lighting to a bare minimum. Ava was enraptured and remarked how wonderful it must have been in olden days when Elizabethan London was lit only by torches. Their companion replied: 'Was it only lit by electric torches then ?' 'Mrs. Wigram', remarked Sir John Anderson, 'is not referring to electricity.' 'Dear me,' said Ava, 'that is the first remark you have made directly to me in your life.' 'I was not speaking *to* you — I was speaking about you,' he replied.

There was unbroken silence in the car until they reached Lord North Street where John displayed surprise and alarm that Ava lived alone. 'It is not right for a young and beautiful woman to live alone,' he declared. 'Are you not acquainted with some older woman with whom you could share your house ?' Upon Ava's protesting that nothing would persuade her to share her house with anybody, he drove off in grim silence.

This strange courtship pursued its curious course. John Anderson became a more and more frequent caller at Lord North Street in the evenings, a fact noted with interest by the private secretaries in the Lord President's office, to whom his whereabouts had always to be known. When there he displayed a certain intolerance — amounting almost to jealousy — of others who might be present and he sustained, with a certain ill grace, Ava's admonishments in this respect.

There came an evening in the summer of 1941 when Ava, having returned to London after a week with her invalid boy Charley at Ditchling, had gone to bed early. As she lay reading the telephone rang. It was John Anderson. 'I've got to see you. I telephoned Ditchling and was told that you were sleeping in London. I'm coming round now.' 'But, Sir John, I'm in bed.' 'Then you must get up out of your bed. I'm coming round.'

Ava got up and went down to receive him. John arrived in the minimum time possible for a car to drive from Whitehall to Westminster. For once he was in a communicative mood. Most unexpectedly he told Ava all of his early life, his first meeting with Chrissie and their courtship, their life together, her final illness and death. All that he had never told to anyone before, he now laid before Ava, clearly, factually, almost dispassionately. Then, when he had finished the recital, he made the strangest of declarations. Mrs. Wigram must, he said, be aware of how overwhelmed he was by his feelings for her. Though he could not, much as he would like to do so, ask her to marry him because the complications involved were too great and too insoluble, he would be faithful to her to the end of time. And would she, he asked, be faithful to him? He was prepared to dedicate himself to her and to her only. It was for this reason that he had told her about his first marriage. From now on all the past had ceased to exist for him.

It was now well into the small hours of the morning and Ava found herself tired, embarrassed and completely puzzled by this singular form of oblique proposal. She refused to respond to John's gesture of dedication, nor could she bind herself to be faithful for eternity. Above all she deprecated his mental jettisoning of his past life. She herself would never cease to think and talk of 'Wigs', whether married or not. She eventually made this clear to John, to his mortification. As he left the house dawn was breaking. 'I'm fearfully vexed', he said as he went down the stairs.

It was now July 1941 and John's suit with Ava could not have appeared less propitious. His somewhat extraordinary proposal of a 'union of souls' based on a mutual promise of faithfulness had been rejected, most understandably, by Ava and clearly a re-appraisal of the situation was necessary. That John was deeply in love is undoubted and he had some reason to believe that there was a degree of reciprocation from Ava's side. Yet at this moment — and indeed to within a month of their marriage — they were addressing one another as 'Sir John' and 'Mrs. Wigram'.

John had said that his circumstances were too greatly complicated to permit of his making a proposal of marriage, but these complications evidently did not include a devotion to the past. This he had been ready to abjure and in the future he was to jettison a number of friendships of long standing connected with his earlier life, a fact which occasioned considerable sadness, and, in some cases, resentment. The seemingly insoluble complexities, therefore, concerned the present, namely his children and Nellie Mackenzie.

It may, perhaps, be asked why John Anderson re-entered matrimony at the age of fifty-nine, and the answer is simpler than might be expected. In the first place there is no doubt that he was lonely and had been so for many years. His children were now grown up and launched on careers of their own and he longed for a home life which would give him companionship and diversion. Then he was very much in love, genuinely and fervently, and not only with his heart but with his head. His sincere love was centred on Ava Wigram but so also was his amused enjoyment of her vivacity, her wit and her ever-fresh and changing focus on the world of men and affairs. These qualities of hers piqued his sense of humour and developed with the years into an indulgent pleasure. Moreover she brought him a sense of social security which he had never experienced in his home life before. The sophisticated way of life, the climate of ideas of the house in Lord North Street, were entirely attuned to that new world which had opened before him on his return from India. Home comforts and good food there were at 4 Lord North Street and these were very acceptable to John, more especially as he had spent many nights sleeping in a minute cubicle in the basement of the Home Office. In the midst of the grave problems of war and State with which he was daily surrounded Ava alone could provide that relaxation and affection for which he felt so great a need. In the weeks that followed he had found this need becoming increasingly urgent and the complications, which had at one time seemed so insurmountable, became more and more capable of solution.

John therefore proposed to Ava in September and was accepted. The effect upon him was magical. 'Do you realize, I wonder, what you have done to me in these last few weeks?', he wrote to her. 'My agricultural friends tell me that when a field that has long lain fallow is suddenly brought under tillage the results may be startling. I feel as if part of my existence which was like a barren hillside covered — not in weeds — but in strong, wiry, perhaps rather prickly growth, had been suddenly transformed into a lovely garden full of gracious forms and seductive perfumes. The pity is that I cannot — & must not — spend much time idling in that garden.'

As to the 'complications', he dismissed them summarily in a letter to his father :

> This will, of course, mean a very considerable upheaval in domestic arrangements. Alastair & Mary have taken it quite well. For Nellie it is a much more radical change but I am sure she will make the best of it & I will naturally do anything I can to ease the position.

AVA ANDERSON ON HER WEDDING DAY

By special permission of King George VI, because of the close association of the office of the Lord President of the Council with the Crown, John and Ava were married in the Chapel Royal, St. James's Palace, on October 30, 1941. The Bishop of Lichfield performed the ceremony and Alastair stood as best man to his father. Ava was attended by her brother and her two stepbrothers, both of whom were later to be killed in action. Her son Charley was represented by his nurse. John's father had felt it too great a journey for a man of his years but his sister Katie and his daughter Mary were there, as also were two links with his past, his devoted friends Geoffrey Russell and William Paterson, of whom the latter had been present at his marriage to Chrissie in Edinburgh thirty-four years before. The honeymoon was spent at Polesden Lacey, which had been lent to them by Mrs. Ronnie Greville.

That John was a devoted lover there is ample evidence in his own letters over the years. 'I can't get along without you, my darling', he once wrote in urging Ava to take good care of her health. 'You *do* realize that, don't you ?' And again as he was about to leave England on a wartime mission : 'Remember always that you have *all* my very devoted love. That is true whatever may pass between us. You are the sweetest, dearest, little "creature" possible & I love you on & on to *eternity* with all my heart.'

To Ava John's solicitude for her son Charley was a source of great comfort. She had feared that this beloved sorrow in her life might in time form a barrier between herself and John — but, at this time, she had not fully comprehended his great capacity for understanding the cares of others. 'It made me sad', John wrote to her, 'when you said you feared that *your* sorrow might cloud my life & lead me to tire of you. I wish I could make you realize how fantastic that is. If I found you always independent & self-sufficient I *might* conclude that you had no real need of me. I like to feel that you lean on me & that I can be some comfort to you. So don't let such unreal thoughts vex your spirit.'

It was, in fact, consideration for Charley's comfort which now wrought a material change in John's domestic arrangements. His marriage to Ava meant that between them they had now three establishments to maintain, her London house, his property at Merstham and the little house near Seaford where Charley lived with his nanny. Manifestly this state of affairs was both unnecessary and uneconomic. With 4 Lord North Street, into which he now moved, as his metropolitan base, he had no further need for 'Picket Wood', which in any case Ava did not like as it was not sufficiently in the country to permit of rural pursuits.

With Alastair's consent and approval, John decided therefore to dispose of 'Picket Wood' and to find some property in Sussex which would accommodate Ava and himself and Charley. In the very meagre leisure which his wartime activities permitted him at week-ends, they set out house-hunting and soon found the place of their hearts at Westdean, near Seaford, where there was an enchanting mid-nineteenth-century house set in the midst of a Saxon village in a fold of the Sussex Downs. Great was their sorrow when it proved impossible to obtain and they had to transfer their quest elsewhere.

John was a born house-hunter. He was not influenced by the charm of beams or fanlights or king-posts, by the height of rooms or the sweep of a staircase. What mattered to him was whether the place had dry rot or not, and he would creep about on his hands and knees making holes with a schoolboy's pocket-knife in floor boards and wainscoting to see whether he could detect the powdery evidence of this hated pest. Eventually they decided upon the Mill House at Isfield. It was far from ideal, being half late fifteenth century and half early 'stockbroker Tudor', but John decreed that it was 'just the thing for Charley' since there were rooms on the ground floor which could be converted for his use.

There they migrated in September 1942, and John at once set about acquiring the appurtenances attendant upon a country property. In quick succession he procured hens, ducks and geese, a cow and some pigs, as well as such more ornamental items as a setting of 'Nun' pigeons and a pair of swans. In a very short space of time he was fully conversant with all their vagaries and deeply interested in their welfare and in the production of eggs, milk and cream. Moreover he became a first-class butter maker. A dispatch rider from Whitehall would come down two or three times during the week-end with red boxes filled with documents for him to deal with, and these he would read sitting in his armchair while winding the butter churn, his papers laid out on a little table beside him at the right level.

The river which wound through the water-meadow below them was a further delight to John. One day he fell off the little bridge which spanned it and swam majestically round in circles with his pork-pie hat, which he always wore in the country, still firmly on his head. Ava became hysterical with laughter and John was incensed at her inability to help him. 'Would you have your husband drown ?' he shouted angrily, but he accepted her advice that he should swim to the bank rather than round and round.

(iii)

The story of the atom bomb, the use of which in August 1945 not only changed the course of the Second World War but of world history, has its origins in France where, as long ago as 1896, the great physicist Henri Becquerel discovered radioactivity, to be followed by Lord Rutherford and Professor Frederick Soddy who first challenged the hitherto accepted theory that atoms of one element could not be converted into those of another. Thence by degrees the challenge developed from theory into practice through the experiments of Rutherford at Cambridge and of his pupils John Cockcroft and Ernest Walton, and of James Chadwick, of the Joliot-Curies in France and their colleagues Hans Halban and Lew Kowarski, and of Hahn and Strassmann in Germany, until in the late 1930's the phenomenon of 'nuclear fission' was established and with it the acknowledged assumption that this phenomenon must be inevitably accompanied by a great release of nuclear energy.[1]

The original experimental achievement of atomic fission occurred in Germany in 1938 and it was known that the Germans had continued their experiments ;[2] but by the beginning of 1939 the problems which remained to be solved before these experiments could be turned into practical achievement were so manifold and so great that few scientists were then prepared to predict the

[1] In so far as security permits, the story of 'Tube Alloys' has been told by Ronald W. Clark in *The Birth of the Bomb* (1961) and by Fletcher Knebel and Charles W. Bailey in *No High Ground* (1961).
[2] The Hon. Henry L. Stimson, 'Decision to use the Atom Bomb', *Harper's Magazine*, February 1947.

imminent danger, or indeed the imminent probability, of an atomic bomb.

Yet there were those, as the international situation grew perceptibly more strained after Hitler's occupation of Prague, whose apprehension ran along these lines, and particularly in regard to the supply of uranium, the key material in atomic experimental activity. The principal source of supply of uranium was in the Katanga province of the Belgian Congo, whence it was sent to Belgium to be processed for the extraction of the radium which it contains. The residue, amounting to hundreds, if not thousands, of tons, had accumulated, containing the vast bulk of the uranium itself — not as metal, for in those days metallic uranium, even in an impure form, was a chemical curiosity, but in the form of some compound.

That this vast supply of uranium should fall into the hands of Germany was a fearfully disturbing thought, especially to those with historical memories who did not doubt that, sooner or later, Hitler would conform to the traditional pattern of German strategy and, once again violating the neutrality of Belgium, would thrust westwards towards the Channel ports and Paris. Amongst these were Professor George Thomson, then at the Imperial College, London,[1] and Kenneth Pickthorn, Member of Parliament for Cambridge University. Professor Thomson sought permission from the Air Ministry to obtain a ton of uranium oxide for purposes of experiments on whether what would now be called a chain reaction could be initiated. He explained that if these experiments were successful they might lead to the possibility of an atomic bomb. Permission was granted and Professor Thomson obtained his uranium, with the result that he and his colleagues were able to establish that a chain reaction was not possible with uranium and ordinary water, though it might be possible with 'heavy water'.

As a result of this line of thought Professor Thomson suggested to Kenneth Pickthorn that some effort should be made to safeguard at least part of the stocks of uranium in Belgium, and Pickthorn, who was under no illusions as to Hitler's designs on the Low Countries, carried the matter to 'Pug' Ismay, then Secretary of the Committee of Imperial Defence. This was in the early summer of 1939, with war growing ever closer. To Ismay Pickthorn spoke

[1] Sir George Thomson, F.R.S., Master of Corpus Christi College, Cambridge.

JOHN AND 'MIRABELLE' AT ISFIELD

of Thomson's belief in the possibility of an atom bomb, its depen-
dence on uranium and the dangerous consequences which would
ensue if Germany became possessed of the Belgian stocks. Like
most people in Whitehall who found themselves confronted with a
difficult problem, 'Pug' went to consult John Anderson, then Lord
Privy Seal. John listened in silence and then, somewhat with the
air of one explaining the alphabet to a child, remarked that an atom
bomb was 'a scientific but remote possibility'. However, his
interest was aroused and, as a result of his intervention, a certain
amount of uranium was obtained from Belgium and made available
for research at British universities.

This was Anderson's first association with the matter of the
atom bomb, but it was an association which was to continue now
throughout his official life as a Cabinet Minister — and beyond.
By the summer of 1941 such progress had been made in nuclear
fission researches that a committee of leading scientists, headed by
Professor Thomson, could report that in their view there was a
reasonable chance of producing an atomic bomb before the end of
the war. Similar research in America had resulted in a like conclusion, and a full interchange of ideas existed between the scientists
of both countries engaged in the work. At this time, however, it
was believed that the Germans were ahead of the Western Powers
in their research and it was naturally considered vital that they
should not be the first to bring atomic weapons into the field of
battle.[1] Moreover, if the Allies should be the first to develop the
weapon, they would have a great new instrument for shortening
the war and minimizing destruction.

Time was therefore, from every point of view, the essence of
the contract and, in view of this, Lord Cherwell,[2] the special
scientific adviser to the Prime Minister, suggested in August 1941
that a Cabinet Minister should be appointed to co-ordinate and

[1] These fears were fortunately groundless but persistent, and as soon as the
liberation of France was fairly under way an American Scientific Mission — ALSOS
— began its search for clues of German progress in atomic research. When the
French captured Strasbourg on November 24, 1944, one of Germany's leading
nuclear physicists fell into Allied hands together with his laboratory, whose records
revealed that the enemy was still a long way from being able to produce an atom
bomb. (Bryant (*op. cit.*), p. 333, f.n.)
[2] Rt. Hon. Frederick Alexander Lindemann, Viscount Cherwell, C.H. ('The
Prof'), was Professor of Experimental Philosophy at the University of Oxford.

U

assume general responsibility for the scientific activities concerned. With this advice Mr. Churchill at once concurred and on August 31 he indited a minute to General Ismay for the Chiefs of Staff :

> Although personally I am quite content with the existing explosives, I feel we must not stand in the path of improvement, and I therefore think that action should be taken in the sense proposed by Lord Cherwell, and that the Cabinet Minister responsible should be Sir John Anderson.
>
> I shall be glad to know what the Chiefs of Staff Committee think.[1]

'The Chiefs of Staff', Mr. Churchill recalls, 'recommended immediate action, with the maximum priority', and John assumed control of the work subject only to reference to the Prime Minister.

It was a singularly happy appointment. John's first love had been science, a field in which he had shown considerable promise as a student. Was there not his brilliant paper on Explosives written at Edinburgh University and the remarkable coincidence that he had investigated the radio-activities of uranium while a post-graduate student at the University of Leipzig? He had never ceased to take an active interest in scientific research of all kinds, and as Lord President had already played a big part in setting up a Scientific Advisory Committee to the War Cabinet, of which Lord Hankey was the first chairman. Hankey was succeeded in 1942 by Sir Henry Dale, President of the Royal Society, who became one of Anderson's closest advisers. 'I do not think that it would be possible to exaggerate the importance to the national interest', Sir Henry has written, 'of having in such a position of authority, behind the dense curtain of official secrecy, a man with so natural an understanding of the meaning of science, and so instinctive a knowledge of, and sympathy for, the possibilities and the difficulties of research.'[2]

John had, of course, the best expert advice available in the country. In addition to his Advisory Committee, a special section was set up in the Department of Scientific and Industrial Research, under Mr. (later Sir Wallace) Akers, of Imperial Chemical Industries,

---

[1] Churchill, *The Hinge of Fate*, p. 340.
[2] *Biographical Memoirs of Fellows of the Royal Society*, vol. 4, November 1958, p. 324.

to handle the technical side of the work, which was carried on in the greatest secrecy under the code name of 'Tube Alloys'. But in what may be called the 'scientific administration' of atomic energy — the responsibility to the Government, the development of research and the inter-Allied dealings — his was the final responsibility for deciding which of the lines of work suggested should be followed up and also for obtaining finance to carry out the policy decided upon.

Now, too, Anderson's talents as a diplomatist were called into play, for the course of true love in Anglo-American relations ran no more smoothly in the sphere of atomic energy than in any other. At their meeting at Hyde Park in June 1942, President Roosevelt and Mr. Churchill reached what the latter at least considered to be 'a very satisfactory agreement . . . about "Tube Alloys"'.[1] This was on the basis of complete equality between the United States and the United Kingdom in the sharing of work, information and ultimate results. In view of the fact that Britain was at that time under frequent bombardment from the air and constant aerial reconnaissance, it was evident that the research plant for the atom bomb experiments could not be sited there. The choice therefore lay between the United States and Canada, which were already possessed of considerable supplies of uranium. 'It was a hard decision to spend several hundred million pounds sterling', Mr. Churchill has written, 'not so much of money as of competing forms of precious war-energy, upon a project the success of which no scientist on either side of the Atlantic could guarantee. Nevertheless, if the Americans had not been willing to undertake the venture we should certainly have gone forward on our own power in Canada, or, if the Canadian Government demurred, in some other part of the Empire.'[2] Mr. Roosevelt was, however, prepared for the United States to shoulder the burden of finance, impressed no doubt by the confidence of British scientists as to the ultimate outcome and the progress which they had already made towards it, and this too was written into the agreement.

Under the terms of the Hyde Park Agreement of June 21, 1942, Anglo-American atomic co-operation continued to function

[1] *Memoirs of Lord Ismay* (1960), p. 254.
[2] Churchill, *The Hinge of Fate*, pp. 341-342.

smoothly until, later in that year, the United States side of the work came under Army control as the 'Manhattan Project'. Thereafter relations deteriorated and had reached a deadlock by the time the President and the Prime Minister met again at Casablanca at the beginning of 1943. Mr. Churchill expressed great concern because the previous Anglo-American co-operation and full exchange of information on research and experimentation seemed to have ended, since the United States War Department were asking to be kept informed of British experiments while refusing altogether to give any information about their own. The issue was turned over to President Roosevelt's *fidus Achates*, Harry Hopkins, for solution and, at the end of February, he called Mr. Churchill, asking that John Anderson should submit a full history of the misunderstanding, since the War Department 'feel that no agreement has been breached'. The Prime Minister was then lying dangerously ill with pneumonia in North Africa, but from his sick bed on February 27 he sent to Hopkins in Washington two long cables based on information supplied by Anderson from London. This exposition, he submitted, was a complete justification for a request that full co-operation should be restored in the work of developing the joint resources of their two countries. 'Urgent decisions about our programme both here and in Canada depend on the extent to which full collaboration between us is restored, and I must ask you to let me have a firm decision on United States policy in this matter very soon.'[1]

Even this appeal was not successful, and by the spring Mr. Churchill was contemplating the 'sombre decision' that Britain would be compelled to go ahead separately in her research in nuclear fission. Nor was the situation greatly improved as a result of the Washington Conference between the two Allied leaders in June. By the end of July relations had become so exacerbated that the War Cabinet decided, at the express request of President Roosevelt, to send John Anderson to Washington in a personal effort to restore Allied understanding. Accompanied by Mr. Gorell-Barnes, he left England by air on August 1 under the somewhat transparent alias of 'Professor Sanderson'.

[1] Robert E. Sherwood, *Roosevelt and Hopkins, an Intimate History* (New York, 1948), pp. 703-704.

This was John's first experience of prolonged air travel and he gave his observations to his father in a letter written after his return. His account will recall to many who made the same trans-Atlantic journey during the war their own impressions of something which was then still somewhat of a phenomenon but which has now become an everyday factor of life, and also of the very human reaction at being released from the rigours of wartime rationing when one egg a week was the order of the day for most of the population!

I set off from Hendon on the Sunday at 4 p.m. Subsequent progress was really fantastic. We did the first part of the journey in a 2 engined machine, a Lockheed, & arrived at Prestwick in Ayrshire punctually to the minute at 6. We stopped there for 4 hours during which all formalities were completed & we had dinner. At 10 p.m. we started off again in the machine that was to take us to our destination, a 4 engined Liberator. The idea when we set out was that we would land after 11 hours at a place called Gander in Newfoundland. However, wind & other conditions being favourable, the pilot announced after 10 hours flight that he was going on to a landing place on the mainland. We expected then to land on Canadian territory. However, when we eventually came down at 12. British time, & 6 a.m. local time, it was to find ourselves on American soil at a place called Presque Isle, in the State of Maine. There everyone was most polite & helpful. We had a wash & breakfast (pineapple juice, followed by two eggs & bacon!) & after 2 hours left again for Washington where we arrived for lunch. The whole journey was made at a height of 9000 feet above any clouds that there were & the main impression was one of great power & stability. There was no rocking or bumping such as one gets in smaller machines & the noise of the engine was not so loud as to prevent conversation. We were in darkness practically all the time we were over the sea but we got a good view of the coast of Prince Edward Island & New Brunswick & had an excellent sight of Boston, New York & Philadelphia. The machine was heated & we were provided with a picnic meal. There were no bunks but our chairs were long & tilted back so that it was possible to sleep fairly comfortably. . . . In the U.S.A. one hardly got the sensation of being in a foreign country & in Canada it seemed exactly like home even in respect of the vegetation.

Arrived in Washington, John found the weather 'decidedly hot', but he had taken the precaution of bringing with him some of his Bengal wardrobe, so he suffered but little, but it was noticed that either his tussore suits had shrunk or that he had put on a little weight since he last wore them!

There was also something of anti-climax. The President's request to the War Cabinet to send their 'top man' had had all the elements of urgency, and John left at a few hours' notice, yet when he arrived he was virtually unexpected. The President himself was off fishing in Canada and the British Ambassador, Lord Halifax, was on leave, the Embassy being in charge of his Minister, Sir Ronald Campbell.[1] John, who had expected to plunge *in medias res* at once, was not best pleased to find that no meeting with the Americans was possible until the following morning. His time was filled by a sightseeing tour with President James Conant of Harvard University, a leading member of Roosevelt's nuclear team, and in shopping for Ava, but the dinner that night at the Mayflower Hotel with Sir Ronald Campbell and Mr. William Hayter [2] was a somewhat frigid affair.

When, however, next day John really got down to business with President Conant and Professor Vannevar Bush and other Americans, he found that he could make swifter progress than had at first been expected. He was quick to see the American point of view and to disabuse their minds of certain well-rooted suspicions. For their part, they found him 'light on his feet', tactful and pleasant. They were impressed by the fact that a British Minister of the Crown and member of the War Cabinet knew enough about science to understand what the scientists were talking about and never tried 'to come it over them'. Within a week accord had been reached on the heads of an agreement for the restoration of full collaboration at all levels and the establishment of a Control Policy Committee in Washington composed of representatives of the United States, the United Kingdom and Canada.

Well satisfied with this achievement, John flew to Ottawa on

[1] Rt. Hon. Sir Ronald Campbell, G.C.M.G., Ambassador to Egypt, 1946–1950.
[2] Sir William Hayter, K.C.M.G., Ambassador to the U.S.S.R., 1953–1957, and now Warden of New College, Oxford.

Saturday, August 7, to spend the week-end with his old friend and colleague, Malcolm MacDonald, then British High Commissioner. He lunched on the Sunday with the Governor-General, Lord Athlone, and Princess Alice at Government House and then drove out to 'Kingsmere', the fantastic home of the Canadian Prime Minister, for further conferences. 'Anderson said he had reached an agreement which he thought the President and Churchill would sign', Mr. Mackenzie King wrote in his famous 'record' that evening: 'It made Canada also a party to the development. . . . He had explained to the Americans that Britain cared nothing about the post-war profit-making industries of the matter, but was concerned for war purposes.'[1] These words were to have an added significance some two years later.[2]

Mr. Churchill arrived at Quebec on the 10th for his conference with President Roosevelt and John reported to him there on the fruits of his mission to Washington. The draft accord which he had drawn up was approved with certain changes by the Prime Minister and the President and was signed as the Quebec Agreement on August 19, 1943. Shortly thereafter British teams joined the Americans in their work on the bomb at Los Alamos, New Mexico, and the Chalk River nuclear project was founded on a joint Canada–United Kingdom basis.

John returned to England by air.

> There was a most beautiful sunset seen to an advantage above [he wrote to his father] & I was interested at the same time to see an iceberg shining in the evening light directly beneath us. It looked small but must have been at least the size of St. Paul's Cathedral.

Ava was waiting at the airport to meet him and there might well have been a spirit of celebration as well as of thankfulness for his safe return, for from that time until the dropping of the atom bomb and the end of the war, Anglo-American relations progressed in the field of nuclear fission with complete amity. 'It is very difficult to say', Lord Bridges has written, 'how all this important development could have been carried out so successfully under the

---

[1] J. W. Pickersgill, *The Mackenzie King Record* (Toronto, 1960), i, p. 532.
[2] See below, pp. 331 *et seq.*

stress of war had there not been a Minister of the Crown with his very special qualifications for the work.'[1]

Personal responsibility fell heavily but sat lightly upon John Anderson's shoulders. He was never at a loss when a decision had to be taken no matter how great the issues involved. When, in the autumn of 1943, British Intelligence received word from occupied Denmark that the celebrated Danish physicist, Professor Niels Bohr, was about to be deported to Germany, they at once reported this important item of news to the Lord President. John saw the picture at once. Bohr was among the greatest nuclear physicists of his day and it was clear to John that his services might well make a valuable contribution to the work of the British team on the 'Tube Alloys' project at Los Alamos. On the other hand, the Germans would certainly put pressure upon him, both physical and mental, to aid them in their own atomic research ; and how long could the most gallant resistance hold out against such methods ? John acted immediately ; Niels Bohr, he directed, must be got out of Denmark at once. And both by hook and by crook this was accomplished by Allied Intelligence. On a night in late September, Bohr and his wife, his four sons and his brother, were spirited out of Copenhagen and across the Sound to Sweden. Thence the Professor and his eldest son were flown in triumph to England, to be welcomed and congratulated by their many friends and colleagues.

The first meeting between Bohr and Anderson was a momentous occasion for both of them. It would be difficult to imagine two more superficially diverse personalities than the hard-headed, somewhat dour Scot, with his feet very firmly on the ground, and the idealistic, romantic, loquacious Dane, with his complete 'otherworldliness'. Yet from the moment of their meeting an affinity was established, forming the basis of a deep and abiding friendship which lasted until Anderson's death, and which caused Bohr to feel 'almost as close to him as to a brother'. This curious relationship was founded upon something more profound than a common interest in science. It was perhaps evoked by the great sense of humanity with which both men were endowed, from which emerged their mutual concept of what an atomic age should be

[1] *Biographical Memoirs of Fellows of the Royal Society*, vol. 4, November 1958, p. 320.

KING GEORGE VI, THE PRIME MINISTER, LORD WOOLTON AND SIR JOHN ANDERSON, AUGUST 3, 1944

and their common fear of what it might become. Anderson attached Bohr and his son as members of the British 'Tube Alloys' team at Los Alamos and retained them there to the end, despite representations from the United States.

For the reactions to Professor Niels Bohr were by no means uniform in character. Some admired him profoundly. To General Smuts, for example, he was a man at the mention of whose name one should stand bareheaded — 'greater than Newton, greater than Faraday'. When Ava Anderson asked Smuts to meet Bohr at luncheon at Lord North Street, the General was greatly moved : 'This is tremendous,' he said, 'as though one was meeting Shakespeare or Napoleon — someone who is changing the history of the world.'

On the other hand, 'the Great Dane' (as he came to be known in Whitehall) proved to be not at all Mr. Churchill's 'cup of tea' and the Americans, with the exception of Mr. Justice Frankfurter, seem generally to have treated him with reserve.

Yet John remained unwaveringly loyal to Bohr and to Bohr's idealism — even to the point of his own detriment. For when, in the summer of 1944, shortly before the Second Quebec Conference, Anderson, acting to some degree under the prompting of the Professor, proposed to Mr. Churchill that the Foreign Office might embark upon a study of the problems of international control of atomic energy after the war and suggested that Russian collaboration might possibly be sought in such a connection, he received a sharp rebuff from the Prime Minister.

In the latest phase of 'Tube Alloys' which concerned the high-level decision to make use of the atom bomb, Anderson bore no part, but on August 7, 1945, the day after the first bomb had been dropped on Hiroshima, he made a broadcast to the people of Britain on the Home Service of the B.B.C., which gave to the layman a vivid idea of the new age which had opened before them and something of the possibilities, as well as the problems and perils, which were inherent in it :

> Yesterday's momentous announcement of the successful delivery of the first atomic bomb marks the culmination of an effort of scientific and industrial organisation unparalleled in the world's history.

The fundamental scientific discoveries from which the whole development springs were made just before the war. The use of sub-atomic energy as an instrument of war was then accepted as a theoretical possibility, and the matter was freely discussed in leading scientific journals in many countries, both belligerent and neutral.

This is, however, one of those instances in which the gulf between theory and practice is very wide. The various forms of matter of which our universe is made up are in general very stable. They do not readily break up and yield their latent energy for man's use. If they did we should lead much more adventurous lives, if indeed such a state of affairs could be compatible with the existence of any organised life on this globe at all.

This then was the problem ; to find means of bringing about a physical reaction, already known to be possible in theory, in such a way that it assumed accumulative form, growing upon itself so to speak. Under pressure of war development has been compressed within the space of a few years which might normally have occupied half a century or more, and the problem has been solved.

At present only a very few substances are known which exhibit under suitable conditions the phenomenon called nuclear fission. The most important of these is the comparatively rare metallic element uranium. But now that a solution has been found, further developments are sure to follow. Means may, for example, be discovered of utilising other less rare elements which would not ordinarily react in this way. And in various ways means may be found of vastly increasing the efficiency of the reaction upon which the use of the material, whether for military or industrial purposes, depends.

All this is, of course, still in the realm of speculation. What is certain is that a vast new field of investigation and development has been opened up in which scientists all the world over will be eager to labour. What must be realised is that this is no mere extension of an existing field of enquiry. A new door has for the first time been prised open. What lies on the other side remains to be seen. The possibilities for good or ill are infinite. There may on the one hand be a veritable treasure-house awaiting fruitful development in the interests of mankind. There might, on the other hand, be only the realisation of a maniac dream of death, destruction and desolation. God grant that it may not prove to be so.

There are problems here calling for statesmanship of the highest order. The establishment of any organ for the maintenance of world peace and security would obviously be sheer mockery if means could not be found of guaranteeing the effective international control of an instrument of war of such potency.

There could be no higher task for the statesmen of the United Nations gathered round the Conference table.

For scientists and industrialists there will be the engrossing problem of finding means of controlling the new and practically limitless sources of energy now seen to be available, so that they may be harnessed in the service of humanity. In this field, so far as I am aware, little or no work has yet been done. It may be many years before efficient methods of using atomic energy for industrial purposes can be devised. There will then still be the question whether the new methods can compete economically with traditional sources of power. What is certain is that we may reasonably look forward to a new era of scientific discovery and development far transcending all experience of the past.

(iv)

In the early morning hours of September 21, 1943, the Chancellor of the Exchequer, Sir Kingsley Wood, died suddenly. His death was a serious blow to the Government. Kingsley Wood was one of those persons, comparatively rare in number, who had enjoyed the friendship of both Mr. Chamberlain and Mr. Churchill. To him Chamberlain had given his confidence to an unwonted degree and Wood had been his loyal supporter and trusted adviser. The advice purveyed, however, had not always been of the highest order. It was Wood who had recommended a dissolution of Parliament after Mr. Chamberlain's return from Munich in 1938 and this suggestion the Prime Minister had wisely rejected in favour of the sager counsel of Lord Halifax.[1] Sir Kingsley had done his much admired leader a greater, albeit an unhappy, service when he fortified Mr. Chamberlain in his decision to relinquish the office of Prime Minister in May 1940. In the post-Munich period,

[1] See above, p. 210.

however, Wood had also become a friend of Mr. Churchill, whose admiration he had earned when, on becoming Secretary of State for Air, he had tackled with assiduity and success the eleventh-hour task of building up the fighting strength of the Royal Air Force. There is no doubt of his important contribution to the readiness of that Service to meet the trial and combat of 1940. In forming the National Government, Mr. Churchill had advanced Wood to the Treasury, where he had successfully introduced three wartime Budgets, historic in their magnitude and scope.

The Prime Minister was at once aware of the heavy loss which he and his colleagues had sustained in the death of the Chancellor and of the difficulties and complications involved in the selection of a successor. His initial preference was for Mr. Oliver Lyttelton,[1] then Minister of Production, who certainly went to bed on the night of September 22 under the impression that he was to be Chancellor of the Exchequer. By the morning, however, Mr. Churchill had had second thoughts. He had decided that he could not dispense with Mr. Lyttelton's invaluable services at the Ministry of Production. In his choice for Chancellor he had turned to John Anderson's 'acute and powerful mind, firm spirit and long experience of widely varied responsibilities'. The appointment was announced on September 24.

Thus John vacated the office of Lord President of the Council, where he was succeeded by Lord Woolton, for the new pastures of the Treasury, while still retaining the over-all responsibility for 'Tube Alloys' and the chairmanship of the Man-Power Committee. In some respects this translation was a pity. The Lord Presidency had suited John ideally. In it his great talents had flowered to their maximum ; his genius for administration and co-ordination had brought forth abundant fruit. He was really better in the rôle of an 'overlord' than in that of a ministerial head of a Government Department. Moreover, as Lord President, his Parliamentary duties had been reduced to a minimum. Now as Chancellor he was perforce called more and more frequently to the House of Commons, where, though he enjoyed the deepest respect, he was never seen at his best.

He was, however, a great success at the Treasury, where he

[1] Now Viscount Chandos.

displayed the usual zeal and acumen of his methodical approach coupled with his habitual distaste for unnecessary drudgery. This combination caused his Private Secretaries something of a headache. The Chancellor of the Exchequer in modern times, whether in peace or in war, carries an immense burden, not merely because of his heavy responsibilities, but because of the volume of work which he has to get through and the mass of paper which he has to read. If his Private Secretaries gave him nightly a box of papers containing everything which he ought to see, or which they thought he would like to see, the load was unreasonable and he obviously felt it to be so, complaining that they had kept him up into the small hours. When, however, they sought to remedy this by a rigorous sifting of what went to him, he would again complain that he had not seen such and such a paper which surely he ought to have seen. No really satisfactory solution for this dilemma was ever evolved, though in course of time it was found moderately possible to equate the burden of paper-work to his capacity to deal with it.

In effect, however, he managed to cope with the burdens of office more successfully, and perhaps with more true economy of effort, than any of his immediate predecessors, and the fact that he did so extended to his private office. It made a parallel economy of effort possible there, an illustration of this being that he was the only Chancellor within thirty years to have fewer than three Private Secretaries.

Sir Richard Hopkins,[1] who worked with Anderson both in the Treasury and as a member of the Port of London Authority, once said that he had served a good many Chancellors of the Exchequer and each had had a different approach when confronted with the taking of a decision : one was concerned with how it would affect his party politically, another with how it would affect the public view of himself, and so on. But John Anderson was different from all the rest. He was the only one who was always searching for the right answer. There could be no finer testimony to a great administrator.[2]

---

[1] See above, p. 45, f.n.

[2] It is not without interest that in the view of Mr. F. N. G. Wilson, the author of the volume on *The Organization of British Central Government*, 1914–1956 (published by the Royal Institute of Public Administration in 1957), the Treasury began to regain its old position in economic affairs from the day that Anderson became Chancellor of the Exchequer (see p. 327, f.n.).

As on previous occasions in his career, Anderson soon earned the unstinted admiration and devotion of his subordinates — and the Treasury is perhaps more reserved and critical in this respect than other Whitehall departments. 'There was never', writes one who served him at this time, 'anything in the nature of a bee in his bonnet, and his approach to every problem was intensely calm and serene while at the same time penetrating. He did less tinkering with other people's work than anyone I have known in this kind of position. A draft was a means to an end and not an end in itself. If it served its purpose, he would leave it alone, even though it must constantly have been very different from the draft which he would have produced himself. He was highly skilled in guiding his subordinates to do their work as he wanted it, and he would often stimulate their efforts by a word of encouragement and praise when he was pleased. I doubt whether he ever did this orally. It was always on the file. His favourite minute for this purpose was the characteristic note — "I am much obliged. J.A." He would also write — "This is very well argued" or "a very good draft".'

John's first act as Chancellor was in effect a posthumous achievement of his predecessor. Kingsley Wood had died on the morning of the day on which he was to have introduced into the House of Commons the Wage Earners' Income Tax Bill which established the 'pay-as-you-earn' (P.A.Y.E.) system of taxation for those in receipt of weekly earnings, an innovation which had been the joint brain-child of Sir Cornelius Gregg [1] and Mr. Paul Chambers, [2] then, respectively, Chairman and Secretary of the Board of Inland Revenue. It fell, therefore, to Anderson to pilot this measure and he did so not only efficiently but with sympathetic understanding and in a spirit of compromise.

The war made many millions of wage earners liable to income tax for the first time. A system of deducting tax from wages (and also salaries) had been set up as early as 1940 but the tax deducted was the tax on wages earned many months before, and this led to difficulties of collection, and often to hardship for the wage earner, if his earnings had fallen in the meantime. Under the plan now proposed the deduction of tax by the employer would not only

---

[1] Sir Cornelius Gregg, K.C.B., K.B.E., had served with Anderson in Dublin Castle as a Treasury official.   [2] Now Chairman of I.C.I. Ltd.

be related to the earnings of the current week but would also take account of the earnings and tax deductions of previous weeks, so that at the end of the year, despite fluctuations in earnings, the right amount of tax would have been paid. The P.A.Y.E. system had caught the popular imagination and there was widespread desire for its extension to all employees. Anderson had reservations as to this on the grounds that the case for P.A.Y.E. for monthly salary earners was by no means so clear as for weekly wage earners, since these earnings were not so liable to fluctuate and the State had much better prospects of getting from them arrears of income tax. Nevertheless he agreed to accept the principle of extension of P.A.Y.E. to salary earners with an income of up to £600 *per annum*. He was pressed, however, from all sides of the House to extend the plan to all salary earners without limit under Schedule E and, though he at first opposed this concession, he announced on November 2 that he accepted it also in principle and would embody it in future legislation. Meanwhile, earners of salaries up to £600 p.a. were brought into the scope of the existing Bill, in addition to weekly wage earners.

Anderson fulfilled his promise to the House in the following February when he introduced a Bill extending the P.A.Y.E. system to all employees, save only members of the armed forces, collection from whom by this system would, he said, prove too great a practical difficulty in war-time.[1]

John Anderson introduced his first Budget on the afternoon of Tuesday, April 25, 1944. He had spent the week-end quietly with Ava in Sussex, and the morning's papers carried photographs of him feeding his pigeons. 'Now he's going to pluck them', remarked one Member lugubriously as the Chancellor took his place on the Front Bench at Question Time. It was noted that he was in a buoyant mood, cracking jokes with P. J. Grigg and Tom Johnston, but in appearance and attire he was severely conventional. He had an easy time with his Questions and neatly side-stepped one which seemed to be an attempt to elicit information which would be in his Budget statement. 'I think I must ask leave to defer to somewhat later in the day anything I may have to say about the national finances', he replied in his most formal manner. Having

[1] Tax was deducted from forces pay, but under a different system.

been filmed at his desk in his room at the House of Commons, he returned to lunch with Ava at Lord North Street. At 2.45 he was again in his place.[1] He displayed no nervousness.

It is traditional for Chancellors of the Exchequer to have some liquid refreshment before them on the Dispatch Box when making a Budget statement. In the past they have displayed diverse tastes. One did it on milk, one even on a glass of water. John's preference remained a secret from the House, for his Parliamentary Private Secretary had provided him with a china tumbler which, of course, was not transparent. In fact, it contained whisky and water.

He spoke for about two hours. It was not a dramatic Budget, though stupendous in figures. The national revenue for the year would be £3,102 million, leaving a deficit of £2,835 million, approximately the same as that of the previous year. As, however, it appeared that the Government would be able to finance this from savings and other non-inflationary sources, it was not necessary for him to introduce any additional taxation and he relieved the apprehension of the House by telling them that his prescription would be 'the mixture as before' — a sally which was received with laughter and loud cheers.

But the Chancellor's statement was not without its note of warning. The policy followed by his predecessors of maintaining stability in the cost of living by means of subsidies, while completely successful, had entailed increasing cost to the Exchequer, yet it could not be denied that the benefits obtained by this policy far outweighed its costs. Nevertheless, the considerable increase in wage rates made it impossible to maintain the cost of living at the figure laid down by his predecessor. This tendency of wages to rise out of proportion to prices was a danger which he, as the guardian of the national exchequer, would have to keep in check. The more incomes were out of line with prices, the more it was

---

[1] This timing may cause some surprise but it will be recalled that, under the special wartime hours of meeting adopted by Parliament because of enemy aerial activity, the House started its work in the morning so as to complete it, as far as possible, in the hours of daylight. Normally, of course, they carried right through ; but, on Budget Day, this would have meant that the Chancellor's Budget Speech would have continued through the luncheon hour. Moreover, it is traditional that details of tax changes, etc., are not announced in the Budget Speech until after 4 o'clock in the afternoon, when the Stock Exchange is closed. On both grounds, therefore, it was more convenient to suspend the sitting for two hours in the middle of the day.

THE CHANCELLOR OF THE EXCHEQUER

necessary to intensify the more inconvenient forces of control, for, should these controls be removed, there was the greater danger of violent price inflation. For these and other reasons he refused to bind himself to maintain the cost of living index within the limit laid down by Sir Kingsley Wood of 25 to 30 per cent above pre-war figures, and he warned the nation that he might have to substitute for this a range of from 30 to 35 per cent.

The Government was also faced at this time with the problem of the re-equipment of industry which would arise at the end of the war. The tax system was not very generous towards the cost of the replacement of capital equipment and yet, with the rise in rates of tax, industry was bound to become increasingly pre-occupied with the difficulty of finding the means to equip itself, or to deal with the world of competition into which it would enter when the war ended.

The outcome of long consideration was contained in the Budget proposals of 1944, which recommended the first major development for nearly a quarter of a century in the handling of the depreciation and replacement of industrial assets. Anderson believed that these proposals were not only desirable but could be defended as based on sound principles of taxation. In his Budget speech of 1944 he proposed that in the reconstruction period the ordinary annual provision for wear and tear should be supplemented by a specially large provision for depreciation at the outset. These 'initial allowances' were fixed at 20 per cent for plant and machinery and 10 per cent for industrial buildings and for mining works. He said 'an allowance of this kind, which will allow one-fifth of the actual expenditure on plant and machinery in any year to be written off forthwith against the profits of that year, as they come under charge for taxation, will represent very substantial financial assistance to industry in carrying out its post-war re-equipment'.[1]

Anderson also commended with special warmth allowances for expenditure on scientific research and, in describing the part which scientific research could play in industrial development, he said :

Research has three aspects. There is the fundamental research of the scientists, whether at the university, or in the laboratories

[1] *House of Commons Debates*, April 25, 1944. Col. 673.

x

attached to industrial establishments or industrial organisations. Successful research is not a mass product. It does not flow merely from numbers of research workers. It requires an imaginative quality of the mind. Without fundamental research there can be no hope of steady progress, and still less of those strange leaps of the creative intelligence which produce in peace no less than in war some of the most important discoveries. But to industry research has a limited value if it stops at the laboratory. There are two further stages. There is what I might describe as the pilot plant stage, where laboratory results are tried out experimentally on a larger scale. Every industrialist knows that it is a real difficulty to translate the delicate skill of the scientific researcher, and the artificial conditions in which he may have worked, into terms of large-scale production. I believe that in this country we have been, perhaps, slow in developing this essential stage. The next and final stage is the commercial production of the product.

These are the three integral parts of the same creative process. To fail on any one is to fail over the whole. Therefore, in considering the help which taxation policy can give to research, my aim has been to help the whole process. It is, I think, most desirable that industry should know in advance the taxation treatment which will be accorded to research expenditure which is undertaken when hostilities cease. I propose, therefore, to include provisions on this matter in the forthcoming Finance Bill.[1]

Both in content and in performance John's first Budget statement was hailed with acclaim. 'There will be only one verdict on the Budget which Sir John Anderson opened yesterday', ran *The Times* editorial next day. 'It could so easily have been a mere humdrum Budget speech : in fact it was all — or almost all — that the occasion called for. . . . The humane and constructive spirit shown throughout the whole statement lends conviction to his balanced confidence in the future.' [2] Many felt that it was the best speech he had ever made and in the debate which followed it was praised on both sides of the House as a really constructive effort to deal with the country's economic problems.

The same was true of the broadcast which John made to the nation on the evening of April 25. Here, in language which the

[1] *House of Commons Debates*, April 25, 1944. Cols. 677-678.
[2] *The Times*, April 26, 1944.

man in the street could not fail to understand and appreciate, he repeated the message of his Budget, a message of mingled caution and exhortation. The response was remarkable. He received many letters of congratulation and gratitude from all sorts and conditions of men, among them a message of warm appreciation from Queen Mary, by the hand of her lady-in-waiting, on his 'wonderful address':

> It made the financial position of the country vividly clear to the lay mind, and Her Majesty particularly appreciated the judicious mixture of warning and encouragement! As a friend of many years' standing, the Queen felt that she could not let the occasion pass without a personal expression of her own interest, appreciation and very real sympathy with you in your heavy and unique responsibility.

Yet within this chorus of praise there were certain cacophonies of criticism. Some Members of Parliament and of the general public were disappointed at Anderson's failure to provide a decrease in taxation and were unmollified by his prescription of 'the mixture as before'. Among these critics was A. P. Herbert, John's fellow University Member and one who had offered so glowing a tribute to him as a 'Tough Boy' four years before.[1] Now he gave vent to his feelings in lines entitled 'A "Good" Budget':

> Thank you, Sir John ; though it's a little strange
> To thank the torturer who makes no change.
> Thank you, Sir John, you've been extremely nice :
> Whisky is still five times the proper price.
>
> 'Thank you, Sir John' ; the compliments resound :
> You still take only ten bob in the pound.
> 'Thank you, Sir John', the cheerful victim brays.
> Never did robbery receive such praise.[2]

The year 1944 marked the isolation of Nazi Germany and the assault upon her by the Allied forces on every side. With the invasion of Italy in September 1943 the war had been brought back to Western Europe and the armies of Britain, the United States and Canada began their attack on the 'soft under-belly of the Axis' —

[1] See above, p. 257.
[2] A. P. Herbert, *Light the Lights* (Methuen, 1945), pp. 14-15. I am indebted to both the author and the publisher for their permission to reproduce these lines here.

though the German resistance at Anzio and Salerno and Cassino proved it not to be so soft after all! In the east the armies of the Soviet Union pressed forward relentlessly.

Meantime in Britain preparations began for the great invasion across the Channel which was to liberate France and the Low Countries. It was in these preparations that the past work of John Anderson became apparent. The organization of British man-power and production, which had been achieved under his direction as Lord President of the Council, now bore abundant fruit, and the great contribution which Britain was able to make to the Allied invasion owed much to the organic structure of the Home Front which John had achieved.

There followed the tremendous events of the summer of 1944 : the overwhelming success of D-Day, the sweep across France, the liberation of Paris and the delivery of Belgium and the southern part of the Netherlands from Nazi occupation. To those who watched from London the advance of the tide of Allied invasion it seemed that the final victory might soon be achieved and with victory would come the problems of peace. Though the consum-mation of these hopes was delayed beyond early expectations the problems entailed by Allied successes soon made their appearance.

With the liberation of France and Belgium and the return of their national governments to Paris and Brussels, there arose financial and economic issues which required both delicate and expert handling. The susceptibilities of both countries were very vulner-able at this time, more particularly in the case of France, and much effort was directed towards building up the self-esteem of the French people and of rehabilitating the French nation to the status of a Great Power. It was for this reason that Mr. Churchill and Mr. Eden made their historic appearance in Paris on November 11-12, 1944, for general talks on political subjects with General de Gaulle, then head of the French Provisional Government. Among other results of these conversations was the admission of France to mem-bership of the European Advisory Committee on equal footing with Britain, the United States and the Soviet Union.[1]

---

[1] The European Advisory Commission was the inter-Allied body set up by the Moscow Conference of 1943, under the chairmanship of Sir William Strang, and charged with the planning for the future treatment of Germany.

A few days later, John Anderson, accompanied by Ava, together with his Private Secretary, Mr. Thomas Padmore,[1] and a detective, arrived in Paris on a further goodwill mission. Negotiations had been in process for some months between British and French Treasury officials for the conclusion of a Monetary Agreement and, although Anderson had had no direct part in these transactions, which had been delegated to the able direction of Sir David Waley, it was thought politic that another senior member of the British War Cabinet should visit Paris for the general purpose of an exchange of views and to show good-will.

Though it would have been well-nigh impossible to prevent Ava from returning at the earliest possible moment to her beloved Paris, her inclusion in the party was exceedingly fortunate. In the first place she was bilingual and, in the second, her knowledge of men and affairs in French politics was almost unrivalled. John was competent in the French language and during the war he had made many friends among the French in exile and had established a remarkable degree of *rapport* with General de Gaulle, but there was no doubt among his colleagues that Ava's presence with him would be an asset in every way. They arrived in Paris on November 29 and stayed with Duff and Diana Cooper at the British Embassy. John had talks with General de Gaulle, with his old friends René Pleven, then Minister of Finance, and Jean Monnet ; with Pierre Mendès-France, the Minister of National Economy, and with the great French scientist, Professor Joliot-Curie, with whom he had been associated in 'Tube Alloys' matters earlier in the war.

After two days Anderson and Padmore, leaving Ava behind in Paris, moved on to Brussels where they spent two and a half days at the British staff headquarters. Here John talked with various dignitaries of the Belgian Government, but he also found time to visit the grave of Ava's half-brother, who had died of wounds received in action a few weeks before and lay buried in a military cemetery near Brussels. Later they visited Field-Marshal Montgomery in his forward headquarters and returned to Brussels.

On the final evening of their visit they were entertained by the Chief of Staff of the 21st Army Group, Major-General Sir Francis de Guingand, and John was initiated into the mysteries of 'vingt

[1] Sir Thomas Padmore, K.C.B., Second Secretary, H.M. Treasury since 1952.

et un', a game he had never played before. He applied himself to
the game with characteristic precision, and to those who watched
it was a memorable spectacle to see that powerful intelligence
addressing itself repeatedly to the grave question whether to 'stick'
or to 'twist', and whether to increase the stake on a particular
hand by one or two matches, each representing five Belgian francs.
Despite his grave application, however, he was down at the end
of the game and had to accept a loan from his Private Secretary !
On the following morning they departed by car for Paris, sustained
on their cold journey by a well-prepared luncheon basket and a
magnum of champagne. After two further days in Paris, the
whole party returned to England on December 5.

Some four months later Anderson was back again in Paris,
this time on a specific mission. Negotiations and discussions on
the Monetary Agreement had continued in the interval and, as
previously, John was kept in close touch, giving decisions on the
major issues as they arose. On February 1, 1945, M. Pleven had
come over to London on a flying visit for penultimate talks with
Anderson and Lord Keynes and by early March almost complete
agreement had been reached. Anderson personally decided that, if
suitable dates could be arranged, the most fitting thing would be for
him to go to Paris for the formal conclusion of the Agreement. He
reported to the War Cabinet on the conclusion of the negotiations
on March 16 and Cabinet approval was given three days later.
The Agreement regularized the monetary relations between the
two countries and cancelled all claims on both sides arising out of
the war, except for the repayment in gold or dollars by France to
Britain of the $58 million (£39 million) representing the French
munitions contracts in the United States which Britain took over
when France capitulated in 1940; it paid over in dollars to the
account of France the dollar payments which the French had
already made in respect of munition contracts prior to the date of
their capitulation. A further source of gold from France to Britain
was provided under the Agreement by one-third of the value of
the payments by France for current supplies being made in gold.
The War Cabinet not only endorsed the Agreement but clearly
thought that Anderson had made a good bargain and was to be
congratulated on it. He flew to Paris on March 27 for the formal

signature, this time accompanied only by Padmore, and returned on the following day.[1]

This journey might well have had a problematical conclusion had it not been for John's intervention. The flight to Paris was made in a Dakota, a roomy aircraft for those days, and John had only Tom Padmore with him. They had not been long airborne when he wandered into the crew's compartment and, having cast a look over the navigation maps, asked why the route marked, instead of being in a pretty straight line, included a semi-circular bulge over the French coast. 'Oh, sir,' replied the navigator, 'that's to avoid flying over Dunkirk' (where the Germans were still holding out with anti-aircraft guns). 'But', said John in his weighty manner, 'why are we going in the region of Dunkirk at all?' 'Because', said the navigator smartly, 'it is on the direct route from London to *Brussels*.' There was a silence in the cabin. Then, after some brisk questioning, it emerged that, with startling efficiency, Transport Command were about to take the Chancellor of the Exchequer to Brussels for the purpose of signing an Agreement with the French Government installed in Paris! Some swift radio work was put in hand and the Dakota was diverted to its proper destination. But had it not been for John's habit of seeing personally that all was well in absolutely all respects, he would duly have arrived at the wrong capital.

That John's idea of coming personally to Paris for the signature of this Agreement was keenly appreciated by the French Government is evident from the conclusion of General de Gaulle's statement at the end of the ceremony:

> *C'est une véritable joie pour moi que mon excellent ami, Sir John Anderson, qui est aussi un grand ami de la France, soit venu le signer avec moi à Paris. Je veux voir dans sa visite une manifestation de plus de la profonde et de la cordiale solidarité franco-britannique, qui se prolongera demain dans la paix pour le plus grand intérêt des deux nations.*

In preparing his second Budget, Anderson proceeded on the reasonable assumption that the war in Europe would come to an

[1] The text of the Anglo-French Financial Agreement was published as a White Paper, Cmd. 6613, on March 28, 1945.

end some time in the early summer. Even so, however, the defeat of Japan remained to be achieved, and it was generally believed that the war in the Orient would continue for at least another eighteen months after the unconditional surrender of Germany. Though John was one of the very few men in Britain who was privy to the development of the atomic bomb and who could, therefore, reasonably look forward to the possibility of an accelerated conclusion of the war against Japan, this was, of course, knowledge which he could not share with Parliament.[1] He, therefore, deemed it prudent to make only a very slight reduction in the Votes of Credit for which he asked. But, on the whole, the situation when he made his Budget statement to the House of Commons on April 24, 1945, called for greater financial optimism than when he had presented the case a year before. The nation's gross revenue showed an increase of £163 million over that of the previous year and the estimated deficit was £25 million less. Nevertheless, though he did not see any reason for introducing additional taxation, he did not feel justified in lightening the burden of taxpayers. For this restraint he gave the House two reasons. In the first place, it would be highly dangerous to increase the pressure of purchasing power on the market before there could be any corresponding increase of supplies ; in the second, he was of the opinion that the nation had not yet reached the stage at which he as Chancellor could begin to consider his task in relation to post-war taxation. As in 1944 the Finance Act had included reliefs for post-war capital expenditure on scientific research, so now in 1945 he proposed similar tax reliefs for capital expenditure on the buildings and other physical assets of productive industry.[2] He warned the House, however, that major reductions in taxation could only be made as a part of a comprehensive review of the probable course of post-war expenditure and of the system of taxation in relation to it, though he indicated that occasion for making such a review might arise before a full year had elapsed.

In point of fact, John's forecast of the duration of the war with

---

[1] The only persons in Britain fully cognizant of the whole matter of 'Tube Alloys' were the King, the Prime Minister, Lord Cherwell and Sir John Anderson.

[2] Both the 1944 and 1945 proposals were not to come into force until the 'appointed day' — which was set at April 6, 1946, in Mr. Dalton's first Budget — Autumn 1945.

Germany proved to be over-cautious. Even as he spoke in Westminster, Field-Marshal Alexander's armies were inflicting a series of stunning defeats upon the enemy in Italy, which culminated in the surrender of the German forces on May 2. Similarly in Germany, Field-Marshal Montgomery's troops entered Bremen on April 26 and Hamburg on May 3. On the following day the Field-Marshal reported to General Eisenhower, the Supreme Allied Commander, that all enemy forces in Holland, north-west Germany and Denmark had surrendered as from 8 a.m. on May 5, and two days later, on May 7 — just thirteen days after Anderson's Budget speech — the unconditional surrender of the German armies was formally signed in the schoolhouse at Rheims at 2.41 a.m.

May 8 — VE Day — was a day of jubilant rejoicing in which John joined whole-heartedly, albeit with the tempering knowledge that there was yet much to be done and many lives to be lost before final victory and peace could be achieved. It was, however, the occasion for a very happy incident in his Parliamentary career.

When the House of Commons met at three o'clock it was in anticipation of a statement by the Prime Minister. But Mr. Churchill was not there. He was broadcasting to the nation and to the Commonwealth and Empire, and there had been some hitch about the time. Question Time came and passed and still there was no Prime Minister. John Anderson was in charge of the Treasury Bench and upon him devolved the responsibility of keeping things going until Mr. Churchill should appear. The House of Commons, justly jealous of its privilege and its dignity, is never at a loss in an emergency of this nature. Some time-honoured precedent, half forgotten, can always be called upon with what sometimes appears to the onlooker as incurable frivolity, but which indeed is not so. It is the House of Commons sense of humour and it stood them in good office on this day.

There is a Bill, known as the Outlawries Bill, which is formally read at the beginning of each session after the King's Speech and is supposed to preserve the right of Members to discuss what they will, whatever topics have been introduced into the Speech by Ministers. The Bill is not printed and nobody has ever seen the text of it, though it is believed to be designed 'for the better prevention of clandestine outlawries'. It was upon this measure that the Member for Oxford University, that splendid jester and re-former Alan Herbert, then a petty-officer in the Navy, fell back as an impromptu curtain-raiser.[1] 'When', he asked, 'do His Majesty's Government propose to proceed with the Outlawries Bill ?' John preserved a complete solemnity, but his eyes twinkled as he replied : 'We fully understand the implications of that question, and my hon. and gallant Friend knows as much about that matter as I do'. Still no Prime Minister. A. P. H. pressed his point and John, whose slow delivery well fitted him for such an emergency, ably seconded him in a noble piece of gagging.

> PETTY-OFFICER HERBERT : Further to my point on Business, and arising out of the most unsatisfactory answer, may I ask by what Minister of the Crown the Outlawries Bill was, in fact, introduced, and why it is that such an important Measure, the first Measure considered in a new Session, is not on the Order Paper ; and further, may I mention the suspicion that this Bill was in fact introduced by one of the Clerks at the Table and, much as we love them, have not things come to a pretty pass if public Bills are to be introduced by the Clerks at the Table without the sanction of the House ?
>
> SIR J. ANDERSON : I thought I was in a position to deal with any matter likely to be raised on the spur of the moment by hon. Friends, but my hon. and gallant Friend's ingenuity has, I must confess, for the moment got the better of me. But I will consult with my right hon. Friend the Home Secretary, who seems definitely to be involved in any question of clandestine outlawries, and perhaps I shall be able to satisfy my hon. and gallant Friend, either privately or in answer to a Question, if he chooses to put one on the Paper.[2]

But still there was no Prime Minister, and even John's capacity for the impromptu was in danger of drying up. He had just offered a somewhat harassed 'No, Sir, I do not know' to a further Supplementary Question when Mr. Churchill came from behind the Speaker's Chair and then, as Sir Alan Herbert recalls, 'We all went mad'.

---

[1] Sir Alan Herbert has given a whimsical account of this incident in his delightful book of parliamentary reminiscences, *Independent Member* (1950), pp. 351-353.
[2] *House of Commons Debates*, May 8, 1945. Col. 1852.

In the afternoon, with his colleagues of the War Cabinet and the Chiefs of Staff, John attended Mr. Churchill to Buckingham Palace to exchange congratulations with King George VI. 'You have brought this country — I may say you have brought the whole world — out of deadly peril', said His Majesty. 'You have won the gratitude of millions and I may add of your Sovereign'.[1]

(v)

Over and above John Anderson's contribution to the government of the country as a Minister of the Crown was the substantial assistance which he afforded the Prime Minister in 'ironing out' the difficulties which inevitably arise in a Coalition Government. Because he was in no sense, either by training or inclination, a Party man and because of his complete lack of any desire to take a leading rôle in political affairs, he had earned the trust and respect of both Conservative and Labour Ministers, and enjoyed the confidence of both Parties to a degree which would not have been accorded to a member of either Party by a member of the other. As a result, he was employed from time to time by Mr. Churchill as a go-between when tension arose between his less impartial colleagues.

The very high regard in which John was held by both his leader and his associates was demonstrated when, early in 1945, King George asked the Prime Minister whom he would recommend to succeed him in the event of his death as a result of enemy action. Mr. Churchill had already tendered formal advice in June 1942 that Mr. Anthony Eden should be entrusted with the formation of a new government, but both he and the Foreign Secretary were to be absent from the country simultaneously in order to attend the Yalta Conference with President Roosevelt and Marshal Stalin. The King now asked for whom he should send if both of them should be killed on this forthcoming journey.

In a letter dated January 28, 1945, Mr. Churchill offered to His Majesty the advice, unusual in itself, that should this eventuality arise, he should entrust the task of forming a government to a person who was neither a professional politician nor a member of

[1] Wheeler-Bennett (*op. cit.*), pp. 625-626.

the Conservative Party. He gave his reasons for this choice clearly
and in detail :

10 Downing Street
Whitehall

Sir,

The Prime Minister, with his humble duty, obeys Your
Majesty's request to tender advice in respect of a successor to
himself if both he and Mr. Eden, whose name has already been
submitted, should be killed during this forthcoming journey.

The Prime Minister feels that this advice should be tendered
by him in relation to the position which would be created if both
he and Mr. Eden were killed at the same time during these next
few months or even weeks when the war against Germany hangs
in the balance and when a National Coalition Government is
functioning. As Your Majesty is no doubt aware, Sir John
Anderson has not declared himself a Member of the Conservative
Party, which has a very large majority over all other Parties in
the House of Commons. He is returned as an Independent
Member for the Scottish Universities. In ordinary circumstances
Mr. Churchill would have advised Your Majesty to make sure
that you send for a man whom the Conservative Party would
choose as Leader, they having the Parliamentary majority. It
may also be considered very probable that any Conservative for
whom Your Majesty might send would immediately be chosen
as Leader of the Conservative Party on account of the profound
respect which that Party bears to the gestures of the Crown.
However, till the end of the German war, it is necessary to consider the maintenance of the present harmonious Coalition whose
services will, the Prime Minister is sure, never be forgotten by
Your Majesty or by the people, having regard to the extraordinary perils through which we have safely passed. It would
therefore seem very appropriate that during the continuance of
the Coalition a Prime Minister should be chosen who would not
necessarily be the Leader of the Conservative Party, though that
might well follow, but would be adapted by character and outlook and, by the general regard attaching to him, well qualified
to sustain the existing all-Party Government.

In this case there can be no doubt that it is the Prime Minister's
duty to advise Your Majesty to send for Sir John Anderson in
the event of the Prime Minister and the Foreign Secretary being
killed.

A new situation would possibly arise after a General Election had been fought. If a Conservative Party were returned with a majority perhaps as large as they have to-day, they might desire that Sir John Anderson should become a Member of their Party or they might choose a Leader of their own. It is very likely that there will be a substantial Conservative majority in the new Parliament ; but it by no means follows that that majority would not accept Sir John Anderson as Prime Minister with or without his acceptance of the Leadership of the Conservative Party. The Prime Minister therefore feels that Your Majesty would be acting[1] not only in harmony with Constitutional usage, but also with the practical needs of the time in sending for Sir John Anderson in the contingency referred to.

It would, of course, in Mr. Churchill's humble opinion, be contrary to the spirit of the Constitution to send for anyone in any way obnoxious to the Party which holds predominance in the House of Commons at the actual moment.

With his humble duty Mr. Churchill remains

Your Majesty's faithful and devoted servant,

WINSTON S. CHURCHILL.[2]

This very remarkable document is of interest in a number of aspects. It is certainly unique that a living Prime Minister should have designated the succession of the premiership, as it were, 'to the third and the fourth generation', and it constitutes an important interpretation of the relative rôles of Sovereign and Minister. That Mr. Churchill was within his rights in tendering his advice there is no shadow of doubt, for the King had specifically asked for it, but it is interesting to speculate on the reception which the recommendation would have been accorded in the event of the King's having to adopt it. The proposal of a non-party man, of distinguished record, to lead a National Government is logical but without precedent and therefore daring, and it is to be wondered whether the King, if he decided to pursue this course, would have consulted the various leaders of the parties composing the coalition

---

[1] It is of noteworthy interest that Lord Birkenhead, writing of what he describes as the 'naked struggle for power' between Professor Lindemann and Sir Henry Tizard, expresses the opinion that had these two men been serving under a strong chairman, 'perhaps a man like Sir John Anderson, these troubles might never have occurred'. (The Earl of Birkenhead, *The Prof. in two worlds* ; *the official life of Professor F. A. Lindemann, Viscount Cherwell* (1961), p. 191.

[2] Wheeler-Bennett (*op. cit.*), pp. 544-546.

before sending for John Anderson, or whether he would have taken Mr. Churchill's counsel *au pied de la lettre* and entrusted him with forming a government without more ado. In either case His Majesty would have been exercising his prerogative with complete correctitude, for the right of appointing his first minister is his unfettered.

It may also be wondered, and perhaps doubted, whether John would have made a very good Prime Minister. He was a born chief but not really a born leader and the great respect in which he was held by the whole House of Commons might not have extended to their following him as Premier. The Conservative Party, which would have suffered the staggering loss of their two principal leaders, might have accepted him provisionally — if for no other reason than sheer inability to agree on an alternative — for he was undoubtedly one of the most outstanding members of the Government. His Labour colleagues in the War Cabinet would also, in all probability, have agreed to serve under him, but whether the Labour Party as a whole would have accepted his leadership is perhaps open to speculation. Moreover, except as the progenitor of the Anderson Shelter, he was virtually unknown in the country at large, and though he was profoundly trusted by all who had served under him, such public contacts as he had had gave more the impression of a portentous Roman figure than of one who could inspire his war-weary countrymen to last out the final lap of the race to victory.

Happily, however, the occasion for a pragmatic solution of these enigmas did not arise, though at the opening of the Potsdam Conference in July 1945, at which Mr. Churchill, Mr. Eden and Mr. Attlee were all present, John Anderson was designated the acting Head of the Government.

With the close of the war in Europe it became evident by many signs and portents that the party truce, which had been so dominant a feature of British national life for the past five years, could not be much longer maintained. The political situation was an unusual one. There had been no general election for nearly ten years, and of the three Prime Ministers who had governed the country during this period only one, Mr. Stanley Baldwin, had been returned by the electorate as the leader of a victorious party. The Parliament of the day was that which had been elected in October 1935 — the same which had rejected the Hoare-Laval Plan, had condoned the re-militarization of the Rhineland, had enthusiastically welcomed Mr. Chamberlain back from Munich, and had as decisively over-thrown him not two years later.

Throughout the war there had been an electoral moratorium. By agreement between the parties the life of Parliament had been annually prolonged beyond the date of its legal expiration in October 1940, and when by-elections became necessary a repre-sentative of the party to which the last occupant of the seat had belonged was by common assent allowed to retain it, in general, without contest. The state of the parties in the House of Commons had, therefore, remained virtually static since September 1939.

The All-Party National Government which Mr. Churchill had formed in May 1940 had worked together loyally and effectively in defeat and victory, and such personal rifts and tensions as had occurred had been in general amicably resolved, very often as a result of John Anderson's good offices as mediator and honest broker. But with the increasing prospects of an early end to the war in Europe there had come a growing strain within this tem-porary partnership. Party differences among Ministers became more apparent when attention began to be focused on problems of post-war reconstruction. So long as the Cabinet were con-cerned solely with the direction of the war they were united by the common aim of victory and coalition government was easy. Once, however, they turned their minds to peace and to the future, while they found it possible to agree on some things — notably the Beveridge Plan and the scheme for a National Health Service — doctrinal differences soon began to emerge ; for example, on matters of post-war industrial organization. It was remarkable that they were able to agree on the principles of a peacetime Employment Policy, but the production of a White Paper on that question showed that there were limits beyond which it would be unprofitable to discuss post-war problems. The differences were too great — and these were matters on which compromise might well have given the worst of both worlds.

Both Mr. Churchill and Mr. Attlee, therefore, were made increasingly aware of the constitutional need for an appeal to the people of Britain by an election. The question to be resolved was when this should take place. Mr. Churchill was hopeful that the National Coalition might remain in being until after the defeat of Japan — which it was generally believed would not be for at least eighteen months after the collapse of Germany — but the great majority of the Labour Party were opposed to its continuation beyond October 1945.

After abortive negotiations with the leaders of the Labour Party, the Prime Minister tendered the resignation of himself and his National Government to the King on May 23. His Majesty bowed to the inevitable and at once invited Mr. Churchill, as the leader of a party which still enjoyed a majority of considerably more than a hundred over all others in the House of Commons, to form a new government. He also granted Mr. Churchill's request for a dissolution of Parliament on June 15.

The 'Caretaker Government' which Mr. Churchill now formed pending the results of the polling to be held on July 5,[1] was composed chiefly of Conservatives, but it also included some National Liberals and Independents, and among the latter was John Anderson, who retained the office of Chancellor of the Exchequer. Once again he was nominated by the Unionist Party of Scotland for one of the three seats of the Scottish Universities, and, as in 1938, he presented himself to his constituents as a non-party candidate. 'I have seen no reason to alter my views in the meantime', he told them in his election address, 'and, as we clearly have still a long way to go before normal conditions are restored, I ask for your votes now on the same footing as before.'

There was, however, a difference between the candidate of 1938 and that of 1945. When John was first elected, his reputation rested on his record as a Civil Servant and a successful proconsul. The ensuing years had been for him an uninterrupted period of high ministerial office and it was against these great achievements that he stood before the electorate. Yet, as he continued in his address,

[1] Because of the delay in getting in the votes of the troops overseas an interval of three weeks separated polling day on July 5 from the declaration of the polls on July 25.

he had not sought, nor would he cling to, high office, but he was ready to serve to the utmost of his capacity so long as the state of the country demanded the whole-hearted collaboration of men of good-will of all ways of thinking.

In a word, I stand for the prosecution of the war against Japan with the utmost vigour, for economic and political collaboration with other peace-loving nations, for the maintenance of stable price and wage levels, the avoidance of inflation and the protection of the people's savings, for the development of our social services in such a way as to satisfy the conscience of our people and to promote our national efficiency, for the encouragement of our trade and industry on the traditional and well-tried basis of private enterprise, and for the progressive easing of the heavy burden of taxation. I prefer practical efficiency to theoretical perfection and I believe sincerely that a broad-based government such as our Prime Minister favours is best suited to our needs in these grave days.

In a broadcast to the nation on June 9, in support of Mr. Churchill's Government, John Anderson reiterated the position which he had made clear in his address to his constituents and followed it up with a survey of what the Government were prepared to do for the people of the United Kingdom in the future. They aimed, he said, at a balanced economy, at a policy of full employment, at a new and expanded system of social insurance and at a programme of better housing. And then he turned to a stirring denunciation of the Labour Party's proposals for nationalization.

I have deliberately left this to the end [he said] for it is the most controversial — free enterprise *versus* State control ; private ownership *versus* public ownership. Let us face this issue squarely. All the measures that I have just been describing assume a system of competitive enterprise and acceptance of the motive of securing reward for our work and efforts — a motive that alike makes Boards of Directors try to earn good dividends, shareholders to criticize balance-sheets and workers to look out for opportunities of securing improved wage scales. We are all affected by it and, if we are honest with ourselves, we will admit this. . . . My admiration for our public services is unbounded ; but nothing in my experience leads me to think that any organization or any

Y

technique has yet been developed inside the machinery of government equal to dealing with all the normal hazards of trade and industry. Therefore I say, let us pin our faith to free enterprise which has served us well in the past, on which our prosperity has been built and which has inspired our spirit of adventure. . . . It is unquestionably to private enterprise that we must look to see us through the problems of the next few years. It would be the height of folly to deny private enterprise fair and favourable conditions for its development. It would be a betrayal of the interests of the nation to secure the worst of every possible world by encouraging a wholly delusive belief in the speedy extension of national control and thereby obscuring the absolute necessity of giving to private enterprise the conditions necessary to its success. . . .

This was as near to the pronouncement of a political credo as John had ever gone. It was a statement of his basic beliefs and a fundamental principle to which he would return again and again in the House of Commons when in opposition. He believed wholeheartedly in the spirit of private enterprise and in the right of every man to enjoy freedom of opportunity for free and equal competition.

The other candidates for the three Scottish University seats were Sir John Graham Kerr (Conservative) and Sir John Boyd Orr (Independent), the food and agricultural expert, both of whom had sat with John in the late Parliament, and, in addition, Dr. H. G. Sutherland (Labour), the Medical Director of the Mass Radiography Centre at Birmingham, and Colonel R. S. Weir (Liberal), the assistant Controller of the Ministry of Labour Region of Scotland.

The election was held under the Proportional Representation system which governed the contests for the university seats. At the final count, after the transfer of surplus 'first preference votes', the figures were as follows :

ANDERSON	8198
BOYD ORR	8198
KERR	8999
SUTHERLAND	4075
WEIR	3319 [1]

Anderson, Kerr and Boyd Orr were therefore declared to be elected.

[1] *The Scotsman*, August 3, 1945.

Thus John was returned to Parliament for the second time, but he shared in the substantial defeat which the Churchill Government suffered at the hands of Labour. Mr. Attlee and his followers achieved an over-all majority of 180 votes in the new House of Commons, and at 7 o'clock on the evening of July 26 Mr. Churchill tendered to his Sovereign the resignation of his short-lived second administration.

So ended John Anderson's tenure of office on the Treasury Bench of the House of Commons. He had served as a Cabinet Minister without intermission from November 1938 to July 1945. He was never to hold ministerial office again.

IX

Shadow Cabinet and House of Lords
1945-1958

(i)

HAVING thus completed nearly seven years as a member of His Majesty's Government, John Anderson now began a six-year period as a member of His Majesty's Loyal Opposition. He was, therefore, only an observer of the tremendous happenings which attended the immediate conclusion of the Second World War, though he was to be an active participant in their sequel.

On July 16, 1945, at 5.30 a.m. (local time), a successful test of a plutonium bomb had taken place on an arid plain some fifty miles from Alamogordo, New Mexico, and the full report of this momentous event, together with photographs of damage effected, reached President Truman at Potsdam on July 21.[1] It was also shown to Mr. Churchill, who described it as 'the Second Coming in wrath'. Together the President and the Prime Minister agreed that the bomb should be used against Japan as soon as it was ready. The responsibility for the decision to use it, however, remained with the President. Marshal Stalin was informed of the bomb by Mr. Truman with 'studied casualness' on July 24. The Marshal appeared to be entirely unimpressed.[2] Mr. Attlee, though present at the

[1] The text of this historic document is made public for the first time by Herbert Feis in *Between War and Peace — the Potsdam Conference* (Princeton, New Jersey, 1960), pp. 165-171.

[2] Such is Mr. Truman's recollection (*Year of Decisions* (New York, 1955), p. 416), but to Mr. Churchill, who was observing the incident at a distance of some five yards, the impression made upon Stalin by the President's casual remark was somewhat different : 'I knew what the President was going to do. What was vital to measure was its effect upon Stalin. I can see it all as if it were yesterday. He seemed to be delighted. A new bomb ! Of extraordinary power ! Probably decisive on the whole Japanese war ! What a bit of luck ! This was my impression at the moment, and I am sure he had no idea of the significance of what he was

Conference as a member of the British delegation, was still in complete ignorance of the bomb's existence.

On the morning of the following day, July 25, Mr. Churchill, Mr. Eden and Mr. Attlee flew back to England for the results of the General Election, and John Anderson surrendered his authority as acting Head of the Government which he had exercised in their absence. The outcome of the election came as a surprise to all and necessitated some very rapid action on the part of Mr. Attlee. By the afternoon of July 28, having accepted the King's mandate to form a government and appointed the senior members of his Cabinet, he was back in Potsdam. In the meantime a Three Power ultimatum had been issued by the United States, Britain and China on July 26, calling upon Japan to accept unconditional surrender or face 'prompt and utter destruction'. The Japanese Government on the 28th elected to ignore this threat and the *tempo* of events now increased to the dramatic climax.[1]

At 8.16 (local time) on the morning of August 6, an aircraft of the United States Air Force, based on the island of Tinian in the Marianas, dropped the first atomic bomb on the Japanese city of Hiroshima with devastating results ; on the following day both Mr. Attlee and John Anderson made radio broadcasts to the British people. The Prime Minister had been so short a time in office that he could do no more than add an introduction to the long announcement that his predecessor had prepared a fortnight before. The voice was the voice of Attlee but the words were the words of Churchill :

> It is now for Japan to realize . . . what the consequences will be of an indefinite continuance of this terrible means of maintaining a rule of law in the world.
>
> This revelation of the secrets nature so long mercifully withheld from man should arouse the most solemn reflections in the mind and conscience of every human being capable of comprehension. We must indeed pray that these awful agencies will

being told' (*Triumph and Tragedy* (1954), pp. 579-580). It is with such problems of conflicting evidence on points of detail that contemporary historians have to contend !

[1] The word used by the Japanese Government in their statement was *mokusatsu* (literally to 'kill with silence'), and this was the term which was broadcast to the people of Japan. American monitors translated it as 'ignore' which was later interpreted officially as 'reject'. It was the latter word which was reported to President Truman at Potsdam. For the full story of this curious episode see Robert J. C. Burtow, *Japan's Decision to Surrender* (Stanford, California, 1954), pp. 145-148.

be made to conduce to peace among the nations and that, instead of wreaking measureless havoc upon the entire globe, they may become a perennial foundation of world prosperity.

John Anderson's message to the nation has been given in full elsewhere in this book.[1] It offered a solemn warning of the potentialities of the bomb and a brief glimpse of the happier future which could, and might, eventuate from this colossal scientific development.

Russia declared war on Japan on August 8 and on the day following the second bomb was dropped on Nagasaki. Already, after the destruction of Hiroshima, the Japanese Government, on the initiative of the Emperor, were ready for peace, but their final surrender had not been made effective. It came now on August 15,[2] the day on which King George VI opened his new Parliament, an occasion on which Anderson made his first appearance on the Opposition Front Bench. VJ Day was celebrated in London with restrained and weary rejoicing. The war was over, but what did the future hold for a humanity stunned by this staggering product of its own ingenuity ?

Though there was general rejoicing that the war had ended, the morrow of VJ Day brought to thinking men deep searching of heart at the manner of its ending. True, the use of the atomic bomb had shortened the war by some fifteen months on the general estimate made on VE Day ; true, too, that hundreds of thousands of British and American lives had been saved — and even more Asiatic lives — for there had been no shadow of doubt that Operations OLYMPIC and CORONET — the two stages of invasion of the Japanese mainland — would have met with fanatical resistance. In addition, there had been the problem of how to bring Japan's overseas armies, strung across Asia from Manchuria to Singapore, to the point of unconditional surrender and this also had been resolved by the situation created immediately upon the dropping of the two atomic bombs.[3] Nevertheless, the fact that the destruction of

---

[1] See above, pp. 297-299.

[2] Even after the Japanese Government had taken their decision to surrender, certain hotheads in the War Ministry and General Staff threatened a military *coup* to nullify this decision. An attempt to use the Imperial Guards Division for this purpose failed on the night of August 14/15. (See Samuel Eliot Morison, *Victory in the Pacific, 1945* (Oxford, 1960), pp. 350-351.)

[3] See Morison (*op. cit.*), pp. 352-353.

Hiroshima and Nagasaki had involved the deaths of some 120,000 persons gave rise to genuine horror. And not this alone. The potentialities of mischief inherent in the atomic bomb could not be overlooked. Had human ingenuity created a demon which human wisdom would be unable to control?

It was this question which caused the most profound misgiving in the hearts and minds of the leaders of the United States and the United Kingdom. 'Ever since Hiroshima I had never stopped thinking about the frightful implications of the atomic bomb', President Truman has written. 'We knew that this revolutionary scientific creation could destroy civilization unless put under control and placed at the service of mankind',[1] and Mr. Attlee expressed similar sentiments in his broadcast on August 7.

The full horror of the bomb had come with appalling suddenness upon these two men who had never known of its existence until suddenly called by fate to the highest position in their respective countries. Mr. Churchill and President Roosevelt had been conditioned to its potentialities through the long years of the struggle and race for its creation, though even they knew nothing of the genetic effects of an atomic explosion. But to Mr. Truman the existence of the bomb had remained unrevealed until he became President of the United States on April 15, 1945, and to Mr. Attlee until after his appointment as Prime Minister on July 26 — less than a month before the first bomb was dropped on Hiroshima. Moreover, on the President had rested the full responsibility for the decision to use the bomb.

While there was no doubt in the mind of either Mr. Truman or Mr. Attlee — nor of any responsible leader in Britain or America — that the Allies were entirely justified in using the bomb to achieve a final victory over Japan, it was the hope of all that the atomic age, which had opened in New Mexico on July 16, 1945, should be memorable for the material benefit which it would confer upon mankind and not for the fact that man had turned upon himself the elemental forces of his own universe.

It was Mr. Attlee who took the initiative. On August 8 — the day before the second bomb was dropped on Nagasaki — he sent a personal telegram to President Truman suggesting that they

[1] Truman (*op. cit.*), p. 523.

should issue a joint statement which might serve to reassure the world. 'There is widespread anxiety', he observed, 'as to whether the new power will be used to save or to destroy civilization. . . . I consider, therefore, that you and I, as heads of the Governments which have control of this great force, should without delay make a joint declaration of our intentions to utilize the existence of this great power, not for our own ends, but as trustees for humanity in the interests of all peoples, in order to promote peace and justice in the world.' The President at once replied that he shared completely the views of the Prime Minister and had prepared a declaration in these terms which he proposed to make shortly. Mr. Attlee concurred, and suggested that a joint declaration should be delayed 'until the means of control and the implications in the field of international relations have been more fully considered between those concerned'. President Truman made his promised statement on August 9 to the effect that plans would be prepared for the future control of the bomb and that he would request Congress to co-operate to the end that its production and use might be regulated and its power be made an overwhelming influence toward world peace. Two days later Mr. Attlee warmly endorsed this statement and pledged His Majesty's Government to use all its efforts in promoting the objects which it foreshadowed.[1]

President Truman had appointed a committee, headed by Mr. Henry L. Stimson, the Secretary for War, to advise him on atomic policy, and Mr. Attlee now proposed to follow a similar course. Coincidentally with his own statement on August 11, he took the decision to create an advisory committee, composed partly of Service and official representatives and partly of scientists, the purpose of which was to be twofold : first, to investigate the implications of the use of atomic energy and to advise the Government what steps should be taken for its development in the United Kingdom either for military or industrial purposes ; secondly, to put forward proposals for the international treatment of this subject and to keep in close touch with the work done by the similar committee which President Truman had set up in the United States.

In choosing a chairman for this Advisory Committee, Mr.

---

[1] Lord Francis-Williams, *A Prime Minister Remembers* (1961), pp. 95-97 ; Truman (*op. cit.*), pp. 523-524.

Attlee saw clearly that it must be someone who had had experience of the problem from the beginning and also knowledge of the long and complicated history of the past negotiations. There was but one man in Britain who possessed these qualifications in their entirety and the Prime Minister turned to him without hesitation, unprejudiced by the fact that, though nominally an Independent Member, he sat on the Opposition Front Bench and was a member of the 'Shadow Cabinet'. On August 14 he offered the chairmanship of the United Kingdom Advisory Committee on Atomic Energy to John Anderson. With equal lack of hesitation, John accepted two days later. The appointment was made public on August 21.

Thus was forged a new partnership over and above the lines of party politics ; a partnership dedicated to the task of controlling, both nationally and internationally, those tremendous forces which held within them such great promise for the future benefit of mankind and such hideous possibilities for its extinction. Great credit redounds both to Clement Attlee and to John Anderson for the parts which they played in this drama, for neither man felt that in trusting to the wisdom and integrity and friendship of the other he was betraying either principles or doctrines, despite the fact that they sat on opposite sides of the House of Commons. The cause which both men served transcended in their minds all petty considerations of party politics. That they failed in achieving the goal which they had set for themselves was no fault of theirs.

To John Anderson the importance of the task which Mr. Attlee had now assigned to him, and the crucial need for it, had long been apparent. From the earliest days of his association with 'Tube Alloys' he had been painfully cognizant of the ultimate and terrible potential consequences inherent in the release of nuclear fission. He had discussed it for hours at a time with Niels Bohr, and had been fortified in his own judgment by the sad prognostications of the noble Dane. To both of them it had long seemed hideous that this vast new force which had been brought forth by human ingenuity should not be placed under international control, its secrets shared and its uses developed for the benefit rather than the destruction of civilization. John now welcomed an opportunity to play a part in this great work.

As the weeks passed it became increasingly clear that the new climate of ideas produced by the use of the atomic bomb was producing serious complications on the international front as a whole, as well as in the more restricted field of Anglo-American relations. The lively doubts as to the future of Soviet policy with which both Mr. Attlee and President Truman had left Potsdam developed into active and well-founded suspicion in the course of the Foreign Ministers' Conference in London on September 11, at which Mr. Molotov gave ample evidence of the non-co-operation and intransigent hostility of his Government. Meantime within the United States a battle royal was developing between the scientists and the Army as to whether the future of atomic energy should be under civilian or military control, and this in its turn had inevitable repercussions on the degree of reciprocal exchange of information between Britain and America.

This question of the sharing of atomic knowledge became immediately one of the vital problems of Anglo-American relations. Doubt at once arose whether the basic arrangement of August 1943, negotiated by John Anderson in Washington and concluded between Mr. Churchill and President Roosevelt in the Quebec Agreement, was to remain the charter of future co-operation between the two countries.[1] It was evident that, although the Quebec Agreement provided for the exchange of information on both military and industrial uses of atomic energy, it was capable of several interpretations.

The basis of the Agreement had been defined in four paragraphs, of which the last three are relevant :

(b) There shall be complete interchange of information and ideas on all sections of the project between members of the Combined Policy Committee and their immediate advisers.

(c) In the field of scientific research and development there shall be full and effective interchange of information and ideas between those in the two countries engaged in the same section of the field.

(d) In the field of design, construction and operation of large-scale plants, interchange of information and ideas shall be regulated by such *ad hoc* arrangements as may, in each section

[1] See above, pp. 287–299.

of the field, appear to be necessary or desirable if the project is to be brought to fruition at the earliest moment; such *ad hoc* arrangements shall be subject to the approval of the Policy Committee.

This followed the wording of the draft contract submitted to Dr. Vannevar Bush by John Anderson on August 4, 1943, and, in accepting it, Dr. Bush, in a memorandum dated August 6, had offered some terms of interpretation :

> In order that we may be sure that there is now no misunderstanding I will comment on a few points [wrote Dr. Bush]. It is our understanding that while members of the Policy Committee will have access to all general information about all phases of the effort, the interchange of information about details of manufacture or construction of plants or of any final weapon will be governed by the provisions of (*d*), and that your suggested provision (*b*) merely is intended to provide that members of the Committee may interchange with their immediate scientific advisers the information they may have, in view of the fact that in some cases members of the Committee may not themselves be scientists.

To this memorandum Anderson replied on the same day : 'Thank you so much for your letter of the 6th August which is entirely satisfactory from my point of view.'[1]

Herein lay the nub of the present situation. In August 1943 all efforts in the field of atomic energy had been concentrated towards one end — the production of the bomb before the enemy produced it first. Indeed the whole project was at that moment only in an advanced stage of scientific research. The possibilities of its development for industrial purposes were even more remote, and it is possible that at Quebec Mr. Churchill paid less attention to them in his discussions with President Roosevelt than might have been considered desirable in the light of subsequent events. The draft agreement which Anderson had reached in Washington had been hard won, and it may well have been thought that no further pressure should be brought to bear on the Americans in the field of 'Tube Alloys'. In any event it was now evident that the terms

---

[1] Truman (*op. cit.*), pp. 535-536. Also see above, p. 295, for Anderson's statement to Mackenzie King that 'Britain cared nothing about the post-war profit-making industries of the matter but was concerned for war purposes'.

of Anglo-American partnership would have to be readjusted, for
President Truman was coming under insistent compulsion from
his advisers, both military and civilian, to retain for the United
States alone the secrets of atomic energy manufacture.

Indeed there were indications that the President was yielding
to this pressure, for on October 3 he announced — almost casually
to a press conference at Tiptonville, Tennessee — that the United
States had no intention of sharing with her Allies the technical
'know-how' which constituted the real secret of the atomic bomb
and, some three weeks later, in a public statement on the foreign
policy of the United States (October 27) he declared that America
would hold in its own hands 'this new power of destruction as a
sacred trust'. Moreover, it was clear that, under pressure of Congressional opinion, the American members of the Combined Policy
Committee were unready and unwilling to give to their British
colleagues the information to which the latter considered they were
entitled under the Quebec Agreement, and this attitude extended
not only to the bomb but also to the development of plants for the
industrial use of atomic energy in peace-time.

To the British Prime Minister, and to John Anderson, it seemed
that this new attitude of the Americans constituted nothing less
than a breach of good faith ; a transgression of the spirit, if not the
letter, of the Quebec and Hyde Park Agreements.[1] If the United
States persisted in following this policy the whole basis of Anglo-
American co-operation in the field of atomic energy would be
destroyed. The situation appeared so critical that Mr. Attlee was
convinced that the time had come for that face-to-face meeting
which he had proposed to President Truman in August and which,
by common consent, had been temporarily postponed. He had
already set matters in train for such a meeting through the channels
of the British Embassy and on September 25 he had sent a private
letter to the President urging the necessity of personal discussions,
which had evoked a warm acquiescent response.[2] Now on

---

[1] The situation was not facilitated by the fact that the text of the Hyde Park
Agreement existed only in the British copy, President Roosevelt having mislaid his
after the meeting with Mr. Churchill. When Mr. Attlee and the President met
with Mr. Mackenzie King in November, the British Embassy had to supply a photo-
stat copy of this document to an embarrassed State Department.

[2] Francis-Williams (*op. cit.*), pp. 97-101 ; Truman (*op. cit.*), p. 534.

October 30 he announced his intention of going to Washington and on November 9 he departed by air, taking John Anderson with him.

It was not only the problem of Anglo-American relations which took the Prime Minister and his chief atomic adviser to Washington. The Conference of Foreign Ministers had dispersed on October 2, after three weeks of desultory wrangling, having achieved precisely nothing except the further disclosure of Soviet intransigence. Observers of the Conference had attributed this intransigence in part to Soviet suspicion of America's monopoly of atomic power and this made it all the more essential in Mr. Attlee's view that means should be found of placing the future use of the bomb under international control.

The British party travelled in two aircraft. That conveying the Prime Minister reached Washington non-stop on the morning of November 10. John's aeroplane, however, had to refuel at New York and was still further delayed by the discovery of some fault in the undercarriage. He reached Washington about three hours after Mr. Attlee and in a state of great anxiety lest word had reached Ava in London of the Prime Minister's solitary arrival. He wrote at once to reassure her, for she had been gravely apprehensive about his journey and could not hide this fact when she came to the airfield to see them off. 'When I saw your dear little face all stricken as I turned to go up the gangway on Friday, it sent a stab through my heart,' wrote John.

While Mr. Attlee was the guest of the President, Anderson stayed with Lord Halifax at the Embassy. The Conference, to which Mr. Mackenzie King had been invited from Ottawa, got under way that morning (November 10) and was at first confined to the Big Three. In the afternoon, they met again with their advisers, but John, who was resting after his flight, did not join them until later. In the evening there was a State Dinner at the White House. 'Not a very impressive affair', he wrote to Ava. 'We had an ordinary 3 course meal & the Pres. & Attlee made short & slightly platitudinous speeches. It was all over by 10.'

On the following day the proceedings were less formal. After the laying of wreaths at Arlington Cemetery on the graves of the American and Canadian Unknown Soldiers and of Field-Marshal

Sir John Dill,[1] the whole party embarked in the Presidential yacht *Williamsburg*. In addition to the President and the two Prime Ministers and John, there were the Secretary of State, James Byrnes, and Admiral Leahy, the President's Chief of Staff, Lord Halifax and the Canadian Ambassador, Lester B. ('Mike') Pearson and the Prime Minister's Secretary, Leslie Rowan.

At first we just sat around & gossiped in little groups while the boat went down stream [John wrote]. I had a good talk with Adm. Leahy whom I liked *very* much. The Pres. was most genial & showed me through two huge albums of photographs of his Potsdam trip. We then lunched on lobster salad, soup, turkey & *soufflé en surprise*. The table was then cleared & a smaller table set out round which we sat thus :

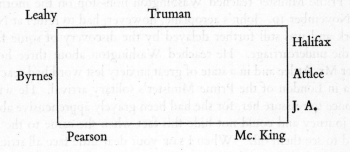

I had a good chance of giving my views & we all seemed fairly well in agreement. Whether it was really so, remains to be seen, but I have just completed a memo. as a basis for further discussion.

The talks continued with the inevitable concomitant of official hospitality. 'Byrnes' dinner last night was at the Mayflower Hotel,' John wrote to Ava — 'huge oysters (each with as much meat as a good-sized hen's egg), prawn curry soup, slabs of roast beef & an ice-pudding. The quantities were quite nauseating.' By November 14 the conference had reached its penultimate — and most difficult — stage.

[1] Field-Marshal Sir John Dill died in Washington on November 4, 1944, while serving as head of the British Joint Staff Mission. He was buried with full military honours in Arlington Cemetery.

By three o'clock [wrote John] we (Attlee, Halifax, myself & Rowan) were back in the President's study, where Mackenzie King & the Canadian Ambassador (Pearson) also gathered. With the President were Byrnes, Leahy & my scientific friend Vannevar Bush. We had a pretty hopeless talk because the Americans had their document, we had ours — quite different — & the Canadians, though they did not table a document, had also been putting their views on paper. As Byrnes, who did most of the talking for the Americans, concentrated entirely on *their* paper we did not make much progress. Finally after about an hour and a half the President suggested that three of us should go away & try to produce a single document which we could all take as a basis for further discussion. The three were Bush, Pearson & myself, so I had the unusual experience of presiding over a little meeting in the Cabinet room of the White House where after about an hour we got something which we were all prepared to recommend subject to amendment in detail.

The final stages of negotiation dragged on late into the night, but at last the conflicting views were harmonized. On the following day (November 15) President Truman announced at a press conference in Mr. Attlee's presence that the three Powers had agreed on the need for international action, under the auspices of the United Nations, for the provision of controls over atomic energy to ensure its use for peaceful purposes only ; to outlaw atomic weapons and other major weapons capable of mass destruction ; and to provide for effective safeguards through inspection.

At the same time the President and the two Prime Ministers had approved the text of a memorandum which ran as follows :

1. We agree that there should be full and effective co-operation in the field of atomic energy between the United States, the United Kingdom and Canada.
2. We agree that the Combined Policy Committee and the Combined Development Trust should be continued in a suitable form.
3. We request the Combined Policy Committee to consider and recommend to us appropriate arrangements for this purpose.[1]

[1] Truman (*op. cit.*), p. 544.

On the face of them, these agreements seemed to be highly satisfactory. John Anderson had played an important and valuable rôle in their negotiation, both as adviser to the Prime Minister and in his own discussions with Dr. Vannevar Bush, Dr. James Conant and others of the President's scientific advisers, with whom he had resumed the relations of friendship and mutual respect which had characterized their wartime dealings.

Mr. Attlee and John, both travelling on this occasion in the same aircraft, returned to London on November 21, after a few days' visit to Ottawa, justifiably satisfied with the results of their mission.[1] It was their hope and their belief that they had taken the first steps towards resolving the suspicion of the Soviet Government by placing atomic energy under the control of the United Nations and that they had restored the basis of Anglo-American co-operation established by John's negotiations in Washington in August 1943 and subsequently ratified by the Quebec Agreement. In both respects they were woefully deceived, though at the outset it seemed that their hopes might be justified.

When the Conference of Foreign Ministers reconvened in Moscow in mid-December, Mr. Molotov accepted the principle of the Three-Power Declaration of Washington and, at the first session of the General Assembly of the United Nations in London a month later, the Soviet delegation joined the unanimous vote of approval on January 24, 1946, which adopted the British resolution establishing the United Nations Atomic Energy Commission with the powers delegated to it by the Washington Declaration. Thereafter, however, the policy of the Soviet Union was directed towards nullifying the work and objectives of this body, a feat in which they were singularly successful.

Similarly, in the field of Anglo-American atomic relations, the fruits of the Washington conversations proved to be but Dead Sea apples. In the months that followed, an Anglo-Canadian-American committee worked steadily at the task of preparing drafts for the

[1] Like all British husbands who went abroad at this time of post-war austerity at home, John had received various shopping commissions from Ava which he had been diligent in fulfilling. 'I am doing my best about your various things', he wrote, '& already I have three large & three small hot water-bottles. I am afraid there is no black velvet but I rang up New York & have a promise of three pairs of shoes which I hope will turn out to be all right. There is nothing in grey & nothing trimmed.'

adaptation of the wartime agreements to post-war conditions. They achieved a fair measure of agreement, subject to some points left for political consideration. But when their drafts finally came to the Combined Policy Committee they encountered a cold wind of hostility which withered them in the bud.

In American politics, as Lord Attlee has ruefully commented, 'The President proposes but Congress disposes'. Mr. Truman had begun his Presidency in the sunshine of Congressional favour but by the close of the year this Washington honeymoon between the White House and Capitol Hill had run its course. When the President had informed his Cabinet of the results of the Washington conversations certain members had commented adversely on the apparent renewal of the Anglo-American agreement for the full exchange of information on atomic energy and this attitude was now reflected in the Senate. Some American scientists, who were opposed to the sharing of the 'know-how' by America with any other country, formed themselves into a surprisingly effective 'lobby' and by the end of December had succeeded in getting the Senate to appoint a Special Committee on Atomic Energy under the chairmanship of Senator McMahon, who shared their views. The Committee immediately introduced a Bill placing atomic energy in the United States under civilian control and prohibiting the disclosure of information to any foreign power.

Mr. Attlee at once foresaw the danger. If the McMahon Bill became law it would deprive the British of the opportunity to share the American knowledge and the advantages derived from years of wartime collaboration on atomic energy to which the British contribution had been very considerable indeed. The Prime Minister informed the American Ambassador in London, Mr. Averell Harriman, that, if the Bill passed, Britain would be forced to undertake her own independent development of atomic energy.[1] To make the position clear he determined to force the issue by instructing Lord Halifax to request detailed information on the construction and operation of atomic energy plants in the United States. The request was made at a meeting of the Combined Policy Committee on April 15, 1946. It was met with a blank refusal.[2]

[1] Truman, *Years of Trial and Hope* (New York, 1956), p. 11.
[2] Francis-Williams (*op. cit.*), p. 110.

Z

There followed an animated and forthright exchange of letters between the Prime Minister and President Truman which, while valuable to the historian as an *exposé* of the points of view of the respective governments, was barren of any other result.[1] Mr. Truman, whatever his personal inclination may have been, was confined within the constrictions of the American Constitution. The Senate passed the McMahon Act on August 1 and on the following day it received the Presidential signature.

The Senators took this action without having ever been informed of the existence of the wartime agreements between Britain and America. Senator McMahon himself had no knowledge of them until enlightened by Mr. Winston Churchill during his visit to Washington in January 1952, when the Prime Minister, while taking him to task about the McMahon Act, showed him the 'top copy' of the Quebec Agreement of 1943, which had been brought from London as a precaution. The Senator confessed his complete ignorance of the document and admitted that, had he and his colleagues on the Senate Atomic Energy Committee known of it at the time of framing their Bill, the measure would never have been passed in its original form.

However, once the McMahon Act had been placed upon the American Statute Book all hope of immediate further co-operation with the United States disappeared. It was more than ten years before the damage inflicted by this piece of legislation was repaired and Anglo-American collaboration regained the same sort of level as had existed hitherto.

Meanwhile Britain was confronted with the task of beginning her own development programme, starting from scratch and without any of the information and assistance which she had felt it her right to expect from the United States. She did so with energy and dispatch. By the autumn of 1946 Parliament had passed the Atomic Energy Act empowering the Minister of Supply to take the necessary action. He had at his disposal the wisdom and counsel of the United Kingdom Advisory Committee on Atomic Energy, of which John Anderson was Chairman.

The results of their efforts were soon disclosed, for they had already been in active operation. As was to be expected, no com-

[1] Francis-Williams (*op. cit.*), pp. 110-117; Truman, *Years of Trial and Hope*, pp. 11-15.

mittee of which John was chairman allowed the grass to grow under its feet. Appointed in August 1945, the Advisory Committee held its first meeting on December 7, shortly after the return of the Prime Minister and Anderson from North America.[1] In pursuance of a decision taken by John's 'Tube Alloys' Committee in the previous April, they urged the Cabinet to press forward with the setting up of a Government-controlled atomic research and experimental establishment and the construction of this was begun at Harwell in Berkshire in April 1946. The first experimental reactor, Gleep, was completed there in August 1947 and the higher powered experimental reactor, Bepo, in July 1948. The 'hot' laboratories for the handling of radioactive substances were completed at Harwell in the following year.

The Advisory Committee also recommended to the Cabinet that a beginning should be made forthwith on the production of plutonium, and an industrial organization for this purpose was formed at the beginning of 1946. A factory was built at Springfields near Preston in Lancashire for making the fuel elements and two air-cooled graphite-moderated reactors were constructed at Windscale in Cumberland, together with the chemical plant for the separation of plutonium from the irradiated fuel elements. In designing this construction work the experience gained in operating the reactors at Harwell was of great value. A programme drawn up and approved by the Advisory Committee in 1947 stated that the first plutonium should be forthcoming in the Windscale reactor in the first quarter of 1952. It was produced exactly to time.

By the beginning of 1948, the Advisory Committee, which had been called into being largely to ensure that continuity with wartime activity should be maintained and to launch the country upon a post-war programme of development, considered that its task had been accomplished. Other committees had come into being — notably the Advisory Council on Scientific Policy and the Defence Research Policy Committee, both under the

---

[1] The hard-core membership of the Advisory Committee consisted of Sir Alan Barlow, Sir Edward Appleton, Mr. (later Sir Neville) Butler, Sir Henry Dale, Professor Blackett, Sir George Thomson, Lord Alanbrooke and Lord Tedder. Others who attended meetings included Sir Alexander Cadogan, Mr. (later Sir Oliver) Franks, Sir Archibald Rowlands, Sir James Chadwick, Sir Robert Robinson, Sir Henry Tizard, Admiral Sir John Cunningham and Mr. (later Sir Roger) Makins.

chairmanship of Sir Henry Tizard — and to these the Cabinet could appropriately look for advice on the broader scientific aspects of atomic energy development, while the Ministry of Supply could keep them informed on the day-to-day operation of the programme of development which the Anderson Committee had set in train.

On January 7, 1948, therefore, Anderson wrote to the Prime Minister tendering his resignation as Chairman of the Advisory Council, and in accepting it Mr. Attlee replied in terms of warm appreciation of the services which he and his colleagues had rendered to the country.[1]

Thus, within two years of the breakdown of Anglo-American co-operation in the field of atomic energy as a result of the passage of the McMahon Act, the United Kingdom was well and truly established as an independent nuclear Power in her own right, and it cannot be denied that considerable credit for this remarkable national achievement was due to the guidance and leadership of John Anderson.

(ii)

The position of John Anderson as a leading member of the Opposition from 1945 to 1950 was, at all odds, remarkable and in certain respects anomalous. As the only 'Independent' in Mr. Churchill's National Government he had had as his colleagues members of the Conservative, Labour and Liberal Parties and even the 'Caretaker Government', in which he had continued to serve as Chancellor of the Exchequer, had maintained the fictional appearance of a coalition by the inclusion of such Liberal elements as Lord Rosebery, Lord Simon and Major Gwilym Lloyd-George,[2] and of John's fellow 'Independent', Arthur Salter. But Mr. Churchill's 'Shadow Cabinet' was a much more closely knit and party-defined body, and here, among the solid Conservative ranks, he was the lone 'Independent'.

Apart from the splendidly anachronistic High Toryism of Mr.

---

[1] *The Times*, January 8, 1948. The Advisory Committee which had not met since May 22, 1947, was disbanded as from January 1948.

[2] Rt. Hon. Gwilym Lloyd-George, second son of the former Prime Minister, sat as a Liberal Member for Pembrokeshire from 1922 till 1924 and from 1929 till 1950 and as a Liberal and Conservative for Newcastle-upon-Tyne North from 1951 to 1957, when he was raised to the peerage as Viscount Tenby.

Churchill, the political thinking of many of the leaders of the Conservative Party had undergone a progression towards the Centre. Most of them would in effect have been happier with the Liberalism of Mr. Gladstone than with the Toryism of Mr. Disraeli ; and had not John been born and bred in the paternal tradition of a Gladstonian Liberal ? Thus, though he affirmed in all sincerity his adherence to the non-party label of 'Independent' and would in due course meet the offer of Conservative seats with a determined refusal, he did not find himself as completely separated in views from his Tory colleagues as might have been expected, and he certainly came under suspicion from some of the Labour backbenchers of 'guilt by association'. There would seem to be no doubt that the basis of his relationship with the Tory leadership was one which permitted them to believe that he would once more take office when a Conservative Government was again returned to power.

Nevertheless his 'Independent' status gave John an exceptionally strong position in Parliament and not least with the leaders of the Government. In those with whom he had served as a colleague in the wartime National Government he continued to inspire deep respect and confidence. Thus Mr. Attlee had not hesitated to seek his advice on matters of atomic energy nor to take him as a trusted counsellor to his discussions with President Truman in November 1945. In the following year, when Lord Halifax returned from six onerous years at the British Embassy in Washington, the Prime Minister and the Foreign Secretary, Mr. Ernest Bevin, considered John Anderson as their first choice for his successor as Ambassador. Their reasons were obvious. Apart from his general distinction, John was especially well qualified for this position at a time when the problems of atomic energy were still very much to the fore, and though it is doubtful whether he could have done anything to remedy the havoc created in Anglo-American co-operation by the provisions of the McMahon Act, it is interesting to speculate what impact his very distinctive personality might have made upon the wider relationship between the two countries. In fact, however, the offer of the post was never made to him. There had been delay in reaching a final decision to make it and by that time John, who had no idea that he was under consideration for the Washington

Embassy, had accepted a position of national importance at home — the Chairmanship of the Port of London Authority.[1]

But his personal good relations with the leaders of the Government did not inhibit John on the Opposition Front Bench, where he was quickly recognized as a formidable opponent. Indeed, it is probably true that as a parliamentarian he gave a better performance as an Opposition speaker than as a Minister. His remarkable memory, his terrifying capacity for accuracy and his widely varied experience of Government departments, surpassed only by that of Mr. Churchill himself, rendered him an adversary to be reckoned with and treated with the greatest wariness.

The Government's majority in the House of Commons made their defeat at the hands of the Opposition a virtual impossibility, yet it was the duty of the Opposition to oppose, and they did oppose the sweeping reform measures of the Labour Party to the best of their ability. In these operations John Anderson, with his extensive knowledge and practical wisdom, played an important part. As a former Chancellor of the Exchequer he denounced Mr. Dalton's demand for a capital levy as 'a crude experiment' and later attacked the economic and financial policies of Sir Stafford Cripps, stigmatizing devaluation as 'a measure of the failure of four years of economic planning and a tragic necessity which would have been avoided by gradual disinflation'. With all the weight of his Home Office experience, both as Secretary of State and Permanent Under-Secretary, he opposed an amendment to the Criminal Justice Bill to insert a provision suspending the death sentence for five years, and his arguments contributed materially to the final vote in which the Government majority was reduced to 23. His acquaintance with the problems of India gained during his Governorship of Bengal caused him to oppugn the Government's policy of accelerating the process of granting independence to India by imposing a time-limit. In moving the Opposition's amendment, John contended that the fixing of an arbitrary date prejudiced the proper development of constitutional arrangements and ignored pledges which had been given in the name of the King-Emperor and the Government of India to certain minorities. He also expressed his profound misgivings as to the Government's negative

[1] See below, pp. 356-360.

policy towards such Indian States as might decide, on reflection, not to cast in their lot with either India or Pakistan.

It was not, however, in mere political manœuvring that John Anderson's opposition to Socialism lay. It was far more fundamental than that. There was no more humane man than he and no-one whose record of life, both public and private, had shown more eloquently a deep sympathy for the underdog and the genuine victim of ill fortune. He was not opposed to those aspects of the Welfare State which brought facilities and benefits within the reach of those who were manifestly entitled to enjoy them. His cardinal opposition was to the doctrinal principle of 'dead-levelling' with which many of those on the Government benches seemed to him to be imbued. He had made his antagonism to this principle very clear in his election broadcast of June 1945 [1] and he took occasion to repeat it at an early date in the history of the new Parliament, during the debate on Dr. Dalton's first Budget on October 24, 1945. His words gained considerable currency at the time and are quoted even to-day :

> My study of the natural sciences has taught me that, in order that energy may expend itself in useful work, it is necessary that there should be inequality — inequality of pressure, of temperature, of electrical potential. Unless you get inequality no work is done. May not something similar be true in human affairs ? May not equality, if we could achieve it, which we never shall, make for stagnation? . . .
>
> I would say this . . . that economic inequality, from a national point of view, is not an evil thing but is positively good, subject to two conditions. The first is that the lowest level is not too low by whatever standard of human needs is judged reasonable. The second condition . . . is that the higher levels are attainable to all, as rewards of character, ability and enterprise. . . .
>
> [The test is] . . . whether your policy creates such incentives as will be of the maximum benefit to the community. [2]

This was in fact a part of John Anderson's credo of life ; the principle upon which he had been reared and nurtured and on

---

[1] See above, pp. 321-322.
[2] *House of Commons Debates*, October 24, 1945. Cols. 2022-2023.

which his whole career had been built, the principle of free and equal competition in the battle of life. To this degree he believed in equality, but to this degree only. Every man, in his view, should enjoy equality of opportunity to compete freely with his fellows and to this extent he sympathized with the social reforms of the Labour Party. But, since competition by definition implied a victor and a loser, he revolted with all his being against those other provisions of the Welfare State which sought, in his opinion, to swaddle the citizen 'from the womb to the tomb' in bands of negative equality. He pinned his faith to the principles and practice of private enterprise.

It must not, however, be thought that John Anderson's contributions to debate were consistently at the expense of the Government. He was unimpugnably sincere in his adherence to his non-party status, and if he not infrequently acted as an official spokesman for the Opposition his basic integrity also led him into expressions of candour which proved highly embarrassing to the Tories.

There was, for example, a hilarious scene in October 1949. In the course of a debate on the economic situation, John opened for the Opposition and, during a long speech, remarked that he did not want to see a repetition of what had happened in Britain in the years after the First World War. Mr. Herbert Morrison at once interrupted with impish glee to welcome this repudiation by Anderson of the financial policy pursued by Mr. Churchill at that time, when Chancellor of the Exchequer. Somewhat bewildered by this interjection Mr. Churchill and John looked enquiringly at each other. Anderson made as if to answer, but his leader was first on his feet, accusing Mr. Morrison of deliberately mixing up two periods of history. Sir John Anderson's remarks, he said, referred to the years immediately after the war whereas a period of four or five years intervened before he, Mr. Churchill, became responsible for the financial administration of the country. This explanation far from satisfied John Anderson, who proceeded to make his own elucidation of his statement. This, he said, referred to the slump in the early 'twenties, which led to further Labour glee. After a brief consultation both men stated their confident belief that the return to the gold standard under Mr. Churchill's Chancellorship had been justified, but by this time the House was

SIR JOHN ANDERSON, OCTOBER 1946

bewildered and the Labour benches exultant.[1]   In replying for the Government, Mr. Attlee remarked that he was never quite sure whether the Rt. Hon. Member for the Scottish Universities was a regular member of the Opposition team or not but that Anderson reminded him (the Prime Minister) of the historical occasion in which 'the Carthaginians employed a heavy, sagacious and most amiable animal called the elephant, but unfortunately the elephant ran the wrong way and disordered the ranks'.[2]

It was in all probability with memories of John's independence of thought that he was not invited to make one of the Conservative Party broadcasts in the election campaigns of 1950 and 1951 lest he should say unpopular things calculated to lose votes for the Party. The omission caused him great disappointment.

John's career as a House of Commons man was, in fact, approaching its end. The Labour Party had come into office pledged, in the words of the Home Secretary, Mr. Chuter Ede, 'to complete the transition to democracy begun in 1832 and to establish the principle of "one man one vote" '.[3] Thus the Representation of the People Bill, which was introduced into Parliament in mid-February of 1948, provided not only for the redistribution of constituencies but for the abolition of those last strongholds of plural voting, the City of London and the Universities.

This declared intention precipitated one of the sharpest differences between the Government and the Opposition ; a difference which turned upon an allegation of bad faith. The matter of the redistribution of seats and the reform of the franchise had been the subject of an all-party conference in 1944, over which the Speaker of the House of Commons had presided. In the course of its deliberations the Conservative representatives had agreed to the 'assimilation' of the parliamentary and local franchises — a step which was calculated to benefit the Labour Party — in return for an understanding that the representation of the City of London and the Universities would remain unaltered. This principle had been incorporated in the Redistribution of Seats Bill which had been passed by the House of Commons in 1944, when specific amendments, moved by Labour Members, to deprive the City of

---

[1] *House of Commons Debates*, October 27, 1949. Cols. 1535-1547.
[2] *Ibid.* Col. 1627.   [3] *Ibid.* February 16, 1948. Col. 839.

London of its special treatment and to abolish separate representation for the Universities had been defeated by substantial majorities.

The determination of the Labour Government four years later to reverse these decisions was the occasion for debates, which Sir Alan Herbert, one of the prospective victims, has described as 'able, obstinate and bitter'.[1]   The Opposition assailed the abolition of the university seats as a breach of honourable obligation binding the Prime Minister and other Ministers who had been members of the Speaker's Conference, and Mr. Churchill did not hesitate to describe it as 'an instance of bad faith . . . to which the history of the House of Commons can, happily, furnish few parallels'.[2]   The Government contended that the provisions of the Speaker's Conference were not binding on future Parliaments and that they had therefore broken no bargain.   They also charged that the Conservatives had themselves broken the agreement by putting Mr. Walter Elliot and Mr. Harry Strauss into safe university seats after they had been defeated in popular constituencies.

John Anderson, among other university representatives, defended his parliamentary *raison d'être* with eloquence, denouncing the decision of the Government to abolish the university franchise when 'universities count for more to-day in our national life than they have ever done':

> University elections — he said — present certain features which they do not share with ordinary territorial elections. There is no canvassing, there are no meetings, there is no emotional appeal. The electors decide upon consideration of a single, balanced statement of the candidates' views. We get — if I may add this — upon a limited scale through the university franchise the undoubted advantages of proportional representation without the grave disadvantages which attach in my view to proportional representation on a universal scale. . . . With the university franchise there is an opportunity of giving representation to electors who are overseas, a not unimportant matter. My view is that the cumulative case against the Government's decision to abolish university representation is overwhelming. . . .
> If the decision of the House and of Parliament is that the Bill shall pass as it is, and that the university franchise shall go, I shall

[1] Herbert (*op. cit.*), p. 194.
[2] *House of Commons Debates*, February 16, 1948. Col. 864.

regret it, and I shall think it a great mistake from a national point of view and from the point of view of the universities. I shall have no personal sense of grievance whatever. My personal feeling will be simply one of great thankfulness that at the end of almost a lifetime of public service, the university franchise gave me the opportunity which I could not otherwise have had of continuing to give such service as I could to my country in a time of great emergency.[1]

But the Government were unmoved by the diverse arguments for the retention of the university vote based on the value of independent and distinguished Members, traditional relations and the utility of variety. They persisted in their claim that they had the right to destroy 'fancy franchises' which weighted the scales in favour of class privilege and the Conservative Party. On March 16, 1948, Mr. Churchill's amendment to retain the university representation was defeated by 328 votes to 198.[2]

By this decision the House of Commons sought to deprive itself in future Parliaments of some of the ablest men who had sat upon its benches : the incisive mind of Wilson Harris, the authoritative and independent voice of Arthur Salter, A. P. Herbert's reforming zeal and inimitable wit, Kenneth Lindsay's passion for education, Walter Elliot's overflowing reservoir of knowledge and Kenneth Pickthorn's wisdom as a constitutional historian — albeit there was no doubting he was a Tory! — the Boanerges voice and downright honesty of Douglas Savory and the legal ability of Harry Strauss. The House was the poorer for this passing.[3]

As for John Anderson, the 'London Correspondence' of the *Manchester Guardian*, that palladium of traditional Liberalism, offered an impartial tribute :

> Whatever may be said for or against the abstract justice of one man, one vote, there is no denying that the sacrifice of University Representation to the principle means a sad loss to the House of Commons on the personal side. There was hardly

[1] *Ibid.* Cols. 889-890.

[2] One Labour Member, Mr. Skeffington Lodge (Bedford) voted against the Government, declaring that 'dead levelling' was not the kind of Socialism in which he believed.

[3] Of the twelve former University representatives, five — Kenneth Pickthorn, Harry Strauss, Walter Elliot, Arthur Salter and Douglas Savory — secured popular seats in the General Election of 1950.

one of the university members in the late Parliament who did not bring a strong individual flavour to its debates, and several of them acquired considerable authority, while one, Sir John Anderson, achieved eminence.

Politics apart, a representative Chamber would have to be very rich in its personnel that could kick Sir John Anderson out without suffering. His unmatched experience in the twin fields of administration and government, coupled with his intellectual honesty, set him quite apart. Labour Members might suspect him of being a crypto-Tory disguised as a Nationalist, but they were wrong. They chose to ignore those candours of his which at times were acutely embarrassing to the Opposition.[1]

What then was to be John Anderson's Parliamentary future? As early as 1946, Mr. Attlee, always an understanding and appreciative friend, had made a tentative suggestion of a peerage. 'John is a just man', he had said to Ava at this time, 'and what is essential to my mind is that he should have a platform when the university seats are abolished.' But John did not want to leave the House of Commons and respectfully declined the advances. A year later the Prime Minister renewed his offer and urged Ava to put pressure on John to accept. It was deplorable, he thought, that the country should be deprived of Anderson's services in Parliament. John, however, remained adamant. He would only go on in Parliament as a Member for the Scottish Universities. If the Labour Party persisted in abolishing the university seats, Mr. Churchill had pledged the Conservative Party to put them back as soon as they returned to power ; he would wait for that. With greater wisdom, Mr. Attlee replied that, whatever pledges had been given, a Conservative Government would not be able to put back the university seats. 'In this country', he said, 'one never puts things back.'

Thus, when the new Parliament, which resulted from the General Election of February 23, 1950,[2] assembled at Westminster, John Anderson was absent from the House of Commons for the first time since March 1938, when he had taken his seat as a private member. He was not greatly perturbed. He was still invited to attend meetings of the Conservative Shadow Cabinet and was

---

[1] *Manchester Guardian*, February 4, 1950.
[2] The Labour Government were returned to power in the General Election of 1950 with an over-all majority of 8.

much absorbed by the responsibilities which he had assumed as Chairman of the Port of London Authority, as a director of the Canadian Pacific Railway and of the Hudson's Bay Company, and as Chairman of Covent Garden.[1] Some of these duties took him far afield to parts of the Commonwealth which he had never visited and where his interests were acutely aroused. The election had shown that the run of popular sentiment had turned against the Labour Party and it was evident that, with their exiguous majority, the Government could not long remain in office. A new election was inevitable in the near future and everything pointed to a Tory victory. Once returned to power the Conservative Party would restore the university seats and he would again offer himself as a candidate for the Scottish Universities. He had already refused an offer from the Ulster Unionists to stand for a safe seat in Northern Ireland — a graceful compliment to the services which he had performed in setting up the Belfast Government in 1922 — on the grounds that he could not accept a 'party label'. His views on Civil Servants becoming party politicians remained unchanged. He reposed complete confidence in Mr. Churchill's pledge to the country to restore the university franchise. He could afford to wait.

With a greater sagacity, born of a wider knowledge and experience of parliamentary history, Mr. Attlee made a third attempt in the spring of 1951 to persuade John to accept a peerage. The occasion was, appropriately enough, the University Boat Race, for which John and Ava always invited a party of friends to follow the crews in the Port of London Authority launch. The Prime Minister repeated to Ava his conviction that the university seats were gone beyond recall and begged her to persuade John to mitigate his intransigence against going to the House of Lords. When Ava reported this conversation to John he weakened to the extent of agreeing to consult Mr. Churchill, which he did at Chartwell a few days later, and received an unqualified reaffirmation from the leader of the Opposition in respect of restoring the university seats. 'Well, there you are, you see', said John to Ava.

It was, therefore, with dismay and bewilderment that a few weeks later Anderson found himself buttonholed by Mr. Churchill, after a meeting of the Shadow Cabinet, with the suggestion that

[1] See below, pp. 354 *et seq.*

he should fight the East Surrey seat in the next General Election, standing as a Constitutionalist.[1] 'But that', said John, 'is a Conservative seat. I'm not a Conservative and I'm not joining the Conservative Party. I'll stand for the university seat or not at all. You know my views about Civil Servants and that they should on no account become politicians.' He was greatly upset and still further disturbed when rumours appeared in the press that he might stand for East Surrey, a possibility which he made haste to deny.

To Ava, with her quick political percipience, this latest development betokened a readiness on the part of the Conservatives to jettison their pledges. 'I think this shows that Clem has always been right and that the university seats will never be put back', she said. But John, displaying a *naïveté* unusual in so shrewd a character, still clung to his belief that a Conservative victory at the polls would mean the restoration of the university franchise.

On October 4, 1951, Mr. Attlee requested and was granted the long-expected dissolution of his short Parliament. The election campaign which followed was fought largely on general lines. The Labour Party claimed that they were the party of peace and coined the slogan : 'You can't trust the Tories'. The Conservatives responded by emphasizing the high cost of living and urged the electorate to 'Look what a mess Labour has made'. Full employment and housing came in the rank of secondary importance in the campaign ; nationalization played little part at all. As the campaign progressed there were few, if any, portents that the virtual stalemate of 1950 might not be repeated, with one or other of the major parties being returned by a bare majority. King George VI sought advice as to how he should proceed in such a contingency and, among other leading statesmen, his Private Secretary, Sir Alan Lascelles, canvassed the view of John Anderson.

In John's view, if the Labour Government should be returned with its present slim majority, the King should warn Mr. Attlee that a continuance of the current state of affairs would be highly detrimental to the country and should suggest that he should try to form a National Government. Should the Prime Minister, however, prefer to face the House of Commons, the only course

---

[1] The East Surrey constituency, considered a safe Conservative seat, had been held in the 1945–1951 Parliaments by the Hon. Michael Astor.

would be to let him do so, even if he had only a majority of one or two. John believed that both Mr. Attlee, and also Mr. Churchill in similar circumstances, would prefer this latter course. Mr. Churchill, he knew, disliked the idea of a coalition government except in time of war and this was also the policy of the Labour Party. On the other hand, he considered it possible that Mr. Churchill might say to the King that, though he himself disliked coalitions, he was ready to make way for some other Conservative leader, such as Mr. Eden, who might feel otherwise. John was confident that, if this were done, the Conservatives would make a genuine effort to form a National Government and to make it work, but if the Labour Party refused to join one, the only remaining possibility was to have another General Election. John himself considered his advice to be somewhat academic as he forecast to Sir Alan Lascelles that the Conservatives would come back with a majority of between thirty and forty.[1]

John proved to be as bad a psephological prophet as he had been naïve in belief in political promises. When the election was held on October 25 the Conservatives were indeed returned to power but with an over-all majority of but sixteen, or just twice that of Mr. Attlee in the previous Parliament. Clearly this could not be construed, even if it were desired to do so, as a mandate to restore the University representation.

When Mr. Churchill was Cabinet-making at Chartwell, John and Ava were at Isfield in Sussex. John was wounded at having been somewhat pointedly ignored during the election campaign, in which he had not been called upon to take any part. Ava was mourning the death of her beloved son Charley, whose sad invalid life had come to an end two months before. She no longer wanted to keep the Isfield house, which was too filled with memories of her boy, and John had recently purchased a property at Westdean, near Seaford, to which they were preparing to move.[2]

The fact that King George VI had but recently undergone a serious operation for the removal of his left lung and was in no very advanced state of convalescence rendered the whole process of filling the ministerial posts somewhat abnormal and protracted. Mr. Churchill was not able to discuss his appointments with the

---

[1] Wheeler-Bennett (*op. cit.*), p. 795.   [2] See below, p. 395.

Sovereign *privatim et seriatim* as is the traditional custom of Prime Ministers, but the senior posts in the Government were filled between October 27 and 30 and John's name was not among them.

The lesser appointments came later. Mr. Harold Macmillan was offered the Ministry of Housing and rang up to inform John that he had accepted. John unhesitatingly confirmed that this was the right decision. 'If Harold is the man I think he is, his Ministry will be the only one that produces something worth while by Christmas', was John's opinion.

At last there came the summons to Chartwell. This time there was no mention of the university seats, or indeed of any seat at all. What Mr. Churchill was now proposing was that John Anderson should accept a peerage, become Chancellor of the Duchy of Lancaster and act as supervising 'Overlord' of the Treasury, the Board of Trade and the Ministry of Supply. John was both shocked and amazed. The concept of 'overlords' in Government was entirely contrary to his beliefs and principles, both as a former Minister and as a former Civil Servant. Though, in a sense, he had occupied an analogous position when Lord President of the Council, this had been a wartime emergency and, in any case, he had been concerned with co-ordinating rather than supervising the activities of the various agencies placed within his aegis. Such a position, he felt, could have no place in the peacetime organization of government. There were Government Departments which were responsible to Ministers, and there were Ministers who answered for their Departments to the House of Commons. This was the established order of things. It was inconceivable to him to have another Minister, floating, as it were, above these Departments and Ministers with no fixed responsibility for either. To John the proposed arrangement would prove intolerable, nor did he think it could possibly work, and he said as much to the Prime Minister.

Mr. Churchill's reply was characteristic : 'I see', he said, 'that the great and romantic Port of London has you in its thrall, and that splendid Canadian Pacific Railway lures you away from us.' John reiterated his objections, but the Prime Minister would not accept his refusal as final until John had consulted Ava, so John came hurrying back to Isfield.

In point of fact Mr. Churchill had hit near to the mark. Anderson was perfectly sincere in his antagonism to the principle of 'overlordship' in government, but there was also something else. As he explained before he left for Isfield to Norman Brook — his valued and trusted Personal Assistant during the war, who by now was Secretary of the Cabinet and in that capacity was in attendance on Mr. Churchill at Chartwell — he was considerably older than Ava and, because he had held ministerial office for so long, he had had little opportunity of building up capital. He was now in the way of doing so and he could barely afford to resign his present array of lucrative directorships as he would have to do if he re-entered the Cabinet. He also made it clear that the Chancellorship of the Duchy of Lancaster offered little attraction to one who had held the offices of Home Secretary, Lord President and Chancellor of the Exchequer.

On his return to Isfield, John recapitulated all that had passed between him and the Prime Minister, but he did not mention the financial aspect. Ava's comment was that if he was not in the Government he might feel very out of things. All the last year he had been a member of the Shadow Cabinet, but now he would be cut off from his intimate life with his colleagues ; he would only know what was happening from the newspapers. When some foreign expert, say, on atomic energy, came to London, or the Secretary of the Treasury from Washington, John would no longer meet such men as a matter of course. Would he not miss all this ?

John was entirely unmoved by this view. His reply was very characteristic : 'Don't fuss yourself. If I require to see anyone from abroad I shall invite him to come and see me — and he'll come. And if you think I am affected by whether Government Hospitality invites me to this or that, you are very much mistaken. Anyhow, this is for me a question of principle. The proposed plan will not work and it's not right.'

So John refused the Chancellorship of the Duchy but accepted the offer of a Viscounty, which is the reversionary right of a retiring Minister of eminence. His peerage was announced in the New Year Honours List of 1952.

The matter of title now arose. What should John call himself ? With that great personal humility which was one of the salient features of his character, he felt it would be out of keeping to call

2 A

himself after any Scottish county or town. Indeed, when there were those who coveted the Thistle for him, he would say that he was not eligible and that this Order was for great landowners of ancient lineage or those whose services had been particularly associated with Scotland. He would have liked to have been Viscount Anderson but this for various technical reasons was unacceptable to the Lord Lyon King of Arms, who suggested 'Inveresk'. Of this idea John was not enamoured. Edinburgh was the city of his birth and upbringing; he had been educated in its schools and at its University and had represented that University, among others, in Parliament. From Edinburgh therefore would he take his title, and, in due course, he was announced as Viscount Waverley, of Westdean in the County of Sussex.

He was introduced into the House of Lords on January 30, 1952, his sponsors being the Viscount Simon and Field-Marshal the Viscount Alanbrooke.

(iii)

With the defeat of Mr. Churchill's Government at the polls in July 1945 and Anderson's consequent release from ministerial duties he was free to re-enter the world of commerce and industry. It was a world which he had known but fleetingly in the brief period between his return from India in December 1937 and his entry into the Cabinet less than a year later. Even this transitory acquaintance, however, had served to imbue him with a fascinated interest in the multiple and complex problems of Big Business and the impact of his own personality in these circles had been forceful and enduring. His return to the City, therefore, was a matter of mutual satisfaction.

John's former associates in I.C.I., Vickers and the Employers' Liability Assurance Corporation welcomed him back to their boards with enthusiasm. There was no question of his rejoining the Midland Bank as he considered it improper for a former Chancellor of the Exchequer to be connected with high finance, but other great concerns competed for his attention. In a short space of time he had become a director of the Hudson's Bay Company, of the Canadian Pacific Railway and briefly, before its nationalization, of the Southern Railway, and last, but by no means least, Chairman of the Port of London Authority.

Anderson has been called acquisitive of directorships and indeed he did amass a formidable array of them, of which the above list is not exhaustive. But it must be remembered that he had spent the greater part of his life in the service of the nation in some capacity or other, none of which was money-making. He was now sixty-three and considerably older than his wife, and almost his sole source of guaranteed income was his pension as a Civil Servant. He needed to make money and there was only a comparatively short span left of his expectation of life in which to do it.

It was with real zest that he flung himself into his new interests, and there was not a board of which he was a director which could complain of his neglect. Utilizing his remarkable memory and his phenomenal powers of concentration, he would pass from meeting to meeting with a complete grasp of the problems involved, never failing to make a contribution of value and importance. His technique at meetings scarcely varied. When there was discussion he would listen to it carefully and then give his opinion which was nearly always accepted because of its intrinsic merits. 'He had a way', wrote one who worked closely with him, 'of being present at a discussion without speaking — except to make summaries, not exactly decisions, but summaries that left only one possible decision.' To his colleagues it was patent that it was always the right answer that he sought, untrammelled by any prejudice, and he became as greatly respected for his integrity as for his wisdom.

There were those of his colleagues and subordinates who found his presence formidable, but this soon proved to be an illusion. It was the outcome, perhaps, of that extraordinary combination of extreme self-confidence, born of the knowledge of his own exceptional powers, and a basic humility, together with that element of shyness that sometimes misleads people into thinking a man aloof, or even pompous, when he is really only reserved. Those, and there were an increasing number in these later years, who could penetrate this façade, never failed to discover behind it a kindliness of heart, a warm humanity and even a pawky Scottish humour which was most endearing.

And he could unbend. In the course of that difficult affair, a staff party, in which all strata of a company, from directors to office boys and warehousemen, mingle once a year for celebration and entertainment, it was John who frequently offered himself as the conjurer's victim, to the intense delight of all present, who viewed with no little pleasure the great Lord Waverley submitting with the utmost good humour and enjoyment to having his pocket-book surreptitiously abstracted and his braces clandestinely removed. Yet — somewhat to the alarm of his fellow-directors — he would refer to their employees as 'minions', using the word in its strictly accurate 'dictionarial' sense.

Of all John's business activities there is little doubt that, though he was deeply interested in each one of them, that from which he derived the greatest satisfaction was the Port of London Authority, one of the most important institutions in the Kingdom. Established in 1909, by an Act of Parliament of the previous year, the Authority was assigned the duties of administering, preserving and improving the Port of London, and to it were transferred various undertakings which had previously been either independent or under some other authority. It became a statutory undertaking independent of Government and municipal authorities, and its board of appointed and elected members was calculated to be representative of all users of the Port.[1]

When John was elected Chairman of the Board in January 1946 it was with a view to the many problems with which the Authority was confronted in a changing post-war world. For example, a third of the total warehousing space of the Port of London had been destroyed by German bombers and some kind of substitute accommodation had to be provided ; in addition, the modernization of existing buildings and equipment, overdue because of the war, had to be put in hand. Moreover, the current relations of the

---

[1] The Port of London Act of 1908 provides for a Board of appointed and elected members. Of the ten appointed members one is nominated by the Admiralty, two by the Ministry of Transport, four by the London County Council, two by the Corporation of the City of London and one by the Corporation of Trinity House. The remaining eighteen members are elected by shipowners and merchants; of these, one represents the public wharfingers and one the owners of river craft. Labour is represented by two members, the Ministry of Transport and the London County Council being required to appoint one each of their representatives after consultation with such organizations representative of labour best qualified to advise them on the matter. The Chairman and Vice-Chairman of the Board are elected by the Authority and may be drawn from outside the ranks of the appointed and elected members. The total membership of the Authority may therefore be thirty.

P.L.A. with its neighbouring and associated authorities had not been always of the happiest.

John's impact upon the Authority was immediate. If he was to be a whole-time Chairman, he said, he must be paid. This had not been so in the case of his predecessors, but the Authority at once understood the position and offered him a salary of £7500 a year, which he accepted, with the stipulation that he must also have a car and a chauffeur at his disposal.

The magnitude and importance of this great mercantile institution appealed at once to Anderson's imagination, just as he at once responded to the challenge presented by its problems. He enjoyed to the full his contacts with the world of shipping and commerce and with the Corporation of the City of London. The very setting was eminently suitable to him. The offices of the Authority had been built shortly after the First World War [1] and are magnificent in the grandeur of the neo-Georgian Romanesque style of that day. The splendours of the walnut-panelled board-room, where each member had his individual desk and the Chairman sat elevated upon a dais with a silver-headed mace behind his chair, gave satisfaction to that strong sense of dignity of office which was one of John's more outstanding characteristics.

It was this highly developed sense of the fitness of things which gave him the very high standard of conduct which he insisted that a Public Authority should adopt in its affairs, both in dealing with the general public and in its relations with other public authorities. These relations must, he persisted, be carried out on a basis of friendly discussion and mutual respect for each other's interests. As a result of his adoption of this cardinal principle, which he himself scrupulously observed, the public relations of the Authority steadily improved under his aegis.

Always one who liked his creature comforts, on assuming office John found the post-war luncheon fare of the Board to be altogether too Spartan for his tastes. He at once set about initiating reforms which should restore the more Lucullan standards of his earlier predecessor Lord Devonport, and succeeded in establishing

---

[1] The building was opened in 1922 by the Prime Minister, Mr. Lloyd George, who, as Chancellor of the Exchequer, had been responsible for introducing the Port of London Authority Act in 1908.

a *cuisine* acknowledged to be one of the best in the City — a reputation which it still deservedly retains. On one occasion the Income Tax authorities endeavoured to arrive at an assessment of the value of these luncheons but they were countered by John with an ease born of a rich and ripe experience not only as a former Chancellor of the Exchequer but as a former Chairman of the Board of Inland Revenue — and no more was heard of this demand!

From the outset Anderson appreciated the closeness of the link between the City of London and the Port of London. Indeed, he believed that the greatness of the City depended in no small part on London's continuing to be a great port. He set himself deliberately to ensure that leaders of the City and of the nation as a whole comprehended the work and importance of the Port. With this end in mind he employed a variety of means whereby many persons in varied walks of life, to whom the Port of London and the majesty of its Authority were virtually unknown, might be made familiar with the romance and importance of an institution which played a vital, if unrecognized, part in the lives of all of them. Of these media that which achieved the greatest measure of success — and indeed of fame — was the cruising round the London Docks in the Authority's yacht, *St. Katharine*, and for this the credit for initiative lay with Ava rather than with John.

The *St. Katharine* — a steam vessel of 353 tons, with a seating capacity of some sixty people — was built as a survey vessel, but since the war had been used solely for the purpose of taking parties of visitors, including Members of Parliament and members of the Board and their wives, through the Port of London.

After Ava's first experience of these cruises she at once saw the potentialities which they offered for social entertaining which should at the same time bring more and more people of importance into contact with the Port of London. John at the outset had some misgivings but these Ava gradually demolished. Her first suggestion of an evening party was severely squashed, but she persuaded John to invite some of their Parliamentary friends to a morning cruise which ended with a pleasant luncheon. Then a few Ambassadors and their wives were added to the list of those invited and little by little Ava gained her point. John consented to an evening party for which she was permitted to choose the food and assist in the selection of the guests. It was an immense success. John was delighted, and a system of 'river parties' was established which became famous in the social life of London. The parties were not confined to the evening but included, for example, an annual Boat Race occasion at which a specially chartered launch followed the crews from Putney to Mortlake and the party was entertained to luncheon.

These gatherings were not merely of social advantage; they were an invaluable asset to the prestige of the P.L.A. Often very few of those invited had any direct connection with the Port of London or its Authority. They represented a cross-section of society: British and foreign diplomatists, prominent Civil Servants and members of both Houses of Parliament, leading figures in art and literature and the theatre, great soldiers and City luminaries, visiting royalty and statesmen from the Commonwealth. All these met together under the pleasantest circumstances, in which the hospitality was princely, the entertainment delightful and the *cuisine* of the most excellent. All became possessed by the spirit of the river and could not fail to be impressed by the prestige of the Authority which could offer them so gay an adventure. Nor was their education neglected, for, on boarding the *St. Katharine*, to each was given, in addition to a list of their fellow-guests, a plan of the Docks and a booklet on the Port of London.

Invitations to these river parties were much sought after and rarely refused. They became famous all the world over and people would write from abroad saying that they would like to arrange their official or business visits to England to coincide with one of John's cruises. He himself delighted in them and became a charming and solicitous host, circulating among his guests and pointing out to them objects of particular interest. On special occasions he would make an admirable little speech, lacking in every respect the more ponderous nature of his official utterances.

Inevitably contretemps would occasionally occur. At the end of one party, Mr. Vincent Massey, then Governor-General of Canada, could not find his hat. A thorough search of the *St. Katharine* failed to produce it and he went home hatless. Next morning John's secretary telephoned to say that every male guest at the previous day's party had been contacted but each seemed to be in possession of his own hat. Vincent Massey bought a new hat and dismissed the matter from his mind. Shortly thereafter he lunched at Lord North Street and to his surprise found his own hat on the hall table. On enquiry it then transpired that John Anderson, who had arrived on board hatless, was himself the culprit. Not only had he unwittingly borne off the property of Vincent Massey but had worn it to be officially photographed!

John brought to the service of the Port of London Authority not only his own great administrative gifts and Ava's social skill but also the full benefit of his scientific knowledge. It was on his initiative that a series of experiments was set on foot which, by utilizing the latest scientific devices, aimed at securing for the first time some exact knowledge of the tidal movements of the River Thames and of the forces which result in the deposit of silt in particular reaches, notably the Black Deep. To do this John called upon the assistance of his old friend and colleague Sir John Cockcroft, the director of the atomic energy centre at Harwell, who found for the Authority a radioactive form of the somewhat rare element scandium, which proved of the greatest assistance in these researches. It is of interest that Anderson himself later gave a learned and technical account of these measures in a discussion before the Institution of Civil Engineers, of which he was an honorary member.[1]

> With his incisive mind [one has written], his massive presence and, under that grave dignity which the ancients called *gravitas*, a profound humanity and understanding of his fellow-men, this calm, wise, courageous Scot, with the immense prestige and fund of goodwill which his character and career had won for him, was perfectly fitted to deal with the exigencies of the time. Expecting of every man the best of which he was capable yet never blaming anyone for inability to do more than his best and himself incapable of injustice, he won from all who worked with him the highest measure of efficiency and loyalty. Resolute, imperturbable and immensely able, of all the great men who have served the Port he was perhaps the greatest.[2]

An aspect of his business career which gave John particular pleasure was the opportunity which it presented for travel in

---

[1] *Proceedings of the Institution of Civil Engineers*, August 1957, vol. 7, pp. 868-869.
[2] Sir Arthur Bryant, *Liquid History* (privately printed, 1960), p. 58.

JOHN ANDERSON IN VINCENT MASSEY'S HAT

countries of the Commonwealth. Apart from his years in India, a few brief trips to the Continent and his official missions to North America on matters of atomic energy, he had a comparatively slight first-hand knowledge of the world at large. Now, however, new horizons spread before him and, with his mind ever avid for fresh knowledge and novel experiences, he enjoyed it to the full.

In the winter of 1950–1951, accompanied by Ava, he went to Australia on Port of London Authority business and to New Zealand as the guest of the Dominion Government. Apart from his interest in the immediate problems with which he was concerned, his imagination was caught and fascinated by the virile pulsating life of Australia and not less by the more compact traditional atmosphere of New Zealand, where he found much to remind him of his Scottish upbringing. In both countries to his intense interest he found flowers and plants unknown to him, though he was accustomed to identify any botanical specimen that he saw, and was fortunate enough to see a lyre bird in the Australian forest — an experience vouchsafed to few. He listened transfixed as this rare fowl gave its amazing exhibition of imitating perfectly the songs of some dozen of the most famous Australian birds while executing a complicated dance. He was also excited by the geology of Australia and the thermal phenomena of New Zealand. It was a sad disappointment both to him and to Ava that she was compelled to cut short her journey and return alone to England on receipt of news from home of the sudden, and ultimately fatal, deterioration in the health of her beloved son Charley.

The Dominion of Canada too now came within John's purview. As a director of the Canadian Pacific Railway and of the Hudson's Bay Company, he visited that great country with Ava on a number of occasions, John relishing the regal state of the private coach which the C.P.R. placed at his disposal. By car and rail and aircraft they traversed the country many times : Upper and Lower Canada with their mixture of French and English stock, the Maritimes with their predominantly Scottish ancestry, the rich wheat lands of the Prairie Provinces, the mighty ranges of the Rocky Mountains and even the frozen tundras of the far north. All these John visited, and as a result of their travels he and Ava were said to have seen more of Canada than most Canadians and certainly more than most visitors from Britain.

Canada meant a great deal to John and he looked forward to his visits with an almost hungry pleasure. His Scottish background gave him an intimate approach, and Canadians, though they found him at first a little pompous, soon discovered that his interest in their affairs was genuine and lively and that he could discuss, for example, the discovery of oil in Alberta with a technical knowledge that astonished them.

The romance of the Hudson's Bay Company particularly appealed to him — its very title, 'the Company of Adventurers of England Trading into Hudson's Bay', was redolent of glamour — and he was destined to express his feeling for it in a particular manner. The Company desired to confer upon Sir Winston Churchill some special title of honour, partly in recognition of his own outstanding services and partly because of his descent from their third Governor, the great Duke of Marlborough. At the meeting of the Board on April 27, 1956, when the matter was discussed, the styles of 'Grand Master' and 'Seigneur' were suggested but were recognized as inadequate. John had listened silently as was his custom. At last he made his contribution : 'I think', he said, 'that in the case of Sir Winston Churchill the title should be "Grand Seigneur"'. And it was so.

(iv)

The association of John Anderson with the world of the arts is not one which springs immediately and spontaneously to mind. Administration he was born to and the art of government came not unnaturally as a corollary. His adaptability to the City was a matter of application of talents already existing and the wide field of scientific development was open to him as of right. But the arts had never been specifically within his field of operations, and yet he was destined to leave his mark upon the artistic life of the nation in at least two notably different aspects.

At the close of the war, the future of music in England, along with many other aspects of our national life, was precarious. The Sadler's Wells Opera and Ballet companies retained intact their fame and their high standard, but orchestral music in London, while well attended despite the disappearance during the war of the Queen's Hall, was mainly confined to the week-ends, and no opera was to be heard in the West End. Indeed, throughout the war, the Covent Garden Opera House had been used as a dance hall.

The expectations of those who cherished hopes for the revival of opera in England were substantially raised by the announcement in Parliament by John, as Chancellor of the Exchequer, in the spring of 1945 that the Government had decided to establish the Council for the Encouragement of Music and the Arts, which had been created as a temporary wartime institution, as the permanent body for administering the Treasury grant in support of the Arts and that it would be incorporated as the Arts Council of Great Britain from the beginning of the new financial year, April 1, 1946.

Fired with new hopes by this promise of Government support, the pioneers in the campaign for the establishment of a national lyric theatre took two important steps which were essential preliminaries to the success of their plans. Through the prompt and courageous action of Messrs. Boosey and Hawkes, the music publishers, a short lease of the property of the Covent Garden Opera House was acquired in 1945 with a view to saving it for opera and ballet and ending its ignoble use as a dance hall. At very considerable cost to themselves Messrs. Boosey and Hawkes not only defrayed the preliminary expenses of the Covent Garden Committee but, in addition to the rent and rates of the building, they undertook to pay certain managerial salaries and running expenses.

The second step was the setting up on February 5, 1946, of the Covent Garden Opera Trust under the inspired chairmanship of Lord Keynes.[1] The aim of the Trust was to revive the glories of opera in London in that great and historic building. Dr. Karl Rankl was appointed Musical Director; Mr. Frederick Ashton, Production Consultant and, later, Chief Choreographer; and Mr. David Webster, Administrator.

Thus were national opera and ballet re-launched in post-war England and established under public control. The Opera House

---

[1] The original Trustees of the Covent Garden Opera House were Lord Keynes, Mr. Samuel Courtauld, Professor E. J. Dent, Sir William Walton, Mr. Leslie Boosey, Mr. Ralph Hawkes, Sir Kenneth Clark, Sir Stanley Marchant and Sir Steuart Wilson.

opened on February 20, 1946, with a distinguished performance of Tchaikovsky's *Sleeping Beauty* and the popular response was immediate and enthusiastic. But, though the new régime was an immediate success and the public were packing the theatre every night, the financial future was far from assured. Money was needed, and needed urgently, not only for current costs but for expenditure entailed by future planning, for the directorate were looking forward to a long period of building up companies and repertoires. In the view of Lord Keynes, Covent Garden should be financed from three sources : the proceeds of the box-office, the Treasury grant and private gifts, and the last of these sources was under immediate threat of extinction.

> The night before the 1946 budget — writes Sir David Webster — he [Keynes] had dined with a man who was prepared to subscribe at least £25,000 a year to the funds of Covent Garden. As Keynes well knew, the next day's budget would make that gift, and any other like it, impossible. Up to that time the man who paid 19/6 in the £ in income tax and surtax could, by paying 6d. to a charity, and through covenanting to pay the same sum for seven years, make it possible for the charity to reclaim the 19/6 in taxation. In 1946 the budget made it impossible for the charity to reclaim the amount paid in surtax. This meant that a man would have to pay 11/6 in the £ to the charity from his private pocket, a totally different picture.[1]

Troubles rarely come singly. The Budget containing this stunning blow to the hopes of the Covent Garden Trustees was introduced by the Chancellor of the Exchequer, Dr. Hugh Dalton, on April 19, and, less than a fortnight later, they suffered the grievous loss of their Chairman. Lord Keynes died suddenly on Easter Sunday, April 21. Clearly this was an emergency of the first order, for the Opera House finances were in immediate danger ; clearly, too, whoever succeeded Keynes must have financial experience, executive ability and sufficient standing to command the respect and co-operation of the Treasury. Where was such a man to be found ? Precious weeks and months went by in an anguished but futile search. Names were discussed but none commended them-

[1] Sir David Webster, 'Viscount Waverley — An appreciation', *Opera*, March 1958.

selves entirely. At length, as the summer drew on, Leslie Boosey, Ralph Hawkes and David Webster reached agreement that the one man who could fulfil all the requirements of a chairman of the Trustees was John Anderson. They placed his name before the Board where it received warm approval and instant acceptance.

It was characteristic of John that when approached he should take time for reflection. This was a new world to him, a world different in many respects from any that he had moved in before. It was, however, not entirely alien to him since it was he who, as Chancellor of the Exchequer in 1945, had authorized the creation of the Arts Council and, indeed, he was largely responsible for the grant of its Royal Charter. He was therefore already interested in the new arrangements for the subsidy of the arts and cognizant of the problems inherent in it and of the manner in which the new budgetary restrictions would intensify them. Typical also was his immediate thought for Ava, who had been 'lobbied' by the Trustees and was immensely anxious for him to accept. He realized how much his acceptance would mean to her and what a fortunate medium of expression Covent Garden would afford her social talents and aesthetic sensibilities. This was a powerful influence with him.

But though John often took counsel with his heart he never allowed it to rule his head. He would not, he said, accept the chairmanship of the Covent Garden Trust until he had received a formal assurance from the Treasury that governmental support would be forthcoming, and to this end he opened personal negotiations with Dr. Dalton. By the end of July these conversations had progressed to the point of an exchange of letters which became historic in the annals of Covent Garden.

26th July, 1946

MY DEAR DALTON,

When I mentioned to you a week or two ago that I had been invited to become Chairman of the Covent Garden Trust in succession to Keynes, I said that I would not feel justified in accepting the suggestion unless I could be assured that the project had been placed on a sound financial basis.

I have seen your recent correspondence with Pooley [1] and

[1] Sir Ernest Pooley. G.C.V.O., then Chairman of the Arts Council of Great Britain.

would certainly not seek to argue that you could reasonably have been expected to commit the Exchequer to a larger annual payment on the facts and figures now available. But in this as in many other matters the future is full of uncertainties. No one knows for example what the trend of orchestral salaries may be during the next few years and there will also be a problem in connection with the renewal of the Lease of the Theatre in some two years' time. Therefore, I want to be assured on two points in particular — First that in expressing your offer in terms of so much a year 'for the quinquennium' you do not in any way rule out the possibility of a larger payment in certain contingencies before the end of that period and, secondly, that you recognise in the arrangements now contemplated that the State will be assuming a definite obligation to see to it that, subject to others playing their part, Opera is not let down.

I would particularly stress this latter point because of references in recent discussions to voluntary contributions. No doubt such contributions are to be welcomed, though the possibilities are, of course, greatly curtailed by your Budget decision on the subject of seven-year covenants, but I am convinced that it would be disastrous if the Trustees were ultimately dependent upon private benefactions for maintaining Opera in this country on a worthy basis. Experience shows how easily undesirable influences can creep in under such conditions. So far as private sources can be tapped it should be for the frills and not the basic requirements of the enterprise.

I ask you, therefore, to review your attitude in the light of these observations, and I venture to hope your answer may be such as to enable me to return a favourable response to the request of the Trustees.

To this letter the Chancellor of the Exchequer replied on August 1.

MY DEAR ANDERSON,

This is in reply to your letter of the 26th July, in which you ask me to review my attitude to the Covent Garden Trust as expressed in my letter to Pooley of the 15th July.

The assistance which the Covent Garden Trust receives from the Exchequer will, of course, come to it through the Arts Council. You will understand that in general I should wish the Council to feel themselves responsible for the allocation of the funds which Parliament puts at their disposal, and to plan their work ahead in the expectation of an assured but limited grant.

I recognise, however, that the magnitude of the Covent Garden undertaking and the difficulty in present circumstances of its future needs places it in a special position, and that the State will be assuming a definite obligation to see to it that, subject to others playing their part, Opera is not let down. I do not therefore rule out the possibility that the fulfilment of this obligation might in certain circumstances make it necessary to increase the Treasury grant to the Arts Council still further than I undertook in my letter of the 15th July. It would, I think, be agreed that these circumstances would not be held to have arisen unless in any year the Trust could show a need for a grant from the Arts Council of an amount exceeding £60,000.

I am sending a copy of this letter to Pooley.

Yours ever,

(signed) HUGH DALTON.

On the following day Anderson forwarded a copy of Dr. Dalton's letter to David Webster. 'I regard the terms of the reply as satisfactory', he wrote, 'and the way is, therefore, open for the Trustees to proceed with my election as Chairman if so minded.'

The Trustees were so minded and John entered upon his new duties with his usual ability and thoroughness. He was now confident of Treasury support and would have recourse to the Dalton Concordat on frequent occasions when it required restating and reaffirming. His attitude to the public purse in relation to Covent Garden was based on two beliefs : first, that while in theory no Chancellor could commit his successor, the whole history of practical politics was based on the fact that he did so, and therefore the Dalton letter was of paramount importance. Secondly, he maintained that the needs of Covent Garden, and of the Arts Council also, were of no budgetary significance : his prevailing *obiter dictum* was : 'You can close Covent Garden but you must not starve it'.

Yet, ironically enough, it was this very magnitude which militated against his complete success in re-establishing the finances of Covent Garden. It was one thing to have an ex-Chancellor of the Exchequer for an advocate with the Treasury, but the reaction of the Treasury officials to this metamorphosis was quite another.

Perhaps because they felt that they must not be 'steam-rollered' by this Immensity, they did not respond to John's proposals as fully as he had hoped. He got considerably less than he asked for, which disappointed him, and there developed within him a certain sense of having been treated unfairly by the Treasury, from whom, 'for old times' sake', he had expected a greater measure of generosity. Despite his ability, his acumen and his influence, the fact remains that, when John died, he had failed to keep the finances of the Opera House on the basis on which he had hoped to keep them when he had assumed the direction of its affairs.

Nevertheless, Anderson's work at Covent Garden was a great tribute to his versatility, for it was not a world in which he ever felt the same degree of security of judgment which was usual with him elsewhere. He really knew nothing about music, nor would he ever make the slightest pretence to *expertise* in criticism of opera or ballet, but he derived real pleasure from the more simple beauties of presentation — the voice of a Callas, the loveliness of a Fonteyn or a Beriosova. He took a deep interest in what was going on. He saw everything that was done at Covent Garden, not once but many times, and he was a rock of sanity and good sense in moments of crisis ; deeply conscious of a public responsibility, he expected everyone else to be the same.

Moreover, John brought to the direction of affairs those great qualities of his and that carefully perfected technique which had served him so well as administrator, in Government and in business. As a chairman he was efficient, firm, just and — to those who did not know him well — rather daunting, but he was most indulgent to those whom he trusted or liked. In general his judgment was very good and, as one of his colleagues has written : 'Looking back, I cannot think that he ever made, or caused to be made, a wrong decision.' Though he has been accused of over-deliberation, there was rarely any fault to be found with his timing.

As in all his past experience of men and affairs his own integrity was his own touchstone. Having accepted his subordinates with confidence he never interfered with them ; demanding only to be perfectly informed, expecting loyalty and giving it generously. Nor did he allow them to be interfered with, for he had always held firmly to the principle of backing up the man who was doing the job. Sir David Webster recalls that on one occasion a man who was giving him trouble announced that he had finished his dealings with the Administrator and was going over his head to the Chairman of the Trustees. 'He will find that it is not very easy to see me', was John's comment when apprised of the matter, and no more was heard of it.

His authority and his prestige were soon needed in a strictly practical quarter. The lease of the Opera House which Messrs. Boosey and Hawkes had so generously acquired in 1945 expired at the close of 1949 and an application to renew it was refused by the Government, who countered by issuing a compulsory purchase order on the owners. After protracted negotiations, in which John Anderson played an important and dominating rôle, an agreement was reached whereby the lease of the Opera House was transferred from Messrs. Boosey and Hawkes to the Ministry of Works, thus achieving for the first time in British history the direct responsibility of the State for a theatre. The Covent Garden Opera Trust disappeared to be replaced by the Royal Opera House, Covent Garden Ltd., which was incorporated on April 1, 1950, and of which John Anderson remained as Chairman of the Board of Directors. This new body became the tenant of the Ministry of Works which, while not interfering with the artistic policy of the concern, undertook to maintain the building for a 42-year period and to ensure that it was used for opera and ballet only. All John's former colleagues followed him on to the board of directors of the new company, and as time passed he invited a further collection of distinguished men to join the board.[1]

The appointment of a new musical director, Mr. Rafael Kubelik, in the summer of 1956, provoked an attack by the late Sir Thomas Beecham, in his most explosive and astringent style, upon the Board of Covent Garden for its choice of a foreigner.[2] Shocked and wounded by the vehemence of the onslaught, Mr. Kubelik offered his resignation, and it was here that John demonstrated once again

---

[1] Amongst those who joined the Board of Covent Garden at John Anderson's invitation were the Hon. James Smith, Lord Wakehurst, the Hon. Edward Sackville-West (later Lord Sackville), Sir Barry Jackson, the Earl of Harewood, Mr. Edric Cundell, Sir Philip Nichols, Sir Arthur Bliss, Viscount Moore (later the Earl of Drogheda), Sir Isaiah Berlin, Sir Oliver Franks (later Lord Franks) and Professor Lionel Robbins (later Lord Robbins).   [2] *The Times*, June 27, 1956.

2 B

his loyalty to those who served under his command. In a brief letter to *The Times* on June 28, he stated the position of himself and his colleagues in reply to the belligerent baronet.

> Sir, — My colleagues and I on the Board of the Royal Opera House, Covent Garden, think it right that the public should know that, after reading the strictures contained in the letter from Sir Thomas Beecham, published in *The Times* yesterday, Mr. Rafael Kubelik formally tendered his resignation on the ground that it appeared that his status as a foreigner might be regarded as an obstacle to the development of a British national opera.
>
> The Board have informed Mr. Kubelik that they are unwilling to accept his resignation. They have assured him that he has their entire confidence and that he can rely on their unstinted support in pursuit of the policy he has outlined during his tenure of his present office.
>
> I am, Sir, yours faithfully,
>
> WAVERLEY.[1]

When the text of this letter was read to Mr. Kubelik, before its dispatch to Printing House Square, he was so touched by its sentiments that he embraced John Anderson warmly. It is one of the few occasions on which John gave the appearance of being nonplussed.

Yet John's great work for Covent Garden could not have achieved its remarkable success without the ardour of his wife, her brilliant gifts and her zealous desire to help him. While he thoroughly enjoyed his association with the Opera House he enjoyed still more the pleasure which Ava derived from it. They were constant in their attendance together and their hospitality in the Royal Box became an established feature of London's social life. Between them they brought to Covent Garden, as to the Port of London Authority, many distinguished people. Members of the Diplomatic Corps, leading statesmen from Commonwealth countries, famous visitors from abroad, all trooped to the Royal Opera House as the guests of John and Ava.

Ava had both a genius and a *penchant* for entertaining ; she made full use of her opportunities, and John delighted in her scintillating

[1] *The Times*, June 29, 1956.

success. Indeed she was a very lucky woman, for who else in this day and age had at her command a steam yacht capable of seating and serving half a hundred guests in splendid elegance, and a permanent lien on the Royal Box at Covent Garden ?

Under the shelter of John Anderson's unshakable stature the venture of British opera grew lusty and acquired stability. If, as is now openly acknowledged, Covent Garden has achieved comparable status with the great international establishments of opera and ballet, posterity will owe a heavy debt to this extraordinary and many-talented man.

Anderson's second experience in the artistic world was almost more of a personal *tour de force* than his association with Covent Garden, for it afforded an even greater demonstration of his own remarkable talent for mastering a subject of which he had no prior knowledge. In October 1950 he accepted the chairmanship of a Committee appointed by the Chancellor of the Exchequer to consider the problem of the export of works of art.

Hitherto the development of the control of such export had been somewhat haphazard. On the outbreak of war in 1939, control of works of art, among other things, had been imposed as a means of conserving national resources, and the powers then taken were used by the keepers and directors of museums and art galleries to advise the Board of Trade in the prevention of national treasures from leaving the country. With the coming of peace and the revival of trade, this practice gave rise to ill feeling among art dealers and even to complaints from governments abroad. As a result, a small committee, composed entirely of civil servants and museum officials, was set up to consider appeals from exporters. Its findings, however, were criticized as not being sufficiently independent and it became evident that the matter required examination on a wider scope and at a higher level. In October 1950, therefore, Sir Stafford Cripps appointed a Committee

to consider and advise on policy to be adopted by His Majesty's Government in controlling the export of works of art, books, manuscripts, armour and antiques, and to recommend what arrangements should be made for the practical operation of the policy.

He invited John Anderson to become chairman of this body and John accepted.[1]

Now John, like any other well-educated man, had a respect for the visual arts and for their place in civilization, but it is to be greatly doubted that he frequently allowed his mind to dwell upon them — natural science was much more his true private love — and it is a certainty that he knew nothing of the *minutiae* of art history. Yet, here he was, charged with the investigation of the most intricate and controversial problems of general policy regarding the arts and museum administration, with connoisseurs, art historians and the trade all straining at the leash — though in different directions — to complain and criticize.

If, at the outset, there were those among Anderson's colleagues who doubted his capacity to cope with this highly complex task they were speedily disillusioned. Just as, thirty years before, John, as a newly appointed Chairman of the Board of Inland Revenue, had astounded a Select Committee of the House of Commons by the scope of his knowledge of his subject,[2] so now he amazed his fellow committee members by his ability within a few weeks to carry out the main examination of the expert witnesses without falling into error.

> Within a meeting or two [writes Lord Robbins] he had so made himself a master of the subject that I would defy the keenest outside observer not to have thought that he had been dealing with it all his life. Only once did my inquisitive ear detect the attribution of a famous painter to a wrong century — and that might have been a slip of the tongue. All was orderly, well-informed, sympathetic and just.

Under John's chairmanship the Committee carried out their instructions in an impartial and thorough manner, giving full weight to the conflicting interests of owners, art dealers, prospective overseas purchasers, and the museums and galleries. As a result,

[1] The other members of the Committee were Professor A. F. (later Sir Anthony) Blunt, the Earl of Crawford and Balcarres, Mrs. Hugh Dalton, Professor Vivian Galbraith, Mr. Christopher Hussey and Professor Lionel Robbins.
[2] See above, p. 45.

the report which they rendered in September 1952 can only be described as a revolution in the attitude of the Government towards museums and the arts generally.[1]

Their conclusion was that export licences should not be given for works of art within limits of age, value and length of domicile in the country, if they were considered by the 'Reviewing Committee' to be of national importance, either because of their aesthetic merit or because of their interest to scholarship or because of their association with the national history and life of Britain. It was, however, recommended that an export licence should only be withheld when a reasonable price was offered by a person or institution in Great Britain. The 'Reviewing Committee' was to consist of a Chairman and three independent members of high standing and experience, and the Chairman was to have a recognized interest in art and learning. This Committee was to keep an eye on the operation of the system generally and to consider each individual case in which a museum director or keeper of a gallery objected to the export of a work of art.

The Report of the Waverley Committee, as it was always known in art circles — John having been raised to the peerage in the course of its deliberations — was implemented virtually as it stood. As a result, the future acquisition policy of most national collections came under review and the official purchasing grants of these collections were increased by 25 per cent to enable them to buy works of art, the export of which might be regarded as being against the national interest. The Treasury was also encouraged to make special grants, when necessary, to assist them in making these purchases.

Although Anderson himself never served on the Reviewing Committee, it is a tribute to the soundness of his Committee's recommendations that there have been no changes in the Reviewing Committee's constitution or *modus operandi* in the eight years of its existence. Indeed, the present members feel that their function is to carry out the principles which the Waverley Report laid down, and they frequently have recourse to its authority for settlement of a disputed point.

---

[1] *Report of the Committee on the Export of Works of Art*, H.M. Stationery Office, 1952.

An outstanding and vivid example of the working of the system established by the Waverley Committee occurred in 1955 when the owner of an El Greco painting, known as 'The Dream of Philip II', applied in January for a licence to export the picture to Liechtenstein on a sale or return basis. Objection to this was raised by the National Gallery, whose Trustees wanted to purchase the picture, on the ground that it would fill a need of the Gallery which had no specimen of this artist's more elaborate religious compositions.

The Reviewing Committee therefore intervened and assessed the sum of £27,000, free of death duty and inclusive of dealer's commission, as a fair price for the picture, but the owner took exception and sought sanction from the Committee for a temporary export licence so that the picture could be sent to Switzerland for inspection by a collector who might make a firm offer for it. This the Committee refused to grant. However, in July of the same year they were informed that a well-known continental collector had not only made a firm offer for the El Greco but had paid over the whole of the purchase price, subject to the granting of an export licence. The collector had been in bona fide negotiation with the owner of the picture at the time of the first application for an export licence and it was clear from the evidence adduced that these negotiations would have matured in a sale at the price stated had not the Committee intervened. In view of these facts and of the great need of the National Gallery for the picture, the Committee reassessed its value on the basis of the price paid by the foreign collector.

The resulting figure of £42,000 was indicative of the great fluctuation in the market value of such works in the course of six months, but the Committee were sustained in their new assessment by the fact that two other El Greco paintings, of inferior importance and beauty, had been exported to the United States at prices which supported their revised judgment.

The sum of £42,000 was therefore paid by the National Gallery, a special contribution of £30,100 being made by the Exchequer.[1] The affair, which was accorded no little notoriety in the press,

[1] The picture is catalogued in the National Gallery as 'The Adoration of the Name of Jesus' instead of under its old fanciful title of 'The Dream of Philip II'.

served to throw into relief the extreme inadequacy of the annual grant-in-aid voted by Parliament to the National Gallery and also the effectiveness of the machinery set up by the Waverley Committee.

(v)

There is a story which, though it perhaps be only *ben trovato*, is nevertheless significant of John Anderson's position in Britain at this time.

There was once — so the story runs — a country of totalitarian persuasion which decided to send a delegation to London for the discussion of various matters of import which were of common interest to them and to the British Government. Now, because the country concerned was a Powerful Influence in world affairs and despite the fact that the Government disapproved of the country's ideological views, it was decided to do their delegation honour, and so the 'V.I.P. treatment' was laid on for them.

The delegation made its arrival, somewhat unusually, by water and, still more unusually, by way of the Thames, and as their craft landed them at the Westminster Stairs they were greeted by the Chairman of the Port of London Authority, Lord Waverley. Later in the day they had an engagement with the Chairman of the United Kingdom Advisory Council on Atomic Energy, and, somewhat to their surprise, found themselves in consultation with Lord Waverley. Later still that same evening, at a party at Buckingham Palace, they again encountered Lord Waverley among the most venerated of the Sovereign's guests. On the following day, matters of coastal defence against flooding claimed their attention and, to their amazement, they found themselves once again in the presence of Lord Waverley, who was conducting an enquiry on behalf of the Government into just this problem. Finally, to their ultimate confusion, when they attended a gala performance given in their honour at Covent Garden, they were received at the entrance to the Royal Opera House by the Chairman of the Board, none other than Lord Waverley. It is said that, in reporting to his government, the leader of the delegation confessed his utter bewilderment : 'This is not, as we thought, a democracy : it is an autocracy run by a man named Waverley.'

This picture of John's ubiquity and versatility in the public life of the nation is no exaggeration. In these post-war years he occupied a unique position. He was a national figure well-known and easily recognized : the heavy face, with its air of a slightly sad bloodhound, the short black coat and pin-stripe trousers, the gold watch-chain, the wing collar and carefully tied cravat. Successive Governments found him ready to accept new responsibilities and to shoulder burdens which others might have hesitated to assume. Thus, for example, his appointment as chairman of two separate and highly important committees, with the most completely diverse terms of reference, was announced in the House of Commons on a single day — April 28, 1953.

The first of these was one for which his previous experiences, both in war and peace, singularly qualified him. As early as November 1951 Mr. Churchill's Government had decided that the time had come when a change should be made in the nature of the control of Britain's atomic energy development. The Atomic Energy Act of 1946 had vested this control in the Ministry of Supply but it was now felt that some other aegis would be more appropriate. The decision to undertake these radical changes was, however, postponed until after the atomic weapon test at Monte Bello in October 1952, but immediately after the successful completion of this experiment a review of the existing conditions was put in hand. Almost inevitably the Prime Minister turned to Lord Waverley in such an event and he, assisted by his old wartime colleague in 'Tube Alloys', Sir Wallace Akers,[1] and by Sir John Woods,[2] was appointed in April 1953 :

> To devise a plan for transferring responsibility for atomic energy from the Ministry of Supply to a non-Departmental organization, due regard being paid to any constitutional and financial implications.

The report which this Committee rendered, of which the recommendations were summarized in a White Paper [3] since their

[1] Sir Wallace Akers, C.B.E., F.R.S., F.R.I.C., F.R.S.A., F.C.S., Director of Atomic Energy Research, 1941–1946.
[2] Sir John Woods, G.C.B., M.V.O., Permanent Secretary, Board of Trade, 1945–1951, Member of Economic Planning Board, 1947–1951.
[3] *The Future Organisation of the United Kingdom Atomic Energy Project*, Cmd. 8986. 1953.

security rating was such as to preclude publication in full, was accepted by the Government virtually *in toto* and, as incorporated in an Act of Parliament of August 1, 1954, constituted the basic pattern of the present United Kingdom Atomic Energy Authority.[1] This was John's last official contribution in the field of atomic energy, with which he had been associated since the earliest days of 'Tube Alloys', but his connection with this fascinating subject did not cease here. He always stood ready to advise, and his wise counsel was of inestimable help in the solution of the difficult problems inherent in the transition to the new organization.

The second of the tasks assigned to John Anderson on April 28, 1953, was also one of considerable complexity and national importance. On the night of January 31/February 1 of that year disastrous floods swept over the east coast of Britain, spreading havoc of varying degree from the Orkneys to Kent. The loss of life was ultimately reckoned to be 307, while the total cost to the country was estimated at between £40 and £50 million.[2] A parallel and simultaneous disaster in the Netherlands resulted in the loss of nearly 1800 lives and of some 50,000 head of cattle, while about 530,000 acres of agricultural land were inundated. The total damage was computed at 1,000,000,000 Dutch guilders (a little less than £100,000,000), a severe blow to a country which was slowly and painfully recovering from its wartime losses and the depredations of enemy occupation. Perhaps the one consoling feature of the disasters was the generous, practical and mutually appreciated assistance which the two nations gave to each other at this time.

The cause of the disaster was said to be the coincidence of a strong north-easterly gale with the peak of the spring tides, but, though both these factors were certainly in evidence, it was felt that, as they must have coincided before and as the damage inflicted far exceeded in extent any recorded figure for the past six hundred years, this explanation seemed inadequate. *The Times*, in an

---

[1] The first Chairman of the Atomic Energy Authority was Sir Edwin (later Lord) Plowden, K.C.B., K.B.E., who was succeeded in 1960 by Sir Roger Makins, G.C.B., G.C.M.G.

[2] A Mansion House Relief Fund opened by the Lord Mayor, Sir Rupert De la Bère, on February 3, 1953, and to which the Government undertook to contribute pound for pound, reached £1 million by February 20 and £5 million by the end of the year.

article of such expertise that it seemed incomprehensible to any but meteorologists, offered a decisive solution :

> On January 31 the peak of a spring tide coincided with a sea surge varying from 6 ft. to 8 ft. Such surges are produced by barometric pressure ; they are incapable of long-term prediction, unlike tides, but they do not often exceed a foot in height. In 1921 a surge of 11 ft. was recorded, but it struck at the time of low water, caused no trouble, and passed unnoticed. There can be no assurance, therefore, that the fatal conditions will not recur in combination at any spring tide, but the incidence might be no more than once in half a century.[1]

It was clear from this and other explanations offered that the causes of the disaster might well recur and that more should be known of them, and it was equally apparent that, in the light of the lessons learned from recent experience, a complete review should be undertaken of the sea defences of the country and also of the system of flood warning. To achieve this a departmental committee was set up under the joint authority of the Home Secretary, the Secretary of State for Scotland, the Minister of Housing and Local Government and the Minister of Agriculture and Fisheries. It was composed of Government officials and experts in the various fields affected by the problem, and Lord Waverley was invited to preside over this expert body.[2]

This was an assignment after John's own heart. It appealed to a number of his interests and gave opportunity for demonstrating his scientific learning, his administrative ability, his capacity as a chairman to get the maximum of co-operation from his colleagues,

---

[1] *The Times*, February 19, 1953.
[2] The Committee was composed of Dr. G. M. B. Dobson, C.B.E., F.R.S., formerly Reader in Meteorology in the University of Oxford ; Sir Donald Ferguson, G.C.B., Permanent Secretary, Ministry of Fuel and Power, 1945–1952 ; Mr. R. D. Gwyther, C.B.E., M.C., an eminent consulting engineer ; Sir Claude Inglis, C.I.E., F.R.S., Director of Hydraulics Research Station, Wallingford, Berks, 1947–58 ; Mr. R. G. Leach, C.B.E., Deputy Financial Secretary, Ministry of Food, 1939–1946 ; Sir Basil Neven-Spence, a member of the Scottish Committee of the Nature Conservancy ; Professor J. Proudman, C.B.E., F.R.S., Professor of Oceanography at Liverpool University, 1933–54 ; Sir Allan Quartermaine, C.B.E., M.C., President of the Institution of Civil Engineers, 1951–1952 ; Lord De Ramsey, T.D., Lord-Lieutenant of Huntingdonshire ; Professor J. A. Steers, Professor of Geography in the University of Cambridge ; Sir Miles Thomas, D.F.C., Chairman of B.O.A.C., 1949–56 ; Sir John Wrigley, K.B.E., C.B., Joint Deputy Secretary, Ministry of Housing and Local Government, 1951–52 ; and Sir Thomas Yates, C.B.E., General Secretary, National Union of Seamen, 1947–60.

and his own technical knowledge gained in the service of the Port of London Authority. He spared neither himself nor his fellow committee members. He made a personal visit to the Netherlands to confer with those engaged in similar investigation there and flew by seaplane over the inundated areas. By July the Committee had presented an interim report making recommendations for a flood warning system, and within a year of their appointment their final report was in the hands of the Government. It was a highly technical document covering exhaustively the terms of reference, and containing proposals ranging from scientific research to be undertaken in close co-operation with Dutch scientists, engineers and government officials, to methods of improving the sea defences of the nation.[1] The Report, which was unanimous, was accepted by the Government in all its principal features, and was subsequently implemented by legislation.

There was, however, one public service which John Anderson was not permitted to perform ; though it was one for which he was eminently well suited. In November 1951 the chairmanship of the Royal Commission on Taxation of Incomes and Profits became vacant through the resignation of Lord Justice Cohen. It seemed to the Prime Minister that the man pre-eminently fitted both by wisdom and by experience to succeed him was John Anderson who, as a former Chairman of the Board of Inland Revenue and Chancellor of the Exchequer, could bring to the problems of the Commission an almost unrivalled expert knowledge of the whole system of taxation. He sounded him forthwith. John was not at first willing to accept these additional burdens of responsibility. His time was amply filled and he looked forward to the new duties entailed in his imminent translation to the House of Lords. He demurred at the original proposal, but under pressure from the Prime Minister and the Chancellor of the Exchequer he allowed himself to be persuaded to accept Mr. Churchill's offer. The

[1] *Report of the Departmental Committee on Coastal Flooding*, Cmd. 916a. Some of the recommendations contained in the Report were novel, among them being that for an urgent investigation into the possibility of providing a suitable structure, capable of being closed, as a means of reducing the maximum water levels higher up the River Thames in time of surge. One method suggested was to interpose this structure across Long Reach between Purfleet and Greenhithe, with 'gates' so as to leave the waterway normally clear. (See Appendix F.)

Queen's approval of his appointment was forthcoming and John took steps to free himself of some of his more routine duties at the Port of London Authority and elsewhere in the City.

What, however, neither Mr. Churchill, nor John himself, had realized was the degree of hostility engendered in the ranks of the Labour Party by Anderson's forthright criticism of their policies. In the Parliament of 1945–1950, he had not hesitated to express both doubt and censure of the precipitate manner in which the Labour Government had initiated the National Health Service and other aspects of the Welfare State which, though he was not antagonistic to them in principle, seemed to him to require a more gradual introduction. On one occasion he had gone so far as to conclude a speech with an appeal to the Government : 'For mercy's sake, stop fooling the people.'[1] Moreover, in his maiden speech in the House of Lords on February 20, John sought to encourage the Conservative Chancellor of the Exchequer, Mr. Butler, to increase his forthcoming Budget surplus — and thereby hasten disinflation — by reducing the food subsidies which had been granted by the Labour Government and which — said John — had come to 'obscure the true facts of our economic position'. He would, he said, think it worth while to get rid of the subsidies altogether 'even if the whole cost had to be redistributed for the benefit of the poorer section of the community who were in danger of suffering hardship on account of their abolition', and, viewed in the light of a social service, he condemned them as 'clumsy and inefficient'.[2]

Now this may have been sound economics but it was certainly not calculated to endear the speaker to the Labour Party nor to secure their approval for his appointment to any such position as the Chairman of the Royal Commission on Taxation. The Party, now in Opposition, had long considered that, though Anderson had persistently and sincerely maintained that he was an independent in politics and free from any party label, he had, in effect, imbibed the doctrines and principles of his Conservative colleagues and that for all practical purposes he must be considered as a Tory.

When, therefore, on Tuesday, February 26, Mr. Churchill announced John's appointment in the House of Commons there

[1] *House of Commons Debates*, October 27, 1949. Col. 1540.
[2] *House of Lords Debates*, February 20, 1952. Col. 121.

was a storm of angry protest from the Opposition benches. The attack was led by Mr. Hugh Gaitskell, who demanded whether the Prime Minister realized the importance of having as Chairman of the Commission 'a man of acknowledged impartiality, of no political bias, and accustomed to the exercise of judicial functions'. He went on to enquire whether Mr. Churchill realized that 'Lord Waverley has shown by his political speeches and by his bearing in the 1945–1950 House of Commons, that he holds strong political opinions corresponding broadly to the right wing of the Conservative Party' and that he was, therefore, 'quite unsuited to fill the post'. The very fact that his name had been put forward, continued Mr. Gaitskell, 'only shows that the Government are determined to influence the conclusions of this Commission for their own party advantage'.[1]

Mr. Churchill's retort to this unexpected onslaught was to describe the ex-Chancellor's observations as 'a diatribe of such a character that it requires no answer except in debate',[2] and the Opposition promptly responded by tabling a motion in the names, amongst others, of Mr. Gaitskell and Dr. Dalton :

> That in view of the strong political views expressed by Lord Waverley on financial, fiscal and social questions, this House regrets that the Prime Minister should have recommended his appointment as chairman of the Royal Commission on the Taxation of Profits and Income, thus departing from the normal practice by which such posts are occupied by persons of acknowledged political impartiality.

John was both shocked and wounded at the bitterness of Labour's attack upon him, which he felt to be both unjustified and unfair, for he still regarded his independent political record as unblemished by any adherence to any political party. He was particularly pained that these accusations should have been made by men with whom he had worked as a loyal colleague in the National Government of 1940–1945 and that other of his former Labour colleagues, though they had not shared in the attack, had condoned it by their silence. His first impulse was to resign immediately, but on reflection he

---

[1] *House of Commons Debates*, February 26, 1952. Cols. 939–940.
[2] *House of Commons Debates*, February 26, 1952. Col. 940.

decided that, despite the Labour aspersions, he would leave the final decision in the hands of the Prime Minister, and he so wrote to Mr. Churchill on February 28. But when he learned of the Labour motion, which was due for debate on the following Monday, March 3, his whole attitude changed. This was intolerable. He would not be placed on trial before the House of Commons, and, deeply mortified, he wrote a second time to the Prime Minister :

February 29, 1952

MY DEAR PRIME MINISTER,

In my letter of yesterday's date I placed myself in your hands, but let you know that despite what had happened in the House of Commons on Tuesday I remained willing to execute her Majesty's commission to the best of my ability.

I confess to you that I have felt very keenly that a question, avowedly of principle, raised by Mr. Gaitskell should have been made the occasion, both in the House of Commons and in the Socialist Press, for what I can only regard as wholly unjustified personal aspersions, but having regard to the dignity and constitutional status of a Royal Commission I resisted my first inclination to tender my resignation.

It has subsequently become clear that the matter is to be pursued by debate in the House of Commons. That alters my attitude. You will recollect that I accepted this heavy obligation under pressure from you and the Chancellor, but I really do not see how the work of the Royal Commission can be conducted in the atmosphere which it is clearly the intention of the Opposition to create.

I need only add that these attacks, made towards the end of a long life of public service, are the more wounding because they appear to have the acquiescence, if not indeed the active support, of wartime colleagues whom I have regarded as personal friends.

In these circumstances I regret to have to ask you to submit to the Queen my resignation of the chairmanship of the Royal Commission.

Yours sincerely,
WAVERLEY.[1]

Mr. Churchill's reply was warmly expressive of the admiration and respect which he had always felt for Anderson and of his anger

---

[1] *The Times*, March 1, 1952.

at the treatment to which this great public servant had been subjected by the Opposition. In view of John's arguments and of the situation created by the Labour motion,[1] however, he could not well press him to withdraw his resignation. He therefore wrote :

February 29, 1952

My DEAR JOHN,

It is with great regret that I have received your letter of February 29. Like many others, I deplore the manner in which you have been treated by the Socialist Party.

Since you were Chairman of the Board of Inland Revenue many years ago, I have watched your public career with admiration. I remember the days when you risked your life in Dublin during the Irish Rebellion. Your distinguished record as Permanent Under-Secretary at the Home Office is well known. The composure with which, as Governor of Bengal, you faced a murderous assault commanded the respect of your many Indian friends as well as of your fellow countrymen. As a member of our wartime National Government you dealt with the gravest and most difficult questions, and were for three years Chancellor of the Exchequer. You have always been regarded as a personality above the turmoil of party politics. After your University seat was taken from you few honours were more well deserved than the peerage which was bestowed upon you.

You have a high expert knowledge of the Income Tax Law and of its administration and are widely respected for your independence of judgment and integrity of character. I am sure that the Royal Commission would have gained in importance by your presiding over it, as you would have done, with strict impartiality. The Royal Commission on Taxation could not have had a more distinguished, experienced and fair-minded chairman. The Chancellor of the Exchequer and I therefore pressed you, much against your wishes, to undertake this additional burden.

Now that you have become the target for organized controversy by the Opposition, I cannot reproach you for seeking

[1] The Opposition motion had also raised doubts in the mind of the Liberal Party — normally supporters of the Government — who now took the view that, whatever Lord Waverley's merits might be, the fact that his appointment was so unacceptable to the Labour Party as to bring about a debate seemed likely to prejudice fair judgment of the Royal Commission's ultimate report and recommendations.

release from new toils. I have therefore informed the Queen of your wish to resign.

Yours sincerely,

WINSTON S. CHURCHILL.[1]

No event in the otherwise serene and successful post-war life of John Anderson caused him such offence and spiritual laceration as this episode. It was, he considered, an affront both to his dignity and his integrity, and a violation of the fundamental principles of truth and fair play. The unjustness of the attack wounded him sorely for, to himself at least, he was still unwaveringly an independent non-party man, but he was hurt more deeply because — as he had written to Mr. Churchill — the attack appeared to have had the acquiescence, if not the active support, of wartime colleagues whom he regarded as his personal friends.

(vi)

There is little doubt that in temperament and manner John, Viscount Waverley, was better attuned to the atmosphere of the House of Lords than Sir John Anderson had been to that of the House of Commons. Of all men in public life he was most serenely possessed of the Roman virtue of *gravitas*, a natural moral power exuding from him in the shape of visible dignity and authority. One of his fellow peers has said of him that he combined in his person the attributes of a Senator of the Roman Republic with those of Aristides the Just, and this formidable amalgam of qualities well fitted him for the detached decorum of the Upper House.

Moreover, he brought to their debates a wealth of knowledge derived from a lifetime of varied experience in the public service upon which he did not hesitate to draw. The House soon learned that his contributions were charged with a discerning authority which was incontrovertible. In the six years of his membership of the House of Lords he never intervened in a debate unless he had something specific and constructive to offer. As Lord Hailsham was later to say of him :

[1] *The Times*, March 1, 1952.

The Rt. Hon. Lord Radcliffe, G.B.E., a Lord of Appeal in Ordinary, was appointed Chairman of the Royal Commission on Taxation of Profits and Income in April 1952.

When he spoke of scientific matters, a graduate of Leipzig University was your adviser.[1] When he spoke of the social services, he had learned his lessons as one of the administrative architects of the reforms of 1911. The economic opinions were those of the ex-Chancellor of the Exchequer ; the imperial policies those of the distinguished proconsul ; the views on terrorism, those of the Irish ex-Secretary and the Bengal Governor ; and, on penal reform, of the man who had been political and administrative head of the Home Office.

Nihil tetigit quod non ornavit.[2]

It is indeed true that on all John touched upon he left the mark of his own distinction of mind and character. There was no debate that was not the richer for his participation ; no discussion that was not elevated by his contribution. It is necessary to take but two examples of these remarkable qualities to demonstrate that the tributes paid to them were in no way exaggerated.

In response to the appeal of the World Health Organization for action in suppressing the heroin 'black market' which supported the vice of drug addiction, the British Government, in April 1955, announced its decision to prohibit the manufacture of heroin as from the end of the current year. This provoked a sharp division of opinion in the medical profession, some doctors holding that there were satisfactory substitutes for the drug, and others maintaining that there were not. A further aspect of the issue was provided by the fact that, although 70 per cent of the world's total lawful supply of heroin was manufactured in Great Britain, which also consumed 54 per cent of it, there were only 54 heroin addicts in this country, as against thousands, for example, in the United States. It seemed doubtful, therefore, whether the prohibition of manufacture of the drug by Britain would make any great contribution to the suppression of what was clearly a non-British vice.

So heated did the controversy become that a debate was initiated on it by Lord Jowitt, the former Socialist Lord Chancellor, in the House of Lords on December 13. It was his contention that, though there was no question as to the motives of the Government, there did exist a doubt as to whether the procedure which they had

---

[1] But see above, p. 15, f.n.
[2] *House of Lords Debates*, January 28, 1958. Cols. 226-227.

adopted under an existing statute was, in fact, legal, and he urged
his fellow peers so to express themselves that the Government
might be constrained to withdraw their prohibition of the manufacture of heroin, extending the period of the existing licences,
pending the institution of further enquiries.

Amongst the several speakers in the ensuing debate were the two
medical peers, Lord Moran and Lord Webb-Johnson, who found
themselves in opposing camps, and also certain informed representatives of lay opinion. Included in the latter was Lord Waverley
who, in a short speech which bristled with knowledgeable argument, came down unequivocally against the decision of the Government to prohibit the manufacture of the drug.[1]

In John's opinion the argument that Britain should take action
to prohibit the manufacture of heroin in order to make effective
an international agreement designed to facilitate the putting down
of drug addiction did not hold water for a moment. What possible
good, he asked, could come to any other country from such a
prohibition? To make the ban effective it would be necessary to
prohibit morphine also, since heroin could be prepared from morphine with the greatest ease, and did the Government propose to
go this far? 'Morphine circulates very freely', he assured his
hearers, 'and it can be converted into heroin without the use of any
appliance or any material which is not most readily available to
any man or woman.' And he continued:

> I speak from my own personal knowledge in this matter,
> and I say that if it were desired to give encouragement to those
> in other countries who are confronted by a most difficult and
> painful situation by 'showing willing' in this country, the proper
> course would be to prohibit the export of heroin, and not that
> alone, but to accompany the prohibition — and as it can be and
> is, I believe, being accompanied — by the most complete and
> effective control of manufacture. Prohibition of export with
> complete control of manufacture can, I believe, effectively
> ensure that no heroin produced in this country can possibly
> contribute to the aggravation of this grave problem by which
> other countries are confronted. Our experience has shown
> that to deal effectively with the problem of addiction requires,

[1] *House of Lords Debates*, December 13, 1955. Cols. 47-49.

first, complete and effective control of manufacture ; second, sound police administration ; and, third (and this is most important), stringent penalties.

My Lords, if I may quote for one moment from my own experience, let me tell you this. Many years ago it was my painful duty to send for the head of one of the most important and highly reputable firms in this country, a firm well known as manufacturers of alkaloids and hypnotics, and to produce to him evidence showing that because of laxity in the organisation under the control of his firm drugs produced under licence were being allowed to pass into illicit channels. And I told him that in those circumstances it would be the duty of His Majesty's Government to withdraw the authority under which that firm — very well known and highly reputable — had been for many years carrying on the manufacture of these drugs and exporting them in large quantities all over the world. The decision was accepted without a murmur because the facts were indisputable. I mention that only as an illustration of the kind of action that has to be taken if the control of these drugs of addiction is to be made effective. That is the sort of line on which, in my humble opinion, other countries have to act. If we wish to show our sympathy, let us by all means not prohibit the manufacture, but prohibit and effectively stop the export to other countries which are not so favourably placed as we are in regard to the control and use of drugs of addiction. That is all I have to say. It gives me no pleasure to express disagreement with the view of a successor of mine at the Home Office, which has been expressed by the noble Lord, Lord Mancroft. I have done so only because I felt that as a matter of duty I had to come here and give the House the result of my own experience.

The balance of the debate seemed to be in accordance with Lord Waverley's views and against the decision to prohibit the manufacture of heroin. The Government agreed to postpone the ban for a year, but in taking this decision it is to be believed that they were less influenced by the merits of a case which they did not accept than by the arguments of Lord Jowitt that their original act of prohibition rested upon an unsure legal foundation.

An even more outstanding contribution by Lord Waverley to the discussions of the Upper House was provided in the debate on capital punishment in July of the following year. The campaign for the abolition of the death penalty had received a fillip at the close of 1955 when, in the course of the Christmas recess, the Home Secretary, Major Gwilym Lloyd-George, granted a free pardon to three men who had been serving sentences after conviction, two years previously, for causing grievous bodily harm to a police constable. The constable recovered from his injuries but, had he died, his three assailants would almost certainly have been hanged. Now, as a result of further investigation of another criminal, who confessed that he and his companions had assaulted the constable, the error of their original conviction was disclosed and the innocent parties were pardoned with a grant in compensation of £300 in two cases and £400 in the third.

This event was, of course, a godsend to the partisans of the abolition of hanging, since one of the salient justifications of capital punishment had always been that no-one was executed if there was a scintilla of doubt as to his guilt. Here, however, were three innocent men who had only escaped the gallows because their alleged victim had not died. The fact that the three wrongfully convicted men were professional criminals who would very likely have been acquitted at the assizes had they not obscured the course of justice by their disclosed perjuries in the witness-box was held to be no answer to this argument.

The Government gave a full day's debate in the House of Commons to the question of capital punishment on February 16, 1956, on a motion which provided for the retention of the death penalty but also for the amendment of the law relating to the crime of murder, and the Home Secretary made it clear that the issue was to be for or against hanging. The Government suffered a defeat, however, on an amendment, moved by the former Labour Home Secretary, Mr. Chuter Ede, which called upon them to introduce legislation forthwith which should abolish or suspend the death penalty for an experimental period. The amendment was carried on a free vote by a majority of 46 ; 48 Conservatives voted in favour of it.

In the meantime Mr. Sydney Silverman,[1] one of the leading advocates of abolishing the death penalty, had introduced a Private

---

[1] Mr. Samuel Sydney Silverman, Labour Member of Parliament for Nelson and Colne since 1935.

Member's Bill to this effect, and to this the Government decided to give facilities for passage if the House on a free vote so willed. It was made clear that the considered opinion of the Government was against the measure. After a series of lively debates, Mr. Silverman's Bill was at length accorded a Third Reading on June 28 by a majority of 19.

The Bill now came before the House of Lords who accorded it a two-day debate on July 9 and 10, in which more than sixty peers took part. All those who favoured the Bill indicated that they preferred a middle course — a course which the Royal Commission on Capital Punishment had recently declared to be impracticable [1] — of amending the law so as to introduce distinctions between capital and non-capital murders, and in this view they were supported by several who favoured the retention of the death penalty.

John was among those who favoured retention. He had already, when on the Opposition Front Bench of the House of Commons, opposed unhesitatingly a previous attempt to secure a temporary abolition of the death penalty,[2] and his judgment remained unchanged. He had no doubt that capital punishment should be retained nor as to its deterrent effect. 'I think a day may well come when it may be safe to abolish the capital penalty', he said, 'I should welcome that, but I am quite convinced that at the moment the balance lies heavily on the side of retention.' He proceeded, with the full weight of his long terms of office as head of the Home Office and as Home Secretary, to attack one of the main arguments in favour of the abolition of the death sentence, namely that it was irrevocable : 'In my view, if the risk of mistake can, for practical purposes, be eliminated, the fact that the death penalty is irrevocable is its main merit.' As for mistakes, he had had experience throughout periods extending over eighteen years during which he had been in close touch with this problem and when it had been his duty to consider every case of the capital penalty and endeavour to form a personal judgment. As far as he was aware there was no case during the whole of these eighteen years in which a mistake had been committed.

---

[1] *Report of the Royal Commission on Capital Punishment, 1949–1953.* Cmd. 8932.
[2] See above, p. 342.

There was, however, an argument which no other opponent of the Bill had introduced and which John was peculiarly well qualified to use, namely the retention of the death sentence as the penalty for political murder. In Ireland and in India he had himself been in frequent danger of assassination and had proved pragmatically the value of the death penalty as a deterrent.

Even if I were convinced, as I am not, that the general arguments for abolition on balance outweighed the arguments against, I would still hesitate before admitting justification for an amendment of the law that would remove entirely the one sanction by which a political crime can be visited, where there is no question of reform, where imprisonment carries no stigma and has no deterrent effect since, according to universal experience, it is invariably curtailed by some amnesty or act of oblivion.

People have said to me rather lightheartedly in that connection, 'Oh, the risk of political crime can be disregarded'. My Lords, can it? I have in mind, as I am sure some noble Lords have, the comparatively recent assassinations of Sir Henry Wilson [1] and Sir Michael O'Dwyer,[2] the latter almost within a stone's throw of this place. I have in mind, too, a case which most of your Lordships will probably have forgotten, the case of the Coventry murders by men called Barnes and Richards, I think, in 1940 when I was Home Secretary.[3] I had to refuse to exercise the Prerogative of mercy in those cases although I received repeated representations from the other side of the Irish Channel and some representations, if the truth must be told, from my own colleagues, who held that the atmosphere would be sweetened if clemency could be shown. That was just the argument that was addressed to me many years ago by the aged Archbishop of Dublin when he was carried up to my room in Dublin Castle to plead for clemency for young Kevin Barry

[1] Field-Marshal Sir Henry Wilson, Bt., G.C.B., D.S.O., M.P., a former Chief of the Imperial General Staff, was assassinated on June 22, 1922, outside his house in Eaton Place by Dunne and O'Sullivan, two Irish gunmen who were subsequently condemned to death and hanged on August 16. The matter has been interestingly treated by Mr. Rex Taylor in his recent book *Assassination* (1961).

[2] Sir Michael O'Dwyer, G.C.I.E., K.C.S.I., a former Lieutenant-Governor of the Punjab, was shot dead by an Indian Muslim on March 13, 1940, at the close of a meeting at the Caxton Hall, Westminster.

[3] On August 25, 1939, a bomb outrage by members of the Irish Republican Army occurred in Coventry, as a result of which five people were killed and twenty gravely injured. Two men, Richards and Barnes, both of the I.R.A., were tried and found guilty of murder on December 15.

who had murdered a British soldier.[1] I had to tell him, to my sorrow, that to do what he had asked would be to proclaim the helplessness of the law . . . and the law was very effective.[2]

John voted against the Bill, which was rejected by 238 votes to 95, but he recorded his hope that an opportunity would arise when the law of capital punishment could be amended to bring it more into accord with practice.

While it cannot be said that, in so large a majority, the Bill owed its rejection to the arguments presented by any particular one of the many speakers who opposed it, it is indisputable that the weighty reasoning and restrained oratory of Lord Waverley materially impressed his fellow peers and reached a wider audience outside the Chamber. The Government took the opportunity of the Queen's Speech from the Throne, at the opening of the new parliamentary session on November 6, to announce their intention of introducing a Homicide Bill which would attempt that distinction peers had advocated in their debate. The new Bill, which finally became law on 21 March, 1957, restricted capital punishment to certain classes of murder and, though 'political murder', *per se*, was not specifically mentioned, the death penalty was retained for 'any murder by shooting or by causing an explosion'. Lord Waverley's arguments may therefore be considered to have been effective, and to this legislation he had made his valuable contribution.

(vii)

This autumnal period of John Anderson's life was perhaps the happiest he had ever known. The splendid sunset years were filled with a serenity of acknowledged accomplishment which brought him great pleasure and satisfaction, and also a softening of his Scottish austerity.

For it was not only his Sovereign who honoured him. In 1945 he was elected a Fellow of the Royal Society under Statute 12, which covers those who have 'rendered conspicuous service to the

---

[1] Kevin Barry, an eighteen-year-old student and a member of the armed forces of Sinn Fein, was executed in Mountjoy Prison, Dublin, on November 1, 1920, for the killing of a British soldier in ambush.

[2] *House of Lords Debates*, July 10, 1956. Cols. 760-761.

cause of science, and whose election would be of signal benefit to the Society'. It is difficult to think of anyone to whom these words could apply more aptly than to John. Academic honours, too, fell thick upon him. The University of Aberdeen had led the way in 1926 with an LL.D. and Cambridge and Edinburgh had made him Honorary Doctor of Civil Law in 1938 on his return from India, with St. Andrews a year later. The Universities of Liverpool, Leeds, Sheffield and London honoured him with LL.D.s, while McGill and Reading accorded him the degree of Honorary Doctor of Science.

The University of Oxford delayed until 1957 to give him an Honorary D.C.L., but eleven years previous to this they had paid him the compliment of the invitation to be the Romanes Lecturer. He chose to speak on 'The Machinery of Government' and delivered a solid and learned discourse which might well serve as a text-book on the subject.[1] It was a topic upon which he was singularly well equipped to discourse. In November 1942 he had been appointed Chairman of a War Cabinet Committee on this very matter, namely 'to enquire into the responsibility of the various departments of the central executive government and to advise in what manner the exercise and distribution by the government of its functions should be improved'.

The Committee examined a wide range of subjects. It looked at the problems of the size of Cabinets, the rôle of supervising Ministers and the number of Standing Committees of the Cabinet, under peacetime conditions. It examined the future of the various wartime Ministries such as the Ministry of Supply, Ministry of Economic Warfare and the Ministry of Food and the future of the Department of Civil Aviation and the Forestry Commission. It looked at the structure of the Home Civil Service after the war, particularly the administrative class, and examined the arrangements for the training of Civil Servants. It spent a good deal of time on the relationship of the Government with Parliament, including the parliamentary control of ministerial orders. It examined the particular problems of Scotland and Wales. It had also to deal with a considerable number of more detailed problems,

---

[1] *The Machinery of Government*, the Romanes Lecture delivered by the Rt. Hon. Sir John Anderson, on May 14, 1946 (Oxford, 1946).

such as departmental responsibility for the care of children deprived
of a normal home life, and which Department should be responsible
for questions of street lighting. It had never been intended that
any general report should be published, but the results of much of
the Committee's labours showed themselves in actions and
announcements made in the ordinary course of administration.

John now drew upon this source of information and upon his
own wide experience. It was the voice of an elder statesman looking backward along the corridors of history. His main thesis was
that while due emphasis should be laid on the departmental responsibility of ministers as a necessary and vital principle, it was also
necessary to stress the importance, as a practical matter, of adequate
machinery for making a reality of collective responsibility.

> The need for this has been proved in two wars and will
> increase now that the Government is so much more concerned
> with economic affairs, with the need for making sure that the
> policies of different departments are consistent with each other
> and form one coherent whole. As means to this end, I would
> rely on the institution, in conjunction with a Cabinet of moderate
> size, of a permanent but flexible system of Cabinet committees,
> on the strengthening of the machinery of the Cabinet secretariat
> and on the association with that secretariat of technical sections
> organized for joint planning and intelligence and for economic,
> statistical and scientific studies.

It is not untrue to say that the process of evolution of Government machinery in the last fifteen years has not differed widely
from that advocated by John Anderson in 1946.

Amid this plenitude of recognition John led as full a life as he
could wish, a life which afforded an unusual diversity of settings :
the dignity of the House of Lords, the variety of public service
which he was asked to perform, the fascination of the City and of
Big Business, the pleasure which he derived from his river parties
in the *St. Katharine*, the administrative problems and the aesthetic
charms of Covent Garden, the new horizons opened up by travel
abroad, and, above all, the happiness of his home life in London
and in Sussex. All these combined to exercise a mellowing effect
upon his temperament. The stiffness and the reserve which had
characterized him in early and middle life and had often filled those

with whom he associated with alarm now gave place to the unforced geniality of a good host and of a man on good terms with himself and with others, with a ready sympathy for younger men and a genuine pleasure in female society.

His sense of humour, which had never been among his more notable traits, also matured during these years, although it rarely lost its solemnity. Once, when Sir Roger Makins, then Ambassador in Washington, was on leave in London, he lunched at 4 Lord North Street. John delivered himself of a considered criticism of the personality and policies of the American Secretary of State, John Foster Dulles, to which the Ambassador offered a defence. Mr. Dulles, said Sir Roger, had the habit of thinking aloud, his ideas developed during this process, which was continuous ; his thoughts thus expressed were not necessarily to be considered as his final judgments. John listened impassively and then announced gravely, but with a twinkle in his eye : 'Well, Roger, you may be right, but don't forget I'm a Presbyterian myself.'

The chief artificer of this later metamorphosis of John was, of course, his wife. His love for Ava, always deep, grew even greater with the passage of time. Secure in his affection for her and of her love for him, gratified by her social success and delighted, with indulgent amusement, by her vivacious personality, he warmed and softened into a more mellifluous maturity.

Indeed, almost the only periods of sadness which he experienced in these later years, apart from the death of his father in 1949, were when he was separated from Ava during her periodic visits to the Embassy in Paris and when she was taking treatment for some weeks at La Preste in the Pyrenees after a painful illness. She was a dilatory correspondent and John was avid for news of her.[1] He wrote nearly every day and telephoned to her frequently when she was in Paris — though he loathed the telephone as a means of communication — but it was for her letters that he hungered. 'No letter' ; 'again no letter', one finds him writing, and at length there was a note of exasperation : 'I am very vexed at not having

[1] As a letter writer, both as regards style and output, Lady Waverley has few equals. This accomplishment had been early fostered and acknowledged by her father. 'You are a perfect correspondent', he wrote to her in April 1913, 'and it is a great thing in these days of telephones, etc. (the mechanical age!) to have mastered in your youth the almost forgotten art of letter-writing.' (Leslie (*op. cit.*), p. 417.)

a letter from you this morning.' Despite his busy days and a full social calendar of engagements, John was filled with solicitude and anxiety during her absences, admonishing her constantly to take great care of herself. He was lonely, too, as he often revealed : 'I am missing you very much' ; 'the house seems strangely empty. I am always expecting to hear a dear little piping voice calling "Johnnie, Johnnie!"'

Yet despite this deep sense of personal affection, John had a curious insensitivity about possessions. It was a part of that strange faculty of his for never mentioning a relation or a friend after death, seemingly relegating them to oblivion. On his marriage to Ava he had at once offered her some of Chrissie's furs and jewellery and, by the same token, he would wear Ralph Wigram's hats and scarfs and use his walking-sticks. This sometimes troubled Ava and, in a moment of exasperation, she once told him that he was quite devoid of deep feeling. 'You don't know anything about sorrow', she said. John was surprised, and completely uncomprehending. 'I can't think what you mean,' he replied, 'I felt terribly about the fall of Hong Kong.' And it was true ; no man took more deeply to heart the public cares and sorrows of his own country.

They were ideally happy together, more especially when, after ten years of patient waiting, they were at last able to purchase the property at Westdean, with which they had both fallen in love soon after their marriage.[1] This square white house, built in the reign of William IV, satisfied both Ava's love of high rooms and John's practical requirements of premises free from dry rot. More-over, he was enchanted with the early Saxon flavour of the village; Alfriston, which was their telephone exchange, was called after Alfric, Master of the Horse to Alfred the Great. Westdean itself possessed one of the earliest parsonages in England, with a priest's secret stairway which delighted John, and the fact that the grey ruins in the village were said to be those of Alfred the Great's palace enthralled him. For early English history was his favourite period, Chaucer his favourite poet, and among his many varied and sur-prising attributes was a knowledge of the Anglo-Saxon tongue.

For Ava too the realization of their long-cherished dream brought balm and healing after the death of her son. The restful

[1] See above, p. 286.

atmosphere of the tiny hamlet and its proximity to the sea ; the quiet evenings when the song of the nightingales was interrupted only by the occasional bark of a fox in the valley below, gave peace to them both and they looked forward to living out the evening of their lives together in these idyllic surroundings.

John loved the Downs. He would stride over the green expanses above the sea in all weathers, looking, as one of the local inhabitants of long standing remarked, like 'the spirit of the Downland in person'. The charm and romance of the open country, with its ever-changing hues and shadows, made up to him for the poverty of the chalky ground in comparison with the rich loam and peat soil of Isfield. His garden and orchard there had meant so much to him and now he had to abandon his much-loved rhododendrons and azaleas. He did not complain, however, and at once set about planting quantities of fruit trees in the arid chalk which, to his intense satisfaction, proved a successful venture.

It was not only John's horticultural interests which were affected by the move from Isfield to Westdean. For various reasons the cows and pigs had to be left behind, but the pigeons, chickens and geese went with them, in addition to a quantity of Muscovy ducks, which had been the gift of Sir Anthony Eden. For these he bought a large bath-tub and sank it into the ground, 'because', he said knowledgeably, 'ducks and geese can't mate without water'. What pleased him most, however, was the greater facility which their new surroundings afforded for the exercising of his bloodhounds.

John's interest in this mighty canine breed dated from 1944. Long years before, Lord Lonsdale had given bloodhounds to Ava, who had been devoted to them and had come to know much of the lore of breeding and pedigree. But they had not figured in her life for a long time and, though she had talked to John about them, he had never displayed more than a polite interest. Now, however, in the autumn of 1944, she sustained the loss of her two half-brothers, both of whom were killed in action. Ava was much attached to these two sons of her father's second marriage. 'My little brothers', she called them, and their deaths caused her sorrow. It was in an effort to distract her mind from her loss that John, who had discovered that near by at Woodingdean was one of the two remaining bloodhound kennels in England, suddenly suggested that they should buy a puppy.

Their first experiment proved unsuccessful, but their second puppy 'Dusk' developed into the mother of champions, having herself, perhaps, one of the finest heads in the history of the blood-hound breed : low-set ears of unparalleled length, high peak of skull, voluminous wrinkles, good depth of lip and great sunken eyes. Her body was exactly right too, with a deep brisket ; only her tail was wrong.

Dusk soon became an acknowledged member of the family both in London and in the country. John loved her and used to take her night and morning to the Embankment Gardens. Ava exercised her in Hyde Park where, with her natural love of children, Dusk persisted in putting up her paws on perambulators, to the delight of the occupants but the manifest disapproval of nurses and mothers.

Like all her kind, Dusk was terrified of traffic and refused to cross a street, cowering down and insisting upon being carried. This was both embarrassing and exhausting, for she was very heavy. Once, when Ava, bowed down with the weight of Dusk in her arms, was waiting on her threshold for the door to be opened, Walter Elliot, espying her from his house on the other side of Lord North Street, rushed across and, without seeming to notice anything strange, cried out : 'You know, Ava, I have come to the conclusion that all people with genius who figure in history were mad. Joan of Arc was mad, Napoleon was mad, Nelson was mad, Pitt was mad. If you count them over you will agree with me.' And he disappeared back into his house, without further remark. Ava recounted this incident to John who, when he next saw Walter, enquired of him : 'If you saw Ava carrying a young giraffe in the street, would you still make no comment ?' Walter Elliot replied : 'I was following my train of thought, and possibly Ava is a case in point, but I'm not sure yet. God moves in a mysterious way His wonders to perform.'

John became deeply devoted to Dusk, assisting at her mating and serving as her midwife. This last adventure was at first disastrous, for he was too inquisitive and she killed off her first-born. When the rest of her litter arrived, however, he was more circumspect and as the puppies grew he was delighted with them, carrying them around in his pockets.

Two of these puppies, Emily and Mighty, became champions and John showed them proudly at Cruft's. He was a tiro at the job, and one of the ring-hands remarked : 'I don't know what that gent. does for a living, but my advice to him would be to go back and do it. He'll never be any good at handling a hound in the ring.' Nevertheless, John being John, he did become an expert handler of hounds. The Anderson kennel not only produced champions but was run at a profit, the puppies selling at as much as £150 a piece, though John hated to part with them. 'It isn't right ; it really isn't right', he would say in anguish as they left him. Equally, of course, John's was one of the few kennels in England which were not afflicted by the fatal bloodhound illness of 'Bloat', and this was because he maintained that the cause of the disease was a deficiency of Vitamin C, and he taught his hounds to eat green vegetables and fruit.

Dusk was devoted to them all but more particularly to the invalid boy Charley. She would take her puppies in her mouth and bring them to him, and her favourite pleasure was to sit beside him when he was being read to and to lie on his bed when he was resting. John, though fond of her, was fonder still of her daughter Emily, upon whom he doted. In contrast to her mother, Emily was remote, shy and undemonstrative. These were the qualities which John admired. 'I love her because she is so reserved', he once said to Ava. This preference nearly ended in tragedy, for Dusk became insanely jealous. When Emily was in whelp and John was taking her for a peaceful saunter, Dusk attacked her daughter with intent to kill and in protecting Emily John was severely bitten, his wounds necessitating anti-tetanus injections and stitches.

There was a pleasantly easy social life at Westdean. John enjoyed motoring about the countryside and visiting those of their friends who lived within easy driving distance — the Macmillans at Birch Grove and Anthony Eden at Binderton. There were visitors from London too who would come down for luncheon on Saturday and Sunday. John, however, disliked 'overnight' guests who, he considered, made too great inroads upon his time.

JOHN AT A DOG SHOW WITH 'EMILY' AND 'MIGHTY'

One exception to this rule was Isaiah Berlin, whose charm and genius and humour delighted John and who achieved the rare distinction of being invited 'to dine and sleep'.

In matters of religion and worship John displayed a certain ambivalence of attitude. The circumstances of Charley's death, with its fortitude and resignation, had impressed him deeply. 'If I had never had any faith at all, the look on that boy's face and what I have seen to-night would have given me belief in an after life', he said to Ava, with tears running down his face, as they stood together by the death-bed. Religion, as such, had never played an important part in his life, though he was always what one would call a religious man, deriving consolation and strength from the worship of God wherever he might be. In London, he attended the Church of Scotland at St. Columba's, Pont Street, but in Sussex he found no difficulty in accepting and participating in the liturgy of the Episcopacy. At the parish church of Westdean he was a regular attendant and resumed the custom, which he had established at Isfield, of reading the lessons each Sunday evening in a fine resonant voice ; but when John began to take Communion it worried Ava's sense of the fitness of things. 'You haven't any real right to do it, you know,' she once said to him. 'You haven't been confirmed.' 'What you do, I want to do,' he answered. 'You want to leave me out.' 'No, Johnnie, I don't ; but it *is* the Church of England and one has to be confirmed before being able to take Communion.' 'Well, I'm not wishing to be confirmed just now,' was John's conclusive reply and he continued to receive Communion from their broadminded friend and rector, the Rev. Spencer Hamilton.[1]

(viii)

Now in his seventy-fifth year, John Anderson appeared to be in excellent health and full of vigour. With the exception of an occasional cold he had never known a day's illness nor had he, save for an injured shoulder in India, ever experienced pain. He was completely assured of his own physical condition and would laugh away Ava's periodic anxieties with : 'You've no need to

---

[1] A further source of pleasure and satisfaction to John Anderson at this time was the marriage of his son Alastair in 1948 to Myrtle Ledgerwood.

worry, I've got a perfect metabolism and longevity is in my blood.' He did indeed seem to have a colossal constitution and had not his father lived to the age of ninety-four ?

In May 1956 an attack of severe abdominal pain whilst travelling in the night train to Edinburgh to attend the General Assembly of the Church of Scotland as the guest of the Lord High Commissioner, Walter Elliot, at Holyroodhouse, caused his doctors some disquiet and considerable anxiety to Ava. He appeared, however, to throw it off completely. He visited Canada alone that year, as Ava was taking treatment at La Preste, but they were both busy with plans to accompany the Royal Ballet to Moscow — John had always wanted to visit Russia — and to attend the festival celebrations at Jamestown, in 1957, which were to mark the 350th anniversary of the founding of the Colony of Virginia and in which John had been invited to take a prominent part.

As the Suez Canal crisis loomed in the autumn of 1956 John watched it with apprehension, and he was frankly critical of the policy of the British Government which culminated in the military operations of December. When Sir Anthony Eden resigned on January 9, 1957, John was unfeignedly delighted at the appointment of Mr. Harold Macmillan as his successor. He had the warmest admiration and affection for him and expressed the utmost confidence in his ability to overcome the very considerable obstacles and difficulties which confronted him on assuming office.

In April John complained of further intestinal discomfort and agreed to be X-rayed, but the examination was completely reassuring. However, he developed a sciatic affection which, despite treatment, remained painful and marred his enjoyment of the Encaenia ceremonies at Oxford on June 26, at which he received an Honorary D.C.L., the Public Orator's Deputy describing him as '*Protea alterum, qui tamen nullum unquam onus, nullum periculum detrectavit*'.[1]

Shortly thereafter he had an attack of jaundice which com-

---

[1] 'A second Proteus, but one who had shirked neither toil nor danger.'

When Sir Norman Brook received the same honour from the University of Oxford at the Encaenia of June 21, 1961, the Public Orator began his citation with the words : '*Nuper mortem deflevimus viri praehonorabilis Johannis Vice-Comitis Waverley, quem abhinc annis fere quattuor honoribus nostris affecimus. Vir qui nunc prodit illi ab epistulis inserviendo ad altissimum in Ministerio Civili fastigium coepit ascendere.*'

AVA AND JOHN AT NO. 4, LORD NORTH STREET

pelled him to forgo a tour of the I.C.I. plants in the North of England in August with Sir Alexander Fleck, the Chairman. John consented to go into St. Thomas's Hospital to be treated for his jaundice and his sciatica, while Ava went on tour to the North in his place. It was agreed between them that on her return they would go together to Vichy for him to take a cure.

On Ava's arrival at Alnwick to stay with the Duke and Duchess of Northumberland she received a telephone message from John's doctor to the effect that he had an obstruction of the gall bladder. An operation was urged as soon as possible, preferably on the following Saturday, August 17, but John had refused his consent, saying that she had promised to take him to Vichy. Ava returned at once to London and found John stubbornly opposed to an operation. Though he had a considerable knowledge of medicine — many thought him a born doctor — he had no experience of illness or of pain, and had developed almost a terror of 'invalidism'. Hospital life revolted him and he resented the ministrations of the nurses. 'It's a fearful thing to be messed about by these women and some quite young girls, too,' he complained.

With considerable difficulty Ava wore down John's objections and persuaded him to have the operation. It was performed on August 17 and disclosed the fact that he had a suspected carcinoma of the pancreas, a verdict which was finally confirmed twelve days later. Ava was informed at once and also his doctor son, Alastair. At her particular wish neither John nor anyone else was told of his condition. Not even his daughter Mary, then on duty with the W.R.A.C. in Norway on a N.A.T.O. mission, was informed ; the only exceptions were the Prime Minister and Lady Dorothy Macmillan, both of whom sustained Ava greatly in her lonely ordeal by their comfort and sympathy.

John meanwhile seemed to be making a remarkable recovery from the effects of his operation. He read the papers avidly, morning and evening, listened to the wireless and watched television. He discussed the affairs of the P.L.A. with Sir Leslie Ford and of Covent Garden with Lord Moore, and was greatly touched by the solicitude displayed. The Queen's Private Secretary telephoned from Balmoral for news of him and he was visited by the Prime Minister and others.

2 D

On September 2, much to the amazement and, to some degree, the alarm of his doctors, John insisted on returning to Lord North Street, and both there and at Westdean his convalescence proceeded very satisfactorily. That he had no qualms as to his own condition, nor knowledge of his complaint, was evident from the fact that he read, with keen but detached critical interest, a series of articles on cancer which appeared at this time in the *Sunday Times*. 'They are on the wrong tack in this country about cancer,' he commented to Ava. 'One of the things I mean to do, when I retire, is to put some notes together on what I believe ought to be done. I've got some theories I wish to submit.'

Ava suffered very greatly at this time. Not only was she bowed down with the burden of her inner secret of John's true illness, a secret which she could share with so very few, but the shock of the news of his cancer had affected her sight. She was now threatened with the loss of the sight of one eye and was advised that total blindness might ensue if she did not rest completely. With real heroism she refused to consider this advice and dedicated herself to the care of John with the utmost devotion and gallantry.

Early in October they went to the Imperial Hotel at Torquay for a further period of recuperation. John seemed to be making good progress and was full of plans for the future. Though he had been persuaded of the wisdom of abandoning his proposed visit to Canada and the United States, he regarded this as merely a postponement and was full of long-range plans for enjoying his retirement. He did not anticipate missing his City life in the least. He proposed to take up the intensive study of botany and to do much research in this field and in others. He had also discussed with Lord Kemsley the writing of his memoirs.

On their return to Lord North Street at the beginning of November John and Ava resumed their normal social life, but it was patent to all but John himself that he was a very sick man indeed. With dogged determination he refused to forgo any ceremony or engagement, despite the fact that he now admitted to increasing fatigue. The State Opening of Parliament on November 5 tired him sorely and he all but fainted at a party at Buckingham Palace two days later. Yet he insisted on watching the Remembrance Sunday ceremonial from the balcony of the Home Office in the biting cold and eventually caught a chill while looking for his car, in which he had left his overcoat, after an official dinner. On November 15 he was readmitted to St. Thomas's Hospital with pneumonia, and in a state of delirium. The pneumonic condition responded effectively to the use of antibiotics, but by December 5 it was clear that there was severe internal haemorrhage ; the end could not be long delayed.

It was now that John Anderson received his last and greatest honour. On November 15 the Prime Minister wrote saying that the Queen wished to confer the Order of Merit upon him. 'I hope very much that you will feel able to accept this,' wrote Mr. Macmillan, 'for it will be a tribute to your long service to the nation in many fields, and will I think give especial pleasure to the Civil Service, with which you have been so long connected and which you served so well.' Ten days later, Her Majesty, by the hand of Sir Michael Adeane, signified her desire of bestowing the Order upon him.[1] John accepted in a touching letter of gratitude on December 2.

This was an honour peculiarly suited to his outstanding record. It is solely within the Queen's own gift and is awarded, so runs its Statute, to those who may have rendered 'exceptionally meritorious service : (*a*) in the Crown Services of Our Empire, or (*b*) may have rendered exceptionally meritorious service towards the adornment of the Arts, Learning, Literature and Science'. 'It is not often', wrote Michael Adeane to John, 'that a recipient qualifies under both headings as you do.'

John was filled with delight and gratitude at the knowledge of this forthcoming honour ; it was characteristic of him that his first reaction should be in connection with that great branch of Government of which he had for so long been a distinguished member. 'The Civil Service will be pleased about this,' was his comment.

It had been the Queen's original intention that the announcement of her award to John Anderson should be made in the New

---

[1] The award of the Order of Merit is in the unfettered gift of the Sovereign independent of the advice of Ministers. This is, however, an interesting example of the minds of the Queen and her Minister working along parallel lines. Her Majesty, as is her right, consulted Mr. Macmillan, and both were agreed upon the eminent suitability of Lord Waverley as a recipient of the Order.

Year Honours List. But, alas, events moved too fast. During the night of December 7 it became plain that his condition was deteriorating so rapidly that without further blood transfusion he would die very soon. The choice lay between letting him slip peacefully away and prolonging his life so that he might enjoy the actual bestowal of his honour. After anxious discussion between the doctors, Ava and Alastair, it was agreed that he should be transfused and the Prime Minister was told that John was so ill that he might not live for another forty-eight hours. At lunch-time on Sunday, December 8, Mr. Macmillan informed Sir Michael Adeane at Windsor of this fact, suggesting that the announcement might be made at once as this would give great comfort to John who, though realizing that he was very ill, did not apparently know that he was dying. The Queen at once agreed and, on her own initiative, instructed Sir Michael to take the insignia of the Order to the hospital that afternoon and confer it upon John in her name.

The problem was to devise the necessary explanation for this emergency action without arousing John's suspicion as to the ultimate gravity of his condition. It was accordingly agreed that he should be told that, as he would shortly be going away to recuperate in a warm climate, Her Majesty did not wish him to come back from the sunshine to the winter cold of England especially for the Investiture nor to keep him waiting until after his return.

Sir Michael Adeane duly carried out Her Majesty's instructions. John seemed perfectly lucid and was deeply touched by the Queen's consideration. — 'It was all her own idea,' he later told Alastair. He entirely accepted the explanation of Her Majesty's action ; he discussed happily the general subject of the Order, expressed his gratification at being numbered among its distinguished members and made a recommendation for a future recipient. As Michael Adeane was leaving he met the Prime Minister on the stairs. Mr. Macmillan was visibly and deeply moved.[1]

[1] There have been two previous occasions on which the Order of Merit has been taken by the Sovereign's Private Secretary to the sick-bed of the recipient : that of Florence Nightingale by Lord Knollys in 1907, and of Admiral of the Fleet Sir Dudley Pound by Sir Alan Lascelles in 1943. King George VI, however, personally conferred the G.C.V.O. upon two of his physicians when on their sick-beds : on Sir Maurice Cassidy in 1949 and on Sir Morton Smart in 1950.

The formal announcement of John's honour was made on the B.B.C. six o'clock news that evening, and in the press on the following day. The newspapers were filled with glowing encomiums of himself and his career, which gave great pleasure both to him and to his family. Congratulations poured in upon him, and by these he was touched immeasurably. One of the letters which gave him particular happiness was from his devoted erstwhile personal assistant, Sir Norman Brook, who in conveying his congratulations had written, not only for himself, but also on behalf of the Civil Service of which he was by now the Head. This letter John kept beside him on the table with his Bible and the morocco case containing his Order.

But he was sinking rapidly. Christmas found him grey and wasted yet able to enjoy the many offerings of flowers which flowed in upon him and Ava, and also the visits of his friends, including the Archbishop of Canterbury, Field-Marshal Lord Alexander, Lord Monckton, Sir Alan Lascelles, Lord Chandos, Lady Diana Duff Cooper and many others. His daughter Mary came to see him on her Christmas leave from Norway and he derived much pleasure from seeing her.

By the New Year, however, he was in great distress and required heavy sedation to keep him tranquil. This was maintained for the remainder of his life. He died with his hand in Ava's at six o'clock on the morning of January 4, 1958.

Lord Waverley was buried at Westdean on January 7, and his Memorial Service took place in Westminster Abbey on January 30. When Parliament reassembled on January 28, the House of Lords was the scene of a number of eulogistic tributes which re-echoed those which had been paid both publicly and privately at the time of his death.

When John Anderson died, a giant passed from among the ranks of men. Trite sayings spring to mind which, when applied to him, suddenly assume an actual significance, a new reality : 'We shall not look upon his like again' ; 'We are all the poorer for his death'. For indeed Anderson did possess a combination of standards and virtues and attributes which were peculiar to his age, and the passing of that age is of loss to us all.

As he was, in a sense, 'the last of the Romans', so also he was to the last a Victorian, and a Scottish Victorian at that ; one who had made his way from humble origins by fierce and honest competition through his own tremendous efforts of intellect and character to the highest positions and honours in the land. His character was formed early in the climate of his own home, the honourable, upright, Protestant upbringing of Scots family life. Thus grounded, he went forward in his own right, his habitual conduct being that of a man of immense moral and physical valour. 'John was a man of great courage, and his services to our country were of the highest order', Sir Winston Churchill wrote of him to Ava.

Wisdom and integrity were, perhaps, the greatest impressions which he gave, the one guided by the other. Everything he did was backed by an unshakable moral certainty, wholly constructive, proceeding by the shortest route from point to point, impelled by an instinctive sense of what was the moral centre of a given situation or problem. This is something which no amount of skill or confidence or ability or wealth or ancestry can produce ; it comes only from stoutness of heart and unswerving human decency.

It is as the last great calm Roman figure of our country that he will be remembered. *Gravitas* he had, but nothing of *hubris*. It was his gravity which misled many to believe him pompous, but those who knew him, those who served with him or under his direction, those who had occasion to ask his aid, can testify that beneath that formidable façade was a deep, human understanding, kindness and justice. 'He could not bear for a sparrow to fall to the ground if it did not deserve to', one of his friends has written.

Yet, Roman though he was, it is to the Greeks that one must turn for a final tribute. As Pericles once said of the Athenian dead :

When great men die, the whole earth is their memorial. In their own country stone monuments describe their praises. But elsewhere, everywhere their fame lives on in the hearts of men, as in a cenotaph not made with hands.

X

EPILOGUE

ON April 19, 1960, John Anderson's family and a group of friends gathered in the little Saxon church of Westdean, that lovely Sussex hamlet where he had been so peacefully happy in the latter years of his life and where he now lies buried. Those present were representative of every facet of John's many-sided life and the occasion was the unveiling of a bronze bust of him by Sir Jacob Epstein. At the close of the service the Prime Minister, Mr. Harold Macmillan, one to whom John had been bound by strong ties of deep mutual respect and affection, spoke these words :

In this beautiful little country church where, in the closing years of his life, he regularly worshipped, we are met to pay tribute to a great man. Our little company gathered here is representative of a large number of men and women, in many and varying walks of life, who felt a deep affection, as well as a profound admiration, for John Anderson — first Viscount Waverley.

Happily the Memorial Bust dedicated today is the work of a great artist. It may seem strange in years far ahead to the casual passer-by to find in this remote Sussex village this striking testimony to the services of one of Scotland's noblest sons who lies buried here. His long and varied life had carried him over a wide field and into many countries. It was here in these peaceful and rural surroundings that he spent his last years in great happiness and content.

At the time of his death many distinguished and talented men wrote and spoke about him, in all parts of the world. Among these I especially recall the tributes published by Lord Salisbury, Lord Salter and Walter Elliot. It would be quite inappropriate for me to try this afternoon to say again what has been already so well said. In any case, we are looking forward to reading the full story of his life, which has fortunately been entrusted to skilled and sympathetic hands.

Throughout his career Lord Waverley displayed an extraordinary versatility — administrator, pro-consul, statesman, scientist, economist, businessman and patron. To all this wide variety of effort he brought not only his unequalled knowledge — he probably knew more on more subjects than any other man of his age — but also his scrupulous and tireless devotion. In everything he undertook he was supremely successful. He began in the Civil Service and rose to the very top. He was generally accepted as the greatest of Civil Servants of his — and perhaps any — age. When the Queen, a few weeks before his death, gave him the Order of Merit, he said to me that he particularly valued the honour as a tribute through him to the Service of which he was so proud. In Ireland he proved not only his ability but his rock-like contempt for danger. He brought this characteristic fortitude as well as his deep humanity to the service of India. Later, as a leading member — one of the key figures — of Churchill's War Administration he played a part second only to our great leader. Indeed without the knowledge that so many of our complicated matters at home were in these safe hands, I do not think that Churchill could have devoted himself so completely to the problems of war overseas. After the war Lord Waverley brought all his ripe experience to the service of the Port of London, and presided over its Authority with conspicuous success. Other business and banking organizations sought his help. To the atomic energy projects he gave all his specialized knowledge and diligence. As Chairman of the Royal Opera House he helped to create what has now become a great national asset.

These were his outward achievements. He was a very great man and had a very great success in his long life. But when we think of John Anderson it is not of all this record of achievement that we think. We think of the man. His was a rare — almost unique — combination of qualities. First, he had absolute and complete courage, both physical and moral. Physical courage — as we many of us here can recall — is not uncommon. Most of us have, in our experience, had knowledge of men endowed with exceptional moral courage. But the combination of the two is always of special and outstanding value. John Anderson was a conspicuous example of both these qualities combined in one man. He was as little moved by the poisoned darts of the columnist as he was by the bullets of the terrorist. His first great characteristic, therefore, was courage — physical and moral.

Secondly, he had absolute integrity of character — the kind of integrity that most of us are fortunate enough to have experienced in our lives — in a parent, or a master, or a friend — and treasure above all other memories. John Anderson was the kind of man in whose presence it was impossible to conceive anything mean, disloyal or dishonourable being proposed or even hinted at. I do not mean he was a prig — far from it. It was simply that he had such a clear and unshakable uprightness that anything base, or even petty, seemed to be impossible in his presence.

Thirdly, he had a sort of majestic simplicity : he was a really companionable man, he liked his fellow men and was especially kind to young men because, in spite of his extraordinary attainments, he was essentially a humble man.

Those who are here at this ceremony to-day are typical of some of the contacts that he had and the great service that he gave to the nation. But we have not come here to-day, to this little Sussex church, merely because of that. It is not just to represent Parliament, or the Cabinet, or the Fighting, Foreign and Civil Services, or the Canadian Pacific Railway, or Imperial Chemical Industries, or the Atomic Energy Board, or the Hudson's Bay Company, or the Port of London, or the Arts Council, or the Royal Society. We have come here because we all admired John Anderson — perhaps more than any man who has come into our lives — and also because we loved him.

BIBLIOGRAPHY

FOR basic reference I have used *The Encyclopaedia Britannica, The Dictionary of National Biography, The Annual Register, The House of Commons Debates* and *The House of Lords Debates.*

(i) OFFICIAL DOCUMENTS

Report of the Northern Nigerian Lands Committee, 1910. Cmd. 5102.
Report of the British West African Colonies and Protectorates Currency Committee, 1912. Cmd. 6426.
Report of the Select Committee on Increase of Wealth (War), 1920.
Report of the Royal Commission on the Rebellion in Ireland, 1916. Cmd. 8279.
Documents Relative to the Sinn Fein Movement, 1921. Cmd. 1108.
Report of the Royal Commission on National Health Insurance, 1928. Cmd. 2596.
Report of the Sankey Commission on the Coal Industry, 1919. Cmds. 359-361.
Report of the Samuel Commission on the Coal Industry, 1926. Cmd. 2603.
Report of the Indian Statutory Commission, 1930. Cmds. 3568-3569.
Report of the Muddiman Committee on the working of Dyarchy, 1928. Cmd. 2360.
Proposals for Indian Constitutional Reform, 1933. Cmd. 4268.
Report of the Joint Committee on Indian Constitutional Reform, 1934.
Report of the Committee on Evacuation, 1938. Cmd. 5837.
Report of the Lord Privy Seal's Conference on Air Raid Shelters, 1939. Cmd. 6006.
Report of Sir William Beveridge on Social Insurance and Allied Services, 1942. Cmd. 6404.
Anglo-French Financial Agreement, 1945. Cmd. 6613.
Report of the Committee on the Export of Works of Art, 1952.
The Future Organization of the United Kingdom Atomic Energy Project, 1953. Cmd. 8986.
Report of the Departmental Committee on Coastal Flooding, 1953. Cmd. 9165.
Report of the Royal Commission on Capital Punishment, 1949-1953. Cmd. 8932.

(ii) GENERAL WORKS

(Except where stated, the books in the following list were published in London)
ANDERSON, Sir John. *Collected Speeches as Governor of Bengal* (Calcutta, 1932–1937).
The Machinery of Government (Oxford, 1946).

ANSON, Sir William. *Laws and Customs of the Constitution* (1892).

ATTLEE, C. R. *As it Happened* (1954).

BÉASLÁI, Piaras. *Michael Collins and the Making of New Ireland* (Dublin, 1926).

BENNETT, Richard. *The Black and Tans* (1959).

BIRKENHEAD, Earl of. *The Prof. in Two Worlds : the Official Life of Professor F. A. Lindemann, Viscount Cherwell* (1961).

BRIDGES, Lord. *Biographical Memoirs of Fellows of the Royal Society*, vol. 4, November 1958.

BROMAGE, Mary C. *De Valera and the March of a Nation* (1956).

BRYANT, Sir Arthur. *Liquid History* (1960).

   Triumph in the West (1959).

BULLOCK, Alan. *The Life and Times of Ernest Bevin*, vol. i (1960).

BUNBURY, Sir Henry N. (Ed.). *Lloyd George's Ambulance Wagon, being the Memoirs of William J. Braithwaite, 1911–1912* (1957).

CALDER, Ritchie. *The Horror of London* (1941).

CHURCHILL, Sir Winston. *Closing the Ring* (1952).

   The Aftermath (New York, 1929).

   The Gathering Storm (1948).

   The Grand Alliance (1950).

   The Hinge of Fate (1951).

   Their Finest Hour (1949).

   Triumph and Tragedy (1954).

CLARKE, Ronald W. *The Birth of the Bomb* (1961).

ERVINE, St. John. *Craigavon, Ulsterman* (1949).

FEILING, Sir Keith. *The Life of Neville Chamberlain* (1946).

FEIS, Herbert. *Between War and Peace, the Potsdam Conference* (Princeton, N.J., 1960).

   Japan subdued : the Atom Bomb and the End of the War in the Pacific (Princeton, N.J., 1961).

FRANCIS-WILLIAMS, Lord. *A Prime Minister Remembers* (1961).

GRIER, Lynda. *Achievement in Education* (1932).

GRIGG, Sir James. *Prejudice and Judgment* (1948).

GWYNN, Denis. *De Valera* (New York, 1933).

HALDANE, J. B. S. *A.R.P.* (1938).

HALIFAX, Earl of. *Fulness of Days* (1957).

HANCOCK, Sir Keith, and GOWING, M. M. *British War Economy* (1949).

HARRIS, R. W. *Not so Humdrum, the Autobiography of a Civil Servant* (1939).

HERBERT, Sir Alan. *Independent Member* (1950).

   Let us be Glum (1941).

   Light the Lights (1945).

IREMONGER, Rev. F. A. *William Temple, His Life and Letters* (1958).

ISMAY, General Lord. *Memoirs* (1960).

JENKINS, Roy. *Sir Charles Dilke, A Victorian Tragedy* (1958).

JONES, Thomas. *A Diary with Letters* (1954).

KEITH, Prof. A. Berriedale. *Letters on Imperial Relations* (1935).
KNEBEL, Fletcher, and BAILEY, Charles. *No High Ground* (1961).
LEASOR, James. *War at the Top* (1959).
LESLIE, Sir Shane. *Memoir of John Edward Courtney Bodley* (1930).
LLOYD GEORGE, David. *The Truth about the Peace Treaties* (1938).
LOCKHART, Sir Robert Bruce. *Your England* (1955).
MACARDLE, Dorothy. *The Irish Republic* (Dublin, 1951).
MACMANUS, M. J. *Eamon de Valera* (Dublin, 1947).
MACREADY, General Sir Nevil. *Annals of an Active Life* (1924).
MARKHAM, Violet. *Friendship's Harvest* (1956).
MAURICE, Major-General Sir Frederick. *Haldane, 1915–1928* (1939).
MINNEY, R. J. *The Private Papers of Hore-Belisha* (1960).
MOOREHEAD, Alan. *The Traitors* (1952).
MORISON, Samuel Eliot. *Victory in the Pacific, 1945* (1960).
MORRISON OF LAMBETH, Lord. *Herbert Morrison : An Autobiography* (1960).
NEILSON, Francis. *The Tragedy of Europe* (Appleton, Wisconsin, 1940–1946).
NICOLSON, Sir Harold. *King George V, His Life and Reign* (1952).
NORWICH, Viscount. *Old Men Forget* (1953).
O'BRIEN, R. Barry. *Dublin Castle and the Irish People* (1912).
O'BRIEN, Terence H. *Civil Defence* (1955).
O'FAOLÁIN, Sean. *De Valera* (1939).
O'SULLIVAN, Donal. *The Irish Free State and its Senate* (1940).
OWEN, Frank. *Tempestuous Journey : Lloyd George, His Life and Times* (1954).
PAKENHAM, Hon. Frank. *Peace by Ordeal* (1935).
PARKER, H. M. D. *Manpower* (1957).
'PERISCOPE.' 'The Last Days of Dublin Castle', *Blackwood's Magazine* (August, 1922).
PICKERSGILL, J. W. *The Mackenzie King Record* (Toronto, 1960).
POSTGATE, Raymond. *The Life of George Lansbury* (1951).
REITH, Lord. *Into the Wind* (1949).
RIDDELL, Lord. *More Pages from My Diary* (1934).
ROBINSON, Sir Henry. *Memories : Wise and Otherwise* (1923).
SADLEIR, Michael. *Sir Michael Sadler* (1949).
SALTER, Lord. *Memoirs of a Public Servant* (1961).
SAMUEL, Viscount. *Memoirs* (1943).
SCOTT, Sir Harold. *Your Obedient Servant* (1959).
SHERWOOD, Robert E. *Roosevelt and Hopkins, an Intimate History* (New York, 1948).
SOMMER, Dudley. *Haldane of Cloan, His Life and Times, 1856–1928* (1960).
STIMSON, Henry L. 'Decision to use the Atomic Bomb', *Harper's Magazine* (February, 1947).
SYMONS, Julian. *The General Strike* (1957).
TAYLOR, H. A. *'Jix' — Viscount Brentford* (1933).
TAYLOR, Rex. *Assassination, the Death of Sir Henry Wilson* (1961).
  Michael Collins (1958).

TEMPLEWOOD, Viscount. *Nine Troubled Years* (1954).

THOMAS, J. H. *My Story* (1937).

THOMSON, Malcolm. *David Lloyd George, the Official Biography* (1948).

TITMUSS, Prof. Richard M. *Problems of Social Policy* (1950).

TRUMAN, Harry S. *Year of Decisions* (New York, 1955).
Years of Trial and Hope (New York, 1956).

VAN KLEFFENS, Elko. *The Rape of the Netherlands* (1940).

WEBSTER, Sir David. 'Viscount Waverley — An Appreciation', *Opera*, March, 1958.

WHEELER-BENNETT, Sir John. *King George VI, His Life and Reign* (1958).

WHITE, Terence de Vere. *Kevin O'Higgins* (1948).

WINANT, John Gilbert. *A Letter from Grosvenor Square* (1947).

YOUNG, G. M. *Stanley Baldwin* (1952).

(iii) NEWSPAPERS AND PERIODICALS

Amrita Bazaar Patrika (Calcutta)

Nature

Proceedings of the Institution of Civil Engineers

Proceedings of the Royal Society

Punch

The Alderley Park Review

Daily Express

Daily Herald

Daily Telegraph

The Economist

Glasgow Herald

The Malvernian (Malvern College)

Manchester Guardian

News Chronicle

The Observer

The Scots Independent (Glasgow)

The Scotsman

The Statesman (Calcutta)

The Times

The Watsonian (George Watson's College)

INDEX

Abercorn, 3rd Duke of, 188

Aberdeen, University of, 392

Act for Restoration of Order in Ireland (1920), 69, 70

Acts of Parliament (U.K.). *See* Act for Restoration of Order in Ireland ; Air Raid Precautions Act, 1937 ; Atomic Energy Act ; Emergency Powers Act; 1920 ; Government of India Acts, 1919 and 1935 ; Home Rule, Ireland ; National Health Insurance, 1914 ; Wage Earners' Income Tax(P.A.Y.E.); Widows, Orphans and Old Age Contributory Pensions, 1925

Adams, Sergeant Jock, 142 n.

Adeane, Sir Michael, 401, 403, 404

Advance (Indian Nationalist paper), 173 n.

Air Raid Precautions and Civil Defence, 96-97, 189-191, 198-207 ; Committee on Evacuation, 199-200, 201-202 ; Anderson Report, 202-205, 212 ; Civil Defence 'Scheme Y', 205-206 ; Anderson appointed Minister for Civilian Defence, 214; problems of organization, 215 ; Civil Defence Bill, 1939, 218 ; Civilian Defence Committees of key industries, 220-221 ; Anderson Shelter, 221-224 ; Hyde Park review of C.D. forces, 227 ; Precautions over aliens, 238-242 ; Defence Regulations, 243-244, 247 n. ; precautions against invasion, 246-247 ; during Blitz, 249-255 ; controversy over deep shelters, 250-255

Air Raid Precautions Act, 1937, 189, 198-199

Aitken, Sir Max (later 1st Baron Beaverbrook), 56

Akers, Sir Wallace, 290, 376 n.

Alanbrooke, Field-Marshal, 1st Viscount, 339 n., 354

Alba, Duke of, 281

Alexander of Tunis, Field-Marshal, 1st Earl, 405

Alice, Princess. *See* Athlone, Countess of

Alison, Dr. John, 5-6, 82

Allied Maritime Transport Council, 42

Amery, Leopold S., 230

Amulree, Lord. *See* Mackenzie, Sir William

Anderson, Alastair David, 2nd Viscount Waverley (son) : birth, 28 ; education, 110-112, joins R.A.F., 232 ; marriage, 399 n. ; mentioned, 48, 108, 110, 117, 149,188,204,208,235,283,284,401,404

Anderson, Ava, Viscountess Waverley, second wife (*née* Bodley ; formerly Mrs. Ralph Wigram) : birth, 277 ; marriage to Ralph Wigram, 278-281 ; courted by Anderson, 281-284 ; marriage, 285 ; home life with Anderson, 286, 295, 297, 303, 304 ; accompanies Anderson to Paris, 309 ; death of son, 351, 361 ; and *St. Katharine* outings, 358 ; accompanies Anderson to Australia, New Zealand and Canada, 361 ; contribution to Covent Garden, 365, 370 ; happiness with Anderson, 395-397; and Anderson's illness, 401-402 ; partial loss of sight, 402; letter to Churchill quoted, 280; mentioned, 333, 348, 350, 352, 353, 360

Anderson, Catherine (Katie) (sister), 2, 10, 11, 26, 126, 182, 285

Anderson, Charles (infant brother), 2

Anderson, Christina (Chrissie), first wife, 8, 10, 11, 12, 13, 14, 15, 16, 19, 46 ; courted by Anderson, 10 ; marries, 26 ; birth of son and daughter, 28 ; character, 10, 26 ; death, 47 ; effect of her death on Anderson, 108

Anderson, Sir David, 222

Anderson, David Alexander Pearson (father), 1, 2, 3, 7, 10, 12, 16, 90-91, 142-143, 228, 285, 394. *See also* Anderson's letters to his father

Anderson, Janet Kilgour *née* Briglmen (mother), 2, 10, 11, 12, 90-91

415

THE END

PRINTED BY R. & R. CLARK, LTD., EDINBURGH